The Scripture Cannot Be Broken

The Scripture Cannot Be Broken

Twentieth Century Writings on the Doctrine of Inerrancy

Edited by
John MacArthur

WHEATON, ILLINOIS

The Scripture Cannot Be Broken: Twentieth Century Writings on the Doctrine of Inerrancy

Published by Crossway
1300 Crescent Street
Wheaton, Illinois 60187

Cover design: Tim Green, Faceout Studio

Cover image: K. Kreto/Shutterstock

First printing 2015

Printed in the United States of America

Scripture quotations marked ASV are from the *American Standard Version* of the Bible.

Scripture quotations marked KJV are from the *King James Version* of the Bible.

Scripture references marked NIV are taken from The Holy Bible, New International Version®, NIV®. Copyright © 1973, 1978, 1984 by Biblica, Inc.™ Used by permission. All rights reserved worldwide.

Scripture quotations marked RV are from the *Revised Version* of the Bible.

Scripture references marked RSV are from *The Revised Standard Version*. Copyright © 1946, 1952, 1971, 1973 by the Division of Christian Education of the National Council of the Churches of Christ in the U.S.A.

In many cases, biblical versions quoted in the original publications were not specified. Crossway Books was unable to identify each version used.

Trade paperback ISBN: 978-1-4335-4865-9
ePub ISBN: 978-1-4335-4868-0
PDF ISBN: 978-1-4335-4866-6
Mobipocket ISBN: 978-1-4335-4867-3

Library of Congress Cataloging-in-Publication Data

The scripture cannot be broken : twentieth century writings on the doctrine of inerrancy / edited by John MacArthur.
pages cm
Includes bibliographical references and index.
ISBN 978-1-4335-4865-9 (tp)
1. Bible—Evidences, authority, etc.—History of doctrines—20th century. I. MacArthur, John, 1939– editor.
BS480.S347 2015
220.1'32—dc23 2014039164

Crossway is a publishing ministry of Good News Publishers.

VP 25 24 23 22 21 20 19 18 17 16 15
15 14 13 12 11 10 9 8 7 6 5 4 3 2 1

Contents

1. God, who is Himself Truth and speaks truth only, has inspired Holy Scripture in order thereby to reveal Himself to lost mankind through Jesus Christ as Creator and Lord, Redeemer and Judge. Holy Scripture is God's witness to Himself.

2. Holy Scripture, being God's own Word, written by men prepared and superintended by His Spirit, is of infallible divine authority in all matters upon which it touches: it is to be believed, as God's instruction, in all that it affirms: obeyed, as God's command, in all that it requires; embraced, as God's pledge, in all that it promises.

3. The Holy Spirit, Scripture's divine Author, both authenticates it to us by His inward witness and opens our minds to understand its meaning.

4. Being wholly and verbally God-given, Scripture is without error or fault in all its teaching, no less in what it states about God's acts in creation, about the events of world history, and about its own literary origins under God, than in its witness to God's saving grace in individual lives.

5. The authority of Scripture is inescapably impaired if this total divine inerrancy is in any way limited or disregarded, or made relative to a view of truth contrary to the Bible's own; and such lapses bring serious loss to both the individual and the Church.

The Chicago Statement on Biblical Inerrancy
"A Short Statement"

Introduction

JOHN MACARTHUR

The most important lessons we ought to learn from church history seem fairly obvious. For example, in the two-thousand-year record of Christianity, no leader, movement, or idea that has questioned the authority or inspiration of Scripture has ever been good for the church. Congregations, denominations, and evangelical academic institutions that embrace a low view of Scripture invariably liberalize, secularize, move off mission, decline spiritually, and either lose their core membership or morph into some kind of political, social, or religious monstrosity. That downhill trajectory (what Charles H. Spurgeon referred to as "the Down Grade") is distinct and predictable. The spiritual disaster looming at the bottom is inevitable. And those who decide to test their skill on the gradient *always* lose control and seldom recover.

Nevertheless, for more than two centuries, an assault on the reliability of Scripture has come in relentless waves from influential voices on the margins of the evangelical movement. Beginning in the late eighteenth century, German *rationalism* gave large precincts of Protestant Christianity a hard push onto the downhill track. Several once-trendy movements have followed the same familiar course. *Modernism* in the nineteenth century, *neoorthodoxy* in the early twentieth century, and *postmodernism* (branded as "Emergent religion") for the past two or three decades have all proved to be high-occupancy on-ramps for the Down Grade. The leaders and cheerleaders in those movements have all employed essentially the same fundamental strategy and tried to make the same basic arguments. They have all claimed that because human authors were involved in the writing of Scripture, we can expect to find errors in what the Bible teaches. They view the historical data of Scripture with suspicion. They regard the ever-shifting opinions of current scientific theory as more trustworthy than divine revelation. Many are perfectly willing to adjust both the moral standards and doctrinal content of Scripture to harmonize with whatever is currently deemed acceptable in secular society.

Those ideas are typically broached subtly, often accompanied by highly nuanced statements that may initially sound like orthodox affirmations of biblical authority. The purveyors of this kind of skepticism are highly skilled at rhetorical sleight of hand. They will often claim, "I firmly believe in biblical inerrancy, *but* . . ."

Whatever follows that conjunction is usually the true indicator of the person's actual view on the authority and reliability of Scripture. Some try to obscure their doubts about inerrancy with a carefully nuanced distinction between "infallibility" and "inerrancy." Others claim they just want to refine and clarify how inerrancy is explained—but what they really want is to soften or dismantle a position they have never really owned. One professor at a leading evangelical seminary wrote an essay arguing that while he personally believes in biblical inerrancy, he thinks evangelicals ought to minimize their emphasis on that article of faith, because the doctrine of inerrancy has sometimes been a stumbling block for seminarians. He feared his students' faith might be shaken when they encounter hard texts, parallel passages that are difficult to harmonize, or biblical claims that are disputed by critical scholars. Another academic author who says he believes the Bible is inerrant recently wrote a similar article, suggesting that evangelical scholars should regard their belief in the truthfulness of Scripture as "provisional."

Lately, some have proposed redefining the word *inerrancy* in a novel way purposely designed to take the teeth out of the 1978 Chicago Statement on Biblical Inerrancy. That is the definitive document on the subject. It is a careful, thorough series of affirmations and denials written in defense of historic evangelicalism's commitment to the inspiration and authority of Scripture. The document was designed to be both thorough and precise, eliminating whatever wiggle room scholars on the evangelical fringe had staked out as a platform from which to challenge biblical inerrancy. The Chicago Statement was drafted and unanimously agreed upon by the founding members of the International Council on Biblical Inerrancy (ICBI). It came at the peak of a controversy that had arisen in the wake of Harold Lindsell's eye-opening 1976 book *The Battle for the Bible.*

Jay Grimstead, one of ICBI's primary founders, says the Chicago Statement is

> a landmark church document . . . created in 1978 by the then largest, broadest, group of evangelical protestant scholars that ever came together to create a common, theological document in the 20th century. It is probably the first systematically comprehensive, broadly based,

> scholarly, creed-like statement on the inspiration and authority of Scripture in the history of the church.[1]

The members of ICBI could see clearly that a significant erosion of confidence in the authority and accuracy of Scripture had infected mainstream evangelicalism. That trend, they believed, posed a serious threat to the health of every evangelical church and academic institution. It severely clouded the testimony of the gospel, and it directly undermined faith itself. They carefully analyzed the controversy and made a list of fourteen specific points of debate that required definitive answers. They commissioned a series of white papers and sponsored a large number of books aimed at a wide spectrum of readers—ranging from simple material written for laypeople to highly technical textbooks for scholars. Within a decade, they had produced a large body of work, most of which was never rebutted by the skeptics. In fact, most of the voices that had been arguing so aggressively against such a high view of Scripture fell silent. In Grimstead's words: "There was deathly silence from the liberal side for several years. Inerrancy was once again popular and respected as the historic, orthodox, and scholarly viewpoint."[2]

In 1987, its work complete and its goals all accomplished, ICBI formally disbanded.

At the time, many seemed to think the bleeding had been permanently stanched. Subsequent history has shown that was not the case. Having won a major skirmish in the conflict over inerrancy, evangelicals quickly turned away from the issue. The next two decades saw the evangelical movement carelessly cede the ground won in the inerrancy battle by capitulating to a more pragmatic philosophy of ministry in which the inerrant truth and authority of Scripture were deliberately downplayed (or completely set aside) under the rubric of "seeker sensitive ministry." Meanwhile, the charismatic movement was making great gains among evangelicals by stirring up an unorthodox interest in private, extrabiblical revelations. Christian publishers produced far more books promoting private, fallible prophecies in the 1990s than on the sufficiency, inerrancy, inspiration, and authority of Scripture. Evangelicals, having decisively won the decade-long debate on biblical inerrancy, seemed to lose interest in Scripture anyway.

Large numbers of today's evangelical leaders are too young to remem-

[1] Jay Grimstead, "How the International Council on Biblical Inerrancy Began," http://www.reformation.net/Pages/ICBI_Background.htm, accessed Aug. 10, 2014.
[2] Ibid.

ber *The Battle for the Bible* and the work of ICBI. And many of them are susceptible (if not outright sympathetic) to the same destructive arguments that prompted the inerrancy debate in the 1970s.

Why is the Down Grade so seductive? Why does a low view of Scripture seem so appealing to men whose job is supposed to be the defense and propagation of "the faith which was once for all handed down to the saints" (Jude 3)?[3] How do old, already-answered arguments, shopworn rhetoric, and failed philosophies continually fool each succeeding generation?

One answer, clearly, is that Christians have never been particularly good at learning the lessons of church history. The church, like Old Testament Israel, seems more prone to repeat the sins of our ancestors than to learn from them. We also have to contend with the noetic effects of sin. Sin so clouds the human heart and intellect that we simply cannot think straight or discern truth clearly if our minds are not governed by both the Word and the Spirit. To those who doubt the truth and authority of Scripture, that poses an insoluble dilemma.

But perhaps the most persistent influence that steers otherwise sound Christians onto the Down Grade is a stubborn craving for approval and esteem from academic elitists. Too many Christian leaders wish the wise men, scribes, and debaters of this world would admire them (cf. 1 Cor. 1:20). That, of course, is a vain and foolish hope. Jesus said, "If you were of the world, the world would love its own; but because you are not of the world, but I chose you out of the world, because of this the world hates you" (John 15:19). He further said, "Woe to you when all men speak well of you, for their fathers used to treat the false prophets in the same way" (Luke 6:26).

For my part, I have no wish to be thought more sophisticated than Jesus, who said, "The Scripture cannot be broken" (John 10:35); "Truly I say to you, until heaven and earth pass away, not the smallest letter or stroke shall pass from the Law until all is accomplished" (Matt. 5:18); "Heaven and earth will pass away, but My words will not pass away" (Matt. 24:35); "It is easier for heaven and earth to pass away than for one stroke of a letter of the Law to fail" (Luke 16:17).

To His opponents, our Lord said, "Have you not even read [the] Scripture . . . ?" (Mark 12:10); "Have you not read in the book of Moses . . . ?" (v. 26); "Have you never read . . . ?" (2:25; Matt. 21:16); "If you believed Moses, you would believe Me" (John 5:46); "If they do not listen to Moses and the Prophets, they will not be persuaded even if someone rises from

[3] All Scripture quotations in the introduction are from *The New American Standard Bible*®. Copyright © The Lockman Foundation 1960, 1962, 1963, 1968, 1971, 1972, 1973, 1975, 1977, 1995. Used by permission.

the dead" (Luke 16:31); and "Is this not the reason you are mistaken, that you do not understand the Scriptures or the power of God?" (Mark 12:24).

It is the solemn duty of everyone in any kind of ministry to "guard, through the Holy Spirit who dwells in us, the treasure which has been entrusted to [us]" (2 Tim. 1:14). That was Paul's admonition to Timothy. It echoes what he said at the end of his first epistle to the young pastor: "O Timothy, guard what has been entrusted to you, avoiding worldly and empty chatter and the opposing arguments of what is falsely called 'knowledge'—which some have professed and thus gone astray from the faith" (1 Tim. 6:20–21). It is clear from the context of both verses that the "treasure" entrusted to Timothy (the deposit that he was commanded to guard) is the full revelation of the gospel, and more specifically, the truth that is recorded for us in Scripture, encompassing both Old and New Testaments. Paul speaks of this treasure as "the standard of sound words which you have heard from me" (2 Tim. 1:13).

That admonition is a plain statement of the central proposition that runs like an unbroken thread through 2 Timothy. Paul is writing his final message to Timothy, and he urges him again and again to stay faithful to the Word of God, handle it carefully, and proclaim it faithfully—because Scripture is God's Word, and it is the only infallible record of the only legitimate message the church has been commissioned to preach. Paul was not speaking to Timothy about some ethereal body of oral traditions; he wanted Timothy to remain faithful to *the written Word of God.*

In other words, Scripture, and Scripture alone, establishes for all eternity "the standard of sound words."

Paul's repeated admonitions on this one central point in 2 Timothy are all familiar: "The things which you have heard from me in the presence of many witnesses, entrust these to faithful men who will be able to teach others also" (2:2); "Be diligent to present yourself approved to God as a workman who does not need to be ashamed, accurately handling the word of truth" (v. 15); "Continue in the things you have learned and become convinced of, knowing from whom you have learned them, and that from childhood you have known the sacred writings which are able to give you the wisdom that leads to salvation through faith which is in Christ Jesus. All Scripture is inspired by God and profitable for teaching, for reproof, for correction, for training in righteousness; so that the man of God may be adequate, equipped for every good work" (3:14–17); and "I solemnly charge you in the presence of God and of Christ Jesus, who is to judge the living and the dead, and by His appearing and His kingdom: preach the word; be ready in season and out of season; reprove, rebuke, exhort, with great patience and instruction" (4:1–2).

One thing is certain: none of the troubles that currently threaten the strength and solidarity of historic evangelicalism can be dealt with apart from a return to the movement's historic conviction that Scripture is the infallible Word of God—verbally inspired, totally inerrant, fully sufficient, and absolutely authoritative. We must recover our spiritual forefathers' confidence in the Bible, as well as their unshakable belief that the Bible is the final test of every truth claim. God's Word is not subject to human revision. It needs no amendment to suit anyone's cultural preferences. It has one true interpretation, and because it proclaims its truth with the full authority of God, the Bible also emphatically declares that all alternative opinions are wrong.

Scripture is therefore not to be handled carelessly, studied halfheartedly, listened to apathetically, or read flippantly. Earlier, we saw that Paul exhorted Timothy to "be diligent to present yourself approved to God as a workman who does not need to be ashamed, accurately handling the word of truth" (2 Tim. 2:15). That, of course, is the solemn and particular duty of every pastor and teacher (James 3:1). But every believer is likewise obliged to study Scripture with the utmost care and diligence.

It is simply not possible to handle Scripture faithfully apart from the unshakable conviction that it is true. How can anyone claim to believe the Bible is the inspired Word of God yet assert that it might contain factual or historical inaccuracies—or regard any other source as more reliable or more authoritative? To suggest that Scripture is God's Word yet possibly in error is to cast doubt on the omniscience, truthfulness, or wisdom of God. The suggestion is filled with mischief, and all who have ever pursued that course to its inevitable end have "suffered shipwreck in regard to their faith" (1 Tim. 1:19).

With the aim of explaining and defending these principles, we have collected this anthology of articles, chosen for their clarity, readability, and relevance to the current discussion. Most of these essays were written and first published a quarter century ago or more. The fact that the same arguments answered in these chapters have resurfaced and need to be answered again today reflects the tenacity of anti-scriptural skepticism. Sadly, it also reveals the failure of evangelicals to learn from their own history and hold tightly to their core convictions. These answers are timeless.

May you understand that Scripture is the very Word of God; may that conviction be strengthened; and may you be equipped to "contend earnestly for the faith which was once for all handed down to the saints" (Jude 3).

Part 1

Historical Perspective

1

"An Historian Looks at Inerrancy"

HAROLD LINDSELL

Evangelicals and Inerrancy

Previously published as "An Historian Looks at Inerrancy," in *Evangelicals and Inerrancy: Selections from the Journal of the Evangelical Theological Society*, ed. Ronald Youngblood (Nashville, TN: Thomas Nelson, 1984), 49–58.

During the summer of 1964, *Christianity Today* polled the membership of the Evangelical Theological Society. Its members were asked to designate the major areas of conflict in the theological arena. Two-thirds of the 112 responders to the poll said that biblical authority is the main theological theme now under review in conservative circles in America. The replies left this writer with the definite impression that the overall theological viewpoint of any man will ultimately be a reflection of his answer to the question, "What is the nature of inspiration and authority?"

Now I am not a theologian in the formal sense of that term. However, this does not disqualify me from speaking on the subject of biblical authority, for I shall deal with it in a perspective consonant with my formal training. Just as a judge must be familiar with the law and make decisions about matters outside the realm of his intimate knowledge, so the historian can come to conclusions about men and movements that operate within complex disciplines outside his own competence but that can be subjected to historical scrutiny competently. I speak therefore as an historian, and as a member of that craft I wish to take a hard look at the inerrancy of the Bible, a subject that is intrinsic to the question of biblical authority.

One of the historian's first conclusions is that in every period in the history of man, some central issue has dominated that age. This is true both for profane and sacred history. We are concerned here with sacred history, and to that area I will limit myself.

Any serious study of the Old and New Testaments will show that the writers devoted little space to the careful formulation of a doctrine of revelation, inspiration, and inerrancy. Nowhere in Scripture is there any reasoned argument along this line such as will be found for justification by faith alone in Romans and for the resurrection of Jesus Christ from the dead in 1 Corinthians. This may appear strange at first until we recognize that this is true for many of the key doctrines of the Christian faith. There is no great apologetic for the existence of God or for the Trinity. Everywhere these truths are enunciated and taken for granted, however. Yet they are not the subject of formal treatment in the same sense that justification by faith and the resurrection from the dead are dealt with.

Search the Gospels and you will find little that deals directly with this question of the Scriptures. Jesus Christ constantly refers to the Old Testament Scriptures, but nowhere does he speak with the view to defend them. Rather, he takes it for granted that the Scriptures are inspired, authoritative, and inerrant, and on the basis of this assumption he interprets the Scriptures and instructs friend and foe alike. He assumes that they, like himself, are controlled by a view similar to his own. Thus when Jesus addresses himself to the Jews concerning his relationship to God, he defends himself and his claim to deity by using the expression, "Scripture cannot be broken." It was this claim that the Jews would not and could not deny. They believed it. What they did not believe was the claim of Jesus to be God. This they held to be blasphemy.

Read the Acts of the Apostles. What do you find there? Surely there is nothing that deals decisively with the phenomena of Scripture. Central to the Acts of the Apostles is their witness to the resurrection of Jesus Christ from the dead, not to that of an inerrant record. Later when Paul deals with the truth or the falsity of the gospel in 1 Corinthians 15, he never makes reference to the authority, inspiration, or inerrancy of Scripture. But he does state that the faith rises or falls on the resurrection of Jesus Christ from the dead.

One can read the balance of the New Testament, and search in vain he must, for anything that suggests that the writers sought to formulate a carefully defined doctrine of an inspired, authoritative, and inerrant revelation. There is adequate material dealing with this subject, but not in the context of a disputed issue and not with the intention of forging an apologetic to answer the opponents of such a viewpoint. Indeed there was no need for the writers of the New Testament to spend much time dealing with this subject. They embraced the common view of the Old Testament held by the Jews of every age. There is a sense in which it may be said that the New Testament deals with the inerrancy of the Scriptures much the same way that it deals with the virgin birth. Both are stated and affirmed. But neither one is the object of real definitive treatment. Both are taken for granted.

In the early centuries of the church, the theologians and church councils faced grave problems. But none of them devoted much time to the question of an inspired and inerrant Bible. The question of Christology agitated every fishmonger in the Eastern church. The philosophically minded Greek world wrestled with the question of the preincarnate Christ. The Arian controversy symbolized this struggle, and from it came decisions that firmly imbedded into the theology of Christendom the teaching that Jesus Christ is coeternal with the Father, of one substance in essence and yet distinct in person.

The Christological controversy did not stop with the preincarnate Christ. It continued as the church sought answers to the questions raised by the incarnation. If Christ is God, is he also true man? Or is his appearance as man simply an appearance and nothing more? Under the guise of docetism, the humanity of Christ was obscured and the church had to fight its way through that miasma of speculation until the formula was devised of one person in two natures, with a human nature and a divine nature, separate and distinct without fusion or confusion. And then it was declared that Christ had both a human and a divine will as over against the teaching of the monothelites.

Still later the church was gripped by the anthropological controversy, better known under the label of Pelagianism and semi-Pelagianism. There, as in the other controversies, the problem was not one that involved the inspiration and inerrancy of the Bible. It was a matter of interpretation. Augustine, of course, was part and parcel of this period of strife, and lines he laid down influenced John Calvin, as any reading of *The Institutes of the Christian Religion* will demonstrate.

The Reformation period did nothing to change the picture materially relative to inspiration and inerrancy. It is true that the Reformation involved the Scriptures, but never was it a question of either the authority or the inspiration of the Scriptures. Both Romanists and Reformers alike held firmly to an inerrant Word of God. The problem did center in the addition of tradition as a source of belief and authority, which addition the Reformers repudiated vehemently. *Sola Scriptura* was the key phrase in the mouths of the Reformers. But it is also true that the question of *interpreting*

Scripture was central in the Reformation. Thus Luther's formula *sola fide*, or justification by faith alone, involved the problem of biblical interpretation, not biblical inspiration and inerrancy, which both Romanists and Reformers accepted cordially. The authority of the Bible alone and without anything else was the formal principle of the Reformers. Justification by faith alone, which repudiated the view that the Church's interpretation of Scripture must prevail, was the material principle of the Reformation.

It may be said without fear of contradiction that the Roman Catholic Church in its official position has always clung to an inerrant Scripture. And this church has constantly defended itself against any other teaching. Thus *The Catholic Encyclopedia* of 1910 (p. 48) says:

> For the last three centuries there have been authors—theologians, exegetes, and especially apologists such as Holden, Rohling, Lenormant, di Bartolo, and others—who maintained, with more or less confidence, that inspiration was limited to moral and dogmatic teaching, excluding everything in the Bible relating to history and the natural sciences. They think that in this way a whole mass of difficulties against the inerrancy of the Bible would be removed. But the Church has never ceased to protest against this attempt to restrict the inspiration of the sacred books. This is what took place when Mgr. d'Hulst, Rector of the Institut Catholique of Paris, gave a sympathetic account of this opinion in "Le Correspondant" of 25 Jan. 1893. The reply was quickly forthcoming in the Encyclical "Providentissimus Deus" of the same year. In that Encyclical Leo XIII said: "It will never be lawful to restrict inspiration to certain parts of the Holy Scriptures, or to grant that the sacred writer could have made a mistake. Nor may the opinion of those be tolerated, who, in order to get out of these difficulties, do not hesitate to suppose that Divine inspiration extends only to what touches faith and morals, on the false plea that the true meaning is sought for less in what God has said than in the motive for which He has said it." In fact, a limited inspiration contradicts Christian tradition and theological teaching.
>
> As for the inerrancy of the inspired text it is to the Inspirer that it must finally be attributed, and it matters little if God has insured the truth of His scripture by the grace of inspiration itself, as the adherents of verbal inspiration teach, rather than by a providential assistance![1]

[1] It should be noted here that the question of the means by which an inerrant Scripture came into being is not the subject of discussion. One can honestly disagree with the person who believes in the mechanical dictation theory as over against the view that God by his Spirit allowed the writers to speak consonant with their linguistic talents and peculiarities. Yet whatever the means were, the end product is the same: an inerrant Scripture.

Luther and Calvin both accepted and taught the doctrine of an inerrant Scripture. This has been documented and is beyond denial.[2] Curiously enough, some of the followers of Luther went beyond anything taught by him and formulated a view that few if any conservative theologians would accept today. I quote: "The Lutherans who devoted themselves to composing the Protestant theory of inspiration were Melanchthon, Chemnitz, Quenstadt, Calov. Soon, to the inspiration of the words was added that of the vowel points of the present Hebrew text. This was not a mere opinion held by the two Buxtorfs, but a doctrine defined, and imposed under pain of fine, imprisonment and exile, by the Confession of the Swiss Churches, promulgated in 1675. These dispositions were abrogated in 1724" *(Catholic Encyclopedia*, p. 48).

The eighteenth century witnessed no radical departure from the view of Scripture that had been normative through the centuries. Indeed in 1729 the Westminster Confession of Faith was adopted. When propounding a doctrine of Scripture, the Confession spoke of "the consent of all the parts . . . and the entire perfection thereof" (chap. 1, sec. 5). The Westminster Confession was used as the basis for the Savoy Declaration of 1658, which became normative for the Congregational churches. And the Baptists in the United States in 1742 adopted what is generally known as the Philadelphia Confession of Faith based upon the Westminster Confession, for the most part, and retaining its statement on the Scriptures. A century later, in 1833, the New Hampshire Confession of Faith was adopted by Baptists in America and included a statement that the Word of God is "without any mixture of error" (Declaration 1).

---

[2] In *Scripture Cannot Be Broken*, Theodore Engelder adduces overwhelming evidence to support this assertion about Luther. Luther endorsed Augustine by saying: "The Scriptures have never erred"; "the Scriptures cannot err"; "it is certain that Scripture cannot disagree with itself." Augustine's famous statement is: "To those books which are already styled canonical, I have learned to pay such reverence and honour as most firmly to believe that none of their authors has committed any error in writing. If in that literature I meet with anything which seems contrary to truth, I will have no doubt that it is only the manuscript which is faulty, or the translator who has not hit the sense, or my own failure to understand" (*A Catholic Dictionary* [New York: Addis & Arnold, 1884], 450). In the case of Calvin there are those who have argued on both sides of the issue. In favor of inerrancy are H. Banke, *Das Problem der Theologie Calvins*; R. E. Davies, *The Problem of Authority in the Continental Reformers*; E. A. Downey, *The Knowledge of God in Calvin's Theology*; A. M. Hunter, *The Teaching of Calvin*; J. Mackinnon, *Calvin and the Reformation*. Mackinnon senses as everyone must that Calvin the scholar over against Calvin the theologian has problems: "When he (the scholar) sees an obvious error in text before him, there is no indication that it makes any *theological* impression on him at all. . . . Again, why, if not because the error is a trivial copyist's blunder, not a misunderstanading of divine 'dictation' by an apostle or prophet?" In other words, Calvin would have been in agreement with Augustine. In both cases it means that they were looking to the autographs, not to copies that were in some measure defective due to copyists' mistakes. Ernest R. Sandeen, of North College, in his paper "The Princeton Theology," *CH* (September 1962), says that Hodge and Warfield "retreated" to "lost and completely useless original autographs" as though this was an innovation. He labels it "the Princeton argument." He failed to see that Hodge and Warfield followed both Augustine and Calvin. Thus the problem was not a new one, but it was "new" in the sense that for the first time in the history of the Church it was *the* central issue being discussed and fought.

Of course there always were dissenting voices that did not believe the Word of God to be infallible and inerrant. But these voices were neither normative nor dominant. They did not exercise a determinative voice in the historic churches at this moment in history. Following the Reformation there was a mighty struggle waged between the Arminians and the Calvinists that extended from the sixteenth well into the nineteenth century. The battle was not waged, however, over the nature of inspiration but over questions relating to a proper understanding and interpretation of the Scriptures.

The eighteenth century marked a definite point of departure on the subject of inspiration. Sparked by the writing of John Locke in the seventeenth century, the next two centuries were characterized by the rise of rationalism, romanticism, evolution, and higher criticism. Many great names are connected with this period of change: Hume, Paley, Paine, Hegel, Kant, Darwin, Nietzsche, Schopenhauer, Spencer, Comte, Marx, and the like. Included in this list should be scores of Germans popularly associated with higher criticism in the nineteenth and twentieth centuries, not to mention the various schools of thought represented by university centers such as Berlin, Tübingen, and Heidelberg. Whereas earlier ages argued whether ultimate religious authority was to be found in the Bible alone, or the Bible through the teaching of the church, or the Bible through the pope, or by the addition of tradition, now there was a direct frontal assault on the Bible itself. Just about everything was questioned and discarded. The Bible under this attack ceased to be a book with the stamp of the divine upon it. It became to the critics a human document composed by men who were no more inspired than other literary figures and certainly not to be fully trusted for ultimate truth in theological or other areas of witness. The storm generated by the higher critics gathered in intensity and seemed to sweep everything before it. Citadels crumbled rapidly; seminaries capitulated; liberalism or modernism with all of its trappings became the order of the day in the twentieth century. In the battle, the fundamentals of the Christian faith that had stood for almost two millennia were discarded. Clifton Olmstead, in his *History of Religion in the United States*, speaks of the resistance forged against this attack on the Bible:

> In the Protestant world the theses of liberal theologians went not unchallenged. Many a theological school, especially those in the Calvinist tradition, produced scholars who were sharply critical of the new currents in religion and clung rigidly to the doctrine of the plenary inspira-

> tion of the Bible. Among the leaders in this camp were the Presbyterians A. A. Hodge, Francis L. Patton, and Benjamin B. Warfield, and the Baptists John A. Broadus and Asahel Kendrick. At the Niagara Bible Conference, which opened in 1876 and continued to meet annually until the end of the century, conservatives regrouped their forces for a frontal attack on the new theology. Their leaders were A. J. Gordon, Arthur Pierson, C. I. Scofield, and James Gray. At the meeting in 1895 the conference formulated its famous "five points of fundamentalism" or necessary standards of belief. They were the inerrancy of Scripture, the Virgin Birth of Jesus Christ, the substitutionary theory of the atonement, the physical resurrection of Christ, and his imminent bodily return to earth. These doctrines were taught as essential at such conservative centers as Moody Bible Institute in Chicago and Los Angeles Bible Institute. In 1909 two wealthy Californians, Lyman and Milton Stewart, financed the publication of twelve small volumes entitled *The Fundamentals: A Testimony of the Truth,* nearly three million copies of which were circulated among ministers and laymen in the United States and abroad. The effect was to stir up a militant antagonism toward liberalism which would reach its height in the decade which followed the First World War. By that time the new theology would have grown old and about to be replaced by theologies which dealt more positively with contemporary issues.

It hardly seems necessary to detail the contributions rendered in the defense of orthodoxy by the Princetonians Hodge, Warfield, and Green. They and others with them constructed an apologetic that has been neither equaled nor surpassed in the last generation. They worked out conservative Christianity's finest defense. Their writings are still the chief source of fact and fuel for contemporary conservative Christianity. The debt that is owed them is almost beyond estimation. It was their work that preserved the Presbyterian church from rapid and complete surrender to the claims of higher criticism. Other denominations were infiltrated and their walls breached, but the onslaughts were thrown back by the Presbyterians. Again Olmstead speaks a word from history about this:

> In several of the major denominations the fundamentalist-modernist controversy grew to gigantic proportions. None was more shaken by the conflict than the Presbyterian, U.S.A. During the painful theological controversies of the late nineteenth century, the church had held to its official position of Biblical inerrancy. In 1910 when a complaint was made to the General Assembly that the New York Presbytery had

> licensed three ministerial candidates whose theological views were somewhat suspect, the Assembly ruled the following articles of faith were necessary for ordination: the inerrancy of Scripture, the Virgin Birth of Christ, the miracles of Christ, the substitutionary atonement, the Resurrection of Christ. No mention was made of premillennialism, a necessary article for fundamentalists. Though the Assembly of 1910 and the Assemblies of 1916 and 1923, which reiterated the five-point requirement, had no intention of reducing the church's theology to these five articles, the conservative element in the church tended to treat the articles in precisely that manner. The general effect was to increase tension and encourage heresy-hunting.

At last the Presbyterian church was breached. J. Gresham Machen and others continued their apologetic for a trustworthy Scripture from without the church. At no time during this struggle within the Presbyterian church could the defenders of an inerrant Scripture be called fundamentalists, nor would they themselves have desired the appellation. It was reserved for another group of theologically conservative people more largely connected with the Bible institute movement and with independent Bible churches throughout the land. It was the accretions to fundamentalism that gave it a bad name among so many people in America. And here one must make a distinction between theological fundamentalism and sociological fundamentalism. At no time could the Machen movement be called sociologically fundamentalist, but it certainly could be called theologically fundamentalist in the best sense of that term.

The Second World War saw the rise of what might be called the "new evangelicalism," which was keenly aware of the plight of a fundamentalism that majored on codes of conduct and defected to liberalism in the area of Christian social ethics. Earlier Carl F. H. Henry's contribution *The Uneasy Conscience of Modern Fundamentalism*, brought some of this into sharp focus. The new evangelicals started with certain presuppositions in mind: (1) a desire to create a new and vigorous apologetic for the conservative position by raising a new generation of well-trained scholars with all of the badges of academic respectability who could speak to the current issues of the day, talk the language of the opposition, and present cogently and compellingly the viewpoint of historic Christianity in the present milieu; (2) a desire to move more vigorously into the area of social ethics and do something about the renovation of society from the vantage point of conservative theology; (3) a desire to meet and overcome the rise of neoorthodoxy, which had replaced the decadent liberalism of the 1920s; (4) a desire to engage in dialogue with those with whom it was in disagreement, based upon the suppositions that the best defense is a good offense and that to man the walls behind barricades had led to nothing constructive in former years; and (5) a desire to move away from the negativism in personal conduct of the older fundamentalism.

This effort began to bear fruit. New and able exponents of the orthodox faith came on the scene. Their names are as familiar to you as they are to me. Books, monographs, and articles were written. Even a magazine like *Time* could conclude, as did its religion editor, that conservative Christianity had depth, strength, scholarship, and something to offer. The evangelistic ministry of Billy Graham, the establishment of *Christianity Today*, the opening of Fuller Theological Seminary, and other events evidenced the new trend. Moreover, the voices of evangelical spokesman were listened to and heard in places where they long had been silent. And all of this was accomplished within the context of a conservative theology that included a belief in an inerrant Scripture.

But now the scene is changing. In getting to the opponents of orthodox Christianity the opponents, in turn, have gotten to some of the new evangelicals. And this is no isolated phenomenon. With the new learning there had come new leaven. And the leaven is to be found in Christian colleges and theological seminaries, in books and articles, in Bible institutes and in conservative churches. The new leaven, as yet, has nothing to do with such vital questions as the virgin birth, the deity of Christ, the vicarious atonement, the physical resurrection from the dead, or the second advent. It involves what it has always involved in the first stages of its development—the nature of inspiration and authority. It could not be otherwise, for one's view of the Bible ultimately determines his theology in all of its ramifications. It is like the Continental Divide in the United States, which marks off the flow of waters either to the Atlantic or the Pacific Oceans depending on which side of the Divide the waters fall. Inexorably and inevitably the waters find their way to their ultimate destiny, just as one's view of the Bible determines ultimately what his theology will be. No man in good conscience or in sanity could hold to an inerrant Scripture after forsaking the deity of Christ, the virgin birth, the vicarious atonement, the physical resurrection from the dead, and the second advent.

Today there are those who have been numbered among the new evangelicals, some of whom possess the keenest minds and have acquired the apparati of scholarship, who have broken, or are in the process of breaking, with the doctrine of an inerrant Scripture. They have done so or are doing so because they think this view to be indefensible and because they do not regard it as a great divide. In order for them to be intellectually honest with themselves, they must do it. Logically, however, the same attitude, orientation, bent of mind, and approach to scholarship that makes the retention of an inerrant Scripture impossible also ultimately makes impossible the retention of the vicarious atonement, imputed guilt, the virgin birth, the physical resurrection, and miraculous supernaturalism.[3] The mediating voices among the new evangelicals who have begun by forsaking inerrancy while retaining inspiration, revelation, authority, and the like still have this hard lesson to learn.

The new-school adherents often feel that those evangelicals who hold to an inerrant Scripture do so because they have "closed minds," or are not truly "scholarly," or are psychologically maladjusted with a defensive mechanism that precludes "openness." What they fail to realize is that the very opinions they hold in regard to those who cling to inerrancy are applied to themselves by those who have not only scrapped inerrancy but also the basic doctrines to which these same people are still committed. Thus they cannot avoid wearing the same labels they apply to the people who adhere to inerrancy, and if they think that by their concession they have really advanced the cause of dialogue with those outside the conservative tradition, they are grossly mistaken.

Moreover the possession of the "closed mind," and the failure to enjoy "openness," and the problem of being truly "scholarly" does not haunt the conservative alone. Liberals are among those who have most thoroughly enjoyed and displayed the very traits they militate against in others. And the mind that is closed because it believes it possesses the truth cannot truly be unscholarly, since the pursuit of truth is the goal of scholarship; and "openness" is not a virtue when it allows for dilution and diminution of the truth one feels he possesses. Of course men may mistakenly but honestly hold to what is false, but unless there is something that is commonly held by all men, neither those who believe nor those who disbelieve can be sure of the rightness or wrongness of their positions unless they have some outside validating authority to which final reference can be made. And this the Word of God is.

---

[3]It is true that men do not always press their views to their logical conclusions. Thus one can hold to an errant Scripture while not forsaking other cardinal doctrines. It is for this reason that those who accept biblical inerrancy should not break with those who disagree with them unless the divergence includes a further departure from other major doctrines of orthodoxy. Perchance the continuance of closest contacts will convince those who reject inerrancy what the logical consequences of such rejection involve.

One can predict with almost fatalistic certainty that in due course of time the moderating evangelicals who deny inerrancy will adopt new positions such as belief in the multiple authorship of Isaiah, the late date of Daniel, the idea that the first eleven chapters of Genesis are myth and saga. And then these critical conclusions will spill over into the New Testament, and when the same principles of higher criticism are applied this can only lead to a scrapping of the facticity of the resurrection, etc. This has ever been the historical movement, and there is nothing to suppose that such a repetitive process will not follow.

Rarely does one hear of a journey from liberalism to orthodoxy, from an errant Scripture to an inerrant Scripture. For the most part it is a one-way street in the wrong direction. It is the opinion of this writer that the moderating proponents among the new evangelicals stand in mortal danger of defecting from the foundation on which the new evangelicalism was built, of evacuating that which it came into being to defend, of surrendering to an inclusive theology that it opposed, and of hiding its deception in a plethora of words, semantically disguised so as to curry favor with those who deny inerrancy and at the same time to retain the allegiance of those who cling to the old doctrine.

This is no obscurantist pose. Nor does it in any sense threaten or underestimate the good in the new evangelicalism. Nor is it intended to downgrade Christian scholarship of the highest order. Rather it is intended to make plain the fact that just as Christology, anthropology, and justification by faith were key issues in the theological struggle of bygone ages, so today the key theological issue is that of a wholly trustworthy or inerrant Scripture. Moreover it is designed to impress upon all that the most significant conservative movement of the twentieth century, labeled by many the new evangelicalism, has already been breached by some and is in the process of being breached by others. And the Evangelical Theological Society that has been such a vital part of the new evangelicalism had better be aware of the turn of events. It has been infected itself, and its own foundations need to be reexamined. For what this society does and how it reacts to this challenge may well determine the direction that churches, denominations, and institutions take in the years immediately before us.

2

"*Apeitheō*: Current Resistance to Biblical Inerrancy"

J. BARTON PAYNE

Evangelicals and Inerrancy

Previously published as "*Apeitheō*: Current Resistance to Biblical Inerrancy," in *Evangelicals and Inerrancy: Selections from the Journal of the Evangelical Theological Society*, ed. Ronald Youngblood (Nashville, TN: Thomas Nelson, 1984), 115–28. Reprinted with permission of Dorothy Payne Woods.

"The whole Bible?" If such an inquiry into their beliefs were to be directed to today's theologians, the response of the large majority would be, "*Apeitheō*: I am not persuaded, I disbelieve." Doubts about Scripture's veracity, moreover, are no longer limited to convinced doctrinal skeptics, whether of an unreconstructed sort of liberalism or of a more repentant kind of neoorthodoxy. They are being currently voiced among theologians generally classified as evangelical, among men who would look to Jesus Christ as Lord and Savior. Furthermore their resistance to the authority of the entire written Word, which the Evangelical Theological Society (ETS) designates as biblical inerrancy, is producing an effect in conservative institutions, conferences and denominations, especially among our more advanced students and younger scholars. But why should those who have been reared in Bible-believing environments now experience attraction to the posture of *apeitheō*? It is not too much to conclude that the very future of the ETS and of the biblical position that it represents lies at stake as we ask how, and why, some of our former colleagues have turned against us and what the Christian's approach to Scripture really ought to be.

The Nature of the Present Declension

Most modern skeptics prefer to cloak their opposition to the Bible beneath words of recognition, or even praise, for its authority. Except for communists and a few atheistic cranks, it is no longer the thing to ridicule scriptural inspiration. Among the more liberal this may be traced to a war-induced disenchantment with man's native capabilities and to an existentialistic yearning for a transcendent point of reference. Among the more conservative, whether they be Roman Catholic or ex-fundamental Protestant, vested interests seem to require their continued use of the term "inerrancy," either to uphold the dogmas of previous popes or to pacify an evangelical constituency that might reduce financial support should the term be discarded. As one of the latter group told me, his institution does not really accept inerrancy, but they keep using the term because otherwise supporters would think they were becoming liberal (!).

But despite this haze in the current theological atmosphere, certain criteria serve as genuine indications of where people stand. (1) Those who resist inerrancy tend to express themselves on the mode of inspiration rather than on its extent. They may protest, for example, that the Bible *is* God's word as well as man's, or that its teachings are ultimately authoritative. But so long as these declaimers refuse to indicate which portions constitute "teaching," their protests decide little or nothing. (2) The parties of resistance may tacitly restrict biblical truth to theological matters. Such delimitation is not infrequently camouflaged, as for example in last June's statement of the Wenham Conference on Inspiration, which affirmed: "The Scriptures are completely truthful and are authoritative as the only infallible rule of faith and practice." Splendid as this affirmation appears at first glance, could it be that the omission of a comma after "completely truthful"—so that this assertion likewise was limited by "as the only infallible rule of faith and practice"—provided the necessary restriction for those present at the conference who limit biblical truthfulness to matters of faith and practice? (3) The resistance likes to remain noncommittal at points where disagreements with other sources are likely to appear. To suggest, for example, that the Bible will not duplicate what can be discovered by scientific research becomes but a backhanded way of setting aside its authority at such points.

The persistent question in all such declension, moreover, concerns the total authority of the Bible. This is not a semantic debate over how one defines "inerrant." Several times during the past year I have received critical inquiries as to what the society means by saying, "The Bible is . . . inerrant," in its doctrinal affirmation. The not-so-veiled suggestion of the inquirers was that if the ETS would only adopt a more latitudinarian interpretation of inerrancy it could retrieve some of its errant colleagues. But this would only gloss over the real issue. Kenneth Kantzer's simple explanation at last year's meeting that an inerrant document "never wanders into false teaching" is quite clear. Could it be that those who oppose the use of the word "inerrancy" in stating their position on the authority and trustworthiness of the Bible are so keenly aware of its meaning that they purposely avoid it? Redefiners of inerrancy seem to contend for some form of partial inerrancy (*sic*), as opposed to the ETS affirmation that the biblical autographs are never errant but that they are authoritative at every point. It boils down to this: that there are some who will no longer believe what they admit that the Bible believes but subscribe rather to *apeitheō*, "not persuaded."

The Reason for Disbelief

When those who resist biblical inerrancy are asked for reasons why, forthrightness seems to come at even more of a premium. But answers are ascertainable. Originally, a rejection of Scripture was concomitant to an antisupernaturalistic opposition against Christianity. Of the disbelieving Pharisees Christ thus asked, "If ye believe not his [Moses'] writings, how shall ye believe my words?" (John 5:47). And to "the father of Old Testament criticism," Johann Gottfried Eichhorn (*Einleitung*, 1780–83), any miracle, including Christ's resurrection, had become absurd. But such is no longer necessarily the case. In the current English-speaking world, at least, the personal piety of Samuel R. Driver (*Introduction*, 1891) pioneered a widespread adoption of negative criticism by men who were otherwise sincerely Christian. Scripture itself, moreover, distinguishes between church membership—"If thou shalt confess with thy mouth Jesus as Lord, and shalt believe in thy heart that God raised him from the dead, thou shalt be saved" (Rom. 10:9)—and church leadership—"For the bishop must . . . hold to the faithful word which is according to the teaching, that he may be able to exhort in the sound doctrine" (Titus 1:9). There may therefore exist opponents of biblical inerrancy whom we could never recognize as legitimate church leaders—for example, by inviting them to share in our class platforms or pulpits—but who could still be brothers, even if inconsistent ones, in Christ.

Yet all resistance to Scripture, whether antisupernaturalistic or not, possesses the common denominator of a subjective authority: an assumption on the part of the critic of his own right to judge, as opposed to the New Testament concept of "bringing every thought into captivity to the obedience of Christ" (2 Cor. 10:5). Irrespective of Christ's actual views on Scripture (see below), current Western thought remains irreconcilably antagonistic to the very idea of "captivity." As observed by H. H. Rowley, Britain's most outstanding present-day Old Testament scholar:

> There were conservative writers who stood outside the general body of critical scholars and who rejected most of their conclusions, but they did not seriously affect the position. While many of them had considerable learning, they made little secret of the fact that they were employing their learning to defend positions which were dogmatically reached. Their work had little influence, therefore, amongst scientific scholars who were concerned only with the evidence, and the conclusions to which it might naturally lead.[1]

"After all," modern man inquires, "does not criticism go awry if subordinated to a presupposition? Do we not live by the scientific method of natural, uninhibited induction and free evaluation? Let the Bible speak for itself: open-minded investigation will surely come out vindicating the truth."

In practice, however, an appeal to the scientific analogy seems unjustifiable, for biblical revelation simply is not amenable to "natural" evaluation. It cannot be placed in a test tube for repeatable experimentation, like the data found in the natural sciences. It can only be appreciated through the testimony of competent witnesses, like the data found in the other historical disciplines. And God himself, through Christ (John 1:18), thus becomes the only authority who can really tell us about his own writing. Supernaturalism therefore replies to modern man: "A truly open-minded scientist must be willing to operate within those methods that are congruous to the object of his criticism, or his conclusions will inevitably go awry." This principle was what made James Orr's inductive attempt to construct a doctrine of inspiration upon the basis of his own evaluation of the observable phenomena of Scripture, with all its various difficulties, basically illegitimate, and it is what made B. B. Warfield's approach of deductively deriving biblical inerrancy from the revealed teaching of

[1] H. H. Rowley, *The Old Testament and Modern Study* (London: Oxford, 1961), *xv*.

Christ and his apostles sound. Evangelicals, in other words, do not insist upon Warfield as though this latter scholar were immune to criticism, as those who resist inerrancy sometimes insinuate, but simply as one whose methodology is consistent with the object of his investigation. Neither do evangelicals wish to minimize the God-given significance of human intelligence or to inhibit those areas of thought that are pertinent to man's Spirit-directed exercise of his own rational responsibility: first, in examining the historical (resurrection) data that lead him to an acceptance of Jesus Christ (1 Cor. 15:1–11); then in seeking an exact understanding of what his Lord taught, specifically concerning Scripture (Luke 24:45); and, lastly, in interpreting with diligence the truths therein contained (2 Tim. 2:15). But evangelicals do deny the right of a man to contradict whatever it is that God may have said that he has said. If I were to do this, I would effectively establish some other criterion over God himself, which amounts to nothing more or less than idolatry. I would then also have to go on to accept the consequences of my rational subjectivism—namely, that doctrines such as the survival of my soul after death, or the atonement of my guilt through vicarious sacrifice, or the proofs for the very existence of my God, are apparently not supported by open-minded judgment in the light of natural evidence.

Yet have not our own Christian colleges, upon occasion, been guilty of conveying to some of their sharpest and most promising students the fallacy that a liberal arts education connotes an all-inclusive liberation with a corresponding responsibility on the part of the individual to reserve to himself the final verdict on any given issue and to insist on his right to say, with *Porgy and Bess*, "It ain't necessarily so"? Within this past year there have arisen cases in one of our evangelical denominations in which, when its assembly resolved to include in its statement of faith an affirmation of biblical inerrancy, some of its leading scholars and pastors indignantly withdrew from fellowship. Such infatuation with academic freedom produces the situation described in Acts 19:9, "Some were hardened and disobedient [*epeithoun*]" (ASV). Now it is true both that in theory the classical meaning of *apeitheō* is "to disobey" and that in practice a man's skepticism in respect to Scripture leads almost inevitably to overt acts of disobedience. But Arndt and Gingrich have searched more deeply and conclude:

> Since, in the view of the early Christians, the supreme disobedience was a refusal to believe their gospel, *apeitheō* may be restricted in some passages to the meaning *disbelieve, be an unbeliever.* This sense . . . seems

> most probable in John 3:36; Acts 14:2; 19:9; Romans 15:31, and only slightly less probable in Romans 2:8.[2]

The heart of the problem is thus an internal one, the primeval sin of pride, the prejudice of rebellious and fallen man, who refuses to go against his own "better judgment" and to take orders but who insists rather on his right to say, "*Apeitheō*, I am not persuaded, I disbelieve" (cf. Acts 19:9 KJV, RSV).

A paradoxical feature in all this is that we who are committed to biblical inerrancy may have contributed, albeit unwittingly, to the current resistance against the Bible's authority. Certain overly zealous Sunday-school materials have invoked a number of subjectively rationalistic bases for belief in Scripture, such as vindications from archaeology or fulfilled prophecies. And, as a result, when our better students uncover similar evidences with the opposite implications, they are rendered an easy prey to rationalistic disbelief. Some of our finest biblical introductions, moreover, contain statements like the following:

> If it [the Bible] presents such data as to compel an acknowledgment that it can only be of divine origin—and it does present such data in abundance—then the only reasonable course is to take seriously its own assertions of infallibility. . . . Human reason is competent to pass upon these evidences . . . in order to determine whether the texts themselves square with the claims of divine origin.[3]

The difficulty, however, is that most of today's outstanding biblical scholars, those who are in the best position (humanly speaking) to know, fail to discover "such data in abundance." On the contrary they tend toward conclusions like the following:

> In the field of the physical sciences we find at once that many mistaken and outmoded conceptions appear in the Bible. . . . Much ink has been wasted also, and is still wasted, in the effort to prove the detailed historical accuracy of the biblical narratives. Archaeological research has not, as is often boldly asserted, resolved the difficulties or confirmed the narratives step by step. Actually they abound in errors, including many contradictory statements. . . . Even in matters of religious concern the Bible is by no means of uniform value throughout.[4]

---

[2] Arndt and Gingrich, *A Greek-English Lexicon of the New Testament and Other Early Christian Literature* (Chicago: University Press, 1959), 82.
[3] G. L. Archer Jr., *A Survey of Old Testament Introduction* (Chicago: Moody, 1964).
[4] M. Burrows, *An Outline of Biblical Theology* (Philadelphia: Westminster, 1946), 44–45, 47.

Moreover, even though most investigations do end up vindicating the Bible as far as inerrancy is concerned, one seeming discrepancy outweighs the significance of ninety-nine confirmations.

Others of our introductions have been more guarded about basing belief in Scripture upon inductive evaluations, cautioning, for example, that "unless we first think rightly about God we shall be in basic error about everything else" (cf. 1 Cor. 2:14 or 2 Cor. 4:3 on the blindness of the unregenerate mind). Yet this same source goes on to declare:

> The Bible itself evidences its divinity so clearly that he is without excuse who disbelieves. . . . Its "incomparable excellencies" are without parallel in any other writing and show most convincingly that the Bible is in a unique sense the Word of God.[5]

But had it not been for New Testament evidence on the canon, could even regenerate Christians have perceived that a given verse in Proverbs or Jeremiah was inspired while similar material from Ecclesiasticus or the Epistle of Jeremy was not? On the other hand, what of Scripture's unexplained difficulties? Are we going too far to say that, on the basis of the evidences presently available, Joshua's asserted capture of Ai or Matthew's apparent attribution (27:9) of verses from Zechariah 11 to Jeremiah favor biblical errancy rather than inerrancy? Candor compels our admission of other cases too for which our harmonistic explanations are either weak or nonexistent. If therefore we once fall into the snare of subjectivism, whether liberal or evangelical, we also may conclude by saying, "*Apeitheō*, I have had it."

The Application of Christian Authority

Turning then to God's own objective testimony in respect to Scripture, what if anything do we find? For we must recognize at the outset that we do not have to find anything. The syllogism "God is perfect, and since the Bible stems from God, then the Bible must be perfect" contains a fallacy, as becomes apparent when we substitute the idea of church for Bible. God lay under no antecedent obligation to ordain inspiration along with his decree for revelation. Even as the church continues to serve as a medium for men's redemption despite its obvious imperfections, so too a Bible of purely human origin could conceivably have proven adequate for human deliverance. Peter, John, and Paul, for example, might have simply recorded their convictions about God's revealed plan of salvation in Christ,

[5] E. J. Young, *An Introduction to the Old Testament*, rev. ed. (Grand Rapids, MI: Eerdmans, 1960), 7, 28–29.

just as modern preachers do, without claiming inspiration (though actually they did: 1 Cor. 2:13; 14:37; 2 Cor. 13:3). Herein, moreover, lies the answer to one of liberalism's more persuasive arguments—namely, that since we today do not need an inerrant KJV, and since the early church did not need an inerrant LXX (Rom. 15:4), therefore the biblical autographs need not have been inerrant either. For evangelicalism refuses to base its commitment to biblical autographic inerrancy upon "needs," whether of God or man, except for that general need of maintaining the truthfulness of Jesus Christ. It is from this latter necessity that Christian authority comes historically into the picture. That is, until a man places his trust in Christ there appears to be no impelling reason why he should believe in the Bible or even in religious supernaturalism, for that matter. But once a man does commit himself to the apostolically recorded person of Jesus, declared to be the Son of God with messianic power by his resurrection from the dead (Rom. 1:4), then his supreme privilege as well as his obligation devolve into letting that mind be in him that was also in Christ Jesus (Phil. 2:5; cf. Col. 2:6; 1 John 2:6), and this includes Christ's mind toward Scripture. Specifically, how Christ's authority is to be applied may then be developed through the following two inquiries.

1. *Did Christ question the Bible?* Affirmative answers at this point seem more common than ever before. It is understandable, moreover, that professed Christians who have felt compelled on rationally subjective grounds to surrender their belief in biblical inerrancy should seek support for their skepticism from some analogy discoverable with Jesus, since nobody really enjoys an inconsistent allegiance. Most modern writers seem content to dismiss inerrancy with generalizations about its being a "sub-Christian" doctrine.[6] Representative of a more straightforward analysis, however, is the Dutch neoorthodox biblical theologian T. C. Vriezen.[7] While granting that "the Scriptures of the Old Testament were for Him as well as for His disciples the Word of God," he adduces three areas in which Jesus "rises above the Holy Scriptures."

> Christ used the traditional text freely, and in doing so He showed Himself superior to all bondage to the letter: [yet the only evidence that Vriezen alleged is that] in Luke iv. 18ff., Isaiah lxi. 2 is quoted without the words "the day of vengeance of our God."

[6] H. R. Mackintosh; cf. A. J. Ungersma, *Handbook for Christian Believers* (Indianapolis: Bobbs-Merrill, 1953), 80–81.

[7] T. C. Vriezen, *An Outline of Old Testament Theology* (Newton, MA: Charles T. Branford, 1960), 2–5.

The example is irrelevant. It is one of those not uncommon instances of successive prophecies in one context: The year of Yahweh's favor, 61:2a, received fulfillment during our Lord's first advent (cf. v. 1), but Christ apparently avoided reference to the day of vengeance described in verse 2b, which was not to achieve fulfillment until his second coming. Real textual freedom, moreover, such as the New Testament use of the LXX no more necessarily subverts inerrancy than does a modern believer's missionary employment of accepted vernacular versions. In John 10:34–35, however, Jesus seemingly went out of his way to associate genuine inerrancy not even with copied manuscripts of the original Hebrew but rather with the autographs themselves: "He [Yahweh] called them gods [judges (?) contemporary with the psalm writer Asaph] unto whom the word of God came [at that time, *egeneto*, aorist] . . . and the scripture cannot be broken." For similar associations of God's inspired words with their inscripturation in the original mss cf. Acts 1:16; 2 Peter 1:21.[8]

Vriezen next says of Jesus:

> Because of His spiritual understanding of the law, He again and again contradicts the Judaic theology of His days derived from it ("them of old time," Matthew v; Mark vii), and even repeatedly contradicts certain words of the law (Matthew v. 38ff.; xix. lff.).

The question, however, revolves in each case about what Christ was really contradicting. In Matthew 19 his opposition was to Pharisaic moral travesty in authorizing a man "to put away his wife for every cause" (v. 2). For while he did go on to contrast Deuteronomic divorce for an *'erwat dābār*, "something indecent" (KB 735a), with Genesis' Edenic situation, he himself came out in favor of the Law because he too limited any absolute prohibition of divorce through his insertion of the words "except for fornication" (v. 9; cf. 5:32). Likewise in the Sermon on the Mount Christ's opposition was directed against Pharisaism. While this sect, moreover, claimed its derivation from the Law, Vriezen's assumption that the words given "to them of old time," which Christ contradicted, must mean the original words of the Law appears gratuitous. In the preceding context our Lord specifically affirmed the inviolability of the Law (5:17) while singling out for criticism only the latter portions of such syndromes as "Love thy neighbor, *and hate thine enemy*" (v. 44); and these latter words, far from

[8] Cf. J. B. Payne, "The Plank Bridge: Inerrancy and the Biblical Autographs," *United Evangelical Action* 24/15 (December 1965): 16–18.

being drawn from the Law, reflected rather those postbiblical traditions that have been found among the self-righteous Qumran sectaries (1QS i 1–10). In the other alleged passages our Lord's opposition, for example, was directed against Pharisaic casuistry in the use of oaths (5:33–37; cf. 23:16–22)—he himself would accept an oath on proper occasion (Matt. 26:63; cf. Heb. 6:16–17)—and against their personally vindictive application of the *lex talionis* (Matt. 5:38–42).

This ties in closely with Vriezen's concluding allegation: "The negative datum that nowhere in the New Testament is mention made of Jesus offering sacrifices may be considered important." Or should it be? For a law to lack particular applicability need not entail its derogation. Vriezen seems, moreover, to have answered his own argument when he states: "In imitation of Christ St. Paul recognized that there were certain commandments of God that were significant only in a certain age and a certain situation."

Ultimately, Vriezen is forthright enough to admit that neither liberals nor conservatives agree with his hypothesis of a Bible-questioning Christ, for he concedes, "This view of Jesus' critical attitude toward the law is contested from both the right and left." Apparently only the neoorthodox, those with strongly vested loyalties toward both Christ and the critics, seem to have persuaded themselves of its validity, and even Vriezen cautions that he must not be understood "to mean that Jesus was 'critical of the Bible' in our sense of the word," or, as far as the present writer has been able to ascertain, in any other negative sense of the word either.

2. *Positively, then, did Jesus affirm the Bible as inerrantly authoritative?* Evangelicals seem at times to have failed to examine with sufficient rigor the exact biblical affirmations of our Lord or to consider with sufficient attention the neoorthodox claim that the Bible does not teach its own inerrancy. Basically such examination demands an attempt to distinguish, and then to interrelate, two differing types of relevant evidence.

(1) *Christ's general statements.* While it seems clear that the prophets and apostles held to an authority of Scripture that was plenary in extent and hence inerrant—cf. 2 Samuel 23:2; Jeremiah 25:13; or Acts 24:14, "believing all things . . . which are written in the prophets"; or 2 Timothy 3:16, "Every Scripture is *theopneustos,* God-breathed"—it remains possible for our Lord's own categorical statements to be so interpreted as to prove deficient, in themselves, of affirming infallibility for the whole Bible. Though they unmistakably teach its broad doctrinal authority, neoorthodox writers have been able to produce explanations that keep them from finally establishing its inerrancy. The five following classic proof texts may

serve as examples. In Matthew 5:18 (cf. Luke 16:16–17) the words, "One jot or one tittle shall in no wise pass away from the law, till all things be accomplished," might be restricted to our Lord's inculcating of total obedience to the Law (cf. the next verse). In Luke 18:31 his affirmation that "all the things that are written through the prophets shall be accomplished unto the Son of man" may well be accepted at face value, without thereby promoting the prophets into anything more than uninspired reporters of valid revelations. The text of Luke 24:25 says, "O foolish men and slow of heart to believe in all that the prophets have spoken"; but the ASV margin reads ". . . *after* all that the prophets have spoken." In Luke 24:44 could Christ perhaps insist that "all things must be fulfilled which are written in the law of Moses, and the prophets, and the psalms, concerning me," without necessarily including all things concerning other subjects? Finally John 10:35, "And the Scripture cannot be broken," might possibly be understood as an ad hominem argument: "If he called them gods . . . and if Scripture cannot be broken (as you believe, whether it actually be true or not), then . . ." The force of the above quotations, in other words, regarding inerrancy remains capable of evasion.

(2) *Christ's specific statements*. It is when our Lord discloses his mind over particular Old Testament incidents and utterances that recognition of his positive belief in the Bible becomes inescapable. At the outset, however, let it again be cautioned that not all of his citations carry equal weight. Christ's references, for example, to Elijah and Elisha (Luke 4:24–27), even when one allows for his confirmation of such factual details as the three years and six months of famine, can yet be treated as mere literary allusions to well-known Old Testament stories, which he need not have considered as more than fictional, though possessed of inherent theological authority. Likewise his identifications of "the book of Moses" (Mark 12:26; Luke 16:29, 31; 24:44) might indicate nothing beyond an awareness of Moses as their central character, much like Samuel in the books of Samuel, without committing our Lord to fixed views on their Mosaic composition.

Yet on the other hand Jesus specifically compared down-to-earth marriage problems of his own and of Moses' days with what was to him the apparently equally real situation of Adam and Eve "from the beginning" (Matt. 19:8; Mark 10:6); he associated Abel with the undeniably historical Zechariah (Luke 11:47–51); he described in detail the catastrophic days of Noah and Lot as transpiring "after the same manner" as the day in which the Son of Man would be revealed (Luke 17:26–30); he lumped

Sodom and Gomorrah together with certain first-century Galilean towns, as subject to equally literal judgments (Matt. 10:15); and he connected the experiences of the Queen of Sheba, Jonah, and the Ninevites with real events in the lives of himself and his contemporaries (Matt. 12:39–41). He equated the narrative description of Genesis 2:24 with the very spoken word of God the Creator (Matt. 19:5). He said that God had uttered the words of Exodus 3:6 to the man Moses (Mark 12:26) and that Moses "gave" Israel the law of Leviticus 12 (John 7:22), "commanded" the law of Leviticus 14 (Matt. 8:4), "wrote" of the Messiah (John 5:46), and indeed "gave you the law" (John 7:19). He affirmed that an actual prophet named Daniel had predicted '"the abomination of desolation" for a period still future to AD 30 (Matt. 25:15) and that David, "in the Holy Spirit," composed the words of Psalm 110:1 (Mark 12:36; Matt. 22:43–45). Even if one allows for the sake of argument that the apostolic writers may not have reproduced Christ's exact phraseology, the impressions that he left about his views on the origin of the Old Testament are still so unmistakable that George Adam Smith felt constrained to confess:

> If the use of his [Isaiah's] name [in the NT quotations] . . . were as involved in the arguments . . . as is the case with David's name in the quotation made by our Lord from Psalm cx, then those who deny the unity of the Book of Isaiah would be face to face with a very serious problem indeed.[9]

But this is just the point. Suppose a man were to go no farther than to acknowledge: "I will, as a Christian, accept biblical authority in respect to those specific matters, and to those alone, which are affirmed by Jesus Christ." He would still find the mind of his Lord so hopelessly opposed to the consensus of modern "scientific" (subjective) criticism that his rationalistic autonomy would suffer automatic forfeit as a principle for biblical research. He might then just as well accept the verdict of the apostles, whom Christ *did* authorize as his representatives (John 14:26; 16:13), on the unified authenticity of Isaiah as well (12:38–41). Furthermore, in the light of Christ's known attitude toward Adam and Abel, it appears rather pointless to question his belief over the literal truth of Elijah and Elisha and of all the other Old Testament matters to which he refers.

(3) *Interrelationships*. In view of Christ's specific statements, his general affirmations (1, above), previously identified as in themselves inconclusive,

---

[9] G. A. Smith, *The Book of Isaiah*, The Expositor's Bible (New York: Hodder & Stoughton, n.d.), 2. 6.

now assume a more comprehensive significance. John 10:35, for example, no longer remains restricted at its ad hominem interpretation, for the unbreakableness of Scripture has been found to correspond to Christ's own beliefs. This Bible reference is therefore depicted on the seal of the Evangelical Theological Society, supported by the cross of Christ breaking in two the sword of criticism. Bernard's liberal International Critical Commentary on John states further that belief in

> the verbal inspiration of the sacred books . . . emerges distinctively in the Fourth Gospel, the evangelist ascribing this conviction to Jesus Himself. We may recall here some Synoptic passages which show that the belief that "the Scripture cannot be broken" was shared by Matthew, Mark, and Luke and that all three speak of it as having the authority of their Master (1. clii).

Older critics such as William Sanday thus conceded:

> When deductions have been made . . . there still remains evidence enough that our Lord while on earth did use the common language of His contemporaries in regard to the Old Testament.[10]

And modern liberals, such as F. C. Grant, freely admit that in the New Testament "it is everywhere taken for granted that Scripture is trustworthy, infallible, and inerrant."[11]

Two concluding questions remain then to be asked. The first directly parallels that which Pilate addressed to the Jewish leaders of his day: "What then shall I do unto Jesus who is called Christ?" (Matt. 27:22). Are we going to recognize his authority, or are we going to take exception to it and deny his reliability by some theory of kenosis? Sigmund Mowinckel, a leading advocate of modern Scandinavian biblical criticism, seems more squarely than most to have faced up to the implications of his views when he concludes:

> Jesus as a man was one of us except that he had no sin (Heb. 4:15). . . . He also shared our imperfect insight into all matters pertaining to the world of sense. . . . He knew neither more nor less than most people of his class in Galilee or Jerusalem concerning history . . . geography, or the history of biblical literature.[12]

---

[10] W. Sanday, *Inspiration* (London: Longmans, Green, 1893), 393.

[11] F. C. Grant, *Introduction to New Testament Thought* (Nashville: Abingdon-Cokesbury, 1950), 75; cf. J. Knox, *Jesus Lord and Christ* (New York: Harper, 1958).

[12] S. Mowinckel, *The Old Testament as Word of God* (New York: Abingdon, 1959), 74.

But can one then really maintain the belief in our Lord's sinlessness? This unreliability cannot be restricted to theoretical matters of incarnate omniscience, which few would wish to assert (cf. Mark 13:32), but it involves Christ's basic truthfulness in consciously committing himself to affirmations about Scriptures that he was under no antecedent obligation even to mention (cf. John 3:34).

In John 15 Jesus himself divided up his contemporaries between bondslaves and friends, distinguishing the latter on the basis of their participation in his own convictions: "For all things that I have heard from my Father I have made known unto you" (John 15:15). What then is to be said of the man who is *apeitheō*, unpersuaded, about what Christ has made known? Is the man who rejects biblical inerrancy simply an inconsistent Christian, perhaps through lack of understanding relative to the mind of Christ? Or having confessed Christ as his Savior is he failing to integrate his scholarship with the teachings of Christ in a logical manner (cf. Col. 2:6)? God alone must judge. In either event, as J. I. Packer has so rightly observed, "any view that subjects the written word of God to the opinions and pronouncements of men involves unbelief and disloyalty toward Christ."[13] It is like Ephraim's worship on the high places after Jehu's removal of Phoenician Baalism: An overt invocation of the name of Yahweh, while persisting in a life opposed to his revealed authority, can result only, as previously suggested, in idolatry. Scripture moreover leaves us all with the wonderful and yet terrible pronouncement: "He that believeth, *ho pisteuon*, in the Son hath eternal life; but he who will not believe, *ho pisteuon*, the Son shall not see life, but the wrath of God abideth on him" (John 3:36).

But there is a second concluding question, which asks, "What are the implications for those who *are* willing to follow Jesus in his allegiance to Scripture?" Returning to John 15, one finds in verse 15 Christ's words: "Greater love hath no man than this, that a man lay down his life for his friends." Christ's love for us was demonstrated on Calvary, but if we have become "friends" of his, then we too should demonstrate our love as we commit our lives to identification with both him and his commitments. For example, this last summer the Committee of Fifteen [formerly N.A.E.-Christian Reformed] on Bible Translation adopted a resolution to require affirmations on biblical inerrancy from all who are to be associated with this major project. Their move took real courage in the face of current re-

[13] J. I. Packer, *"Fundamentalism" and the Word of God* (London: InterVarsity, 1958), 21.

sistance to scriptural authority. Sacrifice, moreover, is entailed, for in verse 19 our Lord goes on to explain, "Because ye are not of the world, but I chose you out of the world, therefore the world hateth you." This committee, as a result of its stand, suffered attack and withdrawal of support. Indeed, we should all take to heart Paul's admonition, "Strive together with me in your prayers to God for me, that I may be delivered from *tōn apeithountōn*" (Rom. 15:30–31), those who will not be persuaded. Yet in verse 27 Christ finished this discourse by observing: "And ye also bear witness, because ye have been with me from the beginning." We are persistently to proclaim submission to Christ, even as our Lord "in the spirit . . . went and preached unto them . . . that aforetime were *apeithēsasin*, unpersuaded, when the longsuffering of God waited in the days of Noah" (1 Pet. 3:20). Should words themselves fail, we are to bear witness by lives of Christian love, so "that if any *apeithousin*, refuse to be persuaded, by the word, they may without the word be gained by the behavior of" (3:1) those who have experienced the power of lives yielded to Christ and to his Bible, the inerrant Scriptures.

Part 2

Scripture

3

"The Attestation of Scripture"

JOHN MURRAY

The Infallible Word

Previously published as "The Attestation of Scripture," in *The Infallible Word: A Symposium*, ed. N. B. Stonehouse and Paul Woolley (1946; repr., Phillipsburg, NJ: P&R Publishing, 2003), 1–54. Reprinted with permission of P&R Publishing Co., P.O. Box 817, Phillipsburg, NJ 08865, www.prpbooks.com.

The Objective Witness

Christians of varied and diverse theological standpoints aver that the Bible is the Word of God, that it is inspired by the Holy Spirit, and that it occupies a unique place as the norm of Christian faith and life. But such general confessions or admissions do not of themselves settle for us the view entertained with respect to the origin, authority, and character of Holy Scripture. A passing acquaintance with the literature on this subject will show that such propositions are made to do service in the expression of wholly diverse views of the nature of Scripture. It becomes incumbent upon us, therefore, to define and examine the statement that the Bible is the Word of God.

Diversity of viewpoint with respect to this proposition has generally, if not always, taken its starting point from the recognition that the Bible has come to us through human instrumentality. Every book of the Bible has had its human author. The Bible did not come to us directly from heaven; in its totality and in all its parts it has come to us through human agency. Since this is the case, every serious student of the Bible has to take cognisance of the human factor in the preparation, composition, and completion of what we know as the canon of Holy Writ.

If, then, human instruments have performed a function in producing the Bible, does it not necessarily follow that the marks of human fallibility and error must be imprinted on the Bible? Since the fall of our first parents, no perfect human being has walked upon this earth. It is true there was one, indeed human, who was holy, harmless, undefiled, and separate from sinners. But he was more than human; he was the eternal Son of God manifest in the flesh. If he had written the Bible, then the question with which we are now faced would not need to be asked. In any case, there would be at hand a very ready answer to the question. The infallibility of Christ's human nature would provide us with a simple answer to the very urgent and difficult question: How can the Bible be the Word of God and at the same time the work of man? The resolution of the apparent antinomy would be provided by the fact that the person who wrote it was himself perfect God and perfect man.

The Lord Jesus Christ, however, did not write the Bible nor any part of it. When he left this world and went to the Father, he left no books that were the product of his pen. So in every case the Bible and all the Bible was written by those who were mere men and therefore by men who, without exception, were themselves imperfect and fallible.

This plain and undisputed fact has led many students of the Bible to the conclusion that the Bible cannot be in itself the infallible and inerrant Word of God. Putting the matter very bluntly, they have said that God had to use the material he had at his disposal and, since the material he had was fallible men, he was under the necessity of giving us his Word in a form that is marred by the defects arising from human fallibility. In the words of Dr. J. Monro Gibson:

> It is important at the outset to remember that the most consummate artist is limited by the nature of his material. He may have thoughts and inspirations far above and beyond what he can express in black-and-white or in colors, in marble or in bronze, in speech or in song; but however perfect his idea may be, it must, in finding expression, share the imperfections of the forms in which he works. If this very obvious fact had only been kept in mind, most of the difficulties which beset the subject of inspiration need never have arisen.[1]

And then Dr. Gibson proceeds to enumerate some of the limitations with which God had to deal, the limitations of human agency, human language, and literary forms.

[1] John Monro Gibson, *The Inspiration and Authority of Holy Scripture* (New York: Revell, n.d.), 146.

It is by plausible argument of this sort that students of the Bible, like Dr. Gibson, have too rashly come to the conclusion that the human factor or, as we should prefer to call it, human instrumentality settles this question and that the Bible, though God's Word, must at the same time be errant and fallible, at least in scientific and historical detail, simply because it came to us through the ministry of men. Dr. Gibson is very jealous that we should follow the facts and let the Bible speak for itself rather than approach the Bible with a preconceived notion of divine infallibility. It is, however, just because we are jealous that the Bible should speak for itself that we must not take it for granted that human authorship necessitates errancy and fallibility.

The fact of human authorship does indeed seem to provide a very easy argument for the errancy and fallibility of Scripture. Or, to state the matter less invidiously, human authorship seems to provide a very easy and necessary explanation of what are alleged to be the facts of errancy and fallibility. We must accept the facts, it is said, rather than hide behind the theory of inerrancy.

Those who thus contend should, however, be aware of the implications of their position. If human fallibility precludes an infallible Scripture, then by resistless logic it must be maintained that we cannot have any Scripture that is infallible and inerrant. All of Scripture comes to us through human instrumentality. If such instrumentality involves fallibility, then such fallibility must attach to the whole of Scripture. For by what warrant can an immunity from error be maintained in the matter of "spiritual content" and not in the matter of historical or scientific fact? Is human fallibility suspended when "spiritual truth" is asserted but not suspended in other less important matters?[2]

Furthermore, if infallibility can attach to the "spiritual truth" enunciated by the biblical writers, then it is obvious that some extraordinary divine influence must have intervened and become operative so as to prevent human fallibility from leaving its mark upon the truth expressed. If divine influence could thus intrude itself at certain points, why should not this same preserving power exercise itself at every point in the writing of Scripture? Again, surely human fallibility is just as liable to be at work in

[2] The phrase "spiritual truth" is used here by way of accommodation to the views of those who in the discussion of this question stress the distinction between the outward form of the Bible and the religious content of which the Bible is the vehicle. Cf., e.g., W. Sanday, *The Oracles of God* (London, 1892), 29f.; R. H. Malden, *The Inspiration of the Bible* (London, 1935), 5f.

connection with the enunciation of transcendent truths as it is when it deals with the details of historical occurrence.

It is surely quite obvious that the appeal to human fallibility in the interest of supporting, or at least defending, biblical fallibility is glaringly inconsequent, if it is maintained that God has at any point given us through human agency an infallible and inerrant Word. Either a priori argument from human fallibility has to be abandoned or the position must be taken that human fallibility has left its mark upon all of Scripture and no part of it can be called the infallible Word of God, not even John 3:16. We cannot too strenuously press the opponents of biblical inerrancy to the implications of their position. Human fallibility cannot with any consistency be pleaded as an argument for the fallibility of Scripture unless the position is taken that we do not have in the Scriptures content of any kind that is not marred by the frailty of human nature.

This plea for consistency does not mean, however, that biblical infallibility is thereby proven. While it is necessary to remove any a priori argument, drawn from human fallibility that would do prejudice to the evidence, the doctrine of biblical inerrancy must rest upon the proper evidence. In this case, as in all other doctrine, the evidence is the witness of Scripture itself. Does the Scripture claim inerrancy for itself and, if so, must this claim be accepted?

It must be freely admitted that there are difficulties connected with the doctrine of biblical infallibility. There appear to be discrepancies and contradictions in the Bible. Naturally we cannot be expected to believe what we perceive to involve a contradiction. Furthermore, disingenuous and artificial attempts at harmony are to be avoided, for they do not advance the cause of truth and of faith. The conscientious student has, therefore, great difficulty sometimes in resolving problems raised by apparent contradictions. It is true that many such resolve themselves when careful study is applied to them, and oftentimes the resolution of the difficulty in the light of the various factors involved becomes the occasion for the discovery of a harmony and fullness of meaning that otherwise would not have been recognized by us. But some difficulties, perhaps many, remain unresolved. The earnest student has no adequate answer, and he may frankly confess that he is not able to explain an apparent discrepancy in the teaching of Scripture.

It might seem that this confession of his own inability to resolve seeming discrepancy is not compatible with faith in Scripture as infallible. This is, however, at the best, very superficial judgment. There is no doctrine of our Christian faith that does not confront us with unresolved difficulties here in this world, and the difficulties become all the greater just as we get nearer to the centre. It is in connection with the most transcendent mysteries of our faith that the difficulties multiply. The person who thinks he has resolved all the difficulties surrounding our established faith in the Trinity has probably no true faith in the triune God. The person who encounters no unresolved mystery in the incarnation of the Son of God and in his death on Calvary's tree has not yet learned the meaning of 1 Timothy 3:16. Yet these unanswered questions are not incompatible with unshaken faith in the triune God and in Jesus Christ, the incarnate Son. The questions are often perplexing. But they are more often the questions of adoring wonder rather than the questions of painful perplexity.

So there should be no surprise if faith in God's inerrant Word should be quite consonant with unresolved questions and difficulties with regard to the very content of this faith.

The defense of the foregoing position that faith is not inconsistent with unresolved questions is far more crucial in this debate than might at first appear. It lies very close to the vital question of what is the proper ground of faith in the Bible as the Word of God. The ground of faith emphatically is not our ability to demonstrate all the teaching of the Bible to be self-consistent and true. This is just saying that rational demonstration is not the ground of faith. The demand that apparent contradictions in the Bible should have to be removed before we accord it our credit as God's infallible Word rests, therefore, upon a wholly mistaken notion of the only proper ground of faith in the Bible. It is indeed true that we should not close our minds and researches to the ever-progressing resolution of difficulties under the illumination of the Spirit of truth, but those whose approach to faith is that of resolution of all difficulty have deserted the very nature of faith and of its ground.

The nature of faith is acceptance on the basis of testimony, and the ground of faith is therefore testimony or evidence. In this matter it is the evidence God has provided, and God provides the evidence in his Word, the Bible. This means simply that the basis of faith in the Bible is the witness the Bible itself bears to the fact that it is God's Word, and our faith that it is infallible must rest upon no other basis than the witness the Bible bears to this fact. If the Bible does not witness to its own infallibility, then we have no right to believe that it is infallible. If it does bear witness to its infallibility, then our faith in it must rest upon that witness, however much difficulty may be entertained with this belief. If this position with respect to the ground of faith in Scripture is abandoned, then appeal to the Bible for the ground of faith in any other doctrine must also be abandoned. The doctrine of Scripture must be elicited from the Scripture just as any other doctrine should be.[3] If the doctrine of Scripture is denied its right to appeal to Scripture for its support, then what right does any other doctrine have to make this appeal? Faith in the Trinity does not have to wait for the resolution of all difficulties that the teaching of Scripture presents to us on this question; it does not have to wait for the resolution of all apparent contradictions in the teaching of Scripture on the Trinity. So neither does faith in Scripture as the inerrant Word of God have to wait for the resolution of all difficulties in the matter of inerrancy.

The real question then becomes: What is the witness of Scripture with reference to its own character? It is important to appreciate the precise scope of this question; it is to elicit from the Scripture the evidence it contains bearing upon its origin, character, and authority. This approach is very different from the approach that too many claim to be the only scientific and inductive approach. It is often said that we must not go to the Bible with an a priori theory of its infallibility, but we must go to the Bible with an open mind and find out what the facts are and frame our theory from the facts rather than impose our theory upon the facts. There is an element of truth in this contention. It is fully granted that we should never approach Scripture with an a priori theory of its character and impose that theory upon the evidence. We just as vigorously repudiate any such method, as do others, and we have to impute to many liberal and radical students the very fault which they are too ready to impute to the orthodox believer. But while the a priori method of approach must on all accounts be condemned, it does not follow that the proper approach is that of the alleged inductive and scientific method. We do not elicit the doctrine of Scripture from an inductive study of what we suppose determines its character. We derive our doctrine of Scripture from what the Scripture teaches with respect to its own character—in a word, from the testimony it bears to itself.

This might seem to be arguing in a circle. It might seem analogous to the case of the judge who accepts the witness of the accused in his own defense rather than the evidence derived from all the relevant facts in the case. We should, however, be little disturbed by this type of criticism. It contains an inherent fallacy. It is fully admitted that normally it would be absurd

[3] W. Sanday states this principle well enough when he says that "we may lay it down as a fundamental principle that a true conception of what the Bible is must be obtained from the Bible itself" (*op. cit.*, 47). But Sanday does not carry out this principle consistently in that he fails to apply it to the express witness Scripture bears to its own character.

and a miscarriage of justice for a judge to accept the testimony of the accused rather than the verdict required by all the relevant evidence. But the two cases are not analogous. There is one sphere where self-testimony must be accepted as absolute and final. This is the sphere of our relation to God. God alone is adequate witness to himself. And our discussion with respect to the character of Scripture belongs to this category. Our discussion is premised upon the proposition that the Bible is the Word of God and therefore premised on the presupposition that it is unique and belongs to the realm of the divine. For this reason the argument from self-testimony is in order and perfectly consistent. Indeed, it is the only procedure that is consistent with the uniqueness of the question with which we are dealing.

This position does not by any means imply that the believer in biblical infallibility can afford to be indifferent neither to the difficulties that may arise in connection with apparent discrepancies nor to the attacks made upon infallibility from various sides on the basis of what are alleged to be disharmonies and contradictions. The believer cannot at any time afford to be obscurantist; and orthodox scholarship must set right criticism over against wrong criticism. The motto of faith must be: "Prove all things, hold fast that which is good." The believer must always be ready to give a reason for the faith that is in him. But he must also remember that the character and content of his faith in Scripture as the Word of God must be dictated by the divine witness bearing directly upon that precise question. What then is the testimony of the Scripture regarding itself? For to this question we must now address ourselves.

First of all, there is the negative evidence. The Scripture does not adversely criticize itself. One part of Scripture does not expose another part as erroneous. It goes without saying that if Scripture itself witnessed to the errancy and fallibility of another part, then such witness would be finality, and belief in the inerrancy of Scripture would have to be abandoned. But it is a signal fact that one Scripture does not predicate error of another. It is true that the Scripture contains the record of much sin and error in the history of men, of Satan, and of demons. The Bible, of course, is to a large extent historical in character and, since history is strewn with sin, the Bible could not fail to record the dark and dismal story. Indeed, the frankness and candor of the Bible in this regard is one of its most striking features. The openness with which it exposes even the sins of the saints is one of the most signal marks of its authenticity. But the condemnation of the very sin and error the Bible records is not witness to its own fallibility. It is rather an integral part of the witness to its own credibility and, so far from constituting any evidence against itself as inerrant Scripture, it thereby contributes evidence that is most germane to the establishment of its infallibility.

It is also true that the Bible fully recognizes the temporary and provisional character of many of the regulations and ordinances which it represents as imposed by divine authority. The most relevant case in point here is the temporary character of many of the regulations of the Mosaic law. That the observance of these preparatory and temporary precepts, rites, and ceremonies has been discontinued with the advent and establishment of the Christian economy is the express teaching of the New Testament. But in such teaching there is no reflection whatsoever on the divinely authoritative character of such provisions under that economy in which they were operative and, far more, no reflection upon the infallibility of that Old Testament Scripture which embodies the revelation to us of that divine institution. For example, when Paul in the epistle to the Galatians writes, "Behold, I Paul say unto you, that if ye be circumcised, Christ shall profit you nothing" (Gal. 5:2), he in no way casts any aspersion on the truth of those Old Testament books which inform us of the institution of circumcision and of its divinely authorized practice among the people of God from Abraham onwards. In fact, the same Paul lends the strongest corroboration to the truth of the Old Testament in this regard when he says elsewhere with reference to Abraham, "And he received the sign of circumcision, a seal of the righteousness of the faith which he had yet being uncircumcised" (Rom. 4:11).

Our thesis at this point will, of course, be vigorously challenged. It will be said that abundant evidence can be produced to show that Scripture does expose as erroneous the distinct representations of other parts of Scripture. To put the opposing argument otherwise, it is said that one part of Scripture says one thing and another part of Scripture dealing with the very same situation says something else. For example, the Pentateuch represents the Levitical laws with respect to sacrifice as ordained by divine revelation and authority after the children of Israel came out of Egypt and while they were sojourning in the wilderness. It cannot be questioned that this is the story of the Pentateuch. But the prophet Jeremiah writes as the word of the Lord, "For I spake not unto your fathers, nor commanded them in the day that I brought them out of the land of Egypt, concerning burnt offerings or sacrifices: but this thing commanded I them, saying, Obey my voice, and I will be your God, and ye shall be my people: and walk ye in all the ways that I have commanded you, that it may be well unto you" (Jer. 7:22–23).

It must be replied that the argument based on this antithesis in the prophecy of Jeremiah fails to appreciate one of the basic principles of biblical interpretation, namely, that a relative contrast is often expressed in absolute terms. What is being protested against in Jeremiah 7:22–23 is the externalism and formalism of Israel. Mere ritual, even when the ritual is of divine institution, is religiously worthless, indeed is hypocrisy, if the real religious import of that ritual is not understood and particularly when the moral requirements of God's law are trampled under foot. Ceremonial ritual without ethical integrity and particularly without regard to spiritual attachment and obedience to the Lord God is mockery. And it is just of this formalism and hypocrisy that Isaiah writes, "Your new moons and your appointed feasts my soul hateth: they are a trouble unto me; I am weary to bear them" (Isa. 1:14).

The objection arising from such passages, however, confuses the precise question of our present thesis. Such passages as these, however great may appear to be the discrepancy in the witness of Scripture, do not fall into the category with which we are now dealing. For they are not, even on the most radical interpretation of the discrepancy, exposures of error on the part of one writer of Scripture of statements made by another writer. Jeremiah in other words does not quote the Pentateuch and then say that the statement concerned is an error and must therefore be corrected. While Jeremiah 7:22–23 constitutes an apparent discrepancy in the testimony of Scripture, Jeremiah does not quote another writer and overtly or impliedly say that this writer was in error. It is in that particular question we are now interested.

The passages in what is generally called the Sermon on the Mount, where Jesus appears to set up an antithesis between his own teaching and the regulatory statutes of the Pentateuch, might plausibly be appealed to in this connection as instituting criticism of some of the Mosaic ordinances. Even though Jesus did not write Scripture, yet the finality of his teaching would make an appeal to his authority quite relevant to the present phase of our discussion. If it could be demonstrated that these passages in Matthew do involve criticism of the Mosaic regulations which Jesus quotes, then the divine character of the Pentateuch would in these particulars be impugned.

It must be recognized at the outset that even if Jesus could be shown to appeal to his own authority as setting aside the Mosaic provisions concerned, this does not establish the errancy of these provisions nor overthrow the fact of their divine authority and sanction under the Mosaic dispensation. We have already shown that the abrogation of the temporary legislation of the Pentateuch does not in the least impugn its authenticity, infallibility, or divine character and authority. So Jesus might well have abrogated the observance of certain Mosaic ordinances and yet not in the least reflect upon their divine origin and character nor upon their divine authority during the period of their application and operation.[4] Surely nothing more than this could with any reason be elicited from these passages in Matthew, and it is obvious that such does not provide us with any evidence that Jesus taught the errancy or fallibility of the five books of Moses.

We must, however, insist that it is not at all apparent that the notion of abrogation is the key to the interpretation of these antitheses. It should be remembered that the preface to this whole section in Jesus' teaching is in these words:

> Think not that I am come to destroy the law, or the prophets: I am not come to destroy, but to fulfill. For verily I say unto you, Till heaven and earth pass, one jot or one tittle shall in no wise pass from the law, till all be fulfilled. Whosoever therefore shall break one of these least commandments, and shall teach men so, he shall be called the least in the kingdom of heaven: but whosoever shall do and teach them, the same shall be called great in the kingdom of heaven. (Matt. 5:17–20)

A careful reading of this passage will show that any reflection upon the character of the law and the prophets or any insinuation of their errancy is entirely out of the question. As we shall see later, the import of such references to the law and the prophets is to the very opposite effect. But, with more precise reference to our present discussion of the idea of abrogation, it would seem very strange indeed that Jesus would have made such an unequivocal appeal to the inviolability of every jot and tittle of the law and to the sanctions attending the breach of one of these least commandments as well as to the divine blessing accruing to the observance of them, and then have proceeded forthwith to teach the abrogation of these very commandments. There would be contradiction in any such view of the sequence and in such an interpretation of the import of the antitheses. We must therefore turn in some other direction for the meaning of Jesus' teaching in these verses. Dr. Stonehouse has admirably shown that

[4] The word "abrogated" in this sentence should not be interpreted as inconsistent with what will be later maintained with respect to the permanent meaning of validity of the law. We are speaking now simply of the discontinuance of the *observance* of certain ordinances.

> understood as illustrations of Jesus' fulfillment of the law, the antitheses then provide no support of the thesis that they involve an abrogation of the objective authority of the law. In the single instance where an enactment through Moses is set aside as provisional, namely, in the instance of the provision for a bill of divorcement, Jesus appeals decisively to the teaching of the law which is not circumscribed by reference to a temporary state of affairs. In the five other cases the design of Jesus is to show that current interpretations are inadequate as abiding by the externals or are in error as to the actual requirements of the law.[5]

These antitheses then constitute no evidence that Jesus taught or even insinuated that any part of the Pentateuch or of the Old Testament was in error and therefore calculated to misinform us as to fact or doctrine.

We must now turn, in the second place, to the positive evidence the Scripture contains with respect to the character of Scripture. However significant and important the absence of evidence calculated to deny the inerrancy of Scripture may be, it is upon positive evidence that the doctrine of biblical infallibility must rest.

In the Old Testament we find a great deal of evidence that bears directly upon the divine character and authority of what is written. Much that is written by the prophets, for example, is, by introductory statements such as "Thus saith the Lord," asserted to be divine in origin, content, and authority. In the most express way the divine seal is attached to what is written. Obviously, if error could be discovered in or predicated of any of the passages bearing this seal, then there are only two alternatives. The claim to be the Word of the Lord must be rejected or fallibility must be predicated of the divine utterance. From the latter every Christian must recoil. The former must reject the testimony of Scripture with respect to the character of its own content. If that is done, then our argument is at an end. The premise of our whole thesis, indeed our thesis itself, is that the doctrine of Scripture must be based upon the witness of Scripture just as any other doctrine in the whole realm of Christian confession. So the adoption of this alternative means the abandonment of the witness of Scripture as the basis of Christian doctrine. If the witness of Scripture is not accepted as the ground of the doctrine of Scripture, if it is not reliable in this department of doctrine, then by what right can its witness be pleaded as the authority in any department of truth?

Again, in the Old Testament the way in which the later books of the

[5] N. B. Stonehouse, *The Witness of Matthew and Mark to Christ* (Philadelphia, 1944), 209.

Old Testament appeal to the laws enunciated in the Pentateuch presupposes the divine authority and sanction of these laws. For example, there is the indictment which the last of the Old Testament prophets, Malachi, brings against his people.

> Ye said also, Behold what a weariness is it! and ye have snuffed at it, saith the Lord of hosts; and ye brought that which was torn, and the lame, and the sick; thus ye brought an offering: should I accept this of your hand? saith the Lord. But cursed be the deceiver, which hath in his flock a male, and voweth, and sacrificeth unto the Lord a corrupt thing: for I am a great King, saith the Lord of hosts, and my name is dreadful among the heathen. (Mal. 1:13–14)

> Even from the days of your fathers ye are gone away from my ordinances, and have not kept them. Return unto me, and I will return unto you, saith the Lord of hosts. But ye said, Wherein shall we return? Will a man rob God? Yet ye have robbed me. But ye say, wherein have we robbed thee? In tithes and offerings. (Mal. 2:7–8)

Such accusations are meaningless on any other assumption than that of the divine authority and obligation of the Levitical law (cf. Mal. 2:4–8). And the endorsement of Moses is put beyond all question when at the end of his prophecy Malachi writes, "Remember ye the law of Moses my servant, which I commanded unto him in Horeb for all Israel, with the statutes and judgments" (Mal. 4:4). It is surely of the greatest weight that the long line of Old Testament prophetic witness should come to its close with so insistent an appeal for devotion to the law of Moses, the Lord's servant, and that the intertestamentary period should be bridged, as it were, by the retrospective and the prospective, the appeal to Moses, on the one hand, and the promise of the resumption of the prophetic voice in him than whom there should not have arisen a greater, namely, John the Baptist, on the other (cf. chap. 4:5).

It is not, however, in the Old Testament that the most cogent evidence of a positive character, relative to this question, appears. For we do not have in the Old Testament any reference on the part of its writers to that collection of canonical writings in its entirety. In the nature of the case, this could not reasonably be expected. Consequently we should not expect in the Old Testament any express predication or witness with respect to the whole collection of Old Testament books looked at in their unity as a fixed canon of sacred writings. In the New Testament the perspective is quite different in this respect. When the New Testament era opens to our view, the Old Testament books comprise a fixed collection of sacred writings. They exist before the speakers and writers of the New Testament period as a distinct corpus of authoritative writings viewed not only in their diversity but also and very distinctly in their unity as the canon of faith. Consequently, we find in the New Testament the most express and distinct estimate of the character of this body of writings viewed in their sum and unity as an entity capable of such characterisation. It is such witness that is most directly pertinent to the present subject. What is the witness of the New Testament to the character of the Old Testament?

When we say "the witness of the New Testament," we mean, of course, the authoritative speakers and writers of the New Testament. First and foremost among such authoritative witnesses is our Lord himself. His word is a finality; on any other supposition the whole superstructure of Christian faith must totter and crumble. What then is our Lord's testimony with respect to the Old Testament?

We have had occasion to quote and discuss the passage in Matthew 5:17–19 in another context. It is relevant to our present purpose in that it provides us with one of the most striking testimonies to the estimate of the Old Testament entertained by Jesus. It is highly probable that when Jesus says "the law or the prophets," he denotes by these two designations the whole of the Old Testament, the law denoting what we know as the Pentateuch and the prophets the rest of the Old Testament. It is possible that by "the prophets" he means the specifically prophetic books of the Old Testament, and by "the law" he may have had in mind the law of Moses in the more specific sense of the legislative economy embodied in the Pentateuch. If he is using these terms in the more specific sense, it would be wholly arbitrary, indeed casuistic and contrary to all of the evidence, to suppose that there is the least hint in such a specific use of the terms "law" and "prophets" that other parts of the Old Testament are in a different category in respect of authority. In this passage, then, Jesus gives us his estimate of at least a very large part of the Old Testament and his conception of the relation that it sustained to his messianic work. He came not to destroy the law or the prophets; he came to fulfill.

The word "destroy" (Καταλύω) is peculiarly significant. It means to abrogate, to demolish, to disintegrate, to annul or, as J. A. Alexander points out, "the destruction of a whole by the complete separation of its parts, as when a house is taken down by being taken to pieces."[6] His emphatic

[6] J. A. Alexander, *The Gospel according to Matthew Explained* (London, 1884), 126.

denial of any such purpose in reference to either the law or the prophets means that the discharge of his messianic mission leaves the law and the prophets intact. He utters, however, not only this emphatic denial but also adds the positive purpose of his coming—he came to fulfill, to complete. And so his work with reference to both law and prophets is completory, not destructive. He who can speak in the immediately succeeding context with such solemn asseveration and imperious authority brings all that is involved in such asseveration and authority to bear upon the confirmation of the abiding validity, stability, and authority of both law and prophets. And not only so, but he also grounds his own mission and task upon such permanent validity and defines his work in terms of fulfillment of all that the law and the prophets provided.

In verse 18 Jesus proceeds to apply the general statement of verse 17 to the very minutiae of the law. It is this application of the general assertion to the minutest details that is particularly pertinent to our present topic. General statements may sometimes not cover, or provide for, certain exceptions in detail. But here Jesus precludes any possibility of discrepancy between the general and the particular. He is saying in effect, "This proposition that I came not to destroy but to fulfill applies not simply in general terms but also to the minutest particulars." And not simply is this the case; the connection expressed by the conjunction is also that the general statement of verse 17 is grounded in the fact that not one jot or tittle, not the minutest detail, will pass from the law till all be fulfilled. To enforce and seal the veracity of this, Jesus uses the formula that combines asseveration and authority, "Verily I say unto you."

The "jot" is the smallest letter of the Hebrew alphabet and the "tittle" is the minute horn or projection that distinguishes consonants of similar form from one another. It would be impossible to think of any expression that would bespeak the thought of the meticulous more adequately than precisely this one used here by our Lord. In respect of the meticulous, our English expression "one letter or syllable" is scarcely equivalent. Could anything establish more conclusively the meticulous accuracy, validity, and truth of the law than the language to which Jesus here attaches his own unique formula of asseveration? Many professing Christians recoil from the doctrine of verbal inspiration, the doctrine which means simply that the inspiration of Scripture extends to the very words as well as to the thoughts. It is difficult to understand why those who assent to inspiration should stumble at *verbal* inspiration. For words are the media of thought and, so far as Scripture is concerned, the written words are the only media of communication. If the thoughts are inspired, the words must be also. But whatever the case may be in the sphere of logic, the antipathy to verbal inspiration has little in common with the very obvious import of Jesus' representation in this passage. The indissolubility of the law extends to its every jot and tittle. Such indissolubility could not be predicated of it if it were in any detail fallible, for if fallible it would someday come to nought. And this is just saying that in every detail the law was in his esteem infallible and therefore indissoluble. It is indeed strange prejudice that professes adherence to the infallibility of Christ and yet rejects the clear implications of his teaching. Nothing could be plainer than this, that in the smallest details he regards the law as incapable of being made void and that in the smallest details it is taken up by him and finds, in his fulfillment of it, its permanent embodiment and validity. By the most stringent necessity there is but one conclusion, namely, that the law is infallible and inerrant.

In our discussion of Matthew 5:17–19, we left open the possibility that Jesus was using the terms "law" and "prophets" in a more restricted and specific sense. It is far from being certain that this interpretation of the scope of his words is justifiable. It is far more reasonable to believe that he had the whole Old Testament in mind. But we must not prejudice the argument by insisting upon this, for the argument we are now pursuing does not rest upon it. The witness of our Lord to the character of the Old Testament is so copious that what is not supplied by one passage is supplied by another. If the books other than those of Moses and the prophets are not expressly alluded to in Matthew 5:17–19, they certainly are in other places. One of the most striking of these is John 10:33–36, and to this part of his witness we may now turn.[7]

The occasion for his speaking these words was that created by the reaction of the Jews to his claim, "I and the Father are one." The Jews rightly interpreted this claim as meaning that Jesus placed himself on equality with God. This they regarded as blasphemy, and they took up stones to stone him. Jesus' claim was, of course, a stupendous one, and there are only two alternatives. Either his claim was true or he did utter blasphemy. Here Jesus did not simply claim to be the Messiah; he claimed to be equal with the Father. The charge brought by the Jews was not a whit too severe if their conception of Jesus was correct. Quite logically on their own presuppositions their charge struck at the centre of Jesus' claim and therefore at the

[7] It is not within the scope of this article to discuss the critical questions that have been raised with respect to the Gospel according to John and other New Testament writings which are appealed to in the subsequent argument.

basis of his mission and work. The charge denied his deity and his veracity. If validated, it would have exposed Jesus' claim as the most iniquitous imposture.

It was a charge with such implications that Jesus had to answer. If ever the resources of effective rebuttal needed to be drawn upon, it was at such a juncture. How did he meet the charge? "Jesus answered them, Is it not written in your law, I said ye are gods? If he called them gods unto whom the word of God came, and the scripture cannot be broken, say ye of him whom the Father sanctified and sent into the world, Thou blasphemest, because I said I am the Son of God." As we read this reply, we are amazed at what appears to be the facility and composure with which it is given as well as at what appears to be its restraint. Indeed, on superficial reading it might appear to be weak and ineffective. But the facility, composure, and restraint, which we believe are real, as well as the apparent weakness, which is not real, all converge to demonstrate the significance for our present purpose of his appeal to Scripture. He staked his argument for the rebuttal of the most serious allegation that could be brought against him upon a brief statement drawn from Psalm 82:6. It is this appeal to Scripture that is the pivot of his whole defence. This cannot be explained on any other basis than that he considered the Scriptures as the unassailable instrument of defence. For "the scripture cannot be broken."

Just as eloquent of Jesus' use of Scripture is, what appears to us, the obscurity of the passage to which he appeals. It would seem to have no direct bearing upon the question at issue. Yet Jesus uses this apparently obscure and less important passage as his argument to answer an attack that was aimed at the very centre of his person and teaching and work. And furthermore, this passage is drawn from that part of the Old Testament that possibly, so far as our argument is concerned, did not come within his purview in Matthew 5:17. Does this not show that his attitude to every jot and tittle of the Psalms was identical with that to every jot and tittle of the law? Upon any other supposition, his appeal to a brief and relatively obscure statement of the book of Psalms would be quite forceless and inconclusive.

Finally, the force of the brief parenthetical clause, "the scripture cannot be broken," has to be noted. It might be plausibly argued that Jesus in his reply to the Jews was simply taking advantage of an ad hominem argument. In the question, "Is it not written in your law?" Jesus is meeting his adversaries on their own assumptions. And so, it might be said, no argument bearing upon Jesus' own view of Scripture could be based on this passage. But Jesus' remark, "the scripture cannot be broken," silences any such contention. In this remark Jesus expresses not simply the attitude of the Jews to Scripture but his own view of the inviolability of Scripture. He appeals to Scripture because it is really and intrinsically a finality. And when he says "the Scripture cannot be broken," he is surely using the word "Scripture" in its most comprehensive denotation as including all that the Jews of the day recognised as Scripture, to wit, all the canonical books of the Old Testament. It is of the Old Testament without any reservation or exception that he says, it "cannot be broken." Here then there can be no question as to how much of the Old Testament came within the purview or scope of his assertion. He affirms the unbreakableness of the Scripture in its entirety and leaves no room for any such supposition as that of degrees of inspiration and fallibility. Scripture is inviolable. Nothing less than this is the testimony of our Lord. And the crucial nature of such witness is driven home by the fact that it is in answer to the most serious of charges and in the defence of his most stupendous claim that he bears this testimony.

In passages such as those with which we have just dealt, our Lord's view of Scripture comes to explicit expression and exposition. It is not, however, in a few passages that his viewpoint is attested. There is a mass of evidence that corroborates the express teaching of the more explicit passages. Indeed, corroboration is too weak a word to do justice to the import of the mass of evidence bearing upon the question. Rather should we say that the teaching of our Lord is so steeped in the appeal to Scripture, so steeped in the use of the formula, "it is written," so pervaded by the recognition that what Scripture says God says, so characterised by the acceptance of the finality of the word of Scripture, that the doctrine of Scripture clearly enunciated in some passages is the necessary presupposition of the correlative evidence. The inescapable fact is that the mass of direct and indirect statement leads to one conclusion that, for our Lord, the Scripture, just because it was *Scripture*, just because it fell within the denotation of the formula, "it is written," was a finality. His attitude is one of meticulous acceptance and reverence. The only explanation of such an attitude is that what Scripture said, God said, that the Scripture was God's Word, that it was God's Word because it was Scripture, and that it was or became Scripture because it was God's Word. That he distinguished between the Word of God borne to us by Scripture and the written Word itself would be an imposition upon Jesus' own teaching wholly alien to the identifications Jesus makes and to the reverence for the letter of Scripture so pervasive in all of his witness.

To institute a contrast between the teaching of our Lord and of his apostles on the question of Scripture would, of course, disrupt the harmony of the New Testament witness. The establishment of such disharmony would admittedly be a serious matter, and it would have far-reaching consequences for the whole construction of Christian truth. Regarding the respective views of Scripture, discrepancy between Jesus and the writers of the New Testament could be sought in either of two directions. It could be sought in the direction of trying to find a more liberal view of Scripture reflected in the writers, or at least in some of the writers, of the New Testament, or it might be sought in the direction of showing that in the writings of the New Testament there is a petrifying and mechanising process at work so that the more organic and elastic view of Jesus is transformed and brought into accord with the allegedly more scholastic and legalistic bias of later developments. We already found what our Lord's teaching was. We found it to be nothing less than that of the infallible character and authority of the Old Testament. A higher view of plenary or verbal inspiration we could not expect to find. If discrepancy between Jesus and the writers of the New Testament is to be sought, it would not be reasonable, in view of the evidence, to seek it in the greater liberalism of Jesus. When we turn in the other direction, do we find any relaxation of the rigidity of Jesus' teaching in those who were his appointed witnesses?

Any adequate examination of this question would lead us far beyond our space in this volume. But is it not of the greatest pertinence that the books of the New Testament show that same characteristic which is so patent in the teaching of Christ, namely, appeal to what had been written? It surely is singular that the New Testament, not only in the reporting of Jesus' teaching but also as a whole, should, as it were, rest its case so frequently upon the adduction of Scripture proof and should authenticate the history of the Old Testament by such copious reference to it. Its witness in general is to the same effect as is summed up in the words of Paul, "For whatsoever things were written aforetime were written for our learning, that we through patience and comfort of the scriptures might have hope" (Rom. 15:4), an appraisal of the whole of the Old Testament that is preceded by a thoroughly typical appeal to the Old Testament as testifying beforehand to the example of Christ that he pleased not himself and as therefore not only witnessing to the fact that Christ pleased not himself but as also supporting the exhortation "Let everyone of us please his neighbour for his good to edification" (Rom. 15:2). It is precisely in such estimation of the Scriptures and in such allusion to them, as not only prophetic of what took place in the fullness of time but also as having direct bearing upon the most practical and abiding of Christian duties, that the New Testament abounds. And this is just saying that the Old Testament is not simply true as history, prophecy, and law but that it is also of abiding validity, application, and authority.

But just as we found in the case of our Lord, that the high view of the inspiration of Scripture not only underlies the formulae and allusions in which his teaching abounds but also comes to explicit expression in specific passages, so is it in the case of the other authoritative New Testament witnesses. The doctrine of Scripture becomes in some passages the subject of express teaching. Perhaps most notable among these is 2 Timothy 3:16, "All scripture is given by inspiration of God."[8]

In the preceding context of this passage, Paul refers to the "holy writings" which Timothy knew from childhood. These "holy writings" can be none other than the sacred Scriptures of the Old Testament. It is with these Scriptures in mind that Paul says, "All scripture is God-breathed." The word that Paul uses predicates of all Scripture or of every Scripture a certain quality. More particularly, the predicate reflects upon its origin; it is the product of God's creative breath. The terseness of Paul's affirmation here must not be allowed to obscure its significance. It is that Scripture, the denotation of which is placed beyond all doubt by the context, is God's mouth, God's breath, and therefore God's oracle. Paul makes no qualifications and no reservations. Every Scripture is God-breathed, and therefore, so far as divine origin and resultant character are concerned, there is no discrimination. And in respect of the benefit accruing to men, all of Scripture is, for the reason that it is God-inspired, also profitable for doctrine, for reproof, for correction, for instruction in righteousness, that the man of God may be perfect, thoroughly furnished unto every good work.

Paul was, of course, well aware that God used human instruments in giving us these Scriptures. In his epistles he makes repeated allusion to the human authors of the sacred books. But the recognition of human instrumentality did not in the least inhibit Paul from making the stupendous affirmation that all Scripture is God-breathed, which means that Scripture is of divine origin and authorship and therefore of divine character and authority.

The predication which Paul here makes is nothing less than the high

[8] See, for a thorough examination of the meaning of θεόπνευστος, B. B. Warfield, "God-Inspired Scripture," in *Revelation and Inspiration* (New York, 1927), 229–80 and, for an exegesis of 2 Tim. 3:16, the same author in *op. cit.*, 79ff.

doctrine of plenary inspiration. For Paul is not here speaking of an inbreathing on the part of God into the writers of holy Scripture nor even into holy Scripture itself. The term Paul uses represents the concept of "breathing out" rather than that of "breathing in" and is far removed from the notion that a human product or witness is so interpenetrated with divine truth or influence that it becomes the Word of God. The whole emphasis is upon the fact that all Scripture proceeds from God and is therefore invested with a divinity that makes it as authoritative and efficient as a word oracularly spoken by God directly to us.

In 2 Timothy 3:16 Paul says nothing with respect to the human authors of Scripture or with respect to the way in which God wrought upon the human authors so as to provide us with God-breathed Scripture. The apostle Peter, however, though not by any means furnishing us with a full definition of the mode of inspiration, does go farther than does Paul in 2 Timothy 3:16 in stating the relation that obtained between the Holy Spirit and the inspired human witnesses. "No prophecy of scripture," he writes, "is of private interpretation. For not by the will of man was prophecy brought aforetime, but as borne by the Holy Spirit men spake from God" (2 Pet. 1:20–21). That Peter's statement here bears upon the agency of the Holy Spirit in the giving of Scripture is obvious from the phrase "prophecy of scripture."

Peter's teaching in this passage is both negative and positive. Negatively, he denies that the prophecy of Scripture owes its origin to human initiative, volition, or determination. It is not the product of individual reflection or imagination. Positively, human instrumentality is asserted. "Men spake from God." False inferences that might be drawn from the absolute terms of the preceding negations are obviated by the recognition of human agency. But while men spake, they spake from God, and it is this datum that harmonises the fact of human agency with the negations of private interpretation and the will of man. They spake from God because they were borne along or borne up by the Holy Spirit.[9] Here there is plainly the conjunction of human and divine agency. But the divine character of the prophecy is insured by the peculiar character of the Spirit's agency. He took up the human agents in such a way that they spoke God's Word, not their own.

In this context it is the stability of the prophetic Word that is being emphasised. The ground upon which this stability rests is that it came

[9] Cf. B. B. Warfield, *op. cit.*, 82f.

from God, that the Holy Spirit was not only operative in the writers of Scripture but carried them to his destination, and that this prophetic Word is not a momentary utterance or passing oracular deliverance but the Word of God that has received through Scripture permanent embodiment and authentication.

Summing up the witness of the New Testament, we find that human authorship or instrumentality is fully recognised, and yet human agency is not conceived of as in any way impairing the divine origin, character, truth, and authority of Scripture. It is divine in its origin because it is the product of God's creative breath and because it was as borne by the Holy Spirit that men spoke from God. For these reasons it bears an oracular character that accords it an authority as real and divine as if we heard the voice of God speaking from heaven. This oracular character is a permanent feature, and so Scripture has an abiding stability and application—it is unbreakable and indissoluble.

The witness with which we have so far dealt confines itself to the express testimony of the New Testament with reference to the Old. What then of the evidence on which may be founded a similar judgment with respect to the character of the New Testament? It must be acknowledged that the great mass of the evidence we possess bearing upon the inspiration of Scripture is the witness of the New Testament with reference to the Old. We do not have from the New Testament writers or authoritative witnesses the same abundance of testimony to the inspiration of the New Testament. That this should be the state of the case should not surprise us. When the New Testament witnesses spoke or wrote, there was no finished New Testament canon to which they could refer as a unified and completed corpus of writings. Particularly is this true of our Lord himself. None of the books of the New Testament was written when he spoke upon earth. Witness to the character of the New Testament as a whole, such as we find in the New Testament with reference to the Old, would have been impossible for any writer of the New Testament except the last and only then as an appendix to his own last canonical writing. This type of witness it would be unreasonable for us to demand as the necessary seal upon the divine character and authority of the entire New Testament.

While we do not have the same mass of testimony to the inspiration of the New Testament as to the Old, and while the circumstances were such that we could not expect the same kind of inclusive characterisation, it does not follow that we have no evidence upon which to maintain the divine origin and character of the New Testament. We have sufficient evidence, and to such we now turn our attention.

The organic unity of both Testaments is the presupposition of the appeal to the authority of the Old Testament and of allusion to it in which the New Testament abounds. This fact of organic unity bears very directly upon the question of the inspiration of the New Testament. For if, as we have found, the authoritative witness of the New Testament bears out the unbreakable and inerrant character of the Old, how could that which forms an organic unit with the Old be of an entirely different character as regards the nature of its inspiration? When the implications of organic unity are fully appreciated, it becomes impossible to believe that the divinity of the New Testament can be on a lower plane than that of the Old. Surely then, if the Old Testament, according to the testimony that in this matter has the greatest relevance or authority, is inerrant, the New Testament must also be.

This argument from organic unity has peculiar force when we properly understand the implications of progressive revelation. The New Testament stands to the Old in the relation of consummation to preparation; it embodies a fuller and more glorious disclosure of God's character and will. This is signalized by the fact that in these last days God hath spoken unto us by his Son, who is the brightness of his glory and the express image of his substance (Heb. 1:1–3). In Paul's language the glory of the New Testament is the glory that excels (2 Cor. 3:10–11). The New Testament Scripture enshrines and conveys to us the content of that new and better covenant, established upon better promises. Is it at all consonant with the completory nature of the New Testament, with the more excellent glory inherent in the New Testament and with the finality attaching to the revelation of God's own Son to suppose that the Scripture of such an economy should be lacking in that inerrancy which the authoritative witnesses—our Lord and his apostles—predicate of the Old Testament? It would be contrary to all sound analogy and reason to entertain such a supposition.[10]

The cogency of this argument is made all the more apparent when we bear in mind the meaning of Pentecost. The Old Testament was God-breathed, possessing unshakable stability and permanent validity, because it was as borne by the Holy Spirit men spoke from God. Yet so much more abundant were the operations of the Spirit introduced by Pentecost that it can be described in terms of "giving" and "sending forth" the Holy

[10] Cf. L. Gaussen, *Theopneustia* (Cincinnati, 1859), 74f.

Spirit. Are we to believe that this greater fullness and abundance of the Spirit's operation gave us a Scripture less reliable and less inerrant than the Scripture that the Spirit gave before the abundant effusion of Pentecost took place? Are we to believe that the Scripture that is the only abiding witness to and embodiment of the full and abundant administration of the Spirit is a Scripture less characterised by the very activity of the Spirit that imparted divinity and authority to the Old Testament? To ask these questions is to show that once the witness of the New Testament to the inspiration and inerrancy of the Old is accepted, once the relations which the two Testaments sustain to one another are understood and appreciated, the infallible character of the Old Testament furnishes us with the most cogent considerations in support of a similar judgment with respect to the character of the New Testament.

We must not think, however, that these considerations constitute the whole basis of faith in the New Testament as inerrant Scripture. For the New Testament is not without direct witness to its own character. It is true that we do not have the mass of testimony that we have in connection with the Old Testament. But in a manner analogous to the witness the Old Testament bears to its own divinity, the New Testament not only bears the unmistakable marks of its divine origin but also bears direct witness to its own divine character and authority.

If the New Testament is the Word of God with all the fullness of meaning that the authoritative witnesses of the New Testament ascribe to the Old, it must be by reason of that same plenary inspiration of the Holy Spirit operative in the writing of the Old Testament. The promises that Christ gave to his disciples with respect to the Holy Spirit have, therefore, the closest bearing upon this question. When Jesus sent out his disciples to preach the kingdom of God, he said to them, "But when they deliver you up, take no thought how or what ye shall speak, for it shall be given you in that hour what ye shall speak. For it is not ye that speak but the Spirit of your Father that speaketh in you" (Matt. 10:19–20; cf. Mark 13:11; Luke 12:12; 21:14–15). Such a promise assures to the disciples that in the "passing exigencies" and "to subserve interests of the narrowest range"[11] there would be afforded to them an inspiration of the Holy Spirit that would make their spoken words not simply their words but the words of the Holy Spirit. This same promise of the Spirit is given greatly increased scope and application when on the eve of his crucifixion Jesus said, "It is

[11] L. Gaussen, *op. cit.*, 77.

expedient for you that I go away. For if I go not away, the Comforter will not come unto you, but if I depart I will send him unto you. . . . He will guide you into all the truth" (John 16:7, 13). After his resurrection Jesus performed what must be construed as the act of official impartation of the Holy Spirit when he breathed on his disciples and said, "Receive ye the Holy Ghost" (John 20:22). And before his ascension he assured them, "Ye shall receive power after that the Holy Spirit is come upon you, and ye shall be my witnesses both in Jerusalem and in all Judea and in Samaria and unto the uttermost part of the earth" (Acts 1:8). The work and functions of the disciples are therefore to be discharged, in accordance with the promise and commission of Christ, by the direction and inspiration of the Holy Spirit. It is no wonder then that we find in the writings of the New Testament a note of authority, of certainty, and of finality that it would be presumptuous for men to arrogate to themselves, a note of authority that is consistent with truth and sobriety only if the writers were the agents of divine authority and the subjects of inspiration by the Holy Spirit. Relevant to the question of inspiration, this note of authority is one of the most significant features of the New Testament.

The passage in 1 Corinthians 7:10–12 is sometimes understood as if Paul were instituting a contrast between the authoritative teaching of Christ and his own unauthoritative judgment on questions bearing upon marriage and separation—"But to the married I give charge, not I but the Lord. . . . But to the rest I say, not the Lord." A careful reading of the whole passage will, however, show that the contrast is not between the inspired teaching of Christ and the uninspired teaching of the apostle but rather between the teaching of the apostle that could appeal to the express utterances of Christ in the days of his flesh, on the one hand, and the teaching of the apostle that went beyond the cases dealt with by Christ, on the other. There is no distinction as regards the binding character of the teaching in these respective cases. The language and terms the apostle uses in the second case are just as emphatic and mandatory as in the first case. And this passage, so far from diminishing the character of apostolic authority, only enhances our estimate of that authority. If Paul can be as mandatory in his terms when he is dealing with questions on which, by his own admission, he cannot appeal for support to the express teaching of Christ, does not this fact serve to impress upon us how profound was Paul's consciousness that he was writing by divine authority, when his own teaching was as mandatory in its terms as was his reiteration of the teaching of the Lord himself? Nothing else than the consciousness of enunciating divinely authoritative law would warrant the terseness and decisiveness of the statement by which he prevents all gainsaying, "And so ordain I in all the churches" (1 Cor. 7:17).

That Paul regards his written word as invested with divine sanction and authority is placed beyond all question in this same epistle (1 Cor. 14:37–38). In the context he is dealing specifically with the question of the place of women in the public assemblies of worship. He enjoins silence upon women in the church by appeal to the universal custom of the churches of Christ and by appeal to the law of the Old Testament. It is then that he makes appeal to the divine content of his prescriptions. "If any man thinketh himself to be a prophet or spiritual, let him acknowledge that the things I write unto you are the commandment of the Lord. And if any man be ignorant, let him be ignorant." Paul here makes the most direct claim to be writing the divine Word and coordinates this appeal to divine authority with appeal to the already existing Scripture of the Old Testament.

In the earlier part of this epistle Paul informs us, in fashion thoroughly consonant with the uniform teaching of Scripture as to what constitutes the word of man the Word of God, that the Holy Spirit is the source of all the wisdom taught by the apostles. "God hath revealed them unto us through the Spirit. For the Spirit searcheth all things, yea, the deep things of God" (1 Cor. 2:10). And Paul appeals here not only to the Holy Spirit as the source of the wisdom conveyed through his message but also to the Spirit as the source of the very media of expression. For Paul continues, "which things also we speak, not in the words which man's wisdom teacheth, but which the Spirit teacheth, combining spiritual things with spiritual" (1 Cor. 2:13). Spirit-taught things and Spirit-taught words! Nothing else provides us with an explanation of apostolic authority.

Much else that supports and corroborates the foregoing position could be elicited from the witness of the New Testament. But in the brief limits of the space available enough has been given to indicate that the same plenary inspiration which the New Testament uniformly predicates of the Old is the kind of inspiration that renders the New Testament itself the Word of God.

Frequently the doctrine of verbal inspiration is dismissed with supercilious scorn as but a remnant of that mediaeval or post-Reformation scholasticism that has tended to petrify Christianity.[12] Such contempt usually

[12] The criticism directed against the doctrine of verbal inspiration, namely, that it involves a theory of mechanical dictation is thoroughly unwarranted. The classic exponents of the doctrine of verbal inspiration have not attempted to define the mode of inspiration. It is true that the word "dictation" sometimes occurs. But it is also obvious that the use of this word was not intended to specify the mode of inspiration as that of dictation. Full allowance is made for the manifold activities and processes by which the books of Scripture

accompanies the claim that open-minded scientific research has made adherence to biblical inerrancy utterly inconsistent with well-informed honesty and therefore untenable. This boast of scientific honesty is plausible, so much so that it is often the password to respect in the arena of theological debate. The plea of the present contribution has been, however, that the summary dismissal of biblical infallibility is lamentably unscientific in its treatment of the very data that bear directly on the question at issue and that such dismissal has failed to reckon with the issues at stake in the rejection of what is established by straightforward scientific exegesis of the witness of Scripture to its own character. If the testimony of Scripture on the doctrine of Scripture is not authentic and trustworthy, then the finality of Scripture is irretrievably undermined. The question at stake is the place of Scripture as the canon of faith. And we must not think that the finality of Christ remains unimpaired even if the finality of Scripture is sacrificed. The rejection of the inerrancy of Scripture means the rejection of Christ's own witness to Scripture. Finally and most pointedly, then, the very integrity of our Lord's witness is the crucial issue in this battle of the faith.

The Internal Testimony

The thesis maintained above in our examination of the objective witness is that Scripture is authoritative by reason of the character it possesses as the infallible Word of God and that this divine quality belongs to Scripture because it is the product of God's creative breath through the mode of plenary inspiration by the Holy Spirit. The rejection of such a position has appeared to many to involve no impairment of the divine authority of the Bible because, even though the infallibility of Scripture has to be abandoned, there still remains the ever abiding and active witness of the Holy Spirit, and so infallible authority is fully conserved in the internal testimony of the Holy Spirit. Scripture is authoritative, it is said, because it is borne home to the man of faith by the internal testimony of the Spirit.

That there is such an activity of the Holy Spirit as the internal testimony is beyond dispute, and that there is no true faith in Scripture as the Word of God apart from such inward testimony is likewise fully granted. It might seem, therefore, that it belongs to the very situation in which we are placed, relative to the Holy Spirit, to say that the divine authority that confronts us is not that emanating from a past and finished activity of the Spirit but

were brought into being and full recognition is given to all the diversity that appears in those who were the human instruments in the production of Scripture. Cf. B. B. Warfield, *op. cit.*, 100–106 and B. B. Warfield, *Calvin and Calvinism*, 62ff.

rather the influence of the Spirit which is now operative with reference to and in us. Does not the positing of divine authority in an activity of the Spirit that to us is impersonal and external, as well as far distant and now inactive, do prejudice to the real meaning of that directly personal and presently operative address of the Holy Spirit to us and in us?

This question is that which defines what is the most important cleavage within Protestantism today. It is the cleavage between what is called Barthianism and the historic Protestant position. The Barthian view is that Scripture is authoritative because it witnesses to the Word of God; it is the vessel or vehicle of the Word of God to us. In that respect Scripture is said to be unique, and in that sense it is called the Word of God. But what makes Scripture really authoritative, on this view, is the ever-recurring act of God, the divine decision, whereby, through the mediacy of Scripture, the witness of Scripture to the Word of God is borne home to us with ruling and compelling power. The Scripture is not authoritative antecedently and objectively. It is only authoritative as here and now, to this man and to no other, in a concrete crisis and confrontation, God reveals himself through the medium of Scripture. Only as there is the ever-recurring human crisis and divine decision does the Bible become the Word of God.

It is apparent, therefore, that for the Barthian the authority-imparting factor is not Scripture as an existing corpus of truth given by God to man by a process of revelation and inspiration in past history, not the divine quality and character which Scripture inherently possesses, but something else that must be distinguished from any past action and from any resident quality. The issue must not be obscured. Barth does not hold and cannot hold that Scripture possesses binding and ruling authority by reason of what it is objectively, inherently, and qualitatively.

An objection to this way of stating the matter is easily anticipated. It is that this sharp antithesis is indefensible. For, after all, it will be said, Scripture is unique. It is the Word of God because it bears witness to God's Word. It occupies a unique category because there was something unique and distinctive about that past activity by which it came to be. It differs radically from other books written at the time of its production and also from all other books. It can, therefore, have no authority in abstraction from that quality that belongs to it as the human witness to the revelation given by God in the past. So, it may be argued, the factor arising from past events and activities enters into the whole complex of factors that combine and converge to invest Scripture with that unique character which makes it the fit medium for the ever-recurring act of divine revelation. It is not then an *either or* but a *both and*.

The objection is appreciated and welcomed. But it does not eliminate the issue. After making allowance for all that is argued in support of the objection, there still remains the fact that, on Barthian presuppositions, it is not the divine quality inherent in Scripture nor the divine activity by which that quality has been imparted to it that makes Scripture authoritative. That past activity and the resultant quality may constitute the prerequisites for the authority by which it becomes ever and anon invested, but they do not constitute that authority. It is rather the ever-recurring act of God that is the authority-constituting fact. This ever-recurring activity of God may be conceived of as the internal testimony of the Spirit, and so it is this testimony that constitutes Scripture authoritative.[13]

It is sometimes supposed that this Barthian construction of the authority of Scripture represents the classic Protestant or indeed Reformed position. Even the Westminster Confession has been appealed to as enunciating this position when it says that "our full persuasion and assurance of the infallible truth and divine authority thereof, is from the inward work of the Holy Spirit bearing witness by and with the Word in our hearts" (I:V). A little examination of chapter I of the Confession will expose the fallacy of this appeal. Indeed, the Westminster Confession was framed with a logic and comprehension exactly adapted not only to obviate but also to meet the Barthian conception. Section V, from which the above quotation was given, does not deal with the nature or ground of the authority of Scripture. The preceding section deals with that logically prior question. It states clearly that the authority of Scripture resides in the fact that it is the Word of God. "The authority of the Holy Scripture, for which it ought to be believed and obeyed, dependeth not upon the testimony of any man, or Church; but wholly upon God (who is truth itself) the author thereof: and therefore it is to be received because it is the Word of God." In one word, Scripture is authoritative because God is its author, and he is its author because, as is stated in Section II, it was given by inspiration of God. Nothing could be plainer than this: that the Confession represents the authority of Scripture as resting not upon the internal testimony of the Holy Spirit but upon the inspiration of the Spirit, a finished activity by which, it is clearly stated, the sixty-six books enumerated were produced and in virtue of which they are the Word of God written.

[13] Cf. Karl Barth, *Die Kirchliche Dogmatik, Die Lehre vom Wort Gottes*, Erster Halbband (München, 1932), 189ff.; English Translation (Edinburgh, 1936), 207ff.

It is, however, by "the inward work of the Holy Spirit bearing witness by and with the Word in our hearts" that we become convinced of that authority. The authority of Scripture is an objective and permanent fact residing in the quality of inspiration; the conviction on our part has to wait for that inward testimony by which the antecedent facts of divinity and authority are borne in upon our minds and consciences. It is to confuse the most important and eloquent of distinctions to represent the former as consisting in the latter. The Confession has left no room for doubt as to what its position is, and in formulating the matter with such clarity it has expressed the classic Reformed conception.

What then is the nature of this internal testimony, and what is the scriptural basis upon which the doctrine rests?

If, as has been shown in the earlier part of this discussion, Scripture is divine in its origin, character, and authority, it must bear the marks or evidences of that divinity. If the heavens declare the glory of God and therefore bear witness to their divine Creator, the Scripture as God's handiwork must also bear the imprints of his authorship. This is just saying that Scripture evidences itself to be the Word of God; its divinity is self-evidencing and self-authenticating. The ground of faith in Scripture as the Word of God is therefore the evidence it inherently contains of its divine authorship and quality. External evidence, witness to its divinity derived from other sources extraneous to itself, may corroborate and confirm the witness it inherently contains, but such external evidence cannot be in the category of evidence sufficient to ground and constrain faith. If the faith is faith in the Bible as God's Word, obviously the evidence upon which such faith rests must itself have the quality of divinity. For only evidence with the quality of divinity would be sufficient to ground a faith in divinity. Faith in Scripture as God's Word, then, rests upon the perfections inherent in Scripture and is elicited by the perception of these perfections. These perfections constitute its incomparable excellence, and such excellence when apprehended constrains the overwhelming conviction that is the only appropriate kind of response.

If Scripture thus manifests itself to be divine, why is not faith the result in the case of everyone confronted with it? The answer is that not all men have the requisite perceptive faculty. Evidence is one thing; the ability to perceive and understand is another. "The natural man receiveth not the things of the Spirit of God: for they are foolishness unto him: neither can he know them, because they are spiritually discerned" (1 Cor. 2:14). It is here that the necessity for the internal testimony of the Spirit enters. The darkness and depravity of man's mind by reason of sin make man blind to the divine excellence of Scripture. And the effect of sin is not only that it blinds the mind of man and makes it impervious to the evidence but also that it renders the heart of man utterly hostile to the evidence. The carnal mind is enmity against God and therefore resists every claim of the divine perfection. If the appropriate response of faith is to be yielded to the divine excellence inherent in Scripture, nothing less than radical regeneration by the Holy Spirit can produce the requisite susceptibility. "Except a man be born again, he cannot see the kingdom of God" (John 3:3). "The natural man receiveth not the things of the Spirit of God" (1 Cor. 2:14). It is here that the internal testimony of the Spirit enters, and it is in the inward work of the Holy Spirit upon the heart and mind of man that the internal testimony consists. The witness of Scripture to the depravity of man's mind and to the reality, nature, and effect of the inward work of the Holy Spirit is the basis upon which the doctrine of the internal testimony rests.

When Paul institutes the contrast between the natural man and the spiritual and says with respect to the latter, "But he that is spiritual judgeth all things, yet he himself is judged of no one" (1 Cor. 2:15), he means that the "spiritual" person is the person endowed with and indwelt by the Holy Spirit. It is only such a one who has the faculty to discern the things revealed by the Spirit. By way of contrast with the natural man, he receives, knows, and discerns the truth.

Earlier in this same chapter Paul tells us in terms that even more pointedly deal with our present subject that the faith of the Corinthians in the gospel was induced by the demonstration of the Spirit and of power. "And my speech and my preaching was not in persuasive words of wisdom, but in demonstration of the Spirit and of power, in order that your faith might not be in the wisdom of men but in the power of God" (1 Cor. 2:4–5). No doubt Paul here is reflecting upon the manner of his preaching. It was not with the embellishments of human oratory that he preached the gospel but with that demonstration or manifestation that is produced by the Spirit and power of God. He is saying, in effect, that the Spirit of God so wrought in him and in his preaching that the response on the part of the Corinthians was the solid faith which rests upon the power of God and not that evanescent faith which depends upon the appeal of rhetorical art and worldly wisdom. It is in the demonstration of which the Holy Spirit is the author that the faith of the Corinthians finds its source. It is, indeed, faith terminating upon the Word of God preached by Paul. But it is faith produced by the accompanying demonstration of the Spirit and manifestation of divine power.

In the first epistle to the Thessalonians Paul again refers to the power and confidence with which he and his colleagues preached the gospel at Thessalonica. "For our gospel came not unto you in word only, but also in power and in the Holy Spirit and much assurance" (1 Thess. 1:5). In this text the reference to power and assurance appears to apply to the power and confidence with which Paul and Silvanus and Timothy proclaimed the Word rather than to the conviction with which it was received by the Thessalonians. The gospel came in the Holy Spirit and therefore with power and assurance. But we must not dissociate the reception of the Word on the part of the Thessalonians from this power and confidence wrought by the Spirit. For Paul proceeds, "And ye became imitators of us and of the Lord, having received the word in much affliction with joy of the Holy Spirit" (v. 6). The resulting faith on the part of the Thessalonians must be regarded as proceeding from this activity of the Holy Spirit in virtue of which the gospel was proclaimed "in power and in the Holy Spirit and much assurance." That the Thessalonians became imitators of the Lord and received the Word with joy is due to the fact that the gospel came not in word only, and it came not in word only because it came in the power of the Holy Spirit. Their faith therefore finds its source in this demonstration of the Spirit, just as the joy with which they received the Word is the joy wrought by the Spirit.

When the apostle John writes, "And ye have an anointing from the Holy One and ye know all things. I have not written to you because ye do not know the truth, but because ye know it, and that no lie is of the truth" (1 John 2:20–21; cf. v. 27), he is surely alluding to that same indwelling of the Spirit with which Paul deals in 1 Corinthians 2:15. This anointing is an abiding possession and invests believers with discernment of the truth and steadfastness in it.

Summing up the conclusions drawn from these few relevant passages, we may say that the reception of the truth of God in intelligent, discriminating, joyful, and abiding faith is the effect of divine demonstration and power through the efficiency of the Holy Spirit, and that this faith consists in the confident assurance that, though the Word of God is brought through the instrumentality of men, it is not the word of man but in very truth the Word of God. We again see how even in connection with the internal testimony of the Spirit, the ministry of men in no way militates against the reception of their message as the Word of God.

This witness of the Holy Spirit has been called the internal "testimony" of the Spirit. The question arises, why is the inward work of the Spirit called *testimony*? There does not appear, indeed, to be any compelling reason why it should be thus called. There is, however, an appropriateness in the word. The faith induced by this work of the Spirit rests upon the testimony the Scripture inherently contains of its divine origin and character. It is the function of the Holy Spirit to open the minds of men to perceive that testimony and cause the Word of God to be borne home to the mind of man with ruling power and conviction. Thereby the Holy Spirit may be said to bear perpetual witness to the divine character of that which is his own handiwork.

The internal testimony of the Spirit has frequently been construed as consisting in illumination or in regeneration on its noëtic side. It is illumination because it consists in the opening of our minds to behold the excellence that inheres in Scripture as the Word of God. It is regeneration on the noëtic side because it is regeneration coming to its expression in our understanding in the response of the renewed mind to the evidence Scripture contains of its divine character. Anything less than illumination in the sense defined above, the internal testimony cannot be.

The question may properly be raised, however, whether or not the notion of illumination is fully adequate as an interpretation of the nature of this testimony. On the view that it consists merely in illumination, the testimony, most strictly considered, resides entirely in the Scripture itself and not at all in the ever-present activity of the Spirit. And the question is, may we not properly regard the present work of the Spirit as not only imparting to us an understanding to perceive the evidence inhering in the Scripture but also as imparting what is of the nature of positive testimony? If we answer in the affirmative, then we should have to say that the power and demonstration with which the Holy Spirit accompanies the Word and by which it is carried home to our hearts and minds with irresistible conviction is the ever-continuing positive testimony of the Spirit. In other words, the seal of the Spirit belongs to the category of testimony strictly considered. If this construction should be placed upon the power and seal of the Spirit, there is a very obvious reason why this doctrine should be called, not only appropriately but necessarily, the internal "testimony" of the Spirit. We must, however, be content to leave this question undetermined. It should not perplex us to do so. There remains in this matter as in the other manifold activities of the Holy Spirit much of mystery that surpasses our understanding.

Whether we view the internal testimony as merely illumination or as illumination plus a positive supplementation construed as testimony in the stricter sense of the word, there is one principle which it is necessary to stress, namely, that the internal testimony does not convey to us new truth content. The whole truth content that comes within the scope of the internal testimony is contained in the Scripture. This testimony terminates upon the end of constraining belief in the divine character and authority of the Word of God and upon that end alone. It gives no ground whatsoever for new revelations of the Spirit.

When Paul writes to the Thessalonians, "Our gospel came not unto you in word only, but also in power and in the Holy Spirit and much assurance," he is surely making a distinction between the actual content of the gospel and the attendant power with which it was conveyed to them and in virtue of which it was carried home with conviction to the hearts of the Thessalonians. In like manner, in 1 Corinthians 2:4–5 the content of Paul's word and preaching will surely have to be distinguished from the demonstration of the Spirit and of power by which Paul's message was effectual in the begetting of faith in the Corinthian believers. And we are likewise justified in recognising a distinction between the truth which John says his readers already knew and the abiding anointing of the Spirit which provided them with the proper knowledge and discernment to the end of bringing to clearer consciousness and consistent application the truth which they had already received (1 John 2:20–27). In each case the illumining and sealing function of the Spirit has respect to truth which had been received from another source than that of his confirming and sealing operations.

The internal testimony of the Spirit is the necessary complement to the witness Scripture inherently bears to its plenary inspiration. The two pillars of true faith in Scripture as God's Word are the objective witness and the internal testimony. The objective witness furnishes us with a conception of Scripture that provides the proper basis for the ever-active sealing operation of the Spirit of truth. The internal testimony insures that this objective witness elicits the proper response in the human consciousness. The sealing function of the Spirit finds its complete explanation and validation in the pervasive witness that Scripture bears to its own divine origin and authority. And the witness to plenary inspiration receives its constant confirmation in the inward work of the Holy Spirit bearing witness by and with the Word in the hearts of believers.

4

"Scripture"

J. I. PACKER

"Fundamentalism" and the Word of God

Previously published as "Scripture," in *"Fundamentalism" and the Word of God: Some Evangelical Principles* (1958; repr., Grand Rapids, MI: Eerdmans, 1972), 75–114. Reprinted by permission of the publisher.

> I want to know one thing, the way to heaven. . . . God Himself has condescended to teach the way. . . . He hath written down in a book. O give me that book: At any price give me the book of God! I have it: here is knowledge enough for me. Let me be Homo unius libri. . . . I sit down alone: only God is here. In His presence, I open, I read His book; for this end, to find the way to heaven. . . . Does anything appear dark and intricate? I lift up my heart to the Father of lights. . . . I then search after and consider parallel passages. . . . I meditate thereon. . . . If any doubt still remain, I consult those who are experience in the things of God: and then the writings whereby, being dead, they yet speak. And what I thus learn, that I teach.
>
> John Wesley

> And now, O Lord God, thou art God, and thy words are true.
>
> 2 Samuel 7:28, RSV

The evangelical view of the Bible has come under fire in this controversy, and it is desirable, as the next step in our argument, to restate it. We have just established the principle that Scripture, "God's Word written," is the final authority for all matters of Christian faith and practice; and we must follow the method which this principle dictates. Accordingly, we shall ask Scripture to give account of itself and test human ideas about it by its own teaching. "Scripture" is a biblical concept; and it is the biblical doctrine of Scripture which evangelicals are concerned to believe. We shall now try to see what the doctrine is; and our story will show us, incidentally, what reply evangelicals should make to those who upbraid them for holding theories of dictation, or inerrancy, or literalism.

We must first be clear as to the nature of our task. Our aim is to formulate a biblical doctrine; we are to appeal to Scripture for information about itself, just as we should appeal to it for information on any other doctrinal topic. This means that our formulation will certainly not give a final or exhaustive account of its subject. All doctrines terminate in mystery; for they deal with the works of God, which man in this world cannot fully comprehend, nor has God been pleased fully to explain. "We know in part"[1]—and only in part. Consequently, however successful our attempt to state the biblical doctrine of Scripture may be, it will not put us in a position where we "have all the answers," any more than a right statement of the doctrine of the Trinity, or providence, would do. We do not, in fact, expect to give all the answers, and a mere complaint that we leave some problems unsolved will not, of itself, be valid criticism of what we say, any more than it ever would be of any theological exposition; for incompleteness is of the essence of theological knowledge. This, of course, is to a greater or less degree the case with all our knowledge of facts. We never know everything about anything. But clearly, when we creatures come to study the Creator and his ways, we must expect our knowledge to be more fragmentary and partial, and further from being exhaustive, than when we study created things. We make no apology, therefore, for leaving some questions unanswered. All that we are trying to do here is simply to find and demarcate the Bible's own attitude and approach to itself, and to present the relevant biblical material from a properly biblical perspective, so that the scriptural way of regarding and employing Scripture may become clear. The sole test of the adequacy of our account will be this: are we putting matters as the Bible itself puts them? Scripture itself is alone competent to judge our doctrine of Scripture.

The relevant evidence for our purpose is the New Testament doctrine of the Old. Since the two Testaments are of a piece, what is true of one will be true of both. The biblical concept of "Scripture" will cover all that falls into the category of Scripture.

Space does not permit a full-length treatment, but we shall try to sketch out at least the main points in the Bible's view of the following three topics: its divine origin; its nature as the word of God; and its interpretation.

[1] 1 Cor. 13:9.

The Divine Origin of Scripture[2]

It is customary to use the term *inspiration* to refer to the divine origin of Scriptures. The biblical warrant for this is the phrase "given by inspiration of God," which is used in the Authorized Version to render the adjective *theopneustos* in 2 Timothy 3:16. As B. B. Warfield showed, this Greek word actually means "breathed out by God"—not so much *in*-spired as *ex*-pired; so that the text explicitly teaches the divine origin of "all Scripture"—here, the written word of the Old Testament.[3] As we have seen already, the divine origin of the Old Testament is everywhere assumed in the New Testament.

When we use the phrase "inspiration of Scripture," the noun may be taken either passively, as meaning "inspiredness," or actively, as denoting the divine activity by which God-breathed Scripture was produced. In this sense, inspiration is to be defined as a supernatural, providential influence of God's Holy Spirit upon the human authors which caused them to write what He wished to be written for the communication of revealed truth to others. It was a divine activity which, whether or not it had any unusual psychological effects (sometimes it did, sometimes it did not), effectively secured the written transmission of saving truth; in this respect, it is something quite distinct from the "inspiration" of the creative artist, which secures no such result, and it is more confusing than helpful to try to relate the two things together. It is true that some of those who were "inspired" in the theological sense were also "inspired" literary artists in the secular sense—Isaiah or John, for instance; but this comparison obscures the point of the idea of inspiration put forward in 2 Timothy 3:16, which is simply of a divine activity that produced Scripture—one, in other words, which involved human writers as a means to an end, but which actually terminated, not on them, but on what they wrote.

Inspiration did not necessarily involve an abnormal state of mind on the writer's part, such as a trance, or vision, or hearing a voice. Nor did it involve any obliterating or overriding of his personality. Scripture indicates that God in his providence was from the first preparing the human vehicles of inspiration for their predestined task,[4] and that he caused them in many cases, perhaps in most, to perform that task through the normal exercise

[2] For a thorough examination of the biblical material, see B. B. Warfield, *The Inspiration and Authority of the Bible* (Marshall, Morgan & Scott, 1951), especially his definitive study of "The Biblical Idea of Inspiration" (chapter III). This study and its companion, "The Biblical Idea of Revelation," also appear as chapters 1 and 2 in *Biblical Foundations,* a symposium of Warfield's writings (Tyndale Press, 1958, 15*s*).

[3] Warfield, *The Inspiration and Authority of the Bible*, 245ff.

[4] Cf. Jer. 1:5; Isa. 49:1, 5; Gal. 1:15.

of the abilities which he had given them. We may not suppose that they always knew they were writing canonical Scripture, even when they consciously wrote with divine authority; and it is not obvious that the writers of, for example, the Song of Solomon, Agur's testament (Proverbs 30), Heman's black psalm (Psalm 88), or Luke's Gospel (written, the author tells us, because "it seemed good to me"), were aware of any directly supernatural prompting at all. Scripture also shows us that inspired documents may be the product of firsthand historical research (as Luke's Gospel is[5]), and of direct dependence on older written sources (as Chronicles depends on Kings), and even of wholesale borrowing (compare 2 Peter and Jude). Moreover, it appears that biblical books may have passed through several editions and recensions over the centuries before reaching their final form, as the book of Proverbs certainly did.[6]

Dictation?

Because evangelicals hold that the biblical writers were completely controlled by the Holy Spirit, it is often supposed, as we saw, that they maintain what is called the "dictation" or "typewriter" theory of inspiration—namely, that the mental activity of the writers was simply suspended, apart from what was necessary for the mechanical transcriptions of words supernaturally introduced into their consciousness.[7] But it is not so. This "dictation theory" is a man of straw. It is safe to say that no Protestant theologian, from the Reformation till now, has ever held it; and certainly modern evangelicals do not hold it. We are glad that Dr. Hebert, at least, recognizes this.[8] It is true that many sixteenth- and seventeenth-century theologians spoke of Scripture as "dictated by the Holy Ghost"; but all they meant was that the authors wrote word for word what God intended. The language of dictation was invoked to signify not the method or psychology of God's guidance of them, but simply the fact and result of it; not the nature of their own mental processes, but the relation of what they wrote to the divine intention. The use of the term "dictation" was always figurative, and the whole point of the figure lay in the fact that it asserted this relation. It was never used with psychological overtones. The proof of this lies in the fact that when these theologians addressed themselves to the question, What was the Spirit's mode of operating in the writers' minds?,

[5] Luke 1:3.

[6] Cf. Prov. 10:1; 24:23; 25:1.

[7] See J. I. Packer, "'Fundamentalists' under Fire," in *"Fundamentalism" and the Word of God* (Grand Rapids: Eerdmans, 1972), 10; Appendix I, 178f.

[8] See Gabriel Hebert, *Fundamentalism and the Church of God* (S.C.M., 1957), 56.

they all gave their answer in terms not of dictation, but of *accommodation*, and rightly maintained that God completely adapted his inspiring activity to the cast of mind, outlook, temperament, interests, literary habits, and stylistic idiosyncrasies of each writer.

Accommodation

Those who credit evangelicals with belief in "dictation" often appeal to the thought of accommodation as the correct alternative to the view, but in so doing they misunderstand the biblical idea of accommodation no less seriously than they misunderstood the biblical idea of complete divine control. They speak as if it were self-evident that a revelation of truth transmitted through the instrumentality of sinful men would suffer in the process. We are told that since the biblical writers were imperfect creatures, morally, spiritually, and intellectually limited, children of their age and children of Adam too, it was inevitable that crudities, distortions, and errors should creep into what they wrote. It is claimed that this is a liberating notion which throws a flood of light on the real character of Scripture and makes possible a great advance in theological understanding. But does it? It certainly gives the theologian an easy way out when he meets passages that do not square with his idea of what the Bible tells us, or ought to tell us; but is the practice of dismissing awkward details as human corruptions of the pure word of God a biblical way of treating Scripture? It is irrelevant and mischievous to appeal in this connection, as some do, to the example of Christ and the apostles in setting aside Old Testament regulations; for they did this because they recognized that the time had ended for which those regulations were meant to be binding, not because they doubted their divine origin.

In fact, this "liberating notion" is a mistaken idea which reflects a thoroughly defective approach to the written Word. For, in the first place, it flatly contradicts the New Testament witness that every part of Scripture has a divine origin and all that is written (*pasa graphe*) is *theopneustos*.[9] And, in the second place, it plainly implies that God was somehow constrained, hampered, and indeed frustrated in his revelatory purpose by the quality of the human material through which he worked. But this is to deny the biblical doctrine of providence, according to which God "worketh all things after the counsel of his own will."[10] The Bible excludes the idea of

[9] Matt. 5:18; 2 Tim. 3:16.
[10] Eph. 1:11.

a frustrated deity. "Whatsoever the Lord pleased, that did he in heaven, and in earth."[11] He was well able to prepare, equip, and overrule sinful human writers so that they wrote nothing but what he intended; and Scripture tells us that this is what in fact he did. We are to think of the Spirit's inspiring activity, and, for that matter, of all his regular operations in and upon human personality, as (to use an old but valuable technical term) *concursive*; that is, as exercised in, through, and by means of the writers' own activity, in such a way that their thinking and writing was *both* free and spontaneous on their part *and* divinely elicited and controlled, and what they wrote was not only their own work but also God's work. Thus, quotations from the Psalms in Acts are described both as David's words, the issue of his own God-given knowledge and God-guided reasoning, and as God's words spoken through David's mouth.[12] David was a sinful man, but his words in these cases were the words of God.

Providence

The twin suppositions which liberal critics make—that, on the one hand, divine control of the writers would exclude the free exercise of their natural powers, while, on the other hand, divine accommodation to the free exercise of their natural powers would exclude complete control of what they wrote—are really two forms of the same mistake. They are two ways of denying that the Bible can be both a fully human and fully divine composition. And this denial rests (as all errors in theology ultimately do) on a false doctrine of God; here particularly, of his providence. For it assumes that God and man stand in such a relation to each other that they cannot both be free agents in the same action. If man acts freely (i.e., voluntarily and spontaneously), God does not, and vice versa. The two freedoms are mutually exclusive. But the affinities of this idea are with deism, not Christian theism. It is deism which depicts God as the passive onlooker rather than the active governor of his world, and which assures us that the guarantee of human freedom lies in the fact that men's actions are not under God's control. But the Bible teaches, rather, that the freedom of God, who works in and through his creatures, leading them to act according to their nature, is itself the foundation and guarantee of the freedom of their action. It is therefore a great mistake to think that the freedom of the biblical writers can be vindicated only by denying full divine control over them; and the

[11] Ps. 135:6.
[12] Acts 1:16; 4:25.

prevalence of this mistake should be ascribed to the insidious substitution of deistic for theistic ideas about God's relation to the world which has been, perhaps, the most damaging effect of modern science on theology. When the critics of evangelicalism take it for granted that evangelicals, since they believe in complete control, must hold the "dictation" theory, while they themselves, since they recognize accommodation, are bound to hold that in Scripture false and misleading words of men are mixed up with the pure word of God, they merely show how unbiblical their idea of providence has become. The cure for such fallacious reasoning is to grasp the biblical idea of God's *concursive operation* in, with, and through the free working of man's own mind.

The Analogy of the Person of Christ

A further way in which some critics try to make the point that they do justice to the human character of the Bible, while evangelicals do not, is by comparing their own position to the orthodox doctrine of the two natures of Christ, and the evangelical view, as they understand it, to the Monophysite heresy. So Dr. Hebert writes: "The Liberals of the last generation, like critical scholars today, were asserting the vital theological truth of the human nature of the Bible, which is analogous to that of the human nature of Christ. They were in fact fighting against the Monophysite heresy which, with its denial of the true humanity of our Lord, is the favourite heresy of orthodox Christians—who are inclined so to exalt Him as their divine Saviour that they lose sight of the fact that He was and is also truly man."[13] The suggestion is that evangelicals fall into an analogous heresy with regard to Scripture. Dr. Hebert goes on to quote some words of Professor R. H. Fuller to this effect, which conclude thus: "All the way through, we have to discern the treasure in the earthen vessels: the divinity in Christ's humanity . . . the Word of God in the fallible words of men." Hebert regards this line of criticism as "very important";[14] but, in fact, he and Professor Fuller misconceive the bearing of the Christological parallel. Insofar as it is valid, it confirms the evangelical view of Scripture as against theirs, as we shall now see. We would make the following observations upon it:

1. At best, the analogy between the divine-human person of the Word made flesh, who is Christ, and the divine-human product of the Word written, which is Scripture, can be only a limited one.

[13] Hebert, *op.cit.*, 76f.
[14] Ibid., 78.

2. If the point of the analogy is merely that human as well as divine qualities are to be recognized in Scripture, we can only agree, and add that it should be clear from what we have already said—which is no more than evangelicals have said constantly for over a century—that we do in fact recognize the reality of both.

3. If we are to carry the analogy further, and take it as indicating something about the character which the human element has by virtue of its conjunction with the divine, we must say that it points directly to the fact that, as our Lord, though truly man, was free from sin, so Scripture, though a truly human product, is truly free from error.[15] If the critics believe that Scripture, as a human book, errs, they ought, by the force of their own analogy, to believe that Christ, as man, sinned.

4. If we are to carry the analogy further still, and take it as indicating something about the reality of the union between the divine and the human, we must say that it is in fact the approach of the evangelicals to Scripture which corresponds to Christological orthodoxy, while that of their critics really corresponds to the Nestorian heresy. Nestorianism begins by postulating a distinction between Jesus as a man and the divine Son, whom it regards as someone distinct, indwelling the man; but then it cannot conceive of the real personal identity of the man and the Son. The right and scriptural place in Christology is to start by recognizing the unity of our Lord's person as divine and to view his humanity only as an aspect of his person, existing within it and never, therefore, dissociated from it. Similarly, the right way to think of Scripture is to start from the biblical idea that the written Scriptures as such are "the oracles of God" and to study their character as a human book only as one aspect of their character as a divine book. Those who start by postulating a distinction between the Bible as a human book and the word of God that is in it are unable, on their own premises, to recognize and exhibit the real oneness of these two things, and when they try to state their mutual relationship they lapse into an arbitrary subjectivism. This is what happens to the critics. (Incidentally, once we see this, we see why they are so ready to accuse evangelicals of Monophysitism; for Nestorians have always regarded orthodox Christology as Monophysite.) We must dissent, therefore, from Professor Fuller's

[15]Warfield works this out in detail: "As, in the case of our Lord's person, the human nature remains truly human while yet it can never fall into sin or error because it can never act out of relation with the Divine nature into conjunction with which it has been brought; so in the case of the production of Scripture by the conjoint action of human and Divine factors, the human factors have acted as human factors, and have left their mark on the product as such, and yet cannot have fallen into that error which we say it is human to fall into, because they have not acted apart from the Divine factors, by themselves, but only under their unerring guidance." *The Inspiration and Authority of the Bible*, 162f.; *Biblical Foundations*, 74f.

Nestorian assertion that our task is to discern the divinity in Christ's humanity and the word of God in the fallible words of man, and suggest that it is rather to appreciate the true manhood of the divine Word incarnate and the authentic human character of the inerrant divine Word written.

The Nature of Scripture

The Unity of Scripture

We come now to discuss the nature of the Bible, considered a single entity—the organism of Scripture, as we may call it. Our first point here is that Scripture is a real *unity*.

The literary historian sees the Bible as a library: a miscellaneous set of more or less occasional writings—public records, legal and liturgical documents, history books, lyric and philosophical poetry and visionary prose, hymns, letters, sermons—put together over a period of a thousand years or more. But it is more than a library of books by human authors; it is a single book with a single author—God the Spirit—and a single theme—God the Son, and the Father's saving purposes, which all revolve round him. Our Lord is therefore the key to Scripture, and its focal centre; there is a sense in which all bears witness of him,[16] and in this common reference the heterogeneous contents of the Bible find their unity. Not that all parts of Scripture are equally important or witness to Christ and the kingdom of God in the same way. But no part of Scripture is without its bearing on these central topics, and no part of Scripture is rightly understood if read without this reference.[17] The course of redemptive history included apostasies, judgments, and captivities, yet that history formed a God-guided unity, and these apparently unproductive episodes served to advance its course toward its predestined goal. And, in the same way, Scripture contains passages which seem unedifying in isolation, yet all these, when set in the context of the whole, contribute something of their own to the biblical message. The structural interrelation of the various parts of the organism of Scripture is certainly complex, but it yields progressively to patient study.

The Word of God

It is customary to speak of the Bible, thus regarded, as *the Word of God*. This phrase is applied in the Old Testament both to individual revelations

[16] John 5:39; Luke 24:27, 44ff.
[17] Cf. 2 Cor. 3:14–16.

to and utterances by the prophets (every such communication being "the word of God" or "of the Lord"), and also to the totality of God's verbal revelation to Israel, as such;[18] and in the New Testament, as we saw, it is used to refer comprehensively to the body of revealed truths which made up the apostolic gospel.[19] The phrase declares the divine origin of that to which it applies: whatever is denominated "the word of God" is thereby affirmed to be a divine utterance. It is for this reason that the phrase is applied to the Bible. The purpose of this usage is to make explicit the biblical conception of Scripture—which is that Scripture is the sum total of divine revelation recorded in a God-breathed written form, and that every scriptural statement is therefore to be received as a divine utterance. The New Testament writers regarded Scripture as the written Word of God, made up of the written words of God—as, in fact, "oracles of God."[20] No clearer proof of this could be given than Warfield's survey of "two classes of passages, each of which, when taken separately, throws into the clearest light their (the New Testament writers') habitual appeal to the Old Testament text as to God himself speaking, while, together, they make an irresistible impression of the absolute identification by their writers of the Scriptures in their hands with the living voice of God. In one of these classes of passages the Scriptures are spoken of as if they were God; in the other, God is spoken of as if he were the Scriptures: in the two together, God and the Scriptures are brought into such conjunction as to show that in point of directness of authority no distinction was made between them.

> Examples of the first class of passages are such as these: Gal. 3:8, "The Scripture, foreseeing that God would justify the heathen through faith, preached before the gospel unto Abraham, saying, In thee shall all the nations be blessed" (Gen. 12:1–3); Rom. 9:17. "The Scripture saith unto Pharaoh, Even for this same purpose have I raised thee up" (Ex. 9:16). It was not, however, the Scripture (which did not exist at the time) that, foreseeing God's purposes of grace in the future, spoke these precious words to Abraham, but God Himself in His own person: it was not the not-yet-existent Scripture that made this announcement to Pharaoh, but God Himself through the mouth of His prophet Moses. These acts could be attributed to "Scripture" only as the result of such

[18] See Ps. 119, where God's "word" (singular: *dabhar* or *imra*, 42 times) is a synonym for His "law" (*torah*, instruction), "testimonies," "precepts," "statutes," "commandments," etc.

[19] See J. I. Packer, "Authority," in *Fundamentalism and the Word of God* (Grand Rapids, MI: Eerdmans, 1972), 42.

[20] Rom. 3:2; see Warfield, *The Inspiration and Authority of the Bible*, chapter 8, for a thorough discussion of this phrase.

> habitual identification, in the mind of the writer, of the text of Scripture with God as speaking, that it became natural to use the term "Scripture says" when what was really intended was "God, as recorded in Scripture, said."
>
> Examples of the other class of passages are such as these: Matt. 19:4, 5, "And he answered and said, Have ye not read that he which made them from the beginning made them male and female, and said, For this cause shall a man leave his father and mother, and shall cleave to his wife, and the twain shall become one flesh?" (Gen. 2:24); Heb. 3:7, "Wherefore, even as the Holy Ghost saith, Today if ye shall hear his voice", etc. (Ps. 95:7); Acts 4:24, 25, "Thou art God, who by the mouth of thy servant David hast said, Why do the heathen rage and the people imagine vain things" (Ps. 2:1); Acts 8:34, 35, "He that raised Him from the dead, now no more turn to corruption . . . hath spoken in this wise, I will give you the holy and sure blessings of David" (Isa. 55:3); "because he saith also in another [Psalm], Thou wilt not give thy holy one to see corruption" (Ps. 16:10); Heb. 1:6, "And when he again bringeth in the first born into the world, he saith, And let all the angels of God worship him" (Deut. 32:43); "and of the angels he saith, Who maketh his angels wings, and his ministers a flame of fire" (Ps. 104:4); "but of the Son, *he saith,* Thy Throne O God, is forever and ever", etc. (Ps. 45:7); and, "Thou, Lord, in the beginning", etc. (Ps. 102:36). It is not God, however, in whose mouth these sayings are placed in the text of the Old Testament: they are the words of others, recorded in the text of Scripture as spoken to or of God. They could be attributed to God only through such habitual identification, in the minds of the writers, of the text of Scripture with the utterances of God that it had become natural to use the term "God says" when what was really intended was "Scripture, the Word of God, says."
>
> The two sets of passages, together, thus show an absolute identification, in the minds of these writers, of "Scripture" with the speaking God.[21]

Now the divine utterances of which Old Testament Scripture was composed were held, as we saw, to coalesce into the unity of a single message. The very use of the terms "Scripture" (*graphé*) and "the Scriptures" (*hai graphai*) in the New Testament proves this. At the conclusion of a careful survey of this usage, Warfield records the following just verdict: "The employment of *graphé* in the NT so far follows its profane usage,

[21] Warfield, *op. cit.*, 299ff.

in which it is prevailingly applied to entire documents and carries with it a general implication of completeness, that in its more common reference it designates the OT to which it is applied in its completeness as a unitary whole. . . . It remains only to add that the same implication is present in the designation of the OT as *hai graphai*, which, . . . does not suggest that the OT is a collection of 'treatises,' but is merely a variant of *he graphe* in accordance with good Greek usage, employed interchangeably with it at the dictation of nothing more recondite than literary habit. Whether *hai graphai* is used, then, or *he graphé*, or the anarthrous *graphé,* in each case alike the OT is thought of as a single document set over against all other documents by reason of its unique Divinity and indefectible authority, by which it is constituted in every passage and declaration the final arbiter of belief and practice."[22]

The biblical concept of Scripture, then, is of a single, though complex, God-given message, set down in writing in God-given words; a message which God has spoken and still speaks. On the analogy of scriptural usage, therefore, it is evident that to describe Scripture as the Word of God written is entirely accurate. Accordingly, if when we speak of "the Bible" we mean not just a quantity of printed paper, but a written document declaring a message—if, that is, we view the inspired volume as a literary product, a verbal expression of thought—then "the Bible" and "Scripture" will be synonyms: it will thus be correct to call the Bible the "Word of God," and to affirm that what it says, God says. If, on the other hand, we are thinking of the Bible simply as a printed book, it will not be wrong to say that the Bible *contains* the word of God, in the same sense in which any other book *contains* the pronouncements of its author. To speak in these terms, however, is to invite misunderstanding, since liberal theologians have been in the habit of using this formula to insinuate that part of what the Bible contains is no part of the Word of God. It is worth guarding our language in order to avoid seeming to endorse so unbiblical a view.

The scriptural approach to Scripture is thus to regard it as God's written testimony to himself. When we call the Bible the "Word of God," we mean, or should mean, that its message constitutes a single utterance of which God is the author. What Scripture says, he says. When we hear or read Scripture, that which impinges on our mind (whether we realize it or not) is the speech of God himself.

Not that the church knows, or ever knew, or will know in this world,

[22] *Dictionary of Christ and the Gospels*, ed. Hastings, s.v. "Scripture" II. 586; reprinted in Warfield, *op. cit.*, 238f.

the full meaning of God's Word. As we shall point out more fully later, the task of biblical interpretation never ends. There is no such thing as an exhaustive exegesis of any passage. The Holy Spirit is constantly showing Christian men facets of revealed truth not seen before. To claim finality for any historic mode of interpretation or system of theology would be to resist the Holy Ghost; there is always more to be said, and the church of each age should echo John Robinson's confidence that the Lord has more light and truth yet to break out of his holy Word. Our point here is simply that the church must receive all teaching that proves to be biblical, whether on matters of historical or of theological fact, as truly part of God's Word.[23]

This shows the importance of insisting that the inspiration of Scripture is *verbal.* Words signify and safeguard meaning; the wrong word distorts the intended sense. Since God inspired the biblical text in order to communicate his Word, it was necessary for him to ensure that the words written were such as did in fact convey it. We do not stress the verbal character of inspiration from a superstitious regard for the original Hebrew and Greek words (like that of Islam for its Koran, which is held to consist essentially of Arabic words, and therefore to be untranslatable); we do so from a reverent concern for the sense of Scripture. If the words were not wholly God's, then their teaching would not be wholly God's.

This consideration suggests a further problem, at which we may here glance: how is it warrantable to treat the Bible as we actually have it as the Word of God, when we have no reason to think that any manuscript or version now existing is free from corruptions? It is sometimes suggested that the evangelical view of Scripture can have no practical application or significance, since the faultless autographs which it posits are not available to us, and that in practice we are involved in an inescapable subjectivism by the necessity of relying on conjectural reconstructions of the text. The suggestion here is that we can have no confidence that any text that we possess conveys to us the genuine meaning of the inspired Word. It is, of course, true that textual corruptions are no part of the authentic Scriptures and that no text is free from such slips. But faith in the consistency of God warrants an attitude of confidence that the text is sufficiently trustworthy not to lead us astray. If God gave the Scriptures for a practical purpose—to

[23] It has been pointed out to me that the use of the phrase "word of God" in this book may cause confusion if it is not explained. The rule is that when "word" is spelt with a capital "W," the reference is to Scripture, or the total biblical message. When it is spelt with a small "w," the reference is to some particular divine utterance, such as the Christian gospel (which is what the phrase denotes in the New Testament, as we saw). Every such word of God is itself part of the Word of God, which is the normative account of all that God says to his church.

make men wise unto salvation through faith in Christ—it is a safe inference that he never permits them to become so corrupted that they can no longer fulfill it. It is noteworthy that the New Testament men did not hesitate to trust the words of the Old Testament as they had it as reliable indications of the mind of God. This attitude of faith in the adequacy of the text is confirmed, so far as it can be, by the unanimous verdict of textual scholars that the biblical text is excellently preserved, and no point of doctrine depends on any of the small number of cases in which the true reading remains doubtful. Professor F. F. Bruce expresses the verdict of scholarship as well as of biblical faith when he writes: "By the 'singular care and providence' of God the Bible text has come down to us in such substantial purity that even the most uncritical edition of the Hebrew or Greek . . . cannot effectively obscure the real message of the Bible, or neutralize its saving power."[24]

This is not to say that textual criticism is needless and unprofitable; but it is to say that, while the work of recovering the original text is not yet finished, and no doubt never will be finished in every minute particular, we should not hesitate to believe that the text as we have it is substantially correct and may safely be trusted as conveying to us the Word of God with sufficient accuracy for all practical purposes. God's faithfulness to his own intentions is our guarantee of that.

Propositional Revelation

The Word of God consists of *revealed truths*. This is nowadays an unfashionable notion. It is commonly said that there are no revealed truths; God revealed himself, not by words, but by the mighty redemptive works through which he became the world's Saviour. Revelation is by action, not by instruction. The Bible is not revelation, but a memorial and legacy of revelation: a record of observations, impressions, and opinions of godly men involved in redemptive history. It has the relative authority of a first-hand account, written with thought and care by men of good faith and great insight, but it has not the absolute authority of truth. Later generations must use their own insight to decide how far its reports may be taken as true, or its theology as adequate. No finality attaches to what it says; it is a source and quarry for theology, but not a standard or criterion for it. It is the work of pious men using their God-given abilities to interpret and

[24] "As Originally Given" (a comment on the reference in the I.V.F. doctrinal basis to "the divine inspiration and infallibility of Holy Scripture, as originally given"), in *The Theological Students' Fellowship Terminal Letter*, Spring 1956, 3. The phrase in inverted commas is from the Westminster Confession, I:8.

explain the acts of God—in other words, a piece of godly speculation; and it forms the jumping-off ground for the religious enquiry and reflection of later ages—which is also, of course, no more than godly speculation. Scriptural statements are simply human testimonies to revelation, fallible and inadequate as all man's words are. They must not be equated with a verbal word of God; there is, in fact, no such word.

But according to Scripture, God reveals himself to men both by exercising power for them and by teaching truth to them. The two activities are not antithetical, but complementary. Indeed, the biblical position is that the mighty acts of God are not revelation to man at all, except insofar as they are accompanied by words of God to explain them. Leave man to guess God's mind and purpose, and he will guess wrong; he can know it only by being told it. Moreover, the whole purpose of God's mighty acts is to bring man to know him by faith; and Scripture knows no foundation for faith but the spoken word of God, inviting our trust in him on the basis of what he has done for us. Where there is no word from God, faith cannot be. Therefore, verbal revelation—that is to say, propositional revelation, the disclosure by God of truths about himself—is no mere appendage to his redemptive activity, but a necessary part of it. This being so, the inspiring of an authoritative exposition of his redemptive acts in history ought to be seen as itself one of those redemptive acts, as necessary a link in the chain of his saving purposes as any of the events with which the exposition deals.

The need for verbal revelation appears most clearly when we consider the person and work of Christ. His life and death were the clearest and fullest revelation of God that ever was or could be made. Yet it could never have been understood without explanation. Whoever could have *guessed*, without being told, that the man Jesus was God incarnate, that he had created the world in which he was crucified, that by dying a criminal's death he put away the sins of mankind, and that now, though gone from our sight, he lives forever to bring penitent sinners to his Father? And who can come to faith in Christ if he knows none of this? No considerations could show more plainly the complete inability of man to "make do" in his religion without a spoken word from God.

In fact, however, there is nothing of which the Bible is more sure than that God has from the first accompanied his redemptive acts with explanatory words—statements of fact about himself and his purposes, warnings, commands, predictions, promises—and that it is in responding specifically to these divine words that obedience consists. Moses, the prophets, Christ, the apostles, all spoke God's words to men; and what they said took the form of statement and inference, argument and deduction.[25] God's word in their mouths was propositional in character. Christ and the apostles regularly appealed to Old Testament statements as providing a valid basis for inferences about God, and drew from them by the ordinary laws of grammar and logic conclusions which they put forward as truths revealed there—that the dead do not perish, that justification is by faith and not by works, that God is sovereign in saving mercy, and so forth.[26] Plainly, they regarded the Old Testament as propounding a body of doctrinal affirmations. And we have seen reasons already for regarding the New Testament as of the same nature as the Old. We conclude, therefore, that, if we are to follow Scripture's own account of itself, we are bound to say that whatever "is either expressly set down in scripture, or by good and necessary consequence may be deduced from scripture"[27] must be regarded as a revealed truth. The Bible confronts us with the conception that the Word of God which it embodies consists of a system of truths, conveying to men real information from God about himself.

Not that the text of Scripture is made up entirely of formal doctrinal statements; of course, it is not. The Bible is not a repository of isolated proof-texts, as the medievals, unconcerned about the literal sense of passages, were prone to think. Comparatively little of Scripture consists of systematic theological exposition; most of it is of a different order. Broadly speaking, the Bible is an interpretative record of sacred history. It reports God's words to Israel, and his dealings with them, down the ages. It includes biographies, meditations, prayers, and praises, which show us how faith and unbelief, obedience and disobedience, temptation and conflict, work out in practice in human lives. It contains much imaginative matter—poetical, rhetorical, parabolic, visionary—which sets before our minds in a vivid, concrete, and suggestive way great general principles, the formal statement of which has often to be sought in other contexts. In fact, Scripture is an organism, a complex, self-interpreting whole, its theology showing the meaning of the events and experiences which it records, and the events and experiences showing the outworking of the theology in actual life. All these items have their place in the total system of biblical truth.

It should be clear, therefore, that when we assert that what Scripture

[25] Bernard Ramm makes a striking observation on Christ's appeal to logic: "With reference to logical forms our Lord used *analogy*, Luke 11:13; *reductio ad absurdum*, Matt. 12:26; *excluded middle*, Matt. 12:30; *a fortiori*, Matt. 12:1–8; *implication*, Matt. 12:28; and law of *non-contradiction*, Luke 6:39." *The Pattern of Authority*, (Grand Rapids, MI: Eerdmans, 1957), 51. The list could be extended.

[26] Cf. Mark 12:26–27; Gal. 3:10–12; Rom. 9:15–18, etc.

[27] Westminster Confession, I:6.

contains is a body of truths, embracing both matters of fact and general principles about God and man, and that these truths together constitute his Word, we are not prejudging the literary character of Scripture as a whole, or of any part of it. There is nothing in this position to cramp one's exegetical style, as some of the critics of evangelicalism seem to fear. We do not suggest that every passage should be treated according to the same prearranged formula (as the medievals did by putting all texts through the same allegorical mincing machine), but rather the very opposite—that we must recognize the complexity of Scripture and do full justice to all the varied types of literary material which Scripture contains.

Infallibility and Inerrancy

Evangelicals are accustomed to speak of the Word of God as *infallible* and *inerrant.* The former term has a long pedigree; among the Reformers, Cranmer and Jewel spoke of God's Word as infallible,[28] and the Westminster Confession of "the infallible truth" of Holy Scripture.[29] The latter, however seems not to have been regularly used in this connection before the nineteenth century. Both have been so variously employed in theological discussion that they now bear no precise meaning at all. Terms which one cannot safely use without first stating what one does not mean by them are of little practical worth, and it might be argued that they, like the word "fundamentalist," would be better dropped. Certainly, they are not essential for stating the evangelical view. If, however, they are construed in the sense intended by those who first applied them to Scripture, they express an important aspect of the approach to Scripture which we are outlining. For this reason, because they have been misunderstood and misused in the present controversy, we shall briefly discuss them here.

"Infallible" denotes the quality of never deceiving or misleading, and so means "wholly trustworthy and reliable"; "inerrant" means "wholly true." Scripture is termed infallible and inerrant to express the conviction that all its teaching is the utterance of God "who cannot lie,"[30] whose word, once spoken, abides forever,[31] and that therefore it may be trusted implicitly. This is just the conviction about Scripture which our Lord was

[28] See Cranmer, *Remains* (Parker Society), 19; Jewel, *Works* (P.S.), I:80; cf. Ridley, *Works* (P.S.), 16, "the infallible word of God." The Latin equivalent is older still: Wycliffe speaks of Scripture as "infallibilis . . . regula veritatis" (*De Veritate Sacrae Scriptural,* XXIV; written 1377–80), and Gerson (*ob.* 1429) in his *Tractatus de Examine Doctrinarum*, II:17, describes Scripture as "tanquam regula sufficiens et infallibilis pro regimine totius ecclesiastici corporis." I owe these references to the Rev. R. T. Beckwith.

[29] Westminster Confession, I:5.

[30] Titus 1:2.

[31] 1 Pet. 1:23–25; Ps. 119:89.

expressing when he said: "The scripture cannot be broken," and, "It is easier for heaven and earth to pass, than one tittle of the law to fail."[32] God's Word is affirmed to be infallible because God himself is infallible; the infallibility of Scripture is simply the infallibility of God speaking. What Scripture says is to be received as the infallible Word of the infallible God and to assert biblical inerrancy and infallibility is just "to confess faith in (i) the divine origin of the Bible and (ii) the truthfulness and trustworthiness of God. The value of these terms is that they conserve the principle of biblical authority; for statements that are not absolutely true and reliable could not be absolutely authoritative.

The infallibility and inerrancy of biblical teaching does not, however, guarantee the infallibility and inerrancy of any interpretation, or interpreter, of that teaching; nor does the recognition of its qualities as the Word of God in any way prejudge the issue as to what Scripture does, in fact, assert. This can be determined only by careful Bible study. We must allow Scripture itself to define for us the scope and limits of its teaching. Too often the infallibility which belongs to the Word of God has been claimed for interpretations of Scripture which are, to say the least, uncertain and which make Scripture pronounce on subjects about which it does not itself claim to teach anything. The Bible is not an inspired "Enquire Within Upon Everything"; it does not profess to give information about all branches of human knowledge in the way that Bradshaw professes to give information about all branches of British Railways. It claims in the broadest terms to teach all things necessary to salvation,[33] but it nowhere claims to give instruction in (for instance) any of the natural sciences, or in Greek and Hebrew grammar, and it would be an improper use of Scripture to treat it as making pronouncements on these matters.

We must draw a distinction between the subjects about which Scripture speaks and the terms in which it speaks of them. The biblical authors wrote of God's sovereignty over his world, and of man's experiences within that world, using such modes of speech about the natural order and human experience as were current in their days, and in a language that was common to themselves and their contemporaries. This is saying no more than that they wrote to be understood. Their picture of the world and things in it is not put forward as normative for later science, any more than their use of Hebrew and Greek is put forward as a perfect model for composition

[32] John 10:35; Luke 16:17; cf. Matt. 5:18.
[33] 2 Tim. 3:16.

in these languages. They do not claim to teach either science or grammar.[34] Sometimes their grammar lapses; often the mental picture of the created order which their phraseology suggests to the twentieth-century mind differs from that of modern science;[35] but these facts do not bear on the inerrancy of the divine Word which the writers' conceptual and linguistic resources were being used to convey. This distinction between the content and the form of the written Word of God needs more discussion than we can give it here, but it seems clear enough in broad outline, although admittedly it is not always easily applied in particular cases. The question which the interpreter must constantly ask is: What is being *asserted* in this passage? The more poetic, imaginative and symbolic the form in which the truth is presented, and the further the truth transcends our present experience and comprehension (as when Scripture tells us of life before the fall, or in heaven), the harder it is to answer that question with exact precision. But the few passages in which it seems impossible to determine the limits of the symbolism with any finality (such as Genesis 2 and 3, or Revelation 21 and 22) are not typical of the Bible as a whole. In most passages, the use of the ordinary rules of exegesis enables us to determine accurately enough the limits of the intended assertions, and to distinguish them from linguistic forms which are simply vehicles for their communication and could be changed without altering their meaning.

This is just to say that the infallibility and inerrancy of Scripture are relative to the intended scope of the Word of God. Scripture provides instruction that is true and trustworthy, not on every conceivable subject, but simply on those subjects with which it claims to deal. We must allow Scripture itself to tell us what these are. The concepts of inerrancy and

---

[34] Attempts to make Scripture teach science, either explicitly or by implication, have occasioned much fruitless labour, from post-Reformation days to the present time. For a review of some of these attempts, and a stimulating outline of the positive relation of Scripture to science, see R. Hooykaas, *Philosophia Libera: Christian Faith and the Freedom of Science* (Tyndale Press, 1957).

[35] This statement should perhaps be illustrated. It is often said that the Bible pictures the universe as like a house, of which the earth is the ground floor (standing on pillars, 1 Sam. 2:8; and having foundations, Job 38:4), heaven the first floor (divided from the earth by a solid firmament, which acts as a ceiling for the earth, Gen.1:8, and a floor for heaven, Ex. 24:10), and Sheol, or Hades, the cellar (the pit into which the dead go down, Ps. 55:15). Water is stored in heaven above the firmament (Gen. 1:7; Ps. 148:4) and rain starts and stops according as holes are opened and shut in the celestial roof (the windows of heaven, Gen. 7:11). Again, it is often said that the Bible thinks of man's consciousness diffused throughout his whole physical structure, so that each part of him is an independent centre of thought and feeling: thus, his bones speak (Ps. 35:10), his bowels yearn (Gen. 43:30), his ear judges (Job 12:11), his kidneys instruct him by night (Ps. 16:7), etc. It may be doubted whether these forms of speech were any more "scientific" in character and intent than modern references to the sun rising, or lightheadedness, or walking on air, or one's heart sinking one's boots, would be. It is much likelier that they were simply standard pieces of imagery, which the writers utilized, and sometimes heightened for poetic effect, without a thought of what they would imply for cosmology and physiology if taken literally. And language means no more than it is used to mean. In any case, what the writers are concerned to tell us in the passages where they use these forms of speech is not the inner structure of the world and men, but the reflection of both to God.

infallibility express one aspect of the conviction that the teaching of Scripture is the authoritative teaching of God and call attention to the fact that it is always a wrong approach to treat anything that Scripture actually says as untrue or unreliable. But they are not hermeneutical concepts and carry no implications as to the character or range of biblical teaching. Those matters can be settled only by honest and painstaking exegesis.

Dr. Hebert misunderstands the position of evangelicals here. The "rigid theory of the factual inerrancy of the Bible"[36] which he attributes to them involves, he supposes, not merely the recognition of its teaching as the Word of a truth-speaking God, but also the imposition upon it of a literalistic mode of interpretation which refuses to take account of the symbolic element in the telling of (for instance) the story of Adam and Eve. The concept of inerrancy, as he sees it, is thus an untheological concept, and one which expresses an essentially untheological interest in vindicating the factual truthfulness of the Bible. This interest, he suggests, results from living in the twentieth century, and hence from being "unconsciously dominated by the materialistic, intellectualistic view of truth which comes so readily to us in a scientific age." It is because of this conditioning "that it seems so plausible to think that if the Bible is true, it must be literally and factually true." Hebert considers that "a style of thinking which is alien to the Bible is being imposed forcibly upon it" by modern evangelicals, and that their preoccupation with factuality inevitably leads to rather wooden and unedifying exposition of the text; he quotes the *New Bible Commentary*[37] as an example of this.[38] On this line of argument, we would make the following comments:

1. The idea that the doctrine of the inerrancy of the Word of God commits its adherents to a literalistic type of exegesis is wholly groundless. There is nothing inconsistent in recognizing that real events may be recorded in a highly symbolic manner, and evangelicals do in fact recognize this. Dr. Hebert has evidently forgotten the passage which he himself quoted from the I.V.F. *New Bible Handbook* in which the use of symbolic modes of representation in the story of Adam and Eve is explicitly acknowledged.[39]

2. The evangelical insistence on the factuality of what Scripture presents as fact is neither new nor untheological. It goes back to the Reformation,

[36] Hebert, *op.cit.*, 43.
[37] InterVarsity Fellowship, 1953.
[38] Hebert, *op.cit.*, 96–98 and chapter 7.
[39] Ibid., 40.

when the allegorical method of exposition was abandoned in favour of the sounder principle that Scripture must be taken in its literal[40] sense. The way in which some have voiced and defended this conviction in recent years may reflect the influence of the modern scientific outlook; but the conviction itself derives, not from modern science, but from the Bible's own claim that what it tells is the truth, no less when it reports historical facts than when it states theological principles. Dr. Hebert confesses it to be his faith (though he gives no satisfying proof) that Scripture errs in matters both of fact and of doctrine;[41] but he did not learn this faith from Christ and the apostles, who, as we saw, uniformly treated Scripture statements in both these categories as truths from God. The authority of Christ requires us to receive as God's Word all that the Bible asserts. No other attitude to biblical assertions is theologically warrantable; the untheological approach in this case is Hebert's own.

Maintaining the evangelical view of Scripture has always involved controversy, and the changing demands of controversy have naturally led to changes of emphasis in stating it. At the time of the Reformation, all the emphasis was laid on the truth of biblical doctrine, for it was only this that the then opponents of evangelicalism—the church of Rome and the Socinian rationalists—would not face. For the past century, however, there has been as much need to insist on the truth of biblical testimony on matters of historical fact as on matters of theology, for liberal Protestants have regularly deemed both. However, this increased emphasis on the factual truthfulness of the Word of God, to which Dr. Hebert calls attention, is not due to the materialistic influence of modern science, but to the characteristic form of modern heresy. So far from indicating a different approach to the Bible from that of the Reformers, as some suppose, it bears witness to an interest in maintaining the authority of the Bible which is identical with theirs.

3. While passing no judgment on modern evangelical standards of biblical exposition, we do not doubt that the approach to Scripture which we are outlining is far more likely to edify the Church than any modern version of the thesis that the written Word of God is true although it is false; that the teaching of Scripture is only roughly right, and that, though we

---

[40] For the meaning of this term, see "Interpreting Scripture Literally" below.

[41] Hebert, *op.cit.*, 139 and chapter 4. His equation of the incompleteness of Old Testament revelation with error is an irrelevance. His repeated assumption of the legitimacy of rejecting, "on critical grounds," such biblical affirmations as that Paul wrote the Pastoral Epistles begs the whole question of critical method; see J. I. Packer, "Reason," in *Fundamentalism and the Word of God* (Grand Rapids, MI: Eerdmans, 1972), and ibid., Appendix II, 182ff.

ought to believe what we suppose the Bible means, we cannot believe all that it actually says. Only highly sophisticated persons could stomach such an approach in any case; but in this case it is simply a wrong approach. Perhaps, after all, the words "inerrancy" and "infallibility" have not yet outlived their usefulness as signposts to point to this fact.

The Interpretation of Scripture[42]

We now come to the third part of this chapter, in which our aim will be to outline the biblical approach to biblical interpretation.

Scripture, as we have seen, is a many-sided interpretative record of an intricate cross-section of world history. The Word of God is an exceedingly complex unity. The different items and the various kinds of material which make it up—laws, promises, liturgies, genealogies, arguments, narratives, meditations, visions, aphorisms, homilies, parables, and the rest—do not stand in Scripture as isolated fragments, but as parts of a whole. The exposition of them, therefore, involves exhibiting them in right relation both to the whole and to each other. God's Word is not presented in Scripture in the form of a theological system, but it admits of being stated in that form, and, indeed, requires to be so stated before we can properly grasp it—grasp it, that is, as a whole. Every text has its immediate context in the passage from which it comes, its broader context in the book to which it belongs, and its ultimate context in the Bible as a whole; and it needs to be rightly related to each of these contexts if its character, scope, and significance are to be adequately understood.

An analogy may help here. A versatile writer with didactic intent, like Charles Williams or G. K. Chesterton, may express his thought in a variety of literary forms—poems, plays, novels, essays, critical and historical studies, as well as formal topical treatises. In such a case, it would be absurd to think any random sentence from one of his works could safely be taken as expressing his whole mind on the subject with which it deals. The point of each sentence can be grasped only when one sees it in the context, both of the particular piece of work from which it comes, and of the writer's whole output. If we would understand the parts, our wisest course is to get to know the whole—or, at any rate, those parts of the whole which tell us in plain prose the writer's central ideas. These give us the key to all his work. Once we can see the main outlines of his thought and have grasped

[42] For an excellent introduction to the discipline of biblical interpretation, see A. M. Stibbs, *Understanding God's Word* (InterVarsity Fellowship, 1950).

his general point of view, we are able to see the meaning of everything else—the point of his poems and the moral of his stories, and how the puzzling passages fit in with the rest. We may find that his message has a consistency hitherto unsuspected, and that elements in his thought which seemed contradictory are not really so at all. The task of interpreting the mind of God as expressed in his written Word is of the same order as this and must be tackled in the same way. The beginner in Bible study often feels lost; he cannot at first grasp the Bible's overall point of view, and so does not see the wood for trees. As his understanding increases, however, he becomes more able to discern the unity of the biblical message, and to see the place of each part in the whole.

Interpreting Scripture Literally

Scripture yields two basic principles for its own interpretation. The first is that the proper, natural sense of each passage (i.e., the intended sense of the writer) is to be taken as fundamental; the meaning of texts in their own contexts, and for their original readers, is the necessary starting point for enquiry into their wider significance. In other words, Scripture statements must be interpreted in the light of the rules of grammar and discourse on the one hand, and of their own place in history on the other. This is what we should expect in the nature of the case, seeing that the biblical books originated as occasional documents addressed to contemporary audiences; and it is exemplified in the New Testament exposition of the Old, from which the fanciful allegorizing practised by Philo and the Rabbis is strikingly absent. This is the much-misunderstood principle of interpreting Scripture *literally.* A glance at its history will be the quickest way of clearing up the confusion.

The medieval exegetes, following Origen, regarded the "literal" sense of Scripture as unimportant and unedifying. They attributed to each biblical statement three further senses, or levels of meaning, each of which was in a broad sense allegorical: the "moral" or "tropological" (from which one learned rules of conduct), the "allegorical" proper (from which one learned articles of faith), and the "anagogical" (from which one learned of the invisible realities of heaven). Thus, it was held that the term "Jerusalem" in Scripture, while denoting "literally" a city in Palestine, also referred "morally" to civil society, "allegorically" to the church, and "anagogically" to heaven, every time that it occurred. Only the three allegorical senses, the medievals held, were worth a theologian's study; the literal record had no value save as a vehicle of figurative meaning. Medieval exegesis was thus exclusively mystical, not historical at all; biblical facts were made simply a jumping-off ground for theological fancies, and thus spiritualized away. Against this the Reformers protested, insisting that the literal, or intended, sense of Scripture was the sole guide to God's meaning. They were at pains to point out, however, that "literalism" of this sort, so far from precluding the recognition of figures of speech where Scripture employs them, actually demands it. William Tyndale's statement of their position may be quoted as typical: "Thou shalt understand, therefore, that the scripture hath but one sense, which is the literal sense. And that literal sense is the root and ground of all, and the anchor that never faileth, whereunto if thou cleave, thou canst never err or go out of the way. And if thou leave the literal sense, thou canst not but go out of the way. Nevertheless, the scripture uses proverbs, similitudes, riddles, or allegories, as all other speeches do; but that which the proverb, similitude, riddle or allegory signifieth, is ever the literal sense, which thou must seek out diligently."

Tyndale castigates the Scholastics for misapplying 2 Corinthians 3:6 to support their thesis that "the literal sense . . . is hurtful, and noisome, and killeth the soul," and only spiritualizing does any good; and he replaces their distinction between the literal and spiritual senses by an equation which reflects John 6:63: "God is a Spirit, and all his words are spiritual. His literal sense is spiritual . . . if thou have eyes of God to see the right meaning of the text, and whereunto the Scripture pertaineth, and the final end and cause thereof.[43] Fanciful spiritualizing, so far from yielding God's meaning, actually obscured it. The literal sense is itself the spiritual sense, coming from God and leading to him.

This "literalism" is founded on respect for the biblical forms of speech; it is essentially a protest against the arbitrary imposition of inapplicable literary categories on scriptural statements. It is this "literalism" that present-day evangelicals profess. But to read all Scripture narratives as if they were eyewitness reports in a modern newspaper, and to ignore the poetic and imaginative form in which they are sometimes couched, would be no less a violation of the canons of evangelical "literalism" than the allegorizing of the Scholastics was; and this sort of "literalism" evangelicals repudiate. It would be better to call such exegesis "literalistic" rather than "literal," so as to avoid confusing two very different things.[44]

---

[43]Tyndale, *Works* (Parker Society, I:304ff. The judicious Richard Hooker was making the same point when he wrote: "I hold it for a most infallible rule in the exposition of Scripture, that when a literal construction will stand, the furthest from the literal is commonly the worst" (*Laws of Ecclesiastical Polity*, V. lix, 2).

[44]For a good, short review of some of the narrative and didactic forms of Scripture, see J. Stafford Wright, *Interpreting the Bible* (InterVarsity Fellowship, 1955).

The modern outcry against evangelical "literalism" seems to come from those who want leave to sit loose to biblical categories and treat the biblical records of certain events as myths, or parables—nonfactual symbols of spiritual states and experiences. Many would view the story of the fall, for instance, merely as a picture of the present sinful condition of each man, and that of the virgin birth as merely expressing the thought of Christ's superhuman character. Such ideas are attempts to cut the knot tied by the modern critical denial that these events really happened, and to find a way of saying that, though the stories are "literally" false, yet they remain "spiritually" true and valuable. Those who take this line upbraid evangelicals for being insensitive to the presence of symbolism in Scripture. But this is not the issue. There is a world of difference between recognizing that a real event (the fall, say) may be symbolically portrayed, as evangelicals do, and arguing, as these persons do, that because the fall is symbolically portrayed, it need not be regarded as a real event at all, but is merely a picture of something else. In opposing such references, evangelicals are contending, not for a literalistic view, but for the very principles of biblical literalism which we have already stated—that we must respect the literary categories of Scripture, and take seriously the historical character of the Bible story. We may not turn narratives which clearly purport to record actual events into mere symbols of human experience at our will; still less may we do so (as has been done) in the name of biblical theology! We must allow Scripture to tell us its own literary character, and be willing to receive it as what it claims to be.

It may be thought that the historic Protestant use of the word "literal" which we have here been concerned to explain is so unnatural on modern lips, and that such a weight of misleading association now attaches to the term, that it would be wisest to drop it altogether. We argued earlier that the word "fundamentalist" should be dropped, as having become a barrier to mutual understanding, and the case may well be the same here. We do not contend for words. We are not bound to cling to "literal" as part of our theological vocabulary; it is not itself a biblical term, and we can state evangelical principles of interpretation without recourse to it (as, indeed, we did in the opening sentences of this section);[45] and perhaps it is better that we should. If we do abandon the word, however, we must not abandon the principle which it enshrines: namely, that Scripture is to be interpreted in its natural, intended sense, and theological predilections must not be allowed to divert us from loyalty to what the text actually asserts.

[45] See "Interpreting Scripture Literally" above.

Interpreting Scripture by Scripture

The second basic principle of interpretation is that Scripture must interpret Scripture; the scope and significance of one passage is to be brought out by relating it to others. Our Lord gave an example of this when he used Genesis 2:24 to show that Moses' law of divorce was no more than a temporary concession to human hard-heartedness.[46] The Reformers termed this principle the "analogy of Scripture"; the Westminster Confession states it thus: "The infallible rule of interpretation of scripture is the scripture itself; and therefore, when there is a question about the true and full sense of any scripture, it must be searched and known by other places that speak more clearly."[47] This is so in the nature of the case, since the various inspired books are dealing with complementary aspects of the same subject. The rule means that we must give ourselves in Bible study to following out the unities, cross-references, and topical links which Scripture provides. Kings and Chronicles throw light on each other; so do the prophets and the history books of the Old Testament; so do the Synoptic Gospels and John; so do the four Gospels and the Epistles; so, indeed, do the Old Testament as a whole and the New. And there is one book in the New Testament which links up with almost everything that the Bible contains: that is the epistle to the Romans, of which Calvin justly wrote in the epistle prefacing his commentary on it: "If a man understands it, he has a sure road opened for him to the understanding of the whole Scripture." In Romans, Paul brings together and sets out in systematic relation all the great themes of the Bible—sin, law, judgment, faith, works, grace, justification, sanctification, election, the plan of salvation, the work of Christ, the work of the Spirit, the Christian hope, the nature and life of the church, the place of Jew and Gentile in the purposes of God, the philosophy of church and of world history, the meaning and message of the Old Testament, the duties of Christian citizenship, the principles of personal piety and ethics. From the vantage point given by Romans, the whole landscape of the Bible is open to view, and the broad relation of the parts to the whole becomes plain. The study of Romans is the fittest starting point for biblical interpretation and theology.

Problems and Difficulties

The scientific study of Scripture is a complicated and exacting task. The biblical languages have their own distinctive idioms and thought forms.

[46] Matt. 19:3–8, dealing with Deut. 24:1.
[47] Westminster Confession, I:9.

Each writer has his own habits of mind, vocabulary, outlook, and interests. Each book has its own character and is written according to stylistic conventions which it is not always easy to see. Each book has its own historical and theological background and must be interpreted against that background; thus, we should not look in the Old Testament for clear statements about the Trinity, or the believer's hope of a future life, for these things were not fully revealed till Christ came. All these factors must be borne in mind, or we shall misinterpret Scripture.

This does not mean that only trained scholars can study the Bible to any profit. Its central message is so plainly stated in the text that the most unlearned of those who have ears to hear and eyes to see can understand it. "The unfolding of thy words gives light; it imparts understanding to the simple."[48] The technicalities of scholarship may be out of the ordinary Bible reader's reach, but nonetheless he can, with God's blessing, grasp all the main truths of God's message. "Those things which are necessary to be known, believed, and observed, for salvation, are so clearly propounded and opened in some place of scripture or other, that not only the learned, but the unlearned, in a due use of the ordinary means, may attain unto a sufficient understanding of them."[49] It is only over secondary matters that problems arise. Here, however, ignorance of the background of biblical statements and allusions, coupled (no doubt) with failure to enter adequately into the writers' minds,[50] leave us on occasion in doubt as to what texts mean, and how they fit in with other texts and with the rest of the Word of God. But these uncertainties affect only the outer fringes of the biblical revelation. And, in fact, this class of problem steadily yields to patient study as our knowledge grows. As in all scientific enquiry, however, the solution of one problem raises another, and we have no reason to expect that all the problems that crop up in biblical exposition will ever be completely solved in this world.

An idea that persistently haunts some people is that the presence in Scripture of passages which are hard to harmonize is an argument against regarding it as God's Word written in the sense we have explained, and that one is not entitled so to regard it until one has first reconciled all the seeming discrepancies to one's own satisfaction. If this were right, every apparent contradiction would be a valid reason for doubting the truth of the biblical doctrine of Scripture. But the idea rests on confusion. Christians

[48] Ps. 119:30 RSV.
[49] Westminster Confession, I:8.
[50] Cf. 2 Pet. 3:16.

are bound to receive the Bible as God's Word written on the authority of Christ, not because they can prove it such by independent enquiry, but because as disciples they trust their divine Teacher. We have pointed out already that no article of Christian faith admits of full rational demonstration as, say, geometrical theorems do; all the great biblical doctrines—the Trinity, the incarnation, the atonement, the work of the Spirit in man, the resurrection of the body, and the renewal of the creation—are partly mysterious, and raise problems for our minds that are at present insoluble. The doctrine of Scripture is no exception to this rule. But that should not daunt, nor even surprise us; for it is the very nature of Christian faith to believe, on the authority of God, truths which may neither be rationally demonstrated nor exhaustively understood. We must remember that God does not tell us everything about his acts and purposes, nor put us in a position to work them all out for ourselves. We shall not reach right views about the things of God by backing our independent judgment, but only by taking his word. We are wholly dependent on him for our knowledge of his ways.

God, then, does not profess to answer in Scripture all the questions that we, in our boundless curiosity, would like to ask about Scripture. He tells us merely as much as he sees we need to know as a basis for our life of faith. And he leaves unsolved some of the problems raised by what he tells us, in order to teach us a humble trust in his veracity. The question, therefore, that we must ask ourselves when faced with these puzzles is not, is it reasonable to imagine that this is so? but, is it reasonable to accept God's assurance that this is so? Is it reasonable to take God's word and believe that he has spoken the truth, even though I cannot fully comprehend what he has said? The question carries its own answer. We should not abandon faith in anything that God has taught us merely because we cannot solve all the problems which it raises. Our own intellectual competence is not the test and measure of divine truth. It is not for us to stop believing because we lack understanding, or to postpone believing till we can get understanding, but to believe in order that we may understand; as Augustine said, "Unless you believe, you will not understand." Faith first, sight afterwards, is God's order, not vice versa; and the proof of the sincerity of our faith is our willingness to have it so. Therefore, just as we should not hesitate to commit ourselves to faith in the Trinity although we do not know how one God can be three persons, nor to faith in the incarnation, although we do not know how the divine and human natures combined in the person of Christ, so we should not hesitate to commit ourselves to faith in Scripture as the infallible Word of the infallible God, even though we cannot solve all the puzzles, nor reconcile all the apparent contradictions, with which in our present state of knowledge it confronts us. On all these articles of faith we have God's positive assurance; and that should be enough.

Accordingly, our methods of interpreting Scripture must be such as express faith in its truth and consistency as God's Word. Our approach must be harmonistic; for we know at the outset that God's utterance is not self-contradictory. Article XX of the Church of England lays down that it is not lawful for the church so to "expound one place of Scripture, that it be repugnant to another"; no more is it lawful for any individual exegete. Not that we should adopt strained and artificial expedients for harmonizing; this will neither glorify God nor edify us. What we cannot harmonize by a natural and plausible hypothesis is best left unharmonized, with a frank admission that in our present state of knowledge we do not see how these apparent discrepancies should be resolved. We may not, with the heretic Marcion and some modern liberals, "criticize the Bible by the Bible," singling out some parts of Scripture as the authentic Word of God and denying the divine character of the rest because it seems to say something different from the parts approved; instead, we should confess the divine origin of all the Scriptures and be guided in interpreting them by Augustine's axiom: "I do not doubt that their authors therein made no mistake and set forth nothing that might mislead. If in one of these books I stumble across something which seems opposed to the truth, I have no hesitation in saying that either my copy is faulty, or the translator has not fully grasped what was said" [Augustine read Scripture in Latin], "or else I myself have not fully understood."[51] We must base our study of Scripture on the assumption that governed the New Testament men in their study of the Old—that God's revealed truth is a consistent unity, and any disharmony between part and part is only apparent, not real.

The Holy Spirit as Interpreter

One final point concerning interpretation remains to be made. Scripture tells us that if we are to understand Scripture, we need, over and above right rules, personal insight into spiritual things. Scripture sets before us spiritual truths—truths, that is, about God, and about created things in relation to God; and to grasp spiritual truths requires spiritual receptiveness. But no man has this by nature. "The natural man receiveth not the things of the Spirit of God: for they are foolishness unto him: neither can he know

[51] *Ep.* 82.

them, because they are spiritually discerned."[52] The habit of mind which enslaves the natural man, Paul tells us, is to set up his own "wisdom" and make it ultimate, and so he is compelled to dismiss as foolishness all that does not accord with it. Without spiritual enlightenment, he will never be able to see the foolishness of his own wisdom, nor the wisdom of the "foolishness of God"[53] proclaimed in the gospel; hence he will never forsake the one for the other. Our Lord confirms this view of man. His repeated diagnosis of the unbelieving Pharisees was that they were *blind*, lacking the capacity to perceive spiritual realities;[54] and he regarded spiritual perception, where he found it, as a supernatural gift from God.[55]

Now, the Holy Spirit has been sent to the church as its Teacher, to guide Christians into truth, to make them wise unto salvation, to testify to them of Christ and to glorify him thereby.[56] To the apostles, he came to remind them of Christ's teaching, to show them its meaning, to add further revelation to it, and so to equip them to witness to all about their Lord.[57] To other men, he comes to make them partakers of the apostolic faith through the apostolic word. Paul indicates the permanent relation between the Spirit, the apostles' word, and the rest of the church in 1 Corinthians 2:10–16. The Spirit, he says, gave the apostles understanding of the gospel: "We have received, not the spirit of the world, but the spirit which is of God; that we might know the things that are freely given to us of God"; "God hath revealed them unto us by his Spirit." Now the Spirit inspires and empowers their proclamation of these things to other men: "which things we speak, not in the words which man's wisdom teacheth, but which the Holy Ghost teacheth"; Paul preaches, and knows that he preaches, "in demonstration of the Spirit and of power."[58] And "he that is spiritual"—he in whom the Spirit abides to give understanding—discerns the meaning of the message and receives it as the testimony of God. This applies no less to the apostolic word written than to the apostolic word preached; and no more to the apostolic writings than to the rest of the written Word of God. The Spirit, who was its author, is also its interpreter, and such understanding of it as men gain is his gift.

Not that the Spirit's presence in men's hearts makes patient study of the text unnecessary. The Spirit is not given to make Bible study needless, but

[52] 1 Cor. 2:14.
[53] 1 Cor. 1:25; see the whole passage, 1:18ff.
[54] Matt. 15:14; 23:16, 17, 19, 26; John 9:39–41.
[55] Matt. 11:25; 16:17.
[56] John 14:26; 15:26; 16:13–14.
[57] John 14:26; 16:12, 13; 17:20.
[58] 1 Cor. 2:4.

to make it effective. Nor can anything in Scripture mean anything when the Spirit interprets. The Spirit is not the prompter of fanciful spiritualizing, or of applications of texts out of their contexts on the basis of accidental associations of words. The only meaning to which he bears witness is that which each text actually has in the organism of Scripture; such witness as is borne to other meanings is borne by other spirits. But without the Spirit's help there can be no grasp of the message of Scripture, no conviction of the truth of Scripture, and no faith in the God of Scripture. Without the Spirit, nothing is possible but spiritual blindness and unbelief.

It follows that the Christian must approach the study of Scripture in humble dependence on the Holy Spirit, sure that he can learn from it nothing of spiritual significance unless he is taught of God. Confidence in one's own powers of discernment is an effective barrier to spiritual understanding. The self-confidence of nineteenth-century critical scholarship was reflected in its slogan that the Bible must be read like any other book; but the Bible is more than a merely human book, and understanding it involves more than appreciating its merely human characteristics. God's book does not yield up its secrets to those who will not be taught of the Spirit. Our God-given textbook is a closed book till our God-given Teacher opens it to us.

A century of criticism has certainly thrown some light on the human side of the Bible—its style, language, composition, history, and culture; but whether it has brought the church a better understanding of its divine message than evangelicals of two, three, and four hundred years ago possessed is more than doubtful. It is not at all clear that we today comprehend the plan of salvation, the doctrines of sin, election, atonement, justification, new birth and sanctification, the life of faith, the duties of churchmanship, and the meaning of church history more clearly than did the Reformers, or the Puritans, or the leaders of the eighteenth-century revival. When it is claimed that modern criticism has greatly advanced our understanding of the Bible, the reply must be that it depends upon what is meant by the Bible; criticism has thrown much light on the human features of Scripture, but it has not greatly furthered our knowledge of the Word of God. Indeed, it seems truer to say that its effect to date has been rather to foster ignorance of the Word of God; for by concentrating on the human side of Scripture it has blurred the church's awareness of the divine character of scriptural teaching, and by questioning biblical statements in the name of scholarship it has shaken confidence in the value of personal Bible study. Hence, just as the medievals tended to equate church tradition with the Word of God, so modern Protestants tend to equate the words of scholars with the Word of God. We have fallen into the habit of accepting their pronouncements at second hand without invoking the Spirit's help to search Scripture and see, not merely whether what they say is so (insofar as the lay Bible student is qualified to judge this), but also—often more important—whether God's Word does not deal with more than the limited number of topics with which scholars at any one time are concerned. The result of this negligence is widespread ignorance among churchmen as to what Scripture actually says. So it always is when the church forgets how to search the Scriptures, acknowledging its own blindness and looking to God's Spirit to teach it God's truth. There is no more urgent need today than that the church should humble itself to learn this lesson once more.

We have now presented in positive outline the biblical approach to Scripture. Its text is word for word God-given; its message is an organic unity, the infallible Word of an infallible God, a web of revealed truths centred upon Christ; it must be interpreted in its natural sense, on the assumption of its inner harmony; and its meaning can be grasped only by those who humbly seek and gladly receive the help of the Holy Spirit.

5

"Scripture Speaks for Itself"

JOHN M. FRAME

God's Inerrant Word

Previously published as "Scripture Speaks for Itself," in *God's Inerrant Word: An International Symposium on the Trustworthiness of Scripture*, ed. John Warwick Montgomery (Minneapolis: Bethany Fellowship, 1974), 178–200. Used by permission of Baker Books, a division of Baker Publishing Group.

What does Scripture say about itself? The question is both momentous and commonplace.

It is momentous: the self-witness of Scripture has been for centuries the cornerstone of the orthodox Christian argument for biblical authority. For one thing, there would never be any such argument unless there were reasons to believe that Scripture *claimed* authority. If Scripture renounced all claim to authority, or even remained neutral on the subject, there would not be much reason for Christians today to claim authority *for* Scripture. But if Scripture *does* claim authority over us, then we are faced with a momentous challenge indeed! Acceptance or rejection of that claim will influence every aspect of Christian doctrine and life.

Furthermore, the authority of Scripture is a doctrine of the Christian faith—a doctrine like other doctrines—like the deity of Christ, justification by faith, sacrificial atonement. To prove such doctrines, Christians go to Scripture. Where else can we find information on God's redemptive purposes? But what of the doctrine of the authority of Scripture? Must we not, to be consistent, also prove *that* doctrine by Scripture? If so, then the self-witness of Scripture must not only be the *first* consideration in the argument; it must be the final and decisive consideration also.

Now of course someone may object that that claim is not competent to establish itself. If the Bible *claims* to be God's word, that does not prove that it *is* God's word. That is true in a sense. Many documents claim to be the word of some god or other. The Koran, the Book of Mormon and countless other books have made such claims. In no case does the claim in itself establish the authority of the book. The claim must be compared with the evidence. But the evidence through the presuppositions furnished by, among other things, our religious convictions. A Christian must look at the evidence with Christian assumptions; a rationalist must look at the evidence with rationalistic assumptions. And the Christian finds his most basic assumptions in the Bible!

As I have argued elsewhere,[1] it is impossible to avoid circularity of a sort when one is arguing on behalf of an *ultimate criterion*. One may not argue for one ultimate criterion by appealing to another. And the argument over scriptural authority is precisely an argument over ultimate criterion!

We must not, of course, simply urge non-Christians to accept the Bible because the Bible says so. Although there is much truth in that simplicity, it can be misleading if stated in that form without further explanation. A non-Christian must start where he is. Perhaps he believes that Scripture is a fairly reliable source, though not infallible. He should then be urged to study Scripture as a historical source for Christian doctrine, as the *original* "source." He will be confronted with the claims of Scripture—about God, about Christ, about man, about itself. He will compare the biblical way of looking at things with his own way. And if God wills, he will see the wisdom in looking at things Scripture's way. But we must not mislead him about the demand of Scripture. He must not be allowed to think that he can become a Christian and go on thinking the same old way. He must be told that Christ demands a *total* repentance—of heart, mind, will, emotions—the whole man. He must learn that Christ demands a change in "ultimate criterion." And thus he must learn that even the evidentiary procedures he uses to establish biblical authority must be reformed by the Bible. He must learn that "evidence" is at bottom an elaboration of God's self-witness; that "proving" God is the same as hearing and obeying him.

So the question of the biblical self-witness is a momentous one indeed. In a sense it is the *only* question. If by "self-witness" we mean, not merely the texts in which the Bible explicitly claims authority, but the whole char-

---

[1] See John Frame, "God and Biblical Language: Transcendence and Immanence," in *God's Inerrant Word: An International Symposium on the Trustworthiness of Scripture*, ed. John Warwick Montgomery (Minneapolis: Bethany Fellowship, 1974), 159–77.

acter of the Bible as it confronts us, then the question of biblical authority is purely and simply the question of biblical self-witness.

On the other hand, the question is also commonplace: simply because it is so important, the question has been discussed over and over again by theologians. Although I feel greatly honored by the invitation to speak and write on such a basic question, I must confess also to a slight feeling of numbness. What can I say that hasn't been said already? What can I say that Gäussen, Warfield, Kuyper, Murray, Young, Van Til, Kline, Ridderbos, Pache, Wenham, Packer, Montgomery, Pinnock, and Gerstner haven't said?[2] Even in this collection, some of the other papers will overlap this topic! No doubt, in a collection of papers of this sort, someone ought to summarize the basic material. But I can't help thinking it might be best just to quote snatches from other authors whose scholarship and eloquence is far superior to my own. It *might* be; but I won't follow that course here, because I do have a few reasons for attempting an individual, if not independent, study.

Past orthodox Christian discussions of this matter have, in my opinion, done a very adequate job on the whole. As in all human endeavors, however, there is room for improvement here. The improvements I have in mind are chiefly two:

1. There needs to be a greater emphasis upon the *persuasiveness* throughout Scripture of the biblical self-witness. As we suggested earlier, there is a sense in which *all* of the Bible is self-witness. Whatever the Bible says, in a sense, it says about itself. Even the genealogies of the kings tell us about the content, and therefore the character of Scripture. The *way* in which the Bible speaks of kings and vineyards and wilderness journeys and

[2] We shall cite some of the most helpful sources on these questions. The classic nineteenth-century work on the subject, still useful, is L. Gäussen, *The Inspiration of the Holy Scriptures*, trans. D. D. Scott (Chicago: Moody, 1949). The most impressive piece of scholarly work in this area to date remains B. B. Warfield, *The Inspiration and Authority of the Bible*, ed. S. G. Craig (Philadelphia: Presbyterian & Reformed, 1948). In relating the doctrine of inspiration to a comprehensive Christian world and life view, Abraham Kuyper's *Principles of Christian Theology*, trans. J. H. DeVries (Grand Rapids: Eerdmans, 1965), is unsurpassed. Almost the only new things that have been said in the last few years about the doctrine have been said by Meredith G. Kline in his *Structure of Biblical Authority* (Grand Rapids: Eerdmans, 1972). A helpful guide through the issues raised by New Testament biblical scholarship is H. Ridderbos, *The Authority of the New Testament Scriptures*, ed. J. M. Kik, trans. de Jongste (Philadelphia: Presbyterian and Reformed Publishing Co., 1963). The soundest overall guide to the theological controversies (in my opinion) is C. Van Til, *A Christian Theory of Knowledge* (Philadelphia: Presbyterian and Reformed Publishing Co., 1969); cf. his "unpublished" syllabus, "The Doctrine of Scripture" (Ripon, CA: Den Dulk Foundation, 1967). For general summaries of the issues, see: *The Infallible Word*, ed. N. R. Stonehouse and P. Woolley, 3rd rev. ed. (Philadelphia: Presbyterian and Reformed Publishing Co., 1967) [the article by John Murray is especially helpful]; *Revelation and the Bible*, ed. Carl F. H. Henry (Grand Rapids: Baker, 1958); and, on the more popular level, but most eloquent and cogent, E. J. Young, *Thy Word Is Truth* (Grand Rapids: Eerdmans, 1957). Other recent works useful in resolving the question of the Bible's self-witness are R. Pache, *The Inspiration and Authority of Scripture*, trans. H. Needham (Chicago: Moody Press, 1969); C. Pinnock, *Biblical Revelation* (Chicago: Moody Press, 1971); and J. W. Wenham, *Christ and the Bible* (Chicago: InterVarsity Press, 1973).

God and man and Christ—its *manner* is a testimony to its character. More specifically: the overall doctrinal structure of Scripture is an important element of the biblical self-witness. For when the Bible speaks of atonement, reconciliation, justification, glorification, it speaks of these in such a way as to presuppose a crucial role for itself. Or to look at redemption from a more historical perspective, from the beginning of God's dealings with men God has taught them to give his words a particular role in their lives, a lesson which is taught again and again through the thousands of years of redemptive history. Now when we neglect this emphasis on the pervasiveness of the biblical self-witness, at least two bad things happen: (a) People can get the idea that the concept of biblical authority is based largely on a few texts scattered through the Bible, texts which may not be very important in the overall biblical scheme of things. They might even get the idea that the doctrine of inspiration is based largely upon a *couple* of texts (2 Pet. 1:21; 2 Tim. 3:16) which liberal scholars dismiss as being late and legalistic. Thus it may seem as though the doctrine of biblical authority is a rather peripheral doctrine, rather easily dispensable for anyone who has even the slightest inclination to dispense with unpalatable doctrines. (b) People can get the idea that Christ and the Bible are separable, that you can believe in and obey Christ without believing in and obeying the Bible. They may think that Scripture is unimportant to the Christian message of redemption.

2. If, as orthodox people maintain, the biblical self-witness to its authority and infallibility is *obvious*, *clear*—and certainly if it is "pervasive"!—then we must face more squarely the question of why not-so-orthodox people see the matter differently. At one level, of course, it is legitimate to say that they fail to see the truth because of their unbelief: the god of this world has blinded their minds.[3] Sin is "irrational"—it turns away from the obvious. But sinners, when they are scholars, at least, generally do things for a *reason*, perverse as that reason may be. And perverse or not, such reasoning is often highly plausible. If orthodox people can identify that reasoning, explain its surface plausibility, and expose its deeper error, then the orthodox view of the biblical self-witness will be stated much more cogently.

In the remaining portion of this essay, I shall present an essentially traditional argument concerning the character of the biblical self-witness; but I shall structure the discussion in such a way as to implement the above two

---

[3] 2 Cor. 4:4.

concerns—not comprehensively, to be sure, probably not adequately—but to greater degree than one might expect in a paper of this length.[4] The first section will examine the role of verbal revelation in the biblical understanding of salvation. The second will discuss the relationship of that verbal revelation to Scripture, and the third will analyse what I take to be the most common and plausible objection to the previous line of reasoning.

Revealed Words and Salvation

We have suggested that the whole Bible is self-witness; but the Bible is not *only* or *primarily* self-witness. It is, first and foremost, not a book about a book, but a book about God, about Christ, about the salvation of man from sin. But that message of salvation includes a message about the Bible. For this salvation requires *verbal revelation.* In saving man, God *speaks* to him.

Lord and Servant

God spoke to man even *before* man fell into sin. The first human experience mentioned in Scripture is the hearing of God's word; for immediately after the account of man's creation we read,

> And God blessed them: and God said unto them, Be fruitful, and multiply, and replenish the earth, and subdue it; and have dominion over the fish of the sea, and over the birds of the heavens, and over every living thing that moveth upon the earth.[5]

It is appropriate that the hearing of these words be presented in Scripture as man's first experience. For this was the experience by which the whole course of man's life was determined. When man heard these words of God, he heard his own *definition.* God was telling man who man was, what his task was. Everything else that man did was to be in obedience to this command. Whether a shepherd, a farmer, a miner, a businessman, a teacher, a homemaker—his main job was to replenish and subdue the earth in obedience to this command. The command covered *all of* life, not just some compartments of it. The command was not to be questioned; it was God's sovereign determination of man's responsibility. The command asserted God's claim to *ultimate* authority; for, paradoxically, while the command declared man to have dominion over the earth, it also declared

[4] As such, the paper will also *fail* to do justice to *other* legitimate concerns.
[5] Gen 1:28.

God's dominion over man! Whatever dominion man enjoys, he receives from God; he enjoys it at God's pleasure; he enjoys it out of obedience to God's command.

Why? Simply because God is God and man is man. God is Lord; man is servant. God commands; man must obey. To have a Lord is to be under authority. A servant is one responsible to obey the *commands* of another. What kind of lordship would there be without commands? The very idea is absurd. Without commands, no obedience; without obedience, no responsibility; without responsibility, no authority; without authority, no lordship.

Man was created in obedience; he fell through disobedience—disobedience to another command, this time the command concerning the forbidden tree.[6] The simplest biblical definition of sin is "lawlessness"[7]—rejection of, disobedience to God's commands. Therefore just as the word of God defines our status as God's creatures and servants, it also defines our status as *fallen* creatures, as sinners.

Redemption, according to Scripture, involves a reassertion of God's lordship. The fall, of course, did not annul God's lordship; God's lordship over fallen man is vividly expressed in divine judgment against sin. But if man is to be saved, he must be brought to realize again that God is Lord and demands man's unconditional obedience. When God saved Israel from Egypt, he called himself by the mysterious name Jehovah which, though its exact meaning is uncertain, clearly asserts his claim to unconditional lordship.[8] And throughout the history of redemption, God continually asserted this claim by making *absolute demands* upon his people.

God's demands are absolute in at least three senses: (1) They *cannot be questioned*. The Lord God has the right to demand unwavering, unflinching obedience. God blessed Abraham because he "obeyed my voice, and kept my charge, my commandments, my statutes, and my laws."[9] He did not waver[10] even when God commanded him to sacrifice his son Isaac, the son of the promise.[11] To waver—even in that horrible situation!—would have been sin. (2) God's demand is absolute also in the sense that it *transcends all other loyalties*, all other demands. The Lord God will not toler-

[6] Gen. 2:17; 3:6, 11f.
[7] 1 John 3:4.
[8] Ex. 3:14; note context. In later years, when this sacred name was considered too sacred to be pronounced, the Jews read the word *Adonai*, Lord, in its place.
[9] Gen. 26:5.
[10] Rom. 4:20.
[11] Gen. 22:18.

ate competition; he demands *exclusive* loyalty.[12] The servant must love his Lord with all his heart, soul, and strength.[13] One cannot serve two masters.[14] One of the most remarkable proofs of the deity of Christ in the New Testament is that, there, Jesus Christ demands—and receives—precisely this kind of loyalty from his followers, the same sort of loyalty which Jehovah demanded of Israel.[15] The Lord demands *first* place. (3) God's demand is also absolute in that it *governs all areas of life*. In the Old Testament period, God regulated not only Israel's worship, but also the diet, political life, sex life, economic life, family life, travel, and calendar of his people. No area of life was immune to God's involvement. To be sure, the New Testament gives us more freedom on a certain sense: the detailed dietary restrictions, uncleanness rituals, animal sacrifices, and other elements of the old order are no longer literally binding. But the New Testament, if anything, is *more* explicit than the Old on the comprehensiveness of God's demand: *whatsoever* we do, even eating and drinking, must be done to the glory of God.[16] We must never shut the Lord out of any compartment of our lives; there must be no areas kept to ourselves. God's lordship involves such *absolute demands*.

Savior and Sinner

But salvation is more than a reassertion of God's lordship. If God merely reasserted his lordship, we would be without hope, for we have turned against him and deserve death at his hand.[17] If God merely spoke to us absolute demands, we would perish, for we have not obeyed these demands. But our God is not only Lord; he is also *Savior*. And he speaks to us not only demands, not only law, but also *gospel*—the good news of Jesus Christ. But we must emphasize that he *speaks* the gospel. The gospel is a *message*, a revelation in words. How can we know that the death of Christ is sufficient to save us from sin? No human wisdom could have figured that out! Only God can declare sinners to be forgiven; only God has the right to promise salvation to those who believe! The same Lord who speaks to demand obedience, also speaks to promise salvation. As Abraham,[18] we are called to believe the gospel simply because it is God's

[12] Ex. 20:3, "Thou shalt have no other gods before me."
[13] Deut. 6:4f; cf. Matt. 22:37ff and parallels in other Gospels.
[14] Matt. 6:22ff.
[15] Matt. 19:16–30; cf. 8:19–22, 10–37, Phil. 3:8.
[16] 1 Cor. 10:31–A New Testament dietary law! Cf. Rom. 14:23; 2 Cor. 10:5; Col. 3:17.
[17] Rom. 3:23; 6:23.
[18] Rom. 4:19f.

own promise. We know that believers in Christ are saved because Jesus has told us they are.[19] Only the Lord can speak the word of forgiveness, that word which declares sinners to be forgiven, and promises eternal life.

Just as there can be no lordship without an absolute demand, so there is no salvation without a gracious and certain promise. Therefore the whole biblical message presupposes the *necessity of verbal revelation.* Without revealed words, there is neither lordship nor salvation. To "accept Christ as Savior and Lord" is to accept from the heart Christ's demand and promise. Let there be no misunderstanding: you *cannot* "accept Christ" without accepting his words! Christ himself emphasizes this point over and over again.[20] If we set aside the words of Christ in favor of a vague, undefined "personal relationship" to Christ, we simply lose the biblical Christ and substitute a Christ of our own imagination.

And not just any words will do! They must be *God's* words—words of divine and not merely human authority; words which cannot be questioned transcend all other loyalties, govern all areas of life. They must be words which *cannot* be contradicted by human philosophies or theologies—or even by the "assured results of modern scholarship"! Without words like *that*, we have no Lord and we have no Savior.

But where can we find words like *that*? No mere philosopher or theologian or scholar speaks such words! Many religions, indeed, claim to have such words; but how are we to judge among these many claims? How do we distinguish the voice of God from the voice of devils and the imaginations of our own hearts?

Revealed Words and Scripture

Scripture tells us to go to Scripture! Or, rather, the *God* of Scripture tells us in Scripture to go to Scripture!

Of course we must note at the outset that the Bible is not the *only* word that God has spoken. God has spoken words to and by his apostles and prophets that are not recorded in the Bible. He has also spoken, in a sense, to the earth, to the storms, to the winds and waves.[21] And in a mysterious sense, the word of God may also be identified with God himself[22] and par-

---

[19] John 5:24.

[20] Matt. 7:24–29; Mark 8:38; Luke 9:26; 8:21; John 8:31, 47, 51; 10:27; 12:47–50; 14:15, 21, 23f.; 15:7, 10, 14; 17:6, 8, 17. The relationship between Christ and his words is essentially the same as that between God and his words in the Old Testament.

[21] Ps. 119:90f.; 147:15–18; 148:5f.; Gen. 1:3; Ps. 33:6, 9; cf. Matt. 8:27.

[22] John 1:1.

ticularly with Jesus Christ.[23] But God does not always tell us what he says to the winds and waves, and he has not always provided us with prophets at a handy distance! Rather, he has directed us to a *book*! That is where we are to go for daily, regular guidance. That is where we may always find the demands of the Lord and the promise of the Savior.

Writing goes back a long way in the history of redemption. The book of Genesis appears to be derived largely from "books of generations."[24] We don't know much about the origin of these books, but it is significant that (1) they include inspired prophecies[25] and (2) they were eventually included among Israel's authoritative writings. From a very early time, God's people began to *record* the history of redemption for their posterity. It was important from the beginning that God's covenants, his demands, and his promises are written down lest they be forgotten. The first explicit reference, however, to a divinely authorized book occurs in connection with the war between Israel and Amalek shortly after the exodus:

> And Joshua discomfited Amalek and his people with the edge of the sword. And the Lord said unto Moses, Write this for a memorial in a book, and rehearse it in the ears of Joshua: that I will utterly blot out the remembrance of Amalek from under heaven. And Moses built an altar, and called the name of it Jehovah-nissi; and he said, the Lord hath sworn: the Lord will have war with Amalek from generation to generation.[26]

Not only does the Lord authorize the writing of the book; the content of it is God's own oath, his pledge. It is the word of God, a word of absolute authority and sure promise. Because God has spoken it, it will surely happen.

But an even more important example of divine writing occurs a few chapters later. In Exodus 20, God speaks the Ten Commandments to the people of Israel. The people are terrified, and they ask Moses to act as mediator between themselves and God. From Exodus 20:22 to 23:33, God presents to Moses further commandments in addition to the ten, which Moses is to convey to the people. In Exodus 24:4, we learn that Moses wrote down all these words and in verse 7 read them to the people. The

[23] John 1:14.

[24] Gen. 5:1; cf. 2:4; 6:9; 10:1; 11:10, 27; 25:12, 19; 36:9; 37:2.

[25] Gen. 9:25–27: though Noah is speaking, he is administering a covenantal blessing and curse which can only take effect under divine sanction. The fulfillment of these words at a much later period shows that these words were in essence the words of God. Cf. Gen. 25:23; 27:27–29; etc.

[26] Ex. 17:13–16. The language here suggests a parallel with the divine "book of life," as though this earthly book were a kind of copy of the divine original.

people received these words as the word of God himself: "All that the Lord hath spoken will we do, and be obedient."[27] They accepted these *written* words as words of absolute demand! But something even more remarkable occurs a few verses later. The Lord calls Moses alone to ascend the mountain, "and I will give thee the tables of stone, and the law and the commandment which I have written, that thou mayest teach them."[28] Note the pronouns in the first person singular! *God* did the writing! In fact, the implication of the tenses is that God had completed the writing before Moses ascended the mountain. Moses was to go up the mountain to receive a completed, divinely written manuscript! Nor is this the only passage that stresses divine authorship of the law. Elsewhere, too, we learn that the tables were "written with the finger of God";[29] they were "the work of God, and the writing was the writing of God, graven upon the tables."[30]

What was going on here? Why the sustained emphasis upon divine writing? Meredith G. Kline[31] suggests that this emphasis on divine writing arises out of the nature of covenant making in the ancient near East. When a great king entered a "suzerainty covenant relation" with a lesser king, the great king would produce a *document* setting forth the terms of the covenant. The great king was the author, because he was the lord, the sovereign. He set the terms. The lesser king was to read and obey, for he was the servant, the vassal. The covenant document was the law; it set forth the commands of the great king, and the servant was bound to obey. To disobey the document was to disobey the great king; to obey it was to obey him. Now in Exodus 20 and succeeding chapters, God is making a kind of "suzerainty treaty" with Israel. As part of the treaty relation, he authors a document which is to serve as the official record of his absolute demand. Without the document there would be no covenant.

Later, more words were added to the document; and we read in Deuteronomy that Moses put all these words in the ark of the covenant, the dwelling place of God, the holiest place in Israel, "that it may be there for

[27] Ex. 24:7.
[28] Ex. 24:12.
[29] Ex. 31:13.
[30] Ex. 32:16; cf. also 34:1; Deut. 4:13; 9:10f.; 10:2–4. Moses too is said to have done some writing in Ex. 34:27f.—probably portions of the law other than the ten commandments. And yet the written work of Moses is no less authoritative than that of the Lord himself—cf. Ex. 34:32. Moses was the mediator of the covenant and as such was a prophet conveying God's word to the people. Cf. Ex. 4:10–17; Deut. 18:15–19. The unique "finger of God" writing therefore is not necessary to the authority of the documents; humanly *written* documents may be equally authoritative, as long as the words are God's. But the "finger of God" picture places awesome *emphasis* upon the authority of the words.
[31] Kline, *op. cit.* in note 2 above.

a witness against thee."[32] The covenant document is not man's witness concerning God; it is God's witness *against* man. Man may not add to or subtract anything from the document;[33] for the document is God's word and must not be confused with any mere human authority.

This divine authority takes many forms. In the extrabiblical suzerainty covenants, certain distinct elements have been discovered:[34] the self-identification of the lord (the giving of his name), the "historical prologue" (proclaiming the benevolent acts of the lord to the vassal), the basic demand for exclusive loyalty (called "love"), the detailed demands of the lord, the curses upon the disobedient, the blessings upon the obedient, and finally the details of covenant administration, use of the document, etc. In the law of God, all of these elements are present. God tells who he is,[35] he proclaims his grace through his acts in history,[36] he demands love,[37] he sets forth his detailed demands,[38] he declares the curses and blessings contingent on covenant obedience,[39] and he sets up the machinery for continuing covenant administration, laying particular emphasis on the use of the covenant book.[40] All of these elements of the covenant are authoritative; all are words of God.

Theologians generally oversimplify the concept of biblical authority. To some theologians, it is God's personal self-manifestation (as in the giving of the divine name) which is authoritative. To others, it is the account of historical events. To others, the demand for love is the central thing. To others it is the divine self-commitment to bless. But the covenantal structure of revelation has room for all of these elements, and what's more, places them in proper relation to one another. There is both love and law, both grace and demand, both kerygma and didache, both

[32] Deut. 31:26.

[33] Deut. 4:2; 12:32; cf. Prov. 30:6; Rev. 22:18f. How, then, could any additions be made to the document? For some additions clearly were made (Josh. 24:26, etc.). Since no man could add or subtract, the addition of a book to the covenant canon carries with it the claim that the addition has *divine* sanction.

[34] Kline, *op. cit.*; we are listing the elements Kline finds in treaties of the second millennium, BC. He regards the Decalogue and the book of Deuteronomy as having this basic structure (thus implying a second millennium date for Deuteronomy!), and he regards the entire Old Testament canon as an outgrowth of these "treaties."

[35] Ex. 20:2, "I am the Lord thy God"; cf. 3:14, etc.

[36] Ex. 20:2, ". . . who brought thee out of the land of Egypt, out of the house of bondage."

[37] Ex. 20:3, "Thou shalt have no other gods before me." Cf. Deut. 6:4f where the term "love" is actually used to denote this exclusive covenant loyalty. The demand for love follows the account of God's gracious acts in history, and is regarded as the vassal's response of gratitude for the Lord's benevolence. Cf. the New Testament emphasis, "We love, because he first loved us," 1 John 4:19.

[38] Ex. 20:12–17. Though the division cannot be sharply made, the first four commandments might be said to represent the fundamental love-requirement, while the last six describe some of its detailed outworkings.

[39] Ex. 20:5f., 12. We have been tracing these covenant elements through the Decalogue, but we could have used many other parts of Scripture as well.

[40] This emphasis is not found in the Decalogue, but it is a major emphasis of Deut. (see 31:24–29) which Kline also identifies as a covenant document.

personal disclosure (stated in "I-thou" form) and objective declarations of facts, both a concept of history and a concept of inspired words. The covenant document contains authoritative *propositions* about history (the servant has no right to contradict the lord's account of the history of the covenant), authoritative *commands* to be obeyed, authoritative *questions* (demanding the vassal's pledge to covenant allegiance), authoritative *performatives* (God's self-commitment to bless and curse).[41] The propositions are infallible; but infallibility is only part of biblical authority. This authority also includes the authority of nonpropositional language as well.

We have seen that the idea of a "canon," an authoritative written word of God, goes back to the very beginning of Israel's history, back to its very creation as a nation. The Scripture is the constitution of Israel, the basis for its existence. The idea of a written word of God did *not* arise in twentieth-century fundamentalism, nor in seventeenth-century orthodoxy, nor in the post-apostolic church, nor in 2 Timothy, nor in postexilic Judaism. The idea of a written word of God is at the very foundation of biblical faith. Throughout the history of redemption, therefore, God continually calls his people back to the written word. Over and over again he calls them to keep "the commandments of the Lord your God, and his testimonies, and his statutes which he hath commanded thee."[42] These are the words of absolute demand and sure promise, the words of the Lord. These were the words that made the difference between life and death. These were the words which could not be questioned, which transcended all other demands, which governed all areas of life. When Israel sinned and returned to the Lord, she returned also to the law of God.[43]

From time to time there were new words of God. Joshua added to the words which Moses had placed in the ark.[44] How could a mere man add to

---

[41] Performatives ("I pronounce you man and wife," "You are under arrest," "Cursed be all who do not obey") do not merely state facts, but "perform" various sorts of actions. When spoken by one in authority, they "accomplish" what they set out to do. Performatives of the Lord in Scripture are uniquely authoritative, but their authority is not *adequately* characterized by the term "infallibility." "Infallibility" is important, but it is only *part* of the meaning of biblical authority. "Infallibility" is, not too strong, but too *weak* a term adequately to characterize authority.

[42] Deut. 6:17; cf. 4:1–8; 5:29–33; 6:24f.; 7:9–11; 8:11; 10:12f.; 11:1, 13, 18ff., 27f.; 12:1, 28; 13:4. In Deuteronomy, almost every page contains exhortations to obey God's commandments and statutes and ordinances! But not only in Deuteronomy! Cf. Josh. 1:8; 8:25–28; Ps. 1:1–3; 12:6f.; 19:7–11; 33:4, 11; 119:1–176; Isa. 8:16–20; Dan. 9:3ff.; 2 Kings 18:6. Read over these and the many similar passages and let the message sink into your heart! The conclusion concerning the authority of the written word is simply inescapable.

[43] 2 Kings 23:2f., 21, 25; Nehemiah 8. The whole Old Testament history is a history of obedience and disobedience: obedience and disobedience to what? To God's commands; and after Exodus 20, to God's written word! The self-witness of the Old Testament is therefore present on every page. "Pervasive," as we said.

[44] Josh. 24:26.

the words of God in view of the command of Deuteronomy 4:2? The only answer can be that Joshua's words were also recognized as God's words. The prophets also came speaking God's words,[45] and some of them were written down.[46]

Thus the "Old Testament" grew. By the time of Jesus there was a well-defined body of writings which was generally recognized as God's word, and which was quoted as supreme authority, as Holy Scripture. Jesus and the apostles did not challenge but rather accepted this view. Not only did they accept it, but they actively testified to it by word and deed. The role of Scripture in the life of Jesus is really remarkable: although Jesus was and is the Son of God, the second person of the Trinity, during his earthly ministry he subjected himself completely to the Old Testament Scripture. Over and over again, he performed various actions "so that the Scripture might be fulfilled."[47] The whole point of his life—his sacrificial death and resurrection was determined beforehand by Scripture.[48] Jesus' testimony to Scripture, then, is not occasional, but pervasive. His whole life was a witness to biblical authority! But listen particularly to what Christ and the apostles *say* concerning the Old Testament! Listen to the way in which they cite Scripture, even in the face of Satan, to "clinch" an argument, to silence objections.[49] Listen to the titles by which they describe the Old Testament: "Scripture," "holy Scripture," "law," "prophets," "royal law of liberty," "the oracles of God."[50] Listen to the formulae by which they cite Scripture: "It is written"; "it says"; "the Holy Spirit says"; "Scripture says." All of these phrases and titles denoted to the people of Jesus' day something far more than a mere human document. These terms denoted nothing less than inspired, authoritative words of God. As Warfield pointed out, "Scripture says" and "God says" are interchangeable![51]

And consider further the explicit *teaching* of Jesus and the apostles concerning biblical authority:

---

[45] Deut. 18:15–19; Isa. 59:21; Jer. 1:6–19; Ezek. 13:2f., 17. The mark of the prophet was the phrase "Thus saith the Lord," which is found over and over again in the prophetic literature. Many theologians hostile to the orthodox view of biblical authority recognize that the prophets *claimed* an identity between their words and God's. See, e.g., E. Brunner, *Dogmatics*, Vol. 1: *The Christian Doctrine of God*, trans. O. Wyon (Philadelphia: Westminster Press, 1950), 18, 27, 31f.

[46] Isa. 8:1; 30:3ff.; 34:16ff.; Jer. 25:13; 30:2; 36:1–31; 51:60ff.; Dan. 9:1f.

[47] Matt. 4:14; 5:17; 8:17; 12:17; 13:35; 21:4; 26:54–56; Luke 21:22; 24:44; John 19:28.

[48] Luke 24:26: "*Behooved* not . . ." Scripture imposes a *necessity* upon Christ!

[49] Matthew 4; 22:29–33; etc.

[50] See Warfield, *op. cit.* (in note 2 above), especially 229–41, 351–407.

[51] Ibid., 229–348.

> 1. Think not that I am come to destroy the law or the prophets: I came not to destroy, but to fulfill. For truly I say to you, Till heaven and earth pass away, one jot or one tittle shall in no wise pass away from the law; until all things are accomplished. Whosoever therefore shall break one of the least of these commandments, and shall teach men so, shall be called least in the kingdom of heaven: but whosoever shall do and teach them, he shall be called great in the kingdom of heaven.[52]

Jots and tittles were among the smallest marks used in the written Hebrew language. Jesus is saying that *everything* in the law and the prophets (equals the Old Testament) carries divine authority. And obedience to that law is the criterion of greatness in the kingdom of heaven.

> 2. Think not that I will accuse you to the Father: there is one that accuses you, even Moses, whom you trust. For if ye believed Moses, ye would believe me; for he wrote of me. But if ye believe not his writings, how shall ye believe my words?[53]

The Jews claimed to believe Moses' writings, but they rejected Christ. Jesus replies that they do not *really* believe Moses; and he urges them to a *greater* trust in the Old Testament. He urges them to believe *all* of the law, and thus come to accept his messiahship. We see here that Jesus did not merely quote Scripture because it was customary among the Jews. Rather, he *criticized* the prevailing custom because it was insufficiently loyal to Scripture. Jesus' view of Scripture was *stronger* than that of the Pharisees and scribes. Jesus sees Moses justly accusing the Jews because of their unbelief in Scripture. Believing Moses is the prerequisite to believing Christ.

> 3. The Jews answered him, For a good work we stone thee not, but for blasphemy; even because thou, being a man, makest thyself God. Jesus answered them, Is it not written in your law, I said, Ye are gods? If he called them gods unto whom the word of God came (and the Scripture cannot be broken), say ye of him whom the Father sanctified and sent into the world, Thou blasphemest; because I said, I am the Son of God?[54]

---

[52] Matt. 5:17–19. For detailed exegesis, see John Murray, *Principles of Conduct* (Grand Rapids, MI: Eerdmans, 1957), 149–57. Cf. also his essay, "The Attestation of Scripture," in *The Infallible Word* (*op. cit.* in note 2 above), 15–17, 20–24 (chapter 3 of present volume).
[53] John 5:45–47.
[54] John 10:33–36; cf. Warfield, *op. cit.*, 138–41.

A difficult passage, this; but note the parentheses. Concerning a fairly obscure psalm, Jesus says that "scripture cannot be broken." It cannot be wrong, it cannot fail, it cannot be rejected as we reject human words.

> 4. For whatsoever things were written aforetime were written for our learning, that through patience and through comfort of the scriptures we might have hope.[55]

Here, the apostle Paul tells us that the Old Testament is relevant, not only for the people of the Old Testament period, but for us as well. It teaches us, gives us patience, comfort, hope. And most remarkably, the *whole* Old Testament is relevant! None of it is dated, none of it is invalidated by more recent thought. Of what human documents may *that* be said?

> 5. And we have the word of prophecy made more sure; whereunto ye do well that ye take heed, as unto a lamp shining in a dark place, until the day dawn, and the day star arise in your hearts: knowing this first, that no prophecy of scripture is of private interpretation. For no prophecy ever came by the will of man: but men spake from God, being moved by the Holy Spirit.[56]

Note the context of this passage: Peter expects to die soon, and he wishes to assure his readers of the truth of the gospel.[57] He knows that false teachers will attack the church, deceiving the flock.[58] He insists that the gospel is not myth or legend, but the account of events which he himself had witnessed.[59] Yet even when the eyewitnesses have left the scene, the believers will still have a source of sure truth. They have the "word of prophecy"—the Old Testament Scriptures—a word which is "more sure."[60] They are to "take heed" to that word and forsake all conflicting teaching; for the word is light, and all the rest is darkness. Moreover, it did not originate through the human interpretative process; it is not a set of human opinions about God; nor did it originate in any human volition. Rather the Holy Spirit carried the biblical writers along, as they spoke for him! The Holy Spirit determined

---

[55] Rom. 15:4.

[56] 2 Pet. 1:19–21; cf. Warfield, *op. cit.*, 135–38.

[57] 2 Pet. 1:12–15.

[58] 2 Peter 2.

[59] 2 Pet. 1:16–18; in the current theological scene it is worth noting that Peter denies any mythological character to the message. It is not *mythos*.

[60] Is the word "more sure" in the sense of being confirmed by eyewitness testimony? Or is it, as Warfield suggests (above reference) "more sure" *than* eyewitness testimony? In either case, the passage places a strong emphasis upon the *certainty* of the word.

their course and their destination. The Bible consists of human writings, but its authority is no mere human authority!

> 6. All Scripture is God-breathed and profitable for doctrine, reproof, correction, instruction in righteousness: that the man of God may be complete, furnished completely unto every good work.[61]

Note again the context, for it is similar to that of the last passage. Paul in this chapter paints a gloomy picture of deceivers leading people astray. How shall we know the truth in all this confusion? Paul tells Timothy to hang on to the truth as he learned it from Paul,[62] but also to the "holy scriptures"[63] (which, we note, are available even to us who have not been taught personally by Paul). This Scripture is "inspired of God" as the KJV says, or more literally "God-breathed"—*breathed out by God.* In less picturesque language, we might say simply "spoken by God"; but the more picturesque language also suggests the activity of the Holy Spirit in the process, the words for "spirit" and "breath" being closely related in the original Greek. Scripture is *spoken* by God; it is *his Word*; and as such it is *all* profitable, and it is *all* that we need to be equipped for good works.

Both Old and New Testaments then pervasively claim authority for the Old Testament Scriptures. But what about the New Testament Scriptures? Can we say that they, also, are the word of God?

We have seen the importance of verbal revelation in both Old and New Testaments. Both Testaments insist over and over again that such words are a necessity of God's plan of salvation. As we have seen, the concepts of lordship and salvation presuppose the existence of revealed words. And in the New Testament, Jesus Christ is Lord and Savior. It would be surprising indeed if Jehovah, the Lord of the Old Testament people of God, gave a written record of his demand and promise, while Jesus, the Lord incarnate of whom the New Testament speaks, left no such record. Jesus told his disciples over and over again that obedience to *his words* was an absolute necessity for kingdom service and a criterion for true discipleship.[64] We *need* the words of Jesus! But where are they!? If there is no written record, no New Testament "covenant document," then has Jesus simply left us to grope in the dark?

---

[61] 2 Tim. 3:16f. For detailed exegesis, see Warfield, *op. cit.*, 133–35, and also 245–96 (a comprehensive treatment of the meaning of "God-breathed").

[62] 2 Tim. 3:14.

[63] 2 Tim. 3:15.

[64] Matt. 7:21ff., 24, 28f.; Mark 8:38; Luke 8:21; 9:26; John 8:47; 10:27; 12:47; 14:15, 21, 23f.; 15:7, 10, 14; 17:6, 8, 17; 18:37; cf. 1 John 2:3–5; 3:22; 5:2f.; 2 John 6; 1 Tim. 6:3; Rev. 12:17; 14:12. Again: look these up, and allow yourself to be impressed by the *pervasiveness* of this emphasis.

Praise God that he has not! Jesus promised to send the Holy Spirit to lead his disciples into all truth.[65] After the Holy Spirit was poured out on the day of Pentecost, the disciples began to preach with great power and conviction.[66] The pattern remains remarkably consistent throughout the book of Acts: the disciples are filled with the Spirit, and *then* they speak of Jesus.[67] They do not speak in their own strength. Further, they constantly insist that the source of their message is God, not man.[68] Their words have absolute, not merely relative, authority.[69] And this authority attaches not only to their spoken words but also to their written words.[70] Peter classes the letters of Paul together with the "other Scriptures"![71] Paul's letters are "Scripture"; and we recall that "Scripture" is "God-breathed"![72]

We conclude, then, that the witness of Scripture to its own authority is *pervasive*: (1) The whole biblical message of salvation presupposes and necessitates the existence of revealed words—words of absolute demand and sure promise; without such words, we have no Lord, no Savior, no hope. (2) Throughout the history of redemption, God directs his people to find these words in written form, in those books which we know as the Old and New Testaments.

Revealed Words and Modern Theologians

Our conclusion, however, raises a serious problem. If the witness of Scripture to its own authority is *pervasive*, then why have so many biblical scholars and theologians failed to see it?

We are not asking why it is that these theologians fail to *believe* the claim of Scripture. The unbelief of theologians is at bottom rather unin-

[65] John 16:13; cf. Acts 1:8.
[66] Acts 2.
[67] Acts 2:4; 4:8, 31; 6:10 (cf. 3 and 5); 7:55; 9:17–20; 13:9f.; 52ff.
[68] 2 Thess. 2:2; Gal. 1:1; 11f., 16; 2:2; 1 Cor. 2:10–13; 4:1; 7:40; 2 Cor. 4:1–6; 12:1, 7; Eph. 3:3; Rom. 16:25.
[69] Rom. 2:16; 1 Thess. 4:2; Jude 17f.; and cf. the passages listed in the preceding and following notes.
[70] Col. 4:16; 1 Thess. 5:27; 2 Thess. 3:14; 1 Cor. 14:37.
[71] 2 Pet. 3:16. Cf. 1 Tim. 5:18 which appears to couple a quotation from Luke with a quotation from the law of Moses under the heading "Scripture."
[72] The question of what books are to be regarded as New Testament Scripture is beyond the scope of this paper, since no actual list can be found as part of the New Testament's self-witness. We may certainly assume, however, on the basis of what has been said, that if revealed words are a *necessary* ingredient of biblical salvation, and if specifically the words of the incarnate Christ and his apostles have such necessity, our sovereign God will "somehow" find a way to enable us to find those words! And surely he has! Although there have been disputes among different churches concerning the *Old Testament* canon, there have never been any church-dividing disputes over the *New Testament* canon! Through history, of course, some New Testament books have been questioned. But once all the facts have gotten before the Christian public, it seems, the questions have always melted away. This is rather amazing, for the Christian church has always been, to its shame, a very contentious body! And yet no serious contentions have ever arisen over the matter of canonicity, a matter which many have found baffling! Try an experiment: read Paul's letter to the Corinthians (canonical), and then read Clement's (noncanonical). *Think* about it; *pray* about it. Is there not an *obvious* difference? Christ's sheep hear his voice!

teresting; it is not much different from the unbelief of anyone else. Yet it is surely possible to disbelieve Scripture's claim while at the same time admitting that Scripture makes such a claim. And some liberal theologians have indeed accepted this option: the Bible *claims* inspiration and authority, but modern men cannot accept such a claim.[73] But others have refused to admit even that Scripture makes that claim! Or more often: they have recognized this claim in some parts of Scripture, but they have judged this claim to be inconsistent with other, more important scriptural teachings, and thus have felt that Scripture "as a whole" opposes the notion of authoritative Scripture in our sense.

Putting the same question differently: Is it possible to construct a sound *biblical* argument for biblical *fallibility?* Some theologians, amazingly enough, have said "yes," despite the evidence to the contrary we and others have adduced. Is this simply a wresting of Scripture in the interest of a heresy? Is it at bottom simply another form of modern unbelief (and therefore as "uninteresting" as the unbelief alluded to earlier)? In the final analysis, I would say, the answer is yes. But some analysis, final or not, is called for. The argument must be scrutinized, lest we miss something important in the biblical self-witness.

We are not here going to argue specific points of exegesis. Some thinkers would question our interpretation of Matthew 5:17–19, arguing that in the Sermon on the Mount and elsewhere Jesus makes "critical distinctions" among the Old Testament precepts. Some, too, would question our reading of the phrase "inspired of God" or "God-breathed" in 2 Timothy 3:16. And indeed, some would argue from 2 Peter 1:21 (but in defiance of 2 Timothy 3:16!) that inspiration pertains only to the writers of Scripture and not to the books which they have written. For enlightenment on these controversies, see the references in the footnotes. In general, we may say that even if it is possible to question a few points of our exegesis, the evidence is so *massive* that the general conclusion is still difficult to avoid:

> The effort to explain away the Bible's witness to its plenary inspiration reminds one of a man standing safely in his laboratory and elaborately expounding—possibly by the aid of diagrams and mathematical formulae—how every stone in an avalanche has a defined pathway and may easily be dodged by one of some presence of mind. We may fancy such an elaborate trifler's triumph as he would analyze the avalanche

[73] Cf. Warfield, *op. cit.*, 115, 175ff, 423f. More recently, F. C. Grant admits that the New Testament writers assume Scripture to be "trustworthy, infallible, and inerrant": *Introduction to New Testament Thought* (Nashville: Abingdon Press, 1950), 75.

> into its constituent stones, and demonstrate of stone after stone that its pathway is definite, limited, and may easily be avoided. But avalanches, unfortunately, do not come upon us, stone by stone, one at a time, courteously leaving us opportunity to withdraw from the pathway of each in turn: but all at once, in a roaring mass of destruction. Just so we may explain away a text or two which teach plenary inspiration, to our own closet satisfaction, dealing with them each without reference to the others: but these texts of ours, again, unfortunately do not come upon us in this artificial isolation; neither are they few in number. There are scores, hundreds, of them: and they come bursting upon us in one solid mass. Explain them away? We should have to explain away the whole New Testament. What a pity it is that we cannot see and feel the avalanche of texts beneath which we may lie hopelessly buried, as clearly as we may see and feel an avalanche of stones![74]

Not even the cleverest exegete can "explain away" the biblical concepts of lordship and salvation and the necessary connection of these concepts with the revealed words of Scripture! No exegete can explain away *all* the verses which call God's people to obey "the commandments, statutes, testimonies, ordinances" of the Lord; *all* the "it is written" formulae; all of the commands delivered by apostles and prophets in authoritative tone.

Rather than such detailed questions, therefore, we shall confine our attention to broader considerations which have carried considerable weight in contemporary theological discussion. For just as we have argued that the biblical concepts of lordship and salvation *require* the existence of revealed words, so others have argued that certain basic biblical concepts *exclude the possibility of* such words!

The primary appeal of these theological views is to the divine transcendence, as the following quotes from Karl Barth and Emil Brunner respectively will indicate:

> Again it is quite impossible that there should be a direct identity between the human word of Holy Scripture and the Word of God, and therefore between the creaturely reality in itself and as such and the reality of God the creator.[75]

[74] Warfield, *op. cit.*, 119f.

[75] Karl Barth, *Church Dogmatics*, Vol. 1: *The Doctrine of the Word of God*, ed. G. W. Bromiley and T. F. Torrance; trans. G. T. Thompson and Harold Knight (New York: Scribner, 1956), pt. 2, 499.

> It is therefore impossible to equate any human words any "speech-about-Him" with the divine self-communication.[76]

Such statements have a kind of primitive religious appeal. God alone is God, and nothing else may be "equated with him." To "equate" or "directly identify" something else with God is idolatry. Now surely we must agree that Scripture endorses this sentiment, for Scripture clearly opposes idolatry and exalts God above all other things! And if this is the case, then it seems that Scripture requires us to distinguish sharply between God himself on the one hand, and language about him on the other; the transcendence of God is surely a central biblical concept! And if transcendence requires us to eliminate all thought of "revealed words," even though other biblical doctrines suggest otherwise, then perhaps we ought to give serious thought to this issue.

However, Barth's concept of "direct identity" is a difficult one, as is Brunner's reference to "equating." What does it mean to assert—or deny—a "direct identity" or "equation" between God and language? Clearly, no one wants to say that "God" and "language about God" are synonymous terms! Nor has anyone in recent memory suggested that we bow down before words and sentences. Even the most orthodox defenders of biblical infallibility maintain that there is *some* distinction to be made between God and language. Further: even the most orthodox agree that the words of Scripture are in some sense creaturely, and thus specifically because of their creatureliness to be distinguished from God. On the other hand, if such words are *God's* words, and not *merely* human, then they are closely related to him, at least as closely as my words are related to me. If God has spoken them, then their truth is his truth; their authority is his authority; their power is his power. Barth is willing to say that from time to time Scripture *becomes* the word of God; therefore he admits that *some* close relation between God and Scripture is essential. The question then becomes: In what way is God "distinct" from this language, and in what way is he "related" to it? A pious appeal to God's transcendence, eloquent though it may be, does not really answer this sort of question. Both the orthodox and the Barthian would like to avoid being charged with idolatry. But *what kind* of distinction between God and language is required by the divine transcendence?

Barth is most reluctant to give any positive description of this relationship. Commenting upon 2 Timothy 3:16, he says:

[76] Emil Brunner, *op. cit.*, 15.

> At the centre of the passage a statement is made about the relationship between God and Scripture, which can be understood only as a disposing act and decision of God Himself, which cannot therefore be expanded but to which only a—necessarily brief—reference can be made. At the decisive point all that we have to say about it can consist only in an underlining and delimiting of the inaccessible mystery of the free grace in which the Spirit of God is present and active before and above and in the Bible.[77]

Inspiration, says Barth, is a mystery, because it is an act of God's grace. We cannot define what it is; we can only assert the graciousness of the process. At another point, however, he does venture to describe inspiration, alluding to the term used in 2 Timothy 3:16:

> *Theopneustia* in the bounds of biblical thinking cannot mean anything but the special attitude of obedience in those [biblical writers] who are elected and called to this obviously special service. . . . But in nature and bearing their attitude of obedience was of itself—both outwardly and inwardly—that of true and upright men.[78]

Inspiration is an act of God to create in men a special attitude of human obedience. It does not give them more than ordinary human powers. Therefore,

> the Bible is not a book of oracles; it is not an instrument of direct impartation. It is genuine witness. And how can it be witness of divine revelation, if the actual purpose, act and decision of God in His only-begotten Son, as seen and heard by the prophets and apostles in that Son, is dissolved in the Bible into a sum total of truths abstracted from that decision—and those truths are then propounded to us as truths of faith, salvation and revelation? If it tries to be more than witness, to be direct impartation, will it not keep from us the best, the one real thing, which God intends to tell and give us and which we ourselves need?[79]

The question, of course, is rhetorical. Barth is appealing to something he thinks his reader will concede as obvious. And this much we will concede: that if the Bible tries to be more than it is, if it exceeds its rightful prerogatives and usurps those of God himself, then it will indeed hide from us the

---

[77] Barth, *op. cit.*, 504.

[78] Ibid., 505; in my view and Warfield's, Barth offers here a most inadequate exegesis of the "God-breathed" of 2 Tim. 3:16.

[79] Barth, *op. cit.*, 507.

real message of God's transcendence. But what *are* the "rightful prerogatives" of Scripture? That must be established before the rhetoric of divine transcendence can have force. The rhetoric of transcendence does not itself determine what those prerogatives are.

It is clear from the last quoted section at least that Barth denies to Scripture one particular prerogative—the prerogative of presenting "truths of revelation in abstraction from" God's saving act in Christ. But what does "in abstraction from" mean in this context? An abstraction is always some sort of distinction or separation, but what kind of distinction or separation? An orthodox theologian will insist that the biblical "truths of revelation" are *not* "in abstraction from" God's act in Christ. On the contrary, we learn about this act, we come to adore this act, because the Bible gives us a true account of it.

I think that in the back of Barth's mind—perhaps in the front of it!—is a concern of many academic people. When we teachers see students cramming for theological exams, stuffing truths into their heads, we sometimes wonder what all of this has to do with the kingdom of God! And the students wonder too! The whole business of "mastering truths" somehow seems "abstract." It almost trivializes the message. Often there is here no real sense of the presence of God, no real spirit of prayer and thankfulness; it seems as if we are taking God's word and making a *game* of it!

Well, theology examinations, theological study *can* be a spiritual trial! But surely if we lose touch with God in studying his truths, it is our fault, not his for providing the truths! And sometimes, at least, the study of truths can be downright inspiring; sometimes, even in the academy, the law of the Lord purifies the soul! The evil in Barth's mind (as I understand him) is not an evil that can be remedied by eliminating the concept of revealed truth. It would be nice if such personal sinfulness could be eliminated by such a conceptual shift! But the sin of trivializing God's word is one of which we are all guilty—Barthians as much as anyone! We cannot eliminate that in Barth's way, nor ought we to try to construct a doctrine of Scripture that will make such trivialization impossible. That is the wrong way to go about constructing doctrinal formulations. Doctrines must not be arbitrarily constructed to counteract current abuses; they must be constructed on the basis of God's revelation.

"Abstraction," then, can't be avoided by renouncing the idea of revealed truths or revealed words. Nor can it be avoided by renouncing biblical infallibility. And in the absence of any other clearly stated threat to God's transcendence in the doctrine we have advocated, we are compelled to stand our ground. The orthodox view does *not* "abstract revelation from God's act," and it does not compromise the greatness and majesty of God. On the contrary: the true greatness of God, his lordship and saviorhood as described in Scripture, *requires* the existence of revealed truths. Without such truths, we have no Lord, no Savior, no basis for piety. Without such truths, all that we say, think, and do will be hopelessly "abstracted" from the reality of God. Without such truths, we have no hope. A Barthian or liberal or "neoliberal" theology can provide no such words; it can locate no words of absolute demands and sure promise. Rather, such a theology retains the right to judge the truth or falsity of *all* words with no divinely authorized criterion. Such theologies must be decisively rejected by the church of Christ, if she is to have any power, any saving message for our time. When Scripture speaks for itself, it claims to be no less than God's own word, and the claim is pervasive and unavoidable. Insofar as we deny that claim, we deny the Lord.[80] Insofar as we honor that word, we honor Christ.[81]

[80] Mark 8:38.

[81] John 8:31, and those passages cited above in our note 64.

Part 3

Inspiration

6

"The Biblical Idea of Inspiration"[1]

BENJAMIN BRECKINRIDGE WARFIELD

The Inspiration and Authority of the Bible

Previously published as "The Biblical Idea of Inspiration," in *The Inspiration and Authority of the Bible*, ed. Samuel G. Craig (Philadelphia: Presbyterian & Reformed, 1948), 131–66.

The word "inspire" and its derivatives seem to have come into Middle English from the French, and have been employed from the first (early in the fourteenth century) in a considerable number of significations, physical and metaphorical, secular and religious. The derivatives have been multiplied and their applications extended during the procession of the years, until they have acquired a very wide and varied use. Underlying all their use, however, is the constant implication of an influence from without, producing in its object movements and effects beyond its native or at least its ordinary powers. The noun "inspiration," although already in use in the fourteenth century, seems not to occur in any but a theological sense until late in the sixteenth century. The specifically theological sense of all these terms is governed, of course, by their usage in Latin theology; and this rests ultimately on their employment in the Latin Bible. In the Vulgate Latin Bible the verb *inspiro* (Gen. 2:7; Wisd. 15:11; Ecclus. 4:12; 2 Tim. 3:16; 2 Pet. 1:21) and the noun *inspiratio* (2 Sam. 22:16; Job 32:8; Ps. 17:16; Acts 17:25) both occur four or five times in somewhat diverse applications. In the development of a theological nomenclature, however, they have acquired (along with other less frequent applications) a technical sense with reference to the biblical writers or the biblical books. The biblical books

[1] Article "Inspiration," from *The International Standard Bible Encyclopedia*, ed. James Orr (Chicago: Howard-Severance, 1915), 3:1473–483.

are called "inspired" as the divinely determined products of inspired men; the biblical writers are called "inspired" as breathed into by the Holy Spirit, so that the product of their activities transcends human powers and becomes divinely authoritative. Inspiration is, therefore, usually defined as a supernatural influence exerted on the sacred writers by the Spirit of God, by virtue of which their writings are given divine trustworthiness.

Meanwhile, for English-speaking men, these terms have virtually ceased to be biblical terms. They naturally passed from the Latin Vulgate into the English versions made from it (most fully into the Rheims-Douay: Job 32:8; Wisd. 15:11; Ecclus. 4:12; 2 Tim. 3:16; 2 Pet. 1:21). But in the development of the English Bible they have found ever-decreasing place. In the English versions of the Apocrypha (both Authorized Version and Revised Version) "inspired" is retained in Wisdom 15:11; but in the canonical books the nominal form alone occurs in the Authorized Version and that only twice: Job 32:8, "But there is a spirit in man: and the inspiration of the Almighty giveth them understanding"; and 2 Timothy 3:16, "All scripture is given by inspiration of God, and is profitable for doctrine, for reproof, for correction, for instruction in righteousness." The Revised Version removes the former of these instances, substituting "breath" for "inspiration"; and alters the latter so as to read: "Every scripture inspired of God is also profitable for teaching, for reproof, for correction, for instruction which is in righteousness," with a marginal alternative in the form of, "Every scripture is inspired of God and profitable," etc. The word "inspiration" thus disappears from the English Bible, and the word "inspired" is left in it only once, and then, let it be added, by a distinct and even misleading mistranslation.

For the Greek word in this passage—θεόπνευστος, *theópneustos*—very distinctly does not mean "inspired of God." This phrase is rather the rendering of the Latin, *divinitus inspirata*, restored from the Wyclif ("Al Scripture of God ynspyrid is . . .") and Rhemish ("All Scripture inspired of God is . . .") versions of the Vulgate. The Greek word does not even mean, as the Authorized Version translates it, "given by inspiration of God," although that rendering (inherited from Tindale: "All Scripture given by inspiration of God is . . ." and its successors; cf. Geneva: "The whole Scripture is given by inspiration of God and is . . .") has at least to say for itself that it is a somewhat clumsy, perhaps, but not misleading, paraphrase of the Greek term in the theological language of the day. The Greek term has, however, nothing to say of *in*spiring or of *in*spiration: it speaks only of a "spiring" or "spiration." What it says of Scripture is, not that it is "breathed into by

God" or is the product of the divine "inbreathing" into its human authors, but that it is breathed out by God, "God-breathed," the product of the creative breath of God. In a word, what is declared by this fundamental passage is simply that the Scriptures are a divine product, without any indication of how God has operated in producing them. No term could have been chosen, however, which would have more emphatically asserted the divine production of Scripture than that which is here employed. The "breath of God" is in Scripture just the symbol of his almighty power, the bearer of his creative word. "By the word of Jehovah," we read in the significant parallel of Psalm 33:6, "were the heavens made, and all the host of them by the breath of his mouth." And it is particularly where the operations of God are energetic that this term (whether רוּחַ, *rūaḥ*, or נְשָׁמָה, *nᵉshāmāh*) is employed to designate them—God's breath is the irresistible outflow of his power. When Paul declares, then, that "every scripture," or "all scripture" is the product of the divine breath, "is God-breathed," he asserts with as much energy as he could employ that Scripture is the product of a specifically divine operation.

1. *2 Timothy 3:16*. In the passage in which Paul makes this energetic assertion of the divine origin of Scripture, he is engaged in explaining the greatness of the advantages which Timothy had enjoyed for learning the saving truth of God. He had had good teachers; and from his very infancy he had been, by his knowledge of the Scriptures, made wise unto salvation through faith in Jesus Christ. The expression, "sacred writings," here employed (v. 15), is a technical one, not found elsewhere in the New Testament, it is true, but occurring currently in Philo and Josephus to designate that body of authoritative books which constituted the Jewish "Law." It appears here anarthrously because it is set in contrast with the oral teaching which Timothy had enjoyed, as something still better: he had not only had good instructors, but also always "an open Bible," as we should say, in his hand. To enhance yet further the great advantage of the possession of these sacred Scriptures the apostle adds now a sentence throwing their nature strongly up to view. They are of divine origin and therefore of the highest value for all holy purposes.

There is room for some difference of opinion as to the exact construction of this declaration. Shall we render "Every Scripture" or "All Scripture?" Shall we render "Every [or all] Scripture is God-breathed and [therefore] profitable," or "Every [or all] Scripture, being God-breathed, is as well profitable?" No doubt both questions are interesting, but for the main matter now engaging our attention they are both indifferent. Whether

Paul, looking back at the sacred Scriptures he had just mentioned, makes the assertion he is about to add, of them distributively, of all their parts, or collectively, of their entire mass, is of no moment: to say that every part of these sacred Scriptures is God-breathed and to say that the whole of these sacred Scriptures is God-breathed, is, for the main matter, all one. Nor is the difference great between saying that they are in all their parts, or in their whole extent, God-breathed and therefore profitable, and saying that they are in all their parts, or in their whole extent, because God-breathed as well as profitable. In both cases these sacred Scriptures are declared to owe their value to their divine origin; and in both cases this their divine origin is energetically asserted of their entire fabric. On the whole, the preferable construction would seem to be, "Every Scripture, seeing that it is God-breathed, is as well profitable." In that case, what the apostle asserts is that the sacred Scriptures, in their every several passage—for it is just "passage of Scripture" which "Scripture" in this distributive use of it signifies—is the product of the creative breath of God, and, because of this its divine origination, is of supreme value for all holy purposes.

It is to be observed that the apostle does not stop here to tell us either what particular books enter into the collection which he calls sacred Scriptures, or by what precise operations God has produced them. Neither of these subjects entered into the matter he had at the moment in hand. It was the value of the Scriptures, and the source of that value in their divine origin, which he required at the moment to assert; and these things he asserts, leaving to other occasions any further facts concerning them which it might be well to emphasize. It is also to be observed that the apostle does not tell us here everything for which the Scriptures are made valuable by their divine origination. He speaks simply to the point immediately in hand and reminds Timothy of the value which these Scriptures, by virtue of their divine origin, have for the "man of God." Their spiritual power, as God-breathed, is all that he had occasion here to advert to. Whatever other qualities may accrue to them from their divine origin, he leaves to other occasions to speak of.

2. *Peter 2:19–21.* What Paul tells here about the divine origin of the Scriptures is enforced and extended by a striking passage in 2 Peter (2:19–21). Peter is assuring his readers that what had been made known to them of "the power and coming of our Lord Jesus Christ" did not rest on "cunningly devised fables." He offers them the testimony of eyewitnesses of Christ's glory. And then he intimates that they have better testimony than even that of eyewitnesses. "We have," says he, "the prophetic word" (Eng-

lish versions, unhappily, "the word of prophecy"): and this, he says, is "more sure," and therefore should certainly be heeded. He refers, of course, to the Scriptures. Of what other "prophetic word" could he, over against the testimony of the eyewitnesses of Christ's "excellent glory" (Authorized Version) say that "we have" it, that is, it is in our hands? And he proceeds at once to speak of it plainly as "scriptural prophecy." You do well, he says, to pay heed to the prophetic word, because we know this first, that "every prophecy of scripture . . ." It admits of more question, however, whether by this phrase he means the whole of Scripture, designated according to its character, as prophetic that is, of divine origin; or only that portion of Scripture which we discriminate as particularly prophetic, the immediate revelations contained in Scripture. The former is the more likely view, inasmuch as the entirety of Scripture is elsewhere conceived and spoken of as prophetic. In that case, what Peter has to say of this "every prophecy of scripture"—the exact equivalent, it will be observed, in this case of Paul's "every scripture" (2 Tim. 3:16)—applies to the whole of Scripture in all its parts. What he says of it is that it does not come "of private interpretation"; that is, it is not the result of human investigation into the nature of things, the product of its writers' own thinking. This is as much as to say it is of divine gift. Accordingly, he proceeds at once to make this plain in a supporting clause which contains both the negative and the positive declaration: "For no prophecy ever came [margin "was brought"] by the will of man, but it was as borne by the Holy Spirit that men spoke from God." In this singularly precise and pregnant statement there are several things which require to be carefully observed. There is, first of all, the emphatic denial that prophecy—that is to say, on the hypothesis upon which we are working, Scripture—owes its origin to human initiative: "No prophecy ever was brought—'came' is the word used in the English version text, with 'was brought' in Revised Version margin—by the will of man." Then, there is the equally emphatic assertion that its source lies in God: it was spoken by men, indeed, but the men who spoke it "spake from God." And a remarkable clause is here inserted, and thrown forward in the sentence that stress may fall on it, which tells us how it could be that men, in speaking, should speak not from themselves, but from God: it was "as borne"—it is the same word which was rendered "was brought" above, and might possibly be rendered "brought" here—"by the Holy Spirit" that they spoke. Speaking thus under the determining influence of the Holy Spirit, the things they spoke were not from themselves, but from God.

Here is as direct an assertion of the divine origin of Scripture as that of

2 Timothy 3:16. But there is more here than a simple assertion of the divine origin of Scripture. We are advanced somewhat in our understanding of how God has produced the Scriptures. It was through the instrumentality of men who "spake from him." More specifically, it was through an operation of the Holy Ghost on these men which is described as "bearing " them. The term here used is a very specific one. It is not to be confounded with guiding, or directing, or controlling, or even leading in the full sense of that word. It goes beyond all such terms, in assigning the effect produced specifically to the active agent. What is "borne" is taken up by the "bearer," and conveyed by the "bearer's" power, not its own, to the "bearer's" goal, not its own. The men who spoke from God are here declared, therefore, to have been taken up by the Holy Spirit and brought by his power to the goal of his choosing. The things which they spoke under this operation of the Spirit were therefore his things, not theirs. And that is the reason which is assigned why "the prophetic word" is so sure. Though spoken through the instrumentality of men, it is, by virtue of the fact that these men spoke "as borne by the Holy Spirit," an immediately divine word. It will be observed that the proximate stress is laid here, not on the spiritual value of Scripture (though that, too, is seen in the background), but on the divine trustworthiness of Scripture. Because this is the way every prophecy of Scripture "has been brought," it affords a more sure basis of confidence than even the testimony of human eyewitnesses. Of course, if we do not understand by "the prophetic word" here the entirety of Scripture described, according to its character, as revelation, but only that element in Scripture which we call specifically prophecy, then it is directly only of that element in Scripture that these great declarations are made. In any event, however, they are made of the prophetic element in Scripture as written, which was the only form in which the readers of this epistle possessed it, and which is the thing specifically intimated in the phrase "every prophecy *of scripture*." These great declarations are made, therefore, at least of large tracts of Scripture; and if the entirety of Scripture is intended by the phrase "the prophetic word," they are made of the whole of Scripture.

3. *John 10:34f.* How far the supreme trustworthiness of Scripture, thus asserted, extends may be conveyed to us by a passage in one of our Lord's discourses recorded by John (John 10:34–35). The Jews, offended by Jesus' "making himself God," were in the act to stone him, when he defended himself thus: "Is it not written in your law, I said, Ye are gods? If he called them gods, unto whom the word of God came (and the scripture cannot be broken), say ye of him, whom the Father sanctified [margin "consecrated"]

and sent unto the world, Thou blasphemest; because I said, I am the Son of God?" It may be thought that this defence is inadequate. It certainly is incomplete: Jesus made himself God (John 10:33) in a far higher sense than that in which "Ye are gods" was said of those "unto whom the word of God came": he had just declared in unmistakable terms, "I and the Father are one." But it was quite sufficient for the immediate end in view—to repel the technical charge of blasphemy based on his making himself God: it is not blasphemy to call one God in any sense in which he may fitly receive that designation; and certainly if it is not blasphemy to call such men as those spoken of in the passage of Scripture adduced gods, because of their official functions, it cannot be blasphemy to call him God whom the Father consecrated and sent into the world. The point for us to note, however, is merely that Jesus' defence takes the form of an appeal to Scripture; and it is important to observe how he makes this appeal. In the first place, he adduces the Scriptures as law: "Is it not written in your law?" he demands. The passage of Scripture which he adduces is not written in that portion of Scripture which was more specifically called "the Law," that is to say, the Pentateuch, nor in any portion of Scripture of formally legal contents. It is written in the book of Psalms; and in a particular psalm which is as far as possible from presenting the external characteristics of legal enactment (Ps. 82:6). When Jesus adduces this passage, then, as written in the "law" of the Jews, he does it, not because it stands in this psalm, but because it is a part of Scripture at large. In other words, he here ascribes legal authority to the entirety of Scripture, in accordance with a conception common enough among the Jews (cf. John 12:34), and finding expression in the New Testament occasionally, both on the lips of Jesus himself, and in the writings of the apostles. Thus, on a later occasion (John 15:25), Jesus declares that it is written in the "law" of the Jews, "They hated me without a cause," a clause found in Psalm 35:19. And Paul assigns passages both from the Psalms and from Isaiah to "the Law" (1 Cor. 14:21; Rom. 3:19), and can write such a sentence as this (Gal. 4:21f.): "Tell me, ye that desire to be under the law, do ye not hear the law? For it is written . . ." quoting from the narrative of Genesis. We have seen that the entirety of Scripture was conceived as "prophecy"; we now see that the entirety of Scripture was also conceived as "law": these three terms, the law, prophecy, Scripture, were indeed, materially, strict synonyms, as our present passage itself advises us, by varying the formula of adduction in contiguous verses from "law" to "scripture." And what is thus implied in the manner in which Scripture is adduced, is immediately afterward spoken out in the most explicit language, because it forms an essential element in our Lord's defence. It might have been enough to say simply, "Is it not written in your law?" But our Lord, determined to drive his appeal to Scripture home, sharpens the point to the utmost by adding with the highest emphasis: "and the scripture cannot be broken." This is the reason why it is worthwhile to appeal to what is "written in the law," because "the scripture cannot be broken." The word "broken" here is the common one for breaking the law, or the Sabbath, or the like (John 5:18; 7:23; Matt. 5:19), and the meaning of the declaration is that it is impossible for the Scripture to be annulled, its authority to be withstood or denied. The movement of thought is to the effect that, because it is impossible for the Scripture—the term is perfectly general and witnesses to the unitary character of Scripture (it is all, for the purpose in hand, of a piece)—to be withstood, therefore this particular Scripture which is cited must be taken as of irrefragable authority. What we have here is, therefore, the strongest possible assertion of the indefectible authority of Scripture; precisely what is true of Scripture is that it "cannot be broken." Now, what is the particular thing in Scripture, for the confirmation of which the indefectible authority of Scripture is thus invoked? It is one of its most casual clauses—more than that, the very form of its expression in one of its most casual clauses. This means, of course, that in the Saviour's view the indefectible authority of Scripture attaches to the very form of expression of its most casual clauses. It belongs to Scripture through and through, down to its most minute particulars, that it is of indefectible authority.

It is sometimes suggested, it is true, that our Lord's argument here is an *argumentum ad hominem*, and that his words, therefore, express not his own view of the authority of Scripture, but that of his Jewish opponents. It will scarcely be denied that there is a vein of satire running through our Lord's defence: that the Jews so readily allowed that corrupt judges might properly be called "gods," but could not endure that he whom the Father had consecrated and sent into the world should call himself "Son of God," was a somewhat pungent fact to throw up into such a high light. But the argument from Scripture is not ad hominem but *e concessu*; Scripture was common ground with Jesus and his opponents. If proof were needed for so obvious a fact, it would be supplied by the circumstance that this is not an isolated but a representative passage. The conception of Scripture thrown up into such clear view here supplies the ground of all Jesus' appeals to Scripture, and of all the appeals of the New Testament writers as well. Everywhere, to him and to them alike, an appeal to Scripture is an appeal to an indefectible authority whose determination is final; both he and they make their appeal indifferently to every part of Scripture, to every element in Scripture, to its most incidental clauses as well as to its most fundamental principles, and to the very form of its expression. This attitude toward Scripture as an authoritative document is, indeed, already intimated by their constant designation of it by the name of Scripture, the Scriptures, that is "the Document," by way of eminence, and by their customary citation of it with the simple formula, "It is written." What is written in this document admits so little of questioning that its authoritativeness required no asserting but might safely be taken for granted. Both modes of expression belong to the constantly illustrated habitudes of our Lord's speech. The first words he is recorded as uttering after his manifestation to Israel were an appeal to the unquestionable authority of Scripture; to Satan's temptations he opposed no other weapon than the final "It is written!" (Matt. 4:4, 7, 10; Luke 4:4, 8). And among the last words which he spoke to his disciples before he was received up was a rebuke to them for not understanding that all things "which are written in the law of Moses, and the prophets, and psalms" concerning him—that is (v. 45) in the entire "Scriptures"—"must needs be" (very emphatic) "fulfilled" (Luke 24:44). "Thus it is written," says he (v. 46), as rendering all doubt absurd. For, as he had explained earlier upon the same day (Luke 24:25ff.), it argues only that one is "foolish and slow at heart" if he does not "believe in" (if his faith does not rest securely on, as on a firm foundation) "all" (without limit of subject matter here) "that the prophets" (explained in v. 27 as equivalent to "all the scriptures") "have spoken."

The necessity of the fulfilment of all that is written in Scripture, which is so strongly asserted in these last instructions to his disciples, is frequently adverted to by our Lord. He repeatedly explains of occurrences occasionally happening that they have come to pass "that the scripture might be fulfilled" (Mark 14:49; John 13:18; 17:12; cf. 12:14; Mark 9:12–13). On the basis of scriptural declarations, therefore, he announces with confidence that given events will certainly occur: "All ye shall be offended [literally "scandalized"] in me this night: *for* it is written . . ." (Matt. 26:31; Mark 14:27; cf. Luke 20:17). Although holding at his command ample means of escape, he bows before oncoming calamities, for, he asks, how otherwise "should the scriptures be fulfilled, that thus it must be?" (Matt. 26:54). It is not merely the two disciples with whom he talked on the way to Emmaus (Luke 24:25) whom he rebukes for not trusting themselves more perfectly to the teaching of Scripture. "Ye search the scriptures," he says to the Jews, in the classical passage (John 5:39), "because ye think that in them ye have eternal life; and these are they which bear witness of me; and ye will not come to me, that ye may have life!" These words surely were spoken more in sorrow than in scorn: there is no blame implied either for searching the Scriptures or for thinking that eternal life is to be found in Scripture; approval rather. What the Jews are blamed for is that they read with a veil lying upon their hearts which he would fain take away (2 Cor. 3:15f.). "Ye search the scriptures"—that is right: and "even you" (emphatic) "think to have eternal life in them"—that is right, too. But "it is these very Scriptures" (very emphatic) "which are bearing witness" (continuous process) "of me; and" (here is the marvel!) "ye will not come to me and have life!"—that you may, that is, reach the very end you have so properly in view in searching the Scriptures. Their failure is due, not to the Scriptures but to themselves, who read the Scriptures to such little purpose.

Quite similarly our Lord often finds occasion to express wonder at the little effect to which Scripture had been read, not because it had been looked into too curiously, but because it had not been looked into earnestly enough, with sufficiently simple and robust trust in its every declaration. "Have ye not read even this scripture?" he demands, as he adduces Psalm 118 to show that the rejection of the Messiah was already intimated in Scripture (Mark 12:10; Matt. 21:42 varies the expression to the equivalent: "Did ye never read in the scriptures?"). And when the indignant Jews came to him complaining of the Hosannas with which the children in the temple were acclaiming him, and demanding, "Hearest thou what these are saying?" he met them (Matt. 21:16) merely with, "Yea: did ye never read, Out of the mouths of babes and sucklings thou hast perfected praise?" The underlying thought of these passages is spoken out when he intimates that the source of all error in divine things is just ignorance of the Scriptures: "Ye do err," he declares to his questioners, on an important occasion, "not knowing the scriptures" (Matt. 22:29); or, as it is put, perhaps more forcibly, in interrogative form, in its parallel in another Gospel: "Is it not for this cause that ye err, that ye know not the scriptures?" (Mark 12:24). Clearly, he who rightly knows the Scriptures does not err. The confidence with which Jesus rested on Scripture, in its every declaration, is further illustrated in a passage like Matthew 19:4. Certain Pharisees had come to him with a question on divorce, and he met them thus: "Have ye not read, that he who made them from the beginning made them male and female, and said, For this cause shall a man leave his father and mother, and shall cleave to his wife; and the two shall become one flesh? . . . What therefore

God hath joined together, let not man put asunder." The point to be noted is the explicit reference of Genesis 2:24 to God as its author: "*He who made them* . . . said"; "what therefore *God* hath joined together." Yet this passage does not give us a saying of God's recorded in Scripture, but just the word of Scripture itself, and can be treated as a declaration of God's only on the hypothesis that all Scripture is a declaration of God's. The parallel in Mark (10:5ff.) just as truly, though not as explicitly, assigns the passage to God as its author, citing it as authoritative law and speaking of its enactment as an act of God's. And it is interesting to observe in passing that Paul, having occasion to quote the same passage (1 Cor. 6:16), also explicitly quotes it as a divine word: "For, The twain, saith he, shall become one flesh"—the "he" here, in accordance with a usage to be noted later, meaning just "God."

Thus clear is it that Jesus' occasional adduction of Scripture as an authoritative document rests on an ascription of it to God as its author. His testimony is that whatever stands written in Scripture is a word of God. Nor can we evacuate this testimony of its force on the plea that it represents Jesus only in the days of his flesh, when he may be supposed to have reflected merely the opinions of his day and generation. The view of Scripture he announces was, no doubt, the view of his day and generation as well as his own view. But there is no reason to doubt that it was held by him, not because it was the current view, but because, in his divine-human knowledge, he knew it to be true; for, even in his humiliation, he is the faithful and true witness. And in any event we should bear in mind that this was the view of the resurrected as well as of the humiliated Christ. It was after he had suffered and had risen again in the power of his divine life that he pronounced those foolish and slow of heart who do not believe all that stands written in all the Scriptures (Luke 24:25); and that he laid down the simple "Thus it is written" as the sufficient ground of confident belief (Luke 24:46). Nor can we explain away Jesus' testimony to the divine trustworthiness of Scripture by interpreting it as not his own, but that of his followers, placed on his lips in their reports of his words. Not only is it too constant, minute, intimate, and in part incidental, and therefore, as it were, hidden, to admit of this interpretation; but it so pervades all our channels of information concerning Jesus' teaching as to make it certain that it comes actually from him. It belongs not only to the Jesus of our evangelical records but as well to the Jesus of the earlier sources which underlie our evangelical records, as anyone may assure himself by observing the instances in which Jesus adduces the Scriptures as divinely authoritative that are recorded in more than one of the Gospels (e.g., "It is written," Matt. 4:4, 7, 10 [Luke 4:4, 8, 10]; Matt. 11:10; [Luke 8:27]; Matt. 21:13 [Luke 19:46; Mark 11:17]; Matt. 26:31 [Mark 14:21]; "the scripture" or "the scriptures," Matt. 19:4 [Mark 10:9]; Matt. 21:42 [Mark 12:10; Luke 20:17]; Matt. 22:29 [Mark 22:24; Luke 20:37]; Matt. 22:56 [Mark 14:49; Luke 24:44]). These passages alone would suffice to make clear to us the testimony of Jesus to Scripture as in its parts and declarations divinely authoritative.

The attempt to attribute the testimony of Jesus to his followers has in its favor only the undeniable fact that the testimony of the writers of the New Testament is to precisely the same effect as his. They, too, cursorily speak of Scripture by that pregnant name and adduce it with the simple "It is written," with the implication that whatever stands written in it is divinely authoritative. As Jesus' official life begins with this "It is written" (Matt. 4:4), so the evangelical proclamation begins with an "Even as it is written" (Mark 1:2); and as Jesus sought the justification of his work in a solemn "Thus it is written, that the Christ should suffer, and rise again from the dead the third day" (Luke 24:46ff.), so the apostles solemnly justified the gospel which they preached, detail after detail, by appeal to the Scriptures, "That Christ died for our sins according to the scriptures" and "That he hath been raised on the third day according to the scriptures" (1 Cor. 15:3, 4; cf. Acts 8:35; 17:3; 26:22, and also Rom. 1:17; 3:4, 10; 4:17; 11:26; 14:11; 1 Cor. 1:19; 2:9; 3:19; 15:45; Gal. 3:10, 13; 4:22, 27). Wherever they carried the gospel it was as a gospel resting on Scripture that they proclaimed it (Acts 17:2; 18:24, 28); and they encouraged themselves to test its truth by the Scriptures (Acts 17:11). The holiness of life they inculcated, they based on scriptural requirement (1 Pet. 1:16), and they commended the royal law of love which they taught by scriptural sanction (James 2:8). Every detail of duty was supported by them by an appeal to Scripture (Acts 23:5; Rom. 12:19). The circumstances of their lives and the events occasionally occurring about them are referred to Scripture for their significance (Rom. 2:26; 8:36; 9:33; 11:8; 15:9, 21; 2 Cor. 4:13). As our Lord declared that whatever was written in Scripture must needs be fulfilled (Matt. 26:54; Luke 22:37; 24:44), so his followers explained one of the most startling facts which had occurred in their experience by pointing out that "it was needful that the scripture should be fulfilled, which the Holy Spirit spake before by the mouth of David" (Acts 1:16). Here the ground of this constant appeal to Scripture, so that it is enough that a thing "is contained in scripture" (1 Pet. 2:6) for it to be of indefectible authority, is plainly enough declared: Scripture must needs be fulfilled, for what is contained in it is the declaration of the Holy Ghost through the human author. What Scripture says, God says; and accordingly we read such remarkable declarations as these: "For the scripture saith unto Pharaoh, For this very purpose did I raise thee up" (Rom. 9:17); "And the scripture, foreseeing that God would justify the Gentiles by faith, preached the gospel beforehand unto Abraham. . . . In thee shall all the nations be blessed" (Gal. 3:8). These are not instances of simple personification of Scripture, which is itself a sufficiently remarkable usage (Mark 15:28; John 7:38, 42; 19:37; Rom. 4:3; 10:11; 11:2; Gal. 4:30; 1 Tim. 5:18; James 2:23; 4:5f.), vocal with the conviction expressed by James (4:5) that Scripture cannot speak in vain. They indicate a certain confusion in current speech between "Scripture" and "God," the outgrowth of a deep-seated conviction that the word of Scripture is the word of God. It was not "Scripture" that spoke to Pharaoh, or gave his great promise to Abraham, but God. But "Scripture" and "God" lay so close together in the minds of the writers of the New Testament that they could naturally speak of "Scripture" doing what Scripture records God as doing. It was, however, even more natural to them to speak casually of God saying what the Scriptures say; and accordingly we meet with forms of speech such as these: "Wherefore, even as the Holy Spirit saith, Today if ye shall hear His voice," etc. (Heb. 3:7, quoting Ps. 95:7); "Thou art God . . . who by the mouth of thy servant David hast said, Why did the heathen rage," etc. (Acts 4:25 Authorized Version, quoting Ps. 2:1); "He that raised him from the dead . . . hath spoken on this wise, I will give you . . . because he saith also in another [place] . . ." (Acts 13:34, quoting Isa. 55:3 and Ps. 16:10), and the like. The words put into God's mouth in each case are not words of God recorded in the Scriptures, but just Scripture words in themselves. When we take the two classes of passages together, in the one of which the Scriptures are spoken of as God, while in the other God is spoken of as if he were the Scriptures, we may perceive how close the identification of the two was in the minds of the writers of the New Testament.

This identification is strikingly observable in certain catenae of quotations, in which there are brought together a number of passages of Scripture closely connected with one another. The first chapter of the epistle to the Hebrews supplies an example. We may begin with verse 5: "For unto which of the angels said he"—the subject being necessarily "God"—"at any time, Thou art my Son, this day have I begotten thee?"—the citation being from Psalm 2:7 and very appropriate in the mouth of God—"and again, I will be to him a Father, and he shall be to me a Son?"—from 2 Samuel 7:14, again a declaration of God's own—"And when he again bringeth in the firstborn into the world he saith, And let all the angels of God worship him"—from Deuteronomy 32:43, Septuagint, or Psalm 97:7, in neither of which is God the speaker—"And of the angels he saith, Who maketh his angels winds, and his ministers a flame of fire"—from Psalm 104:4, where again God is not the speaker but is spoken of in the third person—"but of the Son he saith, Thy throne, O God," etc.—from Psalm 45:6–7 where again God is not the speaker, but is addressed—"And, Thou, Lord, in the beginning," etc.—from Psalm 102:25–27, where again God is not the speaker but is addressed—"But of which of the angels hath he said at any time, Sit thou on my right hand?" etc.—from Psalm 110:1, in which God is the speaker. Here we have passages in which God is the speaker and passages in which God is not the speaker, but is addressed or spoken of, indiscriminately assigned to God, because they all have it in common that they are words of Scripture, and as words of Scripture are words of God. Similarly in Romans 15:9ff. we have a series of citations the first of which is introduced by "as it is written," and the next two by "again he saith," and "again," and the last by "and again, Isaiah saith," the first being from Psalm 18:49; the second from Deuteronomy 32:43; the third from Psalm 117:1; and the last from Isaiah 11:10. Only the last (the only one here assigned to the human author) is a word of God in the text of the Old Testament.

This view of the Scriptures as a compact mass of words of God occasioned the formation of a designation for them by which this their character was explicitly expressed. This designation is "the sacred oracles," "the oracles of God." It occurs with extraordinary frequency in Philo, who very commonly refers to Scripture as "the sacred oracles" and cites its several passages as each an "oracle." Sharing, as they do, Philo's conception of the Scriptures as, in all their parts, a word of God, the New Testament writers naturally also speak of them under this designation. The classical passage is Romans 3:2 (cf. Heb. 5:12; Acts 7:38). Here Paul begins an enumeration of the advantages which belonged to the chosen people above other nations; and, after declaring these advantages to have been great and numerous, he places first among them all their possession of the Scriptures: "What advantage then hath the Jew? or what is the profit of circumcision? Much every way: first of all, that they were intrusted with the oracles of God." That by "the oracles of God" here are meant just the Holy Scriptures in their entirety, conceived as a direct divine revelation, and not any portions of them, or elements in them more especially thought of as revelatory, is perfectly clear from the wide contemporary use of this designation in this sense by Philo, and is put beyond question by the presence in the New Testament of habitudes of speech which rest on and grow out of the conception of Scripture embodied in this term. From the point of view of this designation, Scripture is thought of as the living voice of God speaking in all its parts directly to the reader; and, accordingly, it is cited by some such formula as "it is said," and this mode of citing Scripture duly occurs as an alternative to "it is written" (Luke 4:12, replacing "it is written" in Matthew; Heb. 3:15; cf. Rom. 4:18). It is due also to this point of view that Scripture is cited, not as what God or the Holy Spirit "said," but what he "says," the present tense emphasizing the living voice of God speaking in Scriptures to the individual soul (Heb. 3:7; Acts 13:35; Heb. 1:7, 8, 10; Rom. 15:10). And especially there is due to it the peculiar usage by which Scripture is cited by the simple "saith," without expressed subject, the subject being too well understood, when Scripture is adduced, to require stating; for who could be the speaker of the words of Scripture but God only (Rom. 15:10; 1 Cor. 6:16; 2 Cor. 6:2; Gal. 3:16; Eph. 4:8; 5:14)? The analogies of this pregnant subjectless "saith" are very widespread. It was with it that the ancient Pythagoreans and Platonists and the mediaeval Aristotelians adduced each their master's teaching; it was with it that, in certain circles, the judgments of Hadrian's great jurist Salvius Julianus were cited; African stylists were even accustomed to refer by it to Sallust, their great model. There is a tendency, cropping out occasionally, in the Old Testament, to omit the name of God as superfluous, when he, as the great logical subject always in mind, would be easily understood (cf. Job 20:23; 21:17; Ps. 114:2; Lam. 4:22). So, too, when the New Testament writers quoted Scripture there was no need to say whose word it was: that lay beyond question in every mind. This usage, accordingly, is a specially striking intimation of the vivid sense which the New Testament writers had of the divine origin of the Scriptures, and means that in citing them they were acutely conscious that they were citing immediate words of God. How completely the Scriptures were to them just the word of God may be illustrated by a passage like Galatians 3:16: "He saith not, And to seeds, as of many; but as of one, And to thy seed, which is Christ." We have seen our Lord hanging an argument on the very words of Scripture (John 10:34); elsewhere his reasoning depends on the particular tense (Matt. 22:32) or word (Matt. 22:43) used in Scripture. Here Paul's argument rests similarly on a grammatical form. No doubt it is the grammatical form of the word which God is recorded as having spoken to Abraham that is in question. But Paul knows what grammatical form God employed in speaking to Abraham only as the Scriptures have transmitted it to him; and, as we have seen, in citing the words of God and the words of Scripture he was not accustomed to make any distinction between them. It is probably the scriptural word as a scriptural word, therefore, which he has here in mind: though, of course, it is possible that what he here witnesses to is rather the detailed trustworthiness of the scriptural record than its direct divinity—if we can separate two things which apparently were not separated in Paul's mind. This much we can at least say without straining, that the designation of Scripture as "scripture" and its citation by the formula, "It is written," attest primarily its indefectible authority; the designation of it as "oracles" and the adduction of it by the formula, "It says," attest primarily its immediate divinity. Its authority rests on its divinity, and its divinity expresses itself in its trustworthiness; and the New Testament writers in all their use of it treat it as what they declare it to be—a God-breathed document, which, because God-breathed, as through and through trustworthy in all its assertions, authoritative in all its declarations, and down to its last particular, the very word of God, his "oracles."

That the Scriptures are throughout a divine book, created by the divine energy and speaking in their every part with divine authority directly to the heart of the readers, is the fundamental fact concerning them which is witnessed by Christ and the sacred writers to whom we owe the New Testament. But the strength and constancy with which they bear witness to this primary fact do not prevent their recognizing by the side of it that the Scriptures have come into being by the agency of men. It would be inexact to say that they recognize a human element in Scripture: they do not parcel Scripture out, assigning portions of it, or elements in it, respectively to God and man. In their view the whole of Scripture in all its parts and in all its elements, down to the least minutiae, in form of expression as well as in substance of teaching, is from God; but the whole of it has been given by God through the instrumentality of men. There is, therefore, in their view, not, indeed, a human element or ingredient in Scripture, and much less human divisions or sections of Scripture, but a human side or aspect to Scripture; and they do not fail to give full recognition to this human side or aspect. In one of the primary passages which has already been before us, their conception is given, if somewhat broad and very succinct, yet clear expression. No "prophecy," Peter tells us (2 Pet. 1:21), "ever came by the will of man; *but as borne by the Holy Ghost*, men spake from God." Here the whole initiative is assigned to God, and such complete control of the human agents that the product is truly God's work. The men who speak in this "prophecy of scripture" speak not of themselves or out of themselves but from "God": they speak only as they are "borne by the Holy Ghost." But it is they, after all, who speak. Scripture is the product of man, but only of man speaking from God and under such a control of the Holy Spirit as that in their speaking they are "borne" by him. The conception obviously is that the Scriptures have been given by the instrumentality of men; and this conception finds repeated incidental expression throughout the New Testament.

It is this conception, for example, which is expressed when our Lord, quoting Psalm 110, declares of its words that "David himself said in the Holy Spirit" (Mark 12:36). There is a certain emphasis here on the words being David's own words, which is due to the requirements of the argument our Lord was conducting, but which nonetheless sincerely represents our Lord's conception of their origin. They are David's own words which we find in Psalm 110, therefore; but they are David's own words, spoken not of his own motion merely, but "in the Holy Spirit," that is to say—we could not better paraphrase it—"as borne by the Holy Spirit." In other words, they are "God-breathed" words and therefore authoritative in a sense above what any words of David, not spoken in the Holy Spirit, could possibly be. Generalizing the matter, we may say that the words of Scripture are conceived by our Lord and the New Testament writers as the words of their human authors when speaking "in the Holy Spirit," that is to say, by his initiative and under his controlling direction. The conception finds even more precise expression, perhaps, in such a statement as we find—it is Peter who is speaking, and it is again a psalm which is cited—in Acts 1:16, "The Holy Spirit spake by the mouth of David." Here the Holy Spirit is adduced, of course, as the real author of what is said (and hence Peter's certainty that what is said will be fulfilled); but David's mouth is expressly designated as the instrument (it is the instrumental preposition that is used) by means of which the Holy Spirit speaks the Scripture in question. He does not speak save through David's mouth. Accordingly, in Acts 4:25, "the Lord that made the heaven and earth," acting by His Holy Spirit, is declared to have spoken another psalm "through the mouth of . . . David," His "servant"; and in Matthew 13:35 still another psalm is adduced as "spoken through the prophet" (cf. Matt. 2:5). In the very act of energetically asserting the divine origin of Scripture, the human instrumentality through which it is given is constantly recognized. The

New Testament writers have, therefore, no difficulty in assigning Scripture to its human authors, or in discovering in Scripture traits due to its human authorship. They freely quote it by such simple formulae as these: "Moses saith" (Rom. 10:19); "Moses said" (Matt. 22:24; Mark 7:10; Acts 3:22); "Moses writeth" (Rom. 10:5); "Moses wrote" (Mark 12:19; Luke 20:28); "Isaiah . . . saith" (Rom. 10:20); "Isaiah said" (John 12:39); "Isaiah crieth " (Rom. 9:27); "Isaiah hath said before" (Rom. 9:29); "said Isaiah the prophet" (John 1:3); "did Isaiah prophesy" (Mark 7:6; Matt. 15:7); "David saith" (Luke 20:42; Acts 2:25; Rom. 11:9); "David said" (Mark 12:36). It is to be noted that when thus Scripture is adduced by the names of its human authors, it is a matter of complete indifference whether the words adduced are comments of these authors or direct words of God recorded by them. As the plainest words of the human authors are assigned to God as their real author, so the most express words of God, repeated by the scriptural writers, are cited by the names of these human writers (Matt. 15:7; Mark 7:6; Rom. 10:5, 19, 20; cf. Mark 7:10 from the Decalogue). To say that "Moses" or "David says," is evidently thus only a way of saying that "Scripture says," which is the same as to say that "God says." Such modes of citing Scripture, accordingly, carry us little beyond merely connecting the name, or perhaps we may say the individuality, of the several writers with the portions of Scripture given through each. How it was given through them is left meanwhile, if not without suggestion, yet without specific explanation. We seem safe only in inferring this much: that the gift of Scripture through its human authors took place by a process much more intimate than can be expressed by the term "dictation," and that it took place in a process in which the control of the Holy Spirit was too complete and pervasive to permit the human qualities of the secondary authors in any way to condition the purity of the product as the word of God. The Scriptures, in other words, are conceived by the writers of the New Testament as through and through God's book, in every part expressive of his mind, given through men after a fashion which does no violence to their nature as men, and constitutes the book also men's book as well as God's, in every part expressive of the mind of its human authors.

If we attempt to get behind this broad statement and to obtain a more detailed conception of the activities by which God has given the Scriptures, we are thrown back upon somewhat general representations, supported by the analogy of the modes of God's working in other spheres of his operation. It is very desirable that we should free ourselves at the outset from influences arising from the current employment of the term "inspiration" to designate this process. This term is not a biblical term, and its etymological implications are not perfectly accordant with the biblical conception of the modes of the divine operation in giving the Scriptures. The biblical writers do not conceive of the Scriptures as a human product breathed into by the divine Spirit, and thus heightened in its qualities or endowed with new qualities; but as a divine product produced through the instrumentality of men. They do not conceive of these men, by whose instrumentality Scripture is produced, as working upon their own initiative, though energized by God to greater effort and higher achievement, but as moved by the divine initiative and borne by the irresistible power of the Spirit of God along ways of his choosing to ends of his appointment. The difference between the two conceptions may not appear great when the mind is fixed exclusively upon the nature of the resulting product. But they are differing conceptions and look at the production of Scripture from distinct points of view—the human and the divine; and the involved mental attitudes toward the origin of Scripture are very diverse. The term "inspiration" is too firmly fixed, in both theological and popular usage, as the technical designation of the action of God in giving the Scriptures, to be replaced; and we may be thankful that its native implications lie as close as they do to the biblical conceptions. Meanwhile, however, it may be justly insisted that it shall receive its definition from the representations of Scripture, and not be permitted to impose upon our thought ideas of the origin of Scripture derived from an analysis of its own implications, etymological or historical. The scriptural conception of the relation of the divine Spirit to the human authors in the production of Scripture is better expressed by the figure of "bearing" than by the figure of "inbreathing"; and when our biblical writers speak of the action of the Spirit of God in this relation as a breathing, they represent it as a "breathing out" of the Scriptures by the Spirit, and not a "breathing into" the Scriptures by him.

So soon, however, as we seriously endeavor to form for ourselves a clear conception of the precise nature of the divine action in this "breathing out" of the Scriptures—this "bearing" of the writers of the Scriptures to their appointed goal of the production of a book of divine trustworthiness and indefectible authority—we become acutely aware of a more deeply lying and much wider problem, apart from which this one of inspiration, technically so called, cannot be profitably considered. This is the general problem of the origin of the Scriptures and the part of God in all that complex of processes by the interaction of which these books, which we call the "sacred Scriptures," with all their peculiarities, and all their qualities of whatever sort, have been brought into being. For, of course, these books were not produced suddenly, by some miraculous act—handed down complete out of heaven, as the phrase goes; but, like all other products of time, are the ultimate effect of many processes cooperating through long periods. There is to be considered, for instance, the preparation of the material which forms the subject matter of these books: in a sacred history, say, for example, to be narrated; or in a religious experience which may serve as a norm for record; or in a logical elaboration of the contents of revelation which may be placed at the service of God's people; or in the progressive revelation of divine truth itself, supplying their culminating contents. And there is the preparation of the men to write these books to be considered, a preparation physical, intellectual, spiritual, which must have attended them throughout their whole lives, and, indeed, must have had its beginning in their remote ancestors, and the effect of which was to bring the right men to the right places at the right times, with the right endowments, impulses, acquirements, to write just the books which were designed for them. When "inspiration," technically so called, is superinduced on lines of preparation like these, it takes on quite a different aspect from that which it bears when it is thought of as an isolated action of the divine Spirit operating out of all relation to historical processes. Representations are sometimes made as if, when God wished to produce sacred books which would incorporate his will—a series of letters like those of Paul, for example—he was reduced to the necessity of going down to earth and painfully scrutinizing the men he found there, seeking anxiously for the one who, on the whole, promised best for his purpose; and then violently forcing the material he wished expressed through him, against his natural bent, and with as little loss from his recalcitrant characteristics as possible. Of course, nothing of the sort took place. If God wished to give his people a series of letters like Paul's, he prepared a Paul to write them, and the Paul he brought to the task was a Paul who spontaneously would write just such letters.

If we bear this in mind, we shall know what estimate to place upon the common representation to the effect that the human characteristics of the writers must, and in point of fact do, condition and qualify the writings produced by them, the implication being that, therefore, we cannot get from man a pure word of God. As light that passes through the colored glass of a cathedral window, we are told, is light from heaven, but is stained by the tints of the glass through which it passes; so any word of God which is passed through the mind and soul of a man must come out discolored by the personality through which it is given, and just to that degree ceases to be the pure word of God. But what if this personality has itself been formed by God into precisely the personality it is, for the express purpose of communicating to the word given through it just the coloring which it gives it? What if the colors of the stained-glass window have been designed by the architect for the express purpose of giving to the light that floods the cathedral precisely the tone and quality it receives from them? What if the word of God that comes to his people is framed by God into the word of God it is, precisely by means of the qualities of the men formed by him for the purpose, through which it is given? When we think of God the Lord giving by his Spirit a body of authoritative Scriptures to his people, we must remember that he is the God of providence and of grace as well as of revelation and inspiration, and that he holds all the lines of preparation as fully under his direction as he does the specific operation which we call technically, in the narrow sense, by the name of "inspiration." The production of the Scriptures is, in point of fact, a long process, in the course of which numerous and very varied divine activities are involved, providential, gracious, miraculous, all of which must be taken into account in any attempt to explain the relation of God to the production of Scripture. When they are all taken into account, we can no longer wonder that the resultant Scriptures are constantly spoken of as the pure word of God. We wonder, rather, that an additional operation of God—what we call specifically "inspiration," in its technical sense—was thought necessary. Consider, for example, how a piece of sacred history—say the book of Chronicles, or the great historical work, Gospel and Acts, of Luke—is brought to the writing. There is, first of all, the preparation of the history to be written: God the Lord leads the sequence of occurrences through the development he has designed for them that they may convey their lessons to his people: a "teleological" or "aetiological" character is inherent in the very course of events. Then he prepares a man, by birth, training, experience, gifts of grace, and, if need be, of revelation, capable of appreciating this historical development and eager to search it out, thrilling in all his being with its lessons and bent upon making them clear and effective to others. When, then, by his providence, God sets this man to work on the writing of this history, will there not be spontaneously written by him the history which it was divinely intended should be written? Or consider how a psalmist would be prepared to put into moving verse a piece of normative religious experience: how he would be born with just the right quality of religious sensibility, of parents through whom he should receive just the right hereditary bent, and from whom he should get precisely the right religious example and training, in circumstances of life in which his religious tendencies should be developed precisely on right lines; how he would be brought through just the right experiences to quicken in him the precise emotions he would be called upon to express, and finally would be placed in precisely the exigencies which would call out their expression. Or consider the providential preparation of a writer of a didactic epistle—by means of which he should be given the intellectual breadth and acuteness, and be trained in habitudes of reasoning, and placed in the situations which would call out precisely the argumentative presentation of Christian truth which was required of him. When we give due place in our thoughts to the universality of the providential government of God, to the minuteness and completeness of its sway, and to its invariable efficacy, we may be inclined to ask what is needed beyond this mere providential government to secure the production of sacred books which should be in every detail absolutely accordant with the divine will.

The answer is, nothing is needed beyond mere providence to secure such books—provided only that it does not lie in the divine purpose that these books should possess qualities which rise above the powers of men to produce, even under the most complete divine guidance. For providence is guidance; and guidance can bring one only so far as his own power can carry him. If heights are to be scaled above man's native power to achieve, then something more than guidance, however effective, is necessary. This is the reason for the superinduction, at the end of the long process of the production of Scripture, of the additional divine operation which we call technically "inspiration." By it, the Spirit of God, flowing confluently in with the providentially and graciously determined work of men, spontaneously producing under the divine directions the writings appointed to them, gives the product a divine quality unattainable by human powers alone. Thus these books become not merely the word of godly men but the immediate word of God himself, speaking directly as such to the minds and hearts of every reader. The value of "inspiration" emerges, thus, as twofold. It gives to the books written under its "bearing" a quality which is truly superhuman; a trustworthiness, an authority, a searchingness, a profundity, a profitableness which is altogether divine. And it speaks this divine word immediately to each reader's heart and conscience; so that he does not require to make his way to God, painfully, perhaps even uncertainly, through the words of his servants, the human instruments in writing the Scriptures, but can listen directly to the divine voice itself speaking immediately in the scriptural word to him.

That the writers of the New Testament themselves conceive the Scriptures to have been produced thus by divine operations extending through the increasing ages and involving a multitude of varied activities, can be made clear by simply attending to the occasional references they make to this or that step in the process. It lies, for example, on the face of their expositions, that they looked upon the biblical history as teleological. Not only do they tell us that "whatsoever things were written aforetime were written for our learning, that through patience and through comfort of the scriptures we might have hope" (Rom. 15:4; cf. Rom. 4:23–24); they speak also of the course of the historical events themselves as guided for our benefit: "Now these things happened unto them by way of example"—in a typical fashion, in such a way that, as they occurred, a typical character, or predictive reference impressed itself upon them; that is to say, briefly, the history occurred as it did in order to bear a message to us—"and they were written for our admonition, upon whom the ends of the ages are come" (1 Cor. 10:11; cf. v. 6). Accordingly, it has become a commonplace of biblical exposition that "the history of redemption itself is a typically progressive one" (Küper), and is "in a manner impregnated with the prophetic element," so as to form a "part of a great plan which stretches from the fall of man to the first consummation of all things in glory; and, in so far as it reveals the mind of God toward man, carries a respect to the future not less than to the present" (P. Fairbairn). It lies equally on the face of the New Testament allusions to the subject that its writers understood that the preparation of men to become vehicles of God's message to man was not of yesterday but had its beginnings in the very origin of their being. The call by which Paul, for example, was made an apostle of Jesus Christ was sudden and apparently without antecedents; but it is precisely this Paul who reckons this call as only one step in a long process, the beginnings of which antedated his own existence: "But when it was the good pleasure of God, who separated me, even from my mother's womb, and called me through his grace, to reveal his Son in me" (Gal. 1:15–16; cf. Jer. 1:5; Isa. 49:1, 5). The recognition by the writers of the New Testament of the experiences of God's grace, which had been vouchsafed to them as an integral element in their fitting to be the bearers of his gospel to others, finds such pervasive expression that the only difficulty is to select from the mass the most illustrative passages. Such a statement as Paul gives in the opening verses of 2 Corinthians is thoroughly typical. There he represents that he has been afflicted and comforted to the end that he might "be able to comfort them that are in any affliction, through the comfort wherewith" he had himself been "comforted of God." For, he explains, "Whether we are afflicted, it is for your comfort and salvation; or whether we are comforted, it is for your comfort, which worketh in the patient enduring of the same sufferings, which we also suffer" (2 Cor. 1:4–6). It is beyond question, therefore, that the New Testament writers, when they declare the Scriptures to be the product of the divine breath, and explain this as meaning that the writers of these Scriptures wrote them only as borne by the Holy Spirit in such a fashion that they spoke, not out of themselves, but "from God," are thinking of this operation of the Spirit only as the final act of God in the production of the Scriptures, superinduced upon a long series of processes, providential, gracious, miraculous, by which the matter of Scripture had been prepared for writing, and the men for writing it, and the writing of it had been actually brought to pass. It is this final act in the production of Scripture which is technically called "inspiration"; and inspiration is thus brought before us as, in the minds of the writers of the New Testament, that particular operation of God in the production of Scripture which takes effect at the very point of the writing of Scripture—understanding the term "writing" here as inclusive of all the processes of the actual composition of Scripture, the investigation of documents, the collection of facts, the excogitation of conclusions, the adaptation of exhortations as means to ends and the like—with the effect of giving to the resultant Scripture a specifically supernatural character, and constituting it a divine, as well as human, book. Obviously the mode of operation of this divine activity moving to this result is conceived, in full accord with the analogy of the divine operations in other spheres of its activity, in providence and in grace alike, as confluent with the human activities operative in the case; as, in a word, of the nature of what has come to be known as "immanent action."

It will not escape observation that thus "inspiration" is made a mode of "revelation." We are often exhorted, to be sure, to distinguish sharply between "inspiration" and "revelation"; and the exhortation is just when "revelation" is taken in one of its narrower senses, of, say, an external manifestation of God, or of an immediate communication from God in words. But "inspiration" does not differ from "revelation" in these narrowed senses as genus from genus, but as a species of one genus differs from another. That operation of God which we call "inspiration," that is to say, that operation of the Spirit of God by which he "bears" men in the process of composing Scripture, so that they write, not of themselves, but "from God," is one of the modes in which God makes known to men his being, his will, his operations, his purposes. It is as distinctly a mode of revelation as any mode of revelation can be, and therefore it performs the same office which all revelation performs, that is to say, in the express words of Paul, it makes men wise, and makes them wise unto salvation. All "special" or "supernatural" revelation (which is redemptive in its very idea, and occupies a place as a substantial element in God's redemptive processes) has precisely this for its end; and Scripture, as a mode of the redemptive revelation of God, finds its fundamental purpose just in this: if the "inspiration" by which Scripture is produced renders it trustworthy and authoritative, it renders it trustworthy and authoritative only that it may the better serve to make men wise unto salvation. Scripture is conceived, from the point of view of the writers of the New Testament, not merely as the record of revelations, but as itself a part of the redemptive revelation of God; not merely as the record of the redemptive acts by which God is saving the world, but as itself one of these redemptive acts, having its own part to play in the great work of establishing and building up the kingdom of God. What gives it a place among the redemptive acts of God is its divine origination, taken in its widest sense, as inclusive of all the divine operations, providential, gracious, and expressly supernatural, by which it has been made just what it is—a body of writings able to make wise unto salvation, and profitable for making the man of God perfect. What gives it its place among the modes of revelation is, however, specifically the culminating one of these divine operations, which we call "inspiration"; that is to say, the action of the Spirit of God in so "bearing" its human authors in their work of producing Scripture, as that in these Scriptures they speak, not out of themselves, but "from God." It is this act by virtue of which the Scriptures may properly be called "God-breathed."

It has been customary among a certain school of writers to speak of the Scriptures, because thus "inspired," as a divine-human book, and to appeal to the analogy of our Lord's divine-human personality to explain their peculiar qualities as such. The expression calls attention to an important fact, and the analogy holds good a certain distance. There are human and divine sides to Scripture, and, as we cursorily examine it, we may perceive in it, alternately, traits which suggest now the one, now the other factor in its origin. But the analogy with our Lord's divine-human personality may easily be pressed beyond reason. There is no hypostatic union between the divine and the human in Scripture; we cannot parallel the "inscripturation" of the Holy Spirit and the incarnation of the Son of God. The Scriptures are merely the product of divine and human forces working together to produce a product in the production of which the human forces work under the initiation and prevalent direction of the divine: the person of our Lord unites in itself divine and human natures, each of which retains its distinctness while operating only in relation to the other. Between such diverse things there can exist only a remote analogy; and, in point of fact, the analogy in the present instance amounts to no more than that in both cases divine and human factors are involved, though very differently. In the one they unite to constitute a divine-human person; in the other they coöperate to perform a divine-human work. Even so distant an analogy may enable us, however, to recognize that as, in the case of our Lord's person, the human nature remains truly human while yet it can never fall into sin or error because it can never act out of relation with the divine nature into conjunction with which it has been brought; so in the case of the production of Scripture by the conjoint action of human and divine factors, the human factors have acted as human factors, and have left their mark on the product as such, and yet cannot have fallen into that error which we say it is human to fall into, because they have not acted apart from the divine factors, by themselves, but only under their unerring guidance.

The New Testament testimony is to the divine origin and qualities of "Scripture"; and "Scripture" to the writers of the New Testament was fundamentally, of course, the Old Testament. In the primary passage, in which we are told that "every" or "all Scripture" is "God-breathed," the direct reference is to the "sacred writings" which Timothy had had in knowledge since his infancy, and these were, of course, just the sacred books of the Jews (2 Tim. 3:16). What is explicit here is implicit in all the allusions to inspired Scriptures in the New Testament. Accordingly, it is frequently said that our entire testimony to the inspiration of Scripture concerns the Old Testament alone. In many ways, however, this is overstated. Our present concern is not with the extent of "Scripture" but with the nature of "Scripture"; and we cannot present here the considerations which justify extending to the New Testament the inspiration which the New Testament writers attribute to the Old Testament. It will not be out of place, however, to point out simply that the New Testament writers obviously themselves made this extension. They do not for an instant imagine themselves, as ministers of a new covenant, less in possession of the Spirit of God than the ministers of the old covenant: they freely recognize, indeed, that they have no sufficiency of themselves, but they know that God has made them sufficient (2 Cor. 3:5–6). They prosecute their work of proclaiming the gospel, therefore, in full confidence that they speak "by the Holy Spirit" (1 Pet. 1:2), to whom they attribute both the matter and form of their teaching (1 Cor. 2:13). They, therefore, speak with the utmost assurance of their teaching (Gal. 1:7–8); and they issue commands with the completest authority (1 Thess. 4:2, 14; 2 Thess. 3:6, 12), making it, indeed, the test of whether one has the Spirit that he should recognize what they demand as commandments of God (1 Cor. 14:37). It would be strange, indeed, if these high claims were made for their oral teaching and commandments exclusively. In point of fact, they are made explicitly also for their written injunctions. It was "the things" which Paul was "writing," the recognition of which as commands of the Lord, he makes the Spirit-led man (1 Cor. 14:37). It is his "word by this epistle," obedience to which he makes the condition of Christian communion (2 Thess. 3:14). There seems involved in such an attitude toward their own teaching, oral and written, a claim on the part of the New Testament writers to something very much like the "inspiration" which they attribute to the writers of the Old Testament.

And all doubt is dispelled when we observe the New Testament writers placing the writings of one another in the same category of "Scripture" with the books of the Old Testament. The same Paul who, in 2 Timothy 3:16, declared that "every" or "all scripture is God-breathed" had already written in 1 Timothy 5:18: "For the scripture saith, Thou shall not muzzle the ox when He treadeth out the corn. And, The laborer is worthy of his hire." The first clause here is derived from Deuteronomy and the second from the Gospel of Luke, though both are cited as together constituting, or better, forming part of the "Scripture" where Paul adduces as so authoritative as by its mere citation to end all strife. Who shall say that, in the declaration of the later epistle that "all" or "every" Scripture is God-breathed, Paul did not have Luke, and, along with Luke, whatever other new books he classed with the old under the name of Scripture, in the back of his mind, along with those old books which Timothy had had in his hands from infancy? And the same Peter who declared that every "prophecy of scripture" was the product of men who spoke "from God," being 'borne' by the Holy Ghost (2 Pet. 1:21), in this same epistle (3:16), places Paul's epistles in the category of Scripture along with whatever other books deserve that name. For Paul, says he, wrote these epistles, not out of his own wisdom, but "according to the wisdom given to him," and though there are some things in them hard to be understood, yet it is only "the ignorant and unsteadfast" who wrest these difficult passages—as what else could be expected of men who wrest "also the other Scriptures" (obviously the Old Testament is meant)—"unto their own destruction"? Is it possible to say that Peter could not have had these epistles of Paul also lurking somewhere in the back of his mind, along with "the other scriptures," when he told his readers that every "prophecy of scripture" owes its origin to the prevailing operation of the Holy Ghost? What must be understood in estimating the testimony of the New Testament writers to the inspiration of Scripture is that "Scripture" stood in their minds as the title of a unitary body of books, throughout the gift of God through his Spirit to his people; but that this body of writings was at the same time understood to be a growing aggregate, so that what is said of it applies to the new books which were being added to it as the Spirit gave them, as fully as to the old books which had come down to them from their hoary past. It is a mere matter of detail to determine precisely what new books were thus included by them in the category "Scripture." They tell us some of them themselves. Those who received them from their hands tell us of others. And when we put the two bodies of testimony together, we find that they constitute just our New Testament. It is no pressure of the witness of the writers of the New Testament to the inspiration of the Scripture, therefore, to look upon it as covering the entire body of "Scriptures," the new books which they were themselves adding to this aggregate, as well as the old books which they had received as Scripture from the fathers. Whatever can lay claim by just right to the appellation of "Scripture," as employed in its eminent sense by those writers, can by the same just right lay claim to the "inspiration" which they ascribe to this "Scripture."

LITERATURE.—J. Gerhard, "Loci Theolog.," Locus I; F. Turretin "Instit. Theol.," Locus II; B. de Moor, "Comm. in J. Marckii Comp.," cap. ii; C. Hodge, "Syst. Theol.," New York, 1871, I, 151–86; Henry B. Smith, "The Inspiration of the Holy Scriptures," New York, 1855, new ed., Cincinnati, 1891; A. Kuyper, "Encyclopedie der heilige Godgeleerdheid," 1888–89, II, 347ff., ET; "Enc of Sacred Theol.," New York, 1898, 341–563; also "De Schrift het word Gods," Tiel, 1870; H. Bavinck, "Gereformeerde Dogmatiek," Kampen, 1906, I, 406–527; R. Haldane, "The Verbal Inspiration of the Scriptures Established," Edinburgh, 1830; J. T. Beck, "Einleitung in das System der christlichen Lehre," Stuttgart, 1838, 2nd ed., 1870; A. G. Rudelbach, "Die Lehre von der Inspiration der heil. Schrift," *Zeitschrijt für die gesammte Lutherische Theologie und Kirche*, 1840, 1, 1841, 1, 1842, 1; S. R. L. Gaussen, "Théopneustie ou inspiration plénière des saintes écritures," Paris, 1842, ET by E. N. Kirk, New York, 1842; also "Theopneustia; the Plenary Inspiration of the Holy Scriptures," David Scott's tr., reëdited and revised by B. W. Carr, with a preface by C. H. Spurgeon, London, 1888; William Lee, "The Inspiration of the Holy

Scriptures," Donellan Lecture, 1852, New York, 1857; James Bannerman, "Inspiration: the Infallible Truth and Divine Authority of the Holy Scriptures," Edinburgh, 1865; F. L. Patton, "The Inspiration of the Scriptures," Philadelphia, 1869 (reviewing Lee and Bannerman); Charles Elliott, "A Treatise on the Inspiration of the Holy Scriptures," Edinburgh, 1877; A. A. Hodge and B. B. Warfield, "Inspiration," *Presbyterian Review*, April, 1881, also tract, Philadelphia, 1881; R. Watts, "The Rule of Faith and the Doctrine of Inspiration," Edinburgh, 1885; A. Cave, "The Inspiration of the OT Inductively Considered," London, 1888; B. Manly, "The Bible Doctrine of Inspiration," New York, 1888; W. Rohnert, "Die Inspiration der heiligen Schrift und ihre Bestreiter," Leipzig, 1889; A. W. Dieckhoff, "Die Inspiration und Irrthumlosigkeit der heiligen Schrift," Leipzig, 1891; J. Wichelhaus, "Die Lehre der heiligen Schrift," Stuttgart, 1892; J. Macgregor, "The Revelation and the Record," Edinburgh, 1893; J. Urquhart, "The Inspiration and Accuracy of the Holy Scriptures," London, 1895; C. Pesch, "De Inspiratione Sacrae Scripturae," Freiburg, 1906; James Orr, "Revelation and Inspiration," London, 1910.

7

"Some Reflections upon Inspiration"

EDWARD J. YOUNG

Thy Word Is Truth

Previously published as "Some Reflections upon Inspiration," in *Thy Word Is Truth: Some Thoughts on the Biblical Doctrine of Inspiration* (Grand Rapids, MI: Eerdmans, 1957), 83–109. Reprinted by permission of the publisher.

> ". . . The Scriptures are perfect, inasmuch as they were uttered by the Word of God and His Spirit, though we want the knowledge of their mysteries."
>
> Irenaeus

> ". . . the words of the prophets are the words of God."
>
> Theophilus Of Antioch

> ". . . the records of the gospels are oracles of the Lord, pure oracles as silver purified seven times in the fire."
>
> Origen

In what has been written thus far, we have tried to set forth clearly and simply what the Bible itself has to say about its inspiration. There can be little serious disagreement over whether the Bible actually does teach verbal inspiration. The doctrine expounded in the preceding pages is nothing more than a digest of what Scripture itself teaches. Objection to the doctrine, therefore, is in reality objection to the Scriptures. This is not surprising, since men today do not wish to be guided by the Scriptures in their thinking. They may agree, and they probably will, that we have correctly expounded the scriptural doctrine, but they protest against that doctrine.

Many are the objections which they raise, and it becomes necessary at this point to face some of them. Such a procedure will by no means be without profit, for not only will it enable us to give an answer to many of the current criticisms of the scriptural doctrine of inspiration, but it will also enable us to understand that doctrine more clearly. To these objections, then, let us direct our thought.

One of the best ways to attack something is to demonstrate that it is unimportant, and that is precisely what some writers attempt to accomplish with respect to the biblical doctrine of verbal inspiration. The originals of Scripture are lost, so it is argued, and we cannot completely reconstruct them. Therefore, these originals must have been unimportant. Evidently God did not think that it was necessary for us to have them. If a man wishes to do scholarly work on the Bible, he must use the Greek and the Hebrew texts which are available to him. He cannot obtain the original and must be content with the texts at hand. More than that, the plain man who turns to the Bible for his devotional study must be content with a Bible in his own vernacular. He is removed from the original even a step further. Consequently, all this talk about an inspired and errorless original text is really beside the point. Furthermore, even if there were errors in the original, this would not hinder us from receiving a blessing from the Bible; and we would be foolish indeed if we were to maintain that, unless the original were free of error, we could receive no blessing from the Bible.

But is the doctrine of an errorless autographa of Scripture actually so unimportant after all? A little reflection, we think, will make it clear that such is not at all the case. Let us suppose that the Scriptures actually were given to us by a special revelation of God. In making this supposition we realize full well that we are going counter to the main stream of current thought. Grant, however that such is the case. If the Scriptures are indeed breathed forth from the mouth of God, does it matter whether they contain in them statements which are contrary to fact? To ask the question in this fashion is, of course, to answer it. It matters tremendously, for the veracity of God himself is at stake.

How disturbing is the annoyance of tiny inaccuracies! Upon receiving a letter filled with trifling errors and misspelled words, we are displeased and annoyed; the letter casts reflection upon its writer. In fact, to send such a letter is to do a most discourteous thing. In writing a letter we want to spell our words correctly; also, for the sake of our own reputation, if for nothing else, we want to get our facts straight. If a person does not even take the trouble to do this he may justly be considered a boor or an ignoramus. It is difficult to maintain a high respect for someone who, in writing letters to us, is consistently careless. We do, of course, receive letters from people who are poorly educated, and their errors, even though regrettable, we are willing to pardon. When, however, an educated person writes, and permits minor inaccuracies to characterize his writing, we are disappointed in him, and our respect for him is affected by it.

God has revealed to us his Word. What are we to think of him if this Word is glutted with little annoying inaccuracies? Why could not the omnipotent and omniscient God have taken the trouble to give us a Word that was free from error? Was it not a somewhat discourteous thing for him to have breathed forth from his mouth a message filled with mistakes? Of course, it was discourteous; it was downright rude and insulting. The present writer finds it difficult to have much respect for such a God. Does he expect us to worship him? What kind of a God is he if he has given such an untrustworthy Word to mankind? And this brings us to the heart of the matter. The Scriptures claim to be breathed forth from his mouth; if they partake of error, must not he himself also partake thereof?

He, of course, tells us that his Word is pure. If there are mistakes in that Word, however, we know better; it is not pure. He tells us that his judgments are righteous, but we know better; as a matter of fact, his judgments are mixed with error. He declares that his law is the truth. His law contains the truth, let us grant him that, but we know that it contains error. If the autographa of Scripture are marred by flecks of mistake, God simply has not told us the truth concerning his Word. To assume that he could breathe forth a Word that contained mistakes is to say, in effect, that God himself can make mistakes. We must maintain that the original of Scripture is infallible for the simple reason that it came to us directly from God himself.

It does not follow from this that only an errorless text can be of devotional benefit to Christians, nor do those who believe in the inerrancy of Scripture maintain such a position. Thousands have been brought to a knowledge of the truth and have come to know him whom to know aright is life eternal, and they have had no inerrant text. When one reads some of the arguments that have been raised in opposition to the doctrine of inspiration, one very often receives the impression that there is a good bit of tilting at windmills. Of course an inerrant text is not necessary for the devotional life. There are those who through the King James Version have come to know Christ and have grown in grace daily, yet the King James Version is not inerrant.

Be this as it may, however, the serious student of the Bible will desire to approximate the original insofar as that is possible. We may revert to the illustration of the teacher who had received a letter from the president. When the original was destroyed (shall we say that it is unimportant whether the president of the United States made minor mistakes in his letter?), the teacher had only the copies which the pupils had made. As a result of the ignorance of the children who did the copying, these became imperfect copies. The teacher might have remained satisfied with these imperfect copies. She, however, had great respect for her president. Consequently, she endeavored to the best of her ability to correct each copy so that the exact wording of the original might be restored.

It would be foolish to maintain that because they contained mistakes, the copies were therefore without any value. Anyone could read those copies and learn what the president had written. To obtain the president's message, all one had to do was to read a copy of his letter. So it is with the Bible. The copies of Scripture which are now extant are remarkably accurate, and hence, like the original, they are "profitable for doctrine, for reproof, for correction, for instruction in righteousness" (2 Tim. 3:16). Minor, indeed, are those errors which may be found in the copies of the Bible which we possess, and through careful, scholarly study they are being in remarkable measure removed. Very different, however, was the original. That was the actual God-breathed Word, true to fact in all its statements. Let no one say that it is a matter of indifference whether this original was inerrant; it is a matter of greatest importance, for the honor and veracity of God himself are at stake. If there are actual errors in the original copies of the Bible, the Word which has come forth from the mouth of God is not a perfect Word, and the God of truth is guilty of error. If God has spoken falsely in his Word, he is not the God of truth, and consequently, the Christian religion is a false religion. This conclusion cannot be evaded. It is for this reason that those who embrace the biblical doctrine are so zealous to maintain the absolute perfection of the divine revelation in its original manuscripts.

It should be made clear, however, that if there actually are errors in the original manuscripts, we have no means of knowing where those errors start and where they stop. If God has erred in his speech at one point, how do we know that he has not done so at others? If he has denied the truth once, he might have done it more than once. If in minor matters he has given us falsehood, how do we know that in weightier things—since he is the Author of his Word—he has not done the same thing? This conclusion cannot be avoided. Men may talk all they wish about the unimportance and irrelevance of minor errors in chronology and history; the real truth of the matter is that if God has blundered so badly on those matters in which we can check him, how do we know that he has not also blundered just as badly in speaking to us of himself? It is not an unimportant point. If the original manuscripts of Scripture contain mistakes of fact and statements which are contrary to the truth, then we cannot escape the conclusion that these original manuscripts, since they are inscribed with the outbreathed Word of God, are not trustworthy. If God has lied to us at one point, by what conceivable standard may we say that he has not lied to us at others? If the truth in what are sometimes called "minor matters" is of no importance to him, how do we know that he has any regard for the truth in so-called major concerns? In fact, if he has violated the truth even in these small things, how do we know that he has any concern for the truth at all? If he is the God of truth, he has certainly taken a strange way of showing it. The so-called errors of the extant copies of Scripture, therefore, matters of chronology and the like, must be attributed to those human beings who made copies of the Bible. They are not from the God of Truth himself.

Amazing indeed is the cavalier manner in which modern theologians relegate this doctrine of an inerrant original Scripture to the limbo of the unimportant. Discovering that it is possible for men to be blessed of God without an errorless text, men rush to the conclusion that therefore an infallible Bible is unnecessary and unimportant. So dogmatic are they in this procedure, so confident are their assertions that the doctrine of an inerrant Scripture is unimportant, that they seem not to realize what they are doing. It is obvious, we are sometimes told, that the great doctrines of the Christian faith can be formulated from the copies of the Bible which are now in our possession. The church never had an infallible copy of the Bible with which to work. Consequently, it is asked, why should we bother with such a doctrine? We do not have the original copies of Scripture. How can we know what they were like? We can say nothing about them. Hence, the modern theologian is very eager to maintain his silence concerning them or, if he does not maintain it, to declare that even in the original copies of Scripture there were errors. He seems to be sure that the originals of Scripture were not infallible.

There is, of course, one means that is very widely adopted in order to escape from the difficulty of maintaining an originally inerrant Bible. It consists simply in equating the revelation of God with his ordinary providential working. In God's providence there have arisen, for example, those writings, the *Iliad* and the *Odyssey*, which we know as the works of Homer. Without entering into the question how much Homer actually had to do with their composition, other than to remark that we believe that they display the marks of one great mind, we may say that in a certain sense, these works were given to us from God. Who can read the *Iliad* and the *Odyssey* without being greatly impressed by their magnificence? Surely the genius which went into their composition was a gift from none other than God himself. Homer—assuming that he was the author—was a highly gifted and endowed man, and we may thank God for the talent that was given to him. At the same time, we would not say that the very words of either the *Iliad* or the *Odyssey* were taught to the poet by God. We certainly would not maintain that he, as he wrote, was borne by the Holy Spirit. Nor would we feel for an instant that, if there were serious errors in the original copies of the *Iliad* and *Odyssey*, such mistakes were a reflection upon God himself. Rather, we do not particularly care whether there were errors in the originals of Homer. Whoever wrote those originals made the errors, and it is not too important who that author was. The originals were not given to the poet by a direct, special revelation. It is in similar fashion that some would also treat the Bible. They would regard its composition as a mere act of God's providence, and would in effect deny any special revelation. The composition of the Bible, therefore, on this view, would not differ in any essential respect from that of the great poetry of ancient Greece.

If this conception of the origin of the Bible be correct, it of course follows that the Bible is in reality no different from any other book. The men who wrote the Bible may indeed have been serious-minded men; they were not, however, borne by the Spirit of God as they wrote, nor were the words which they penned God-breathed. They were men of their own time, subject to the ignorance and limitations of their time.

Serious-minded these authors may have been; that they were good men, however, is open to question. The words which they wrote were given to the world as words which the writers received by direct revelation from God. If, in a matter so fundamental as that of the origin of their words, the writers of Scripture did not tell the truth, how can we even say that they were good men. They were not good men, but deceivers. If the Bible arose as other books arise, merely in the ordinary providence of God, the Bible is not a good book, for the Bible *claims* to be a special revelation of God.

These are the implications that one cannot escape if he is to accept the Bible as being no different in respect to its origin from other books. Those who thus treat the Bible say not a word that would lead one to believe that they themselves seriously consider the words of the Scriptures to be God-breathed. They do not come to grips with the question whether the original of the Bible was breathed forth from the mouth of God himself. If the Bible came to us in the ordinary way through God's providential working—if, in other words, the Bible came to us just as other books do—then, it goes without saying, that it matters not one whit whether the originals of the Bible were free from error. If, on the other hand, (foreign and uncongenial as the thought is to the mind of the modern theologian) the Bible was given to man by special revelation of the one living and true God, it makes all the difference in the world whether the Bible came to us free from error. If the Bible is indeed the Word of God, is that Word free from error, or is God bound by the limitations and errors that adhere to sinful humanity? There is the issue, and it cannot be evaded.

If we are going to reject the Bible as God's special revelation, that is one thing. If, however, we are going to cleave to the doctrine of inspiration, let us face the claims of the Bible honestly. The Bible asserts that it is the very Word of God. If we believe that assertion, let us accept it and follow its implications where they lead. It would be a great boon to the entire religious situation if those who no longer believe in the scriptural doctrine of inspiration would cease speaking and writing as though they did so believe. When a man says that he considers the Bible to be the Word of God, the humble Christian will likely take his words at face value and think that he intends them in the same sense as does the Bible itself. Such, of course, is not the case at all. Merely for the sake of simple honesty, it would be a great advantage if in the present religious situation men would make it clear what they mean by their usage of scriptural terminology.

If, however, we do accept the teaching of the Bible, God grant that we may not be ashamed of that teaching! The Bible, in manifold ways, has proclaimed and asserted its divinity. It has emphatically declared that in a unique manner it has come to us from God. If, in professing to believe the Bible, we are going to be serious, let us accept its claims and not try to explain them away! Let us follow our God, who cannot lie; and since he cannot lie, let us believe that his Word is truth itself. Those copies of Scripture which came forth from God Almighty were infallible and inerrant. No matter what men may say to the contrary, no matter how much they may seek to obscure the issue, in the very nature of the case it could not have been otherwise.

An Objection

At this point it may be well to consider briefly an objection which is sometimes raised. Since, as we have maintained, God cannot err, the Word which comes forth from his mouth must also itself be inerrant. This conclusion, it is said by way of objection, need not at all follow. We might as well argue that, since Christ is the perfect Son of God, therefore he could not die. As a matter of fact, however, he did die. And because the sinless Son of God did die, we cannot maintain that the Holy Ghost could not have condescended to use the poverty, error, and sin of the biblical writers whom he employed. To this objection several things need to be said. Basically, however, it appears to confuse sin and the consequences of sin. All that God speaks, because God is Truth itself, must also be true and in accordance with fact. To maintain that God may have uttered words that are false or that do not square with the facts is in effect to make of God a liar. What, however, shall we say about the death of Christ? Jesus Christ, according to the Bible, is God become man. When the second person of the ever-blessed Trinity took to himself our human nature, he took that nature apart from sin. Hence the importance of the doctrine of the virgin birth. That holy Babe which was born of Mary was the Son of God. Although he became flesh and dwelled among us, although he became man in the truest sense of the word, he nevertheless became a sinless man. Holy, harmless, and undefiled, he lived his blessed life upon this earth in our midst. Why, then, did he die? Does not death come only upon those who have sinned? But he was not a transgressor of the law. Why then did he die? The answer is that the guilt of our sin was laid to his account, and as our substitute he bore the penalty of our sin. He was, in other words, punished in our stead. It was our sin for which he was smitten. How wondrously the prophet has set it forth: "He *was* wounded for our transgressions, he *was* bruised for our iniquities: the chastisement of our peace *was* upon him; and with his stripes we are healed" (Isa. 53:5). What Isaiah says is the same thing that the apostle sets forth so beautifully in his second epistle to the Corinthians (5:21): "For he hath made him *to be* sin for us, who knew no sin; that we might be made the righteousness of God in him." If Christ had taken unto himself a sinful nature, and so had died as a consequence of his own sins, then, indeed, there might be force in the objection which we are now considering. Such, however, was not the case. Not for his own sins did he die, but for the sins of others.

> What thou, dear Lord, hast suffered
> Was all for sinners' gain;

Mine, mine was the transgression,
But thine the deadly pain.

In those words we find the correct statement of the case. The transgression was not his but that of his people; the deadly pain, however, fell upon him, for in their stead he was punished.

If he were a sinner, then, indeed, we should expect him to die. Sin brings forth death, and sin also issues in error and fallibility. To say that God has erred is to say that he has sinned; to assert, however, that Christ died is not necessarily to say that he has died for his own sin. The death of Christ in no way implies that he himself was a sinful man, and hence an appeal to the death of our Lord, such as we have just considered, in no wise militates against the biblical doctrine of inerrancy.

A New View

Is not, it may be asked, this doctrine of an inerrant original text comparatively new? Was it not developed during the last century by orthodox Protestant theologians? Luther and Calvin, it is often claimed, did not hold anything similar to it. More than that, the Fathers of the church certainly did not teach it. Therefore, the conclusion seems to be, the doctrine is one which belongs not to catholic Christianity but only to a small segment of the church.

Modern writers like to cast their scorn upon this view and to declare how recent it is. Of course, it might as well be noted in passing, a doctrine is not necessarily false because its implications were only recently realized. The church existed for many centuries before Luther saw the force of the scriptural doctrine of justification by faith. Despite that fact, however, men have always been justified by faith. The doctrine was true long before Luther saw its force and implications. If, therefore, it should be true that only in recent years men have begun to see the implications of the doctrine of inspiration, that in itself is no condemnation.

Is this doctrine, however, something which has just been developed during the last century? Our answer is, as we have been seeking to show, that it is found in the pages of the Scriptures themselves. It is perfectly true that its full implications were not set forth before the Reformation. During the sixteenth and the seventeenth centuries men who deeply loved the Lord Jesus Christ and his church worked out some of the implications of the scriptural teaching on inspiration. They did this, not because they had a bent of mind inclined toward philosophical speculation and sophistical niceties and wished to give satisfaction thereto, but because they faced a powerful foe, a foe which would deny to the Bible its position of supreme and final authority and would substitute therefore the church. That foe was Rome, and the issue which was raised was vital, and one which struck at the very roots of the Christian religion. To which ultimate authority is the humble and devout believer to listen? Is he to listen to what the church has to say? Is the church to tell him what he is to believe and how he is to live? To these questions Rome said yes, and its reply was fortified and buttressed by strong and powerful arguments. To listen to the church, however, would be a return to the fiction of a merit religion such as had characterized the Middle Ages and would close the door upon the gospel of the free grace of a merciful God and lead the soul into that bondage against which the great Reformers, Luther and Calvin, had so valiantly struggled.

There were those however, who refused to take the retrograde step into the darkness and superstition of the Middle Ages. To listen to the church, they believed, would be to shut one's ears to the voice of God. It must be shown that the church was usurping a place which did not belong to her, a place which was God's alone. Was this blessed Book, this Book which had led Luther out of the dark night of sacerdotalism and priestcraft into the glorious light of the grace of God, a Book whose claims could be trusted? The Book itself asserted, and that in no uncertain manner, that it was the Word of God. In what sense, however, was it the Word of God? Was it merely a secondary authority to be used as a support for whatever the church thought men should believe? That was the way in which, in effect, it was regarded by Rome. Or was it the Word of God in a different sense? Was it the final court of appeal to which men must harken if they would be saved?

At this crucial period there were not wanting men whose hearts God had touched, who knew that Christ had died for them, who loved the Savior because he had delivered them from their sins, and these men could not sit by and watch the Bible be relegated to a secondary position. They were desirous that the Bible should receive its full recognition. Hence, they made earnest and careful study of the Bible in order to discover what it had to say for itself. As a result the church has been enriched by their writings. We have, for example, the magnificent treatise on the Scriptures which Francis Turretin has left. There are those who could condemn that treatise and others of a similar nature by labelling them with the word "scholasticism." However, he who will take the trouble to work through what Turretin has written will make the discovery that here was a heart aflame with devotion to the Christ who had died for him and seeking only to be true to what God had revealed concerning his Holy Word.

It is certainly true that during the sixteenth and seventeenth centuries the implications of the doctrine of biblical inspiration were worked out more fully than before. And we may humbly give thanks to God that he gave men of such devotion to his church. We could do far worse today than to study these great masters of Protestant theology.

This does not mean that we must agree with everything that they wrote. We must, rather, test what they wrote to see whether it actually is taught in the Bible. No doubt there are references and allusions in the writings of the Protestant scholastics which are not particularly relevant today. No doubt there may have been a tendency on the part of some to a certain formalism in statement, and possibly also to over-refinement in argument. With all their faults, however, these men rendered a great service, and we may thank God that he saw fit to give them to his church.

It is also true that as a counter to the destructive criticism of the nineteenth century, a criticism which wrought such havoc in the church of Christ, even further thought was given to the doctrine of inspiration. We may thank God for men such as Charles Hodge, A. A. Hodge, and Benjamin B. Warfield. If students for the ministry would study the writings of these men instead of those of the present neoorthodox writers, the church would find itself in a far healthier condition.

The two following quotations will give the reader an inkling of the penetrating insight and fidelity to Scripture manifested by A. A. Hodge and B. B. Warfield:

> We believe that the great majority of those who object to the affirmation that Inspiration is verbal are impelled thereto by a feeling, more or less definite, that the phrase implies that Inspiration is, in its essence, a process of verbal dictation, or that, at least in some way, the revelation of the thought, or the inspiration of the writer, was by means of the control which God exercised over his words. And there is the more excuse for this misapprehension because of the extremely mechanical conceptions of Inspiration maintained by many former advocates of the use of this term "verbal." This view, however, we repudiate as earnestly as any of those who object to the language in question. At the present time the advocates of the strictest doctrine of Inspiration, in insisting that it is verbal, do not mean that, in any way, the thoughts were inspired by means of the words, but simply that the divine superintendence, which we call Inspiration, extended to the verbal expression of the

> thoughts of the sacred writers, as well to the thoughts themselves, and that, hence, the Bible considered as a record, an utterance in words of a divine revelation is the Word of God to us. Hence, in all the affirmations of Scripture of every kind, there is no more error in words of the original autographs than in the thoughts they were chosen to express. The thoughts and words are both alike human, and, therefore subject to human limitations, but the divine superintendence and guarantee extends to the one as much as to the other.[1]

What a matchless statement of inspiration is found in the following words:

> The Bible, moreover, being a work of the Spirit for spiritual ends, each writer was prepared precisely for his part in the work by the personal dealings of the Holy Spirit with his soul. Spiritual illumination is very different from either revelation or inspiration, and yet it had under the providence of God a large share in the genesis of Scripture, contributing to it a portion of that Divine element which makes it the Word of God. The Psalms are divinely inspired records of the religious experiences of the writers, and are by God himself authoritatively set forth as typical and exemplary for all men forever. Paul and John and Peter largely drew upon the resources, and followed the lines of their own personal religious experience in the intuitional or the logical development of their doctrine, and their experience had, of course, been previously divinely deemed for that very purpose. And in determining their religious experience, God so far forth determined their contributions to Scripture. And He furnished each of the Sacred writers, in addition to that which came to him through natural channels, all the knowledge needed for his appointed task, either by vision, suggestion, dictation or elevation of faculty, or otherwise, according to His will. The natural knowledge came from all sources, as traditions, documents, testimonies, personal observations and recollections; by means also of intuitions, logical processes of thought, feeling, experience, etc., and yet all were make under the general direction of God's providence. The supernatural knowledge became confluent with the natural in a manner which violated no law of reason or of freedom. And throughout the whole of His work the Holy Spirit was present, causing His energies to flow into the spontaneous exercises of the writer's faculties, elevating and directing where need be, and everywhere securing the errorless expression in language of the thought designed by God. This last element is what we call Inspiration.[2]

[1] "Inspiration," by A. A. Hodge and B. B. Warfield, in *The Presbyterian Review*, No. 6 (April 1881): 232–33.
[2] Ibid., 230–31.

Thank God for men who have been concerned to study the church's doctrines and to discover what are the implications of those doctrines! Would that our present day could boast of such painstaking Bible study as that which characterized the labors of the men just mentioned. Let us freely grant and rejoice in the fact that there has indeed been development in the understanding of this precious doctrine.

What, however, about the period before the Reformation? As we read over the history of the Christian church, there is one thing that impresses us, namely, the reverence in which the Holy Scriptures were held. Consider Justin Martyr as he appeals to the Scriptures to prove the deity of Jesus Christ. Why should he thus employ the Scriptures, were it not that he believed them to be the final court of appeal? Or hear Origen as, from the Bible, he endeavors to refute the specious attacks of a Celsus upon Christianity. Whatever errors Origen may have entertained, and he certainly had his share of them, the Scriptures, as his own practice makes clear, were to him the last and ultimate court of appeal. He may in effect have nullified this fact by the allegorizing with which he covered the Scriptures but, nevertheless, he at least thought that he was appealing to the Bible. Where they spoke, he was willing to listen; what they enjoined, he would put into practice. And it might be noted that the tremendous labor which he expended upon his sixfold version of the Bible, the Hexapla, is a tribute to his devotion to the Bible. More than that, however, the twenty-odd years in which he was engaged in this study, and particularly, his careful transcription of the Hebrew Old Testament in Greek characters, is, say what one will, a remarkable tribute to his belief in the verbal inspiration of the Bible.

This monumental work of Origen's was no mere antiquarian pursuit, wrought for the sake of scholarship as such. Origen was not interested primarily in scientific research. Rather, it was as a servant of Jesus Christ, a minister of the gospel, that he labored. By means of the Hexapla, he hoped that the church would have a better text of the Bible and, consequently, that the gospel might be more faithfully preached. From such deep devotion to the text of Scripture and its actual words, one receives the impression that Origen, were he alive today, would be one of the staunchest defenders of verbal inspiration.

Nor does Origen stand alone in his devotion to the Scriptures. One might find example after example of trust in the final authority of the Bible. The question is not what books of Scripture were regarded as inspired; there were indeed differences of opinion as to the extent of the canon. What is at issue is that throughout the course of church history, men appealed to that which they regarded as Scripture. If they considered a book to be Scripture, then they knew that they were bound to that book as to the very Word of God.

Valiant is the stand which Luther took upon this question. Hear him as he asserts, "Arguments based upon reason determine nothing, but because the Holy Ghost says it is true, it is true."[3] Well known are his brave words, spoken at Worms:

> Unless I am convinced by testimony from Scripture or evident reason—for I believe neither the Pope nor the Councils alone, since it is established that they have often erred and contradicted themselves—I am conquered by the writings cited by me, and my conscience is captive to the Word of God; recant I will not, since it is neither safe nor honest to do ought against conscience.[4]

And again,

> I have learned to ascribe this honor [i.e., infallibility] only to books which are termed canonical, so that I confidently believe that not one of their authors erred, but the other authors, no matter how distinguished by great sanctity and teaching, I read in this way, that I do not regard them as true because they themselves judged in this wise but in so far as they could convince me through the authority of the canonical writings or other clear deductions.[5]

From the time of the apostles until the present, God's people have loved his Word. In times of sorrow, they have found solace in its promises; in days of sadness, they have been comforted and strengthened by its testimonies; in the midst of happiness, they have rejoiced in its commands, and always has this been so because they have regarded this Word as God's Word; its words, indeed, have been a blessing to their souls. Thus, even though many of its implications have only been worked out since the days of the Reformation, the idea of verbal inspiration has been present from the beginning. One thing at least is clear: the doctrine of verbal inspiration, which Bible believers are defending today, is a doctrine which has been defended since the days of the apostles. It is indeed the very view which the apostles and, above all, our Lord himself maintained. The views of modernism, neoorthodoxy, and destructive criticism do not represent a natural development

[3] M. Reu, *Luther and the Scriptures*, 1944, 16.
[4] Ibid., 28.
[5] Ibid., 24.

of the attitude toward the Bible which has characterized the church since the time of its inception. Those who espouse the doctrine of verbal inspiration and scriptural infallibility are in a true apostolic succession.

Is the Bible Infallible Only in Faith and Practice?

Another objection, however, lies ready to hand. In stressing the fact that the Scriptures in matters of historical and geographical detail are infallible, we are charged with going too far. The Bible, it is acknowledged, is of course the only infallible rule of faith and practice, but that is as far as its infallibility goes. There are those who are willing to subscribe to the statement that the Scriptures are the only infallible rule of faith and practice, and by that declaration they mean, if we may employ the language of Charles A. Briggs,

> they are infallible in all matters of divine revelation, in all things where men need infallible guidance from God. We do not thereby claim that a writer dwelling in Palestine had an infallible knowledge of countries he had never visited, of dates of events beyond his own experience where he had to rely upon tradition or doubtful or imperfect human records. We do not affirm that he gave an exact and infallible report of words spoken centuries before, which had never been previously recorded; or an infallible description of events that happened in distant lands and ages; removing from the traditional report every excess of color and every variation in detail. We do not thereby claim that the writer of the poem of the creation knew geology and astronomy, and natural history better than the experts of modern science, but teach us the science of God and redemption, and the art of having holy, godlike lives. The Bible is the only infallible rule of faith and practice.[6]

In the words of this quotation Briggs has stated, perhaps as well as anyone, the objection of those who think they can limit the infallibility of Scripture to faith and practice. The objection, however, does not get at the root of the matter. It is an objection that has a certain pious ring to it and appears to possess a certain amount of plausibility. Plausible as it is, however, it cannot stand. Several things must be remarked concerning it.

In the first place, it is an objection that does not understand the true nature of faith. We do not believe, say these objectors, that the Bible is infallible in anything but faith and practice. It is not infallible in philosophy;

[6] Charles Augustus Briggs, *The Bible, The Church and The Reason* (1892), 93–94.

it is not infallible in astronomy; it is not infallible in other sciences; it is infallible only when it tells us what we are to believe. When, however, we come to examine the question what we are to believe, we discover that the doctrines which Scripture commends are rooted and grounded upon that which was done in history. The Christian faith, as it is revealed in the Bible, is not a mass of abstractions divorced from history. It is not eternal truths and ideals but rather the account of something that God did for us upon this earth in history. Hence, it becomes very important to us to know whether what the Bible has to say about these historical matters is correct or not.

According to the Bible our salvation depends upon the death of Jesus Christ at Calvary and upon his subsequent resurrection from the dead. Now, it is quite important to know certain details about the tomb in which he was laid. Was that tomb empty upon the third day? Was there an actual historical resurrection or not? Questions such as these intrude themselves into our consideration and will not be pushed aside. Is the Bible, therefore, correct in what it has to say of these historical details or not? If the historical framework in which the great redemptive acts of God took place is a framework which is not to be trusted, how do we know that we have a true and correct account of those redemptive acts themselves?

History and faith cannot be divorced the one from the other. Remove its historical basis and faith vanishes. To understand our faith properly we must study history, and this history is offered to us in the Bible. To say that what the Bible relates of history is fallible, but what it relates of faith is infallible is to talk nonsense. Apart from history there is no faith. The separation between the two which some seek to make is impossible. The only faith that can legitimately bear the name Christian is one that is rooted in historical events. From these it cannot be separated.

This brings us to another consideration. Who is to say what is faith and what is not? Those who claim that the Bible is infallible only as a rule of faith do not define where faith begins and where it ends. This fact may be illustrated by an appeal to the first chapter of Genesis. With respect to this chapter, how far does the infallibility of the Bible extend? Is everything that is related in this important chapter necessarily in error? Or are some statements true and some false? What is infallible and what is not infallible? Where does "faith" end and historical details begin? What, in other words, are the precise limits of "faith" in this first chapter of Genesis? What are the matters of "faith" herein revealed concerning which we may say that the Bible is infallible? And more than that, we would ask, who is to tell us what is and what is not a matter of faith? On these important questions the advocates of the view that the Bible is infallible only in matters of faith and practice are strangely silent. It will probably be acknowledged that in telling us that God is the Creator, the Bible is infallible. No doubt Dr. Briggs, from whom we have just made a rather lengthy quotation, would at least maintain such a position. Others, however, do not wish to join Dr. Briggs in this belief. They are indeed willing to employ the words of the first verse of Genesis and they are also willing to speak of God as the Creator. Their language, however, bears a different connotation from that of Dr. Briggs, for they also make it clear that they do not believe in creation in the sense intended by Genesis 1. Both Dr. Briggs and those who reject the first verse of Genesis would doubtless wish to be known as Christians. Dr. Briggs, we think, would say that the doctrine of creation as taught in the Bible is a necessary article of faith. Others, on the contrary, would say that as it is taught in the Bible, the doctrine is not necessary at all to faith. Not only is it not necessary, they would furthermore maintain, but it is even positively harmful. Who, then, is to settle the issue? Who is to tell us what is and what is not of faith? Dr. Briggs may have certain ideas as to what faith is; others however, have quite different ideas. When, therefore, it is declared that the Bible is an infallible rule of faith, we may be pardoned if we ask the simple question, What is this faith? It should be clear that those who assert that only in matters of faith and practice, as distinguished, for example, from historical statements, is the Bible infallible, are in fact erecting the human mind as the ultimate judge of what is and what is not faith. We are, of course, far from maintaining that the human writers of the Scriptures were of themselves infallible in all their knowledge. We are far from holding that Moses, to take an example, possessed advanced knowledge of modern science. If Moses had depended upon his own ideas of science, he would have produced an account of creation that would have been anything but infallible. In writing of creation, however, Moses did not depend upon his own ideas but wrote only that which was revealed to him by God.

Thus we come to the heart of the objection which we are now considering. Those who assert that only in matters of faith the Bible is infallible do not seem to appreciate the fact that the Bible is a revelation of God. In asserting that the Bible is infallible, we are not basing this infallibility upon the knowledge of the human writers of Scripture. It may be that Moses, Isaiah, John, and Paul were all men whose views of astronomy are today outmoded. Probably they held opinions on many other matters which would now be regarded as out of date. The Bible, however, is not simply the work of Moses and Isaiah, John and Paul. If it were, what a jumble of confusion and error it would be! It might then be little better than the works of other great men of antiquity. The Bible, however, is the revelation of God. The information which it offers to us is information which was communicated to its human writers by God. The reason, therefore, why the first chapter of Genesis reads as though it were written only yesterday is that the information contained therein was revealed to Moses by God. Much as men today like to talk about the prescientific character of the Bible, there is no one who can prove the presence of an error in the first chapter of Genesis.

The Bible, it is often said, is not a textbook of astronomy. That we freely grant. The Bible nowhere claims to be such a textbook. It is, however, a textbook of the philosophy of astronomy; when the Bible speaks, as in Genesis 1, upon astronomical matters, it is absolutely in accord with fact in what it says. It may be that through misunderstanding and fallible interpretations of our own, we have obscured what the Bible has to say. When, however, the true meaning of the Scripture is obtained, we have the truth upon that particular subject about which the Scripture is speaking. The Bible is not a textbook of geography; when, however, it speaks upon a geographical matter, it speaks with absolute authority. The Bible is not a textbook of geology; when, however, it speaks upon matters of geology, it is infallible in what it says. Human theories of astronomy, geology, and geography have changed and do change. The Bible, in what it says upon these subjects, is not in any sense in disharmony with the facts. That it may disagree with certain theories is, of course, granted; it does not disagree with the facts, since those facts also were given of God. The Bible, we must conclude, is infallible in all that it says, or we cannot be sure that it is infallible in anything. We cannot with any consistency maintain that only in the realm of faith and practice is it without error.

Do Protestants Misuse the Bible?

One frequently hears the assertion these days that Luther set Christendom free from the Roman pope, and now the time has arrived for someone to set Christendom free from the paper pope. Until the time of the Reformation, it is maintained, the church was considered infallible; now, however, the Bible has taken its place. The Bible is given the position of authority which once was occupied by the church. In rejecting an infallible church Protestantism has simply substituted an infallible book. This is bad, we are told, because the Bible does not claim such a place for itself. There is only one who should have supreme authority, namely, Jesus Christ. Protestants have put the Bible in the place of Jesus Christ, and that is one of the great weaknesses of Protestantism.

Plausible words are these; plausible, but utterly false. Before a little sober reflection they lose their force entirely. Despite that fact, however, they are often voiced in such a way as to give the impression that those who are uttering them had made some new and great discovery. They must not stand unchallenged, however, for they represent a perversion of the facts.

In the first place, it must be insisted that the picture offered by this objection is an oversimplification of the facts. It will not do to declare that until the time of the Reformation the church was accepted as an infallible authority, and then with the Reformation the Bible was presented as a substitute. A modern writer sets it forth thus:

> When the Reformation set the cat among the ecclesiastical pigeons, it was almost inevitable that the Bible should before long be given as spurious an eminence as the Church itself had enjoyed.[7]

It is true, of course, that through the long years of development the authority of the church was receiving ever greater and more prominent recognition. At the same time, the church claimed to reverence the Scriptures, and in her definition of doctrine did appeal to the Scriptures. The supreme authority of the Bible, however, was more and more pushed into the background. What the Reformation did was simply to clear the air and reestablish the Scriptures as the sole authority. One has but to read the writings of the New Testament in order to see that the church had begun with the belief that the Scriptures were that sole authority. Tradition, however, slowly but surely, began to usurp the place that at the beginning had belonged to the Bible. The Reformation swept away that tradition and once more called men to the Scriptures as the infallible authority. In other words, what the Reformation did was nothing more or less than to reestablish the rightful position of the Bible as the sole authority. The Reformation, in the providence of God, was a mighty purifying process. Gone was the error of human tradition and superstition which had grown during the Middle Ages, and in its place shone forth, once again, in all its purity, the infallible Word of God.

[7] William Neil, *The Rediscovery of the Bible* (London, 1954), 31.

In calling men back to the Bible, however, did the Reformers place the Bible in a position which belonged to Jesus Christ? Did they, in their endeavor to unite Protestantism against Rome, set up an authority other than Christ himself? Did they, in effect, supplant Christ with the Bible? Has the Bible, therefore, come between Christian faith and its Author? Has a false biblicism engulfed Protestantism? Strangely enough, through what we believe to be a misunderstanding of his teaching, Luther is sometimes omitted from the charge which we are now discussing. Be that as it may, we are told that the Reformers, at least Calvin and some of the others, were guilty of attributing to the Bible a position of priority which belonged to Christ alone.

How, we should like to ask, can the Bible possibly supplant the authority of Christ? We today would probably know nothing of Christ were it not for the Bible. Where do these modern theologians who claim to be zealous for the absolute authority of Christ receive their knowledge of Him? They receive it, humbling as the thought may be, from the *words* of the Bible. They do not receive it from some mysterious, nebulous Word which is to be separated from the actual words of Scripture. Much as modern theology may dislike the words of the Bible, it is from those despised words, and from them alone, that we learn of Jesus Christ. It would be well if that rather evident fact were kept in mind as we discuss this question.

What we are saying is so patent that there would seem to be no cause for discussion. Little children sing from the heart what the modern theologian seems unable to comprehend:

> Jesus loves me, this I know,
> For the Bible tells me so.

It is but a child's hymn, but it has a far more profound insight into the truth of the matter than has many a modern theologian who thinks that he can make a disjunction between Christ and his God-breathed Word. Were it not for the *words* of the Bible we would know nothing of the love of Jesus for lost sinners, nothing of his atoning death and his triumphant resurrection, nothing of the gift of his blessed Spirit, nothing of the promises of his sure return. Is it any wonder that children love to sing:

> Holy Bible, Book divine,
>   Precious treasure, thou art mine:
> Mine to tell me whence I came;
>   Mine to tell me what I am.

Mine to chide me when I rove,
Mine to show a Saviour's love,
Mine thou art to guide and guard;
Mine to punish or reward?

There may be some who will regard these words as expressing a mere bibliolatry. Those, however, who, because his Book has told them of him, know Jesus Christ, will dismiss all such cries as vain. Is this bibliolatry? Do Protestants worship a book? For our part we know of none who do. Protestants do not worship the paper and ink and the leather cover that goes to make up a Bible. It is true enough that the very form of the Word of God means a great deal to the true believer. Do we not all possess Bibles that have been with us throughout our lives? At home and abroad, they have been our constant companions, and a certain attachment, no doubt, is to be found in our hearts toward them. But our love for the Bible is something far deeper than the attachment one has toward an ancient and comfortable piece of furniture. We love this Book because of its message. Its very words are treasured in our hearts because we believe that these words were given by God himself. How deeply our love to God has grown when we could meditate during the early hours of the morning upon passages of the Scripture! We have repeated the words to ourselves over and over again, rejoicing in the blessing of the truth which they bring. Is this to dethrone Jesus Christ from his position of absolute authority? Those who speak thus evince little understanding of the true relationship between Jesus and his Word. It is through these blessed, divinely revealed *words* that our sinful hearts are brought closer to the Lord Jesus Christ.

The Reformers did not substitute the infallible Bible for an infallible Christ. By giving to the world an open Bible the Reformers preached Jesus Christ. When Calvin wrote his classic *Institutes,* he simply opened up the way for a serious and devout soul to come to a deeper knowledge of the Lord of Glory. And what about Luther; did he obscure Jesus Christ? When, after his vigorous stand at Worms, he was kidnapped and shut up in an old castle, what means did he employ to preach Jesus Christ as the absolute authority? If the modern theologians are correct, Luther did a very foolish thing. Thank God, however, that Luther did such a foolish thing. Luther translated the New Testament into the German language so that the people might hear the very words which Jesus Christ spoke. Luther knew nothing of this modern distinction between the Word of God and the words of the Bible. Luther, honest soul that he was, thought that the best way to get

Christ to the people was to give them the Bible in their own language. And since the people had this Word of God, they came to know Jesus Christ as their Lord and Savior. By giving his people the Bible, Luther thus gave them Jesus Christ.

We have a suspicion that those who are so concerned lest the Bible occupy a position which belongs to Christ have also themselves an "absolute" or "infallible" authority which they, whether they realize it or not, would themselves place upon the throne. It is the "infallible" mind of man. Not an infallible church, and not an infallible Bible, they tell us. Do they not, however, in their turn, demand an infallible "human mind" before which our Christianity must bow? Also, who is this Jesus Christ whose position has supposedly been dethroned by the Bible? We do not know him. Is he the eternal Son of God, the second person of the Holy Trinity, who, for our salvation, took unto himself human nature, without sin, being born of the Virgin Mary, to live upon this earth a sinless life, and, as our High Priest, to die upon the cross in our stead and to rise from the dead? Is that the Christ about whom the modern theologian is concerned? Has the position of this Christ been usurped by the Bible? We think not, for that blessed Christ is the one of whom the *words* of Holy Scripture speak. No, it is not that historic Christ which the Bible displaces, but some Christ whom we know not. There are many who say, "I am Christ." Is he for whom modern theologians seem so concerned one of these? If so, we know that he is at best but a fabrication of the human mind; he is not the divine Christ of Scripture. Is he but a name for worldly urbanity, for sentimental good cheer; is he but a slogan; is he the majority vote of the church council? We know him not, nor do we have any particular desire to know him. He cannot save us from our sins, sins which we have come to know through reading the words of the Scripture. Concerning all false Christs the Scriptures have said, ". . . see that ye be not troubled: for all *these things* must come to pass, but the end is not yet" (Matt. 24:6). Any Christ other than the historic Savior, the Christ of the Bible, is a Christ whom man has devised; and may we be spared from an "infallible" human mind which will tell us what Christ we are to worship.

The issue in the church today is not between those who maintain that the original manuscripts of the Bible were inerrant and those who believe that the original manuscripts may have contained errors, but who, nevertheless, are ardent believers in the doctrines of an evangelical, supernatural Christianity. If that ever were the situation in Christendom, it certainly is not so at the present day. It may have been that at one time there were staunch believers in the other doctrines of Scripture who nevertheless held that the original copies of the Bible contained errors. If there were such, however, they have given way. Certainly there are few today who hold to such a position. The errors of the Bible which men now say they find are not minor at all. If they were only minor the situation would not be so desperate. The time has come, however, when men do not want to accept the biblical witness to itself, but rather would be guided by the dictates of human reason.

There is, consequently, a refusal to do justice to the biblical doctrine of inspiration. The real reason why men oppose the doctrine of an infallible Scripture is that they are not willing to embrace the biblical doctrine of inspiration. There is no such thing as inspiration which does not carry with it the correlate of infallibility. A Bible that is fallible—and we speak of course of the original—is a Bible that is not inspired. A Bible that is inspired is a Bible that is infallible. There is no middle ground. Many are the attempts, indeed, which have been made to discover such a middle ground. They are, however, vain. Futile indeed are the efforts of those who wish to hold to some doctrine of inspiration without at the same time accepting belief in infallibility. It soon becomes apparent that the type of inspiration to which they are cleaving is not one that is taught in Scripture itself.

In the city of Geneva, there is a monument to the Reformation, and on this monument are carved the figures of some of the great Reformers. Underneath their figures are inscribed the words *Post tenebras lux*—"After the darkness, light." It is a stirring inscription. After the darkness of the Middle Ages, when, to all intents and purposes at least, the Bible was a closed and chained Book, light came. And light came in a most strange manner. Light came when the pages of the Bible were once more opened and its truths preached and believed in the hearts of the people.

Today also darkness is covering the land and gross darkness the people. If light is to come, it will not be through the work of man but through the work of God's Holy Spirit. And light will come, we believe, when the Spirit once more causes the men of our day to turn from the superficiality of so much of modern religious life to the Word of the one living and true God. Then will the pages of the Bible once more be opened and men will turn to its life-giving words, for, being the words of God, they are "profitable for doctrine, for reproof, for correction, for instruction in righteousness: that the man of God may be perfect, thoroughly furnished unto all good works.

8

"Verbal Inspiration in Church History"

R. LAIRD HARRIS

Inspiration and Canonicity of the Scriptures

Previously published as "Verbal Inspiration in Church History," in *Inspiration and Canonicity of the Scriptures: An Historical and Exegetical Study* (1995; repr., Greenville, SC: A Press, 1996), 55–64 (a revised and updated edition of *Inspiration and Canonicity of the Bible*, published in 1957 and 1969 by Zondervan Publishing House).

In this section, only a survey of the acceptance of this doctrine through the great periods of church history will be attempted. That the doctrine was so accepted is clear and is freely admitted by many—even of those unfriendly to the doctrine. We shall consider only the post-Reformation era, the Reformers themselves, and the times of the early church.

It is safe to say that there is no doctrine, except those of the Trinity and the deity of Christ, which has been so widely held through the ages of church history as that of verbal inspiration. This, however, is by no means the common conception of the situation. Occasionally an effort is made to picture this doctrine as a recent growth, the product of the Hodge-Warfield-Machen School of Princeton Seminary. This was the contention of men in the Presbyterian church in the U.S.A. who defended the Auburn Affirmation of 1924. They asserted that in 1923 the General Assembly of that church had erred when it readopted five basic points, including the doctrine of verbal inerrancy, as essential to Presbyterian standards. They maintained that the Westminster Standards teach that the Bible is "our only infallible rule of faith and practice," that is to say, an infallible guide in spiritual matters. But the Auburn Affirmation argued that "the doctrine of inerrancy of Scripture, intended to enhance the authority of the Scriptures, in fact impairs their supreme authority for faith and life."[1] It was argued that inerrancy is not found in the Westminster Standards but was a new development adopted by the General Assembly under pressure from the fundamentalist groups of the early 1900s.

This argument had already been considered by Warfield and dealt with at length.[2] Philip Schaff had written in 1893, at about the time of the heresy trial of his colleague, C. A. Briggs, that "the theory of a literal inspiration and inerrancy was not held by the Reformers."[3] Warfield goes on to consider the argument by Briggs and others that the Westminster Confession does not teach this doctrine. The Confession, of course, devotes its first chapter to the Scriptures and declares that the canonical books and these alone are of authority. The Apocrypha are not, but are mere "human writings." The authority of Scripture depends "upon God (who is truth itself, the author thereof); and therefore it is to be received, because it is the Word of God." "Nothing at any time is to be added" to Scripture. There is a wonderful "consent of all the parts" among its "many other incomparable excellencies." "The Old Testament in Hebrew . . . and the New Testament in Greek . . . being immediately inspired by God . . . are therefore authentical . . . the Church is finally to appeal unto them."

It would seem that the Confession speaks positively enough, although the word "inerrant" is not used. Why the word "inerrant" is not used is easy to see. Three hundred fifty years ago the modern critical problems and the "conflict" of science and the Bible or serious questions of historical accuracy had not yet arisen. The Confession does speak of "the infallible truth" of the Word of God, and this should be sufficient. "Inerrant" means "without mistake"; "infallible" means "incapable of error." It is actually a stronger word. In 1645 there had not yet arisen the distinction which liberal theologians now attempt to draw between spiritual truth and historical error. The old creed therefore does not specifically say that the Bible is true also in matters of history and science as well as in the spiritual sphere. It simply emphasizes that the Bible is all true. As Chapter XIV of the Westminster Confession puts it, "By this faith [saving faith], a Christian believeth to be true whatsoever is revealed in the Word, for the authority of God Himself speaketh therein." It is also to be noted that the matter

[1] Point one of the Auburn Affirmation. See R. Laird Harris, "Introduction," in *Inspiration and Canonicity of the Scriptures* (Greenville, SC: A Press, 1996), 29–30.
[2] B. B. Warfield, *The Westminster Assembly and Its Work* (New York: Oxford, 1931), 261–333.
[3] Quoted by Warfield, ibid., 261.

of self-contradiction in the Bible had repeatedly arisen, but that here the Confession took its stand with the other Reformation creeds to insist that there are no contradictions in Scripture.[4] It mentions "the consent of all the parts." So the Westminster standards actually teach biblical inerrancy, even though they do not use the modern terminology which has been developed to meet a new attack.

Warfield carefully considers this in the above mentioned article, but, with his characteristic thoroughness, he does even more. He treats in detail the writings of eminent Westminster divines that have been preserved for us and shows that they clearly deny the possibility of mistakes in Scripture. He quotes John Ball's catechism, which declared that "the Holy Scriptures in the Originals were inspired both for matter and for words."[5] Richard Capel is quoted also as saying that the original writers of Scripture were "indued with the infallible Spirit" and "might not err."[6] The great Richard Baxter is briefly quoted to the same effect. "No error or contradiction is in it, but what is in some copies, by the failing of preservers, transcribers, printers, or translators."[7]

Warfield quotes many of the other authors of the Westminster Confession to the same effect, much to the detriment of the contrary view which C. A. Briggs had set forth in his book *Whither*? Warfield showed how Briggs had, in a serious manner, taken quotations of these men out of context. They believed precisely what we believe when we affirm the doctrine of verbal inerrancy today.[8]

Happily, in this point Warfield's argument is usually admitted today. The tendency now is to say that the awful doctrine of verbal inspiration was the product of an atrophied orthodoxy of the century after the Reformation, when the high character of the Reformers had been superseded by the sterile intellectualism and cold orthodoxy of the creed-making age.

Barth speaks almost as if this doctrine were the invention of the post-Reformation era: "The historistic conception of the Bible with its cult of heroes and the mechanical doctrine of verbal inspiration are products of

[4] The antagonists of the early church fathers had pointed out a number of alleged contradictions which are still stock in trade for the objectors, though most have long ago been satisfactorily dealt with. Justin and Irenaeus are quoted below as holding that apparent contradictions are reconcilable. An interesting old book with regard to the Old Testament is *The Conciliator* by R. Manasseh ben Israel (d. 1657), trans. E. H. Lindo (reprint New York: Herman Press, 1972) which in spite of its age deals quite well with many such problems. It does not use textual criticism to solve textual problems.

[5] Warfield, *Westminster Assembly*, 266.

[6] Ibid., 268.

[7] Ibid., 273.

[8] To the same effect are other creeds of the century previous to the Westminster Divines. The Thirty-Nine Articles of the Church of England and the Scotch Confession of 1560 may be mentioned.

the same age and the same spirit. They have this in common, that they stood for the means by which men of the Renaissance claimed to control the Bible."[9] He speaks of the "period of orthodoxy (subsequent to Calvin) which was the counterpart of the fatal doctrine of inspiration."[10]

Emil Brunner speaks a bit more accurately and at length. His view is that Luther had come to the grand conclusion that it is not the Bible that counts but Christ contained therein. We should note that this position invents a false antithesis. It is our view that the Bible counts because it is the true revelation of Christ. And as to Luther's view, which has been much discussed, Marcus Reu has admirably drawn together the evidence from the great Reformer's writings to show that he fully believed in verbal inspiration.[11] But, Brunner declares, "Calvin is already moving away from Luther toward the doctrine of verbal inspiration. His doctrine of the Bible is entirely the traditional, formally authoritative, view. From the end of the sixteenth century onwards there was no other 'principle of Scripture' than this formally authoritarian one."[12] Brunner here at least agrees with Warfield and disagrees with Briggs and older liberals when he declares that verbal inspiration has been the teaching of the Protestant church and its creeds. Most students of the Reformation will be astonished at the suggestion that Calvin believed anything else. Luther has been quoted as questioning the doctrine because of his oft mentioned remark that James is a "right strawy Epistle." It should be noted, however, that Luther's problem was not one of inspiration but of canonicity. Luther had denied the Apocryphal books of the Old Testament, a denial in which he was on solid ground and had much support from previous as well as contemporary scholars. But it need not be wondered at too much if, in facing the problem of the reconciliation of the epistle of James with Luther's essential doctrine of justification by faith, Luther was perhaps tempted to solve it too easily, simply by questioning the canonicity of James. After all, the epistle had actually been questioned in certain circles of the early church, and its apostolic origin was not thoroughly demonstrated. Luther, a pioneer, might well have questioned it. However, in Luther's defense it should further be said that he kept the book of James in every edition of his Bible. Actually, the context of his reference to James shows that he only argues that James is an "epistle of straw" in comparison with the greater and more basic books of

---

[9] Karl Barth, *Doctrine of the Word of God*, vol. 1, part 1 of *Church Dogmatics* (Edinburgh: T&T Clark, 1936), 126f.
[10] Ibid., 128.
[11] Martin Reu, *Luther and the Scriptures* (Chicago: Wartburg, 1944).
[12] Emil Brunner, *The Christian Doctrine of God* (Philadelphia: Westminster Press, 1950), 111.

the Gospels, major Pauline epistles, etc. In this we admit that he was right. Verbal inspiration as a doctrine by no means teaches that Obadiah is as important as Genesis. It merely insists that the entire Bible is true. Luther plainly accepted the doctrine of verbal inspiration.

Brunner makes the further admission that the doctrine is an ancient one: "The doctrine of verbal inspiration was already known to pre-Christian Judaism . . . and was probably also taken over by Paul and the rest of the apostles."[13] He proceeds to argue that the doctrine was of no great consequence through the medieval period because the principle of allegorical interpretation allowed the scholastics to make what they would out of the Bible. The doctrine was revived in the Reformation. Probably Brunner does not realize the import of what he is here saying. He says that this doctrine of verbal inspiration—which he cordially castigates—was the legacy of Judaism, accepted by the apostles, and held by the early church through the years of her strength down to the times of Origen and Augustine, who set the pattern of allegorical interpretation for a thousand years. The loss of this doctrine as a practical element in theology (though it was by no means lost in theory) corresponded with the Dark Ages. After the Reformation, the doctrine lasted through three centuries of the church's strength till the rise of higher criticism. It was held by the church which spread abroad in the great missionary movement of the nineteenth century. It has been denied by the scholars of the late nineteenth century and by the laity and churchmen of the twentieth. This terrible doctrine seems to be absent in the times of the church's apostasy and present in the times of her power. At least Brunner is historically rather accurate. One might well here wish that Brunner had reconsidered and embraced a doctrine evidently so productive of spiritual power and blessing![14]

With these admissions it perhaps is a work of supererogation to search the old Christian writings to prove that the early church was faithful in following its Lord in this doctrine. The evidence has been set forth in some detail by Sanday in his Bampton Lectures on "Inspiration," especially in his first chapter, where he gives a great number of brief references to the writers of the early centuries, especially after AD 200.[15]

It might be of interest to quote Warfield's estimate of Sanday's work: "Dr. Sanday, in his recent Bampton Lectures on 'Inspiration'—in which,

[13] Ibid., 107.

[14] To the same effect, Alan Richardson, *A Preface to Bible Study* (Philadelphia: Westminster Press, 1944), remarks that "from the second century to the eighteenth this theory [of verbal inspiration] was generally accepted as true," although Richardson finds that "few better educated Christians" hold to it anymore (p. 23).

[15] William Sanday, *Inspiration, Bampton Lectures for 1893* (London: Longmans, 1901), especially 28–42.

unfortunately, he does not teach the Church doctrine—is driven to admit that not only may 'testimonies to the general doctrine of inspiration' from the earliest Fathers 'be multiplied to almost any extent'; but (that) there are some which go further and point to an inspiration which might be described as "verbal" . . . nor does this idea,' he adds, 'come in tentatively and by degrees, but almost from the very first.' He might have spared the adverb 'almost.' The earliest writers know no other doctrine."[16] With this we heartily agree. Sanday did not hold to verbal inspiration. But, like Brunner, quoted above, he was constrained to admit that this has been the teaching cherished by Christians through the ages. He is an unwilling witness to the fact that the early Fathers believed in a verbally inspired Scripture. Much of the evidence is referred to also by Gaussen in his book *Theopneusty*,[17] but the quotations are not printed nor classified as conveniently as in Sanday.

A very few of these early statements should be given. The *First Epistle of Clement*, written near the end of the first century AD, speaks of the Old Testament with the greatest reverence and tells also of the inspiration of the apostles and their high authority. Several times Clement quotes from the Old Testament and ascribes the words of the human author to God, Christ, or the Holy Ghost.[18] It is called the "Scripture," "Sacred Scriptures," the "Holy Word," etc. Specifically he says, "Look carefully into the Scriptures, which are the true utterances of the Holy Spirit. Observe that nothing of an unjust or counterfeit character is written in them."[19]

Ignatius, the bishop of Antioch, who was martyred about AD 117, has left us a similar witness. By this time references to the New Testament abound, and an exceedingly high view of the apostles is held. He speaks rather deprecatingly of the Jewish law, but it is plainly the Judaizing doctrine that is meant, for he commends the prophets. However, he emphasizes that the word of the new dispensation is far superior. He remarks concerning those who ignorantly deny Jesus that "these persons neither have the prophets persuaded nor the law of Moses nor the Gospel even to this day."[20] The way in which he here places the gospel on a par with the Old Testament is very instructive. Of these prophets he says, "The divinest prophets

[16] B. B. Warfield, *The Inspiration and Authority of the Bible*, ed. Samuel G. Craig (Philadelphia: Presbyterian & Reformed, 1948), 108.

[17] S. R. L. Gaussen, *Theopneusty, or Plenary Inspiration* (reprint Chicago: Moody, 1949), 343.

[18] Clement (of Rome), chaps. 8, 13, 16, 22, etc. The Epistle is conveniently found in *ANF*, vol. 1. The standard translation of the Loeb Classical series (Cambridge: Harvard, 1985) has the Greek text with the translation done by Kirsopp Lake.

[19] Ibid., chap. 45 in *ANF*, vol. 1, 62.

[20] Ignatius, *To the Smyrneans*, chap. 5, in *ANF*, vol. 1, 88.

lived according to Christ Jesus. On this account also they were persecuted, being inspired by his grace to fully convince the unbelieving that there is one God, who has manifested Himself by Jesus Christ His Son."[21] He says also that we who have received the things of the new dispensation should follow Christ when the "prophets themselves in the Spirit did wait for Him as their teacher." Again he uses such terms when he urges us to flee to "the Gospel as to the flesh of Jesus, and to the apostles as to the presbytery of the church. And let us also love the prophets because they, too, have proclaimed the Gospel, and placed their hope in Him, and waited for Him; in whom also, believing, they were saved, through union to Jesus Christ, being holy men, worthy of love and admiration, having had witness borne to them by Jesus Christ."[22] Ignatius is full of the thought that the new is better than the old. But he does not hint that the new is truer than the old. For him, as he says, "It is written" refers not only to the old dispensation but applies equally well to the gospel.[23]

Polycarp, the great martyr and disciple of John, writes near the beginning of the second century, just after Ignatius' martyrdom, "Whosoever perverts the oracles of the Lord to his own lusts, and says that there is neither a resurrection nor a judgment, he is the firstborn of Satan."[24] Polycarp here is probably speaking of the New Testament. His opinion of the apostles is most high: "For neither I nor any other such one can come up to the wisdom of the blessed and glorified Paul. He, when among you, accurately and steadfastly taught the word of truth."[25] The prophets—surely the Old Testament authors—are said to have "proclaimed beforehand the coming of the Lord,"[26] thus evidencing a belief in predictive prophecy. The quotation from Psalm 4:4, "In your anger do not sin," and from Ephesians 4:26, "Do not let the sun go down while you are still angry," are linked together and called Sacred Scriptures.[27] (Ephesians 4:26 quotes Psalm 4:4, verbatim from the Septuagint, and possibly Polycarp is taking the whole quotation from Ephesians; the alternative is that he was quoting the psalm and then quoting Paul's additional word as also Scripture.) In this short epistle Polycarp has comparatively few references to the Old Testament, but his doctrine of Scripture is clearly the standard one of complete belief therein.

---

[21] Ibid., *To the Magnesians*, chap. 8, in *ANF*, vol. 1, 62.
[22] Ibid., *To the Philadelphians*, chap. 5, in *ANF*, vol. 1, 82.
[23] Ibid., *To the Philadelphians*, chap. 8, in *ANF*, vol. 1, 84.
[24] Polycarp, *To the Philippians*, chap. 7, in *ANF*, vol. 1, 34.
[25] Ibid., Chap. 3, in *ANF*, vol. 1, 33.
[26] Ibid., Chap. 6, in *ANF*, vol. 1, 34.
[27] Ibid., Chap. 12, in *ANF*, vol. 1, 35.

There are a few other fragments and short writings from authors of this early time which do not speak so positively as these, but it must be remembered that neither they nor any of the rest of the authors quoted give any hint that the Scriptures, either Old Testament or New, are not to be trusted. Rather, the spirit of their extant remains is in full agreement with the doctrine so widely witnessed in the apostolic writings that the Holy Scriptures are true and without the slightest mistake.

When we come to the great authors of the latter half of the second century where the witness abounds, we also find full testimony to belief in a doctrine of inspiration that must be described as verbal. Justin Martyr wrote just after the middle of the second century. His dates are not certain, but he seems to have been born about AD 115 and he died a martyr in 165. His writing would therefore have been mid-century. Commonly quoted on the subject of inspiration is Justin's description of the inspiration of "the holy men" who would "present themselves pure to the energy of the Divine Spirit, in order that the divine plectrum itself, descending from heaven, and using righteous men as an instrument like a harp or lyre, might reveal to us the knowledge of things divine and heavenly. Wherefore, as if with one mouth and one tongue, they have in succession, and in harmony with one another, taught us both concerning God, and the creation of the world, and the formation of man . . ."[28] Note that this quotation gives an illustration which is perhaps unfortunate and is by no means a part of our doctrine, but it also points out that the product is divine and true, without contradictions. This last point is made more explicit in another passage: "I am entirely convinced that no Scripture contradicts another; I shall admit rather that I do not understand what is recorded, and shall strive to persuade those who imagine that the Scriptures are contradictory to be rather of the same opinion as myself."[29] To this end he was arguing with Trypho, a Jew whom he was trying to convert to the new faith.

A final quotation from Justin's *First Apology* tells of the rise of the Old Testament: "There were, then, among the Jews certain men who were prophets of God, through whom the prophetic Spirit published beforehand things that were to come to pass, ere ever they happened." These prophe-

[28] Justin Martyr, *Hortatory Address to the Greeks*, chap. 8, in *ANF*, vol. 1, 276. This *Address to the Greeks* is thought by some not to be genuine, and indeed, the famous illustration of the plectrum on the lyre is slightly embarrassing as being too mechanical. But the mechanics of the illustration need not be pushed and in any case the *Address* represents very early testimony.

[29] Justin Martyr, *Dialogue with Trypho*, chap. 65, in *ANF*, vol. 1, 230. This dialogue is put at about AD 135 by F. F. Bruce because Trypho was a refugee from the disaster of the second Jewish revolt at that time, *BCS*, 65.

cies, he says, were "carefully preserved when they had been arranged in books by the prophets themselves in their own Hebrew language."[30] Justin then presents two or three pages of Old Testament citations predicting Christ's coming and work. A great deal of this material is equal to much that is written on the subject today, and it is all from the point of view of one who accepts without question the supernatural inspiration of the authors of Scripture so that it can be trusted entirely even in small details.

Next to be considered is Irenaeus, the disciple of the aged Polycarp and therefore closely linked to the apostle John, under whom Polycarp sat. He complains that these men, "when . . . they are confuted from the Scriptures, they turn round and accuse these same Scriptures, as if they were not correct."[31] But Irenaeus declares that they are correct in whole and in part. He objects to the fact that Marcion and Valentinus use only a part of Luke: "It follows then, as a matter of course, that these men must either receive the rest of his narrative or else reject these parts also. For no person of common sense can permit them to receive some things recounted by Luke as being true and to set others aside, as if he had not known the truth."[32] He maintains that the author of Matthew was so endowed with the Holy Ghost that he, "foreseeing the corruptors," wrote certain words and not others so as to preclude the Gnostic heresy.[33] He declares that the apostles after the resurrection "were invested with power from on high when the Holy Spirit came down (upon them), were filled from all (his gifts), and had perfect knowledge."[34] A final quotation may be given from the many more which could be cited. He says with the humility of true faith, "If, however, we cannot discover explanations of all those things in Scripture which are made the subject of investigation, yet let us not on this account seek after any other God besides Him who really exists. For this is the greatest impiety. We should leave things of that nature to God who created us, being most properly assured that the Scriptures are indeed perfect, since they were spoken by the Word of God and His Spirit."[35] What good advice from the second century to the twentieth!

During the immediately following period of the third century our witnesses are abundant. Sanday says, "Indeed on both sides, the side of doctrine and the side of practice, the authoritative use of Scripture—the

[30] Justin Martyr, *First Apology*, chap. 31, in *ANF*, vol. 1, 173.
[31] Irenaeus, *Against Heresies*, iii.2.1, in *ANF*, vol. 1, 276.
[32] Ibid., iii.14.4, in *ANF*, vol. 1, 439.
[33] Ibid., iii.16.2, in *ANF*, vol. 1, 441.
[34] Ibid., iii.1.1, in *ANF*, vol. 1, 414.
[35] Ibid., ii.28.2, in *ANF*, vol. 1, 399.

New Testament equally with the Old—underlies the whole of the Christian literature of this period. Not only might we quote it for page after page of Irenaeus, Clement of Alexandria, Tertullian, Hippolytus, Origen . . . but—what is of even more importance—the method is shared alike by orthodox writers and heretical."[36] We may summarize the matter by citing a quotation from Augustine a bit later, who says of the canonical Scriptures that he "firmly believes that no one of their authors has erred in anything, in writing."[37]

Sanday strangely tries to add a caveat that side by side with this view was a lower opinion which he imagines to be "in closer contact with the facts."[38] This lower view of Scripture he finds in the fragments of Papias, the preface to Luke's Gospel, and the *Muratorian Canon*. His main substantiation for this idea is apparently a willful misunderstanding of what is involved in verbal inspiration. He assumes that verbal inspiration involves that the authors did not study or use sources for their work.

No one who reads his Bible at all would wish to claim that the human authors were entirely passive in the process of inspiration. God did not lay hold of a Persian to write Hebrew nor of a mystical John to write the logical epistles of Paul. God chose John to write according to his nature, but superintended his writing. Paul, trained in the schools of Jerusalem, reflects his background, but writes only God's truth. If human industry in preparation of material precludes inspiration, then no one from Moses to the apostle John was inspired. Of course Moses counted the Israelites before he wrote the book of Numbers. The census (or mustering of the troops) was not a matter of revelation to Moses, but it is nonetheless true and a part of God's Word. Of course Mark took care to gather his material carefully from Peter just as Papias says, and Luke worked industriously, as he outlines in Luke 1:1–4. But hard labor is not antithetic to usefulness for God! God would probably not have chosen Paul as a vessel of inspiration and an author of Scripture if he had not been one who would labor more abundantly than all. Very few indeed have been the theologians who have held that verbal inspiration involved a trancelike receptivity and mechanical dictation of the Word without human activity. None of the great creeds so define it. To liken the fundamentalist view to a mechanical thing such as Mohammed claimed is only to evidence a lack of knowledge of what one's opponents believe and what the church has so widely held. These

---

[36] Sanday, *Inspiration*, 38.
[37] Augustine, *Epistle to Jerome*, 82.3. Quoted by Warfield, *Inspiration*, 108.
[38] Sanday, *Inspiration*, 45.

misconceptions are so unnecessary and yet frequent that they can only be called willful. They have been considered above.[39]

Others have objected that such incidental details as the apostle's asking for his cloak left at Troas (2 Tim. 4:13) or requesting lodging (Philem. 22) surely cannot be considered as inspired because they are too mundane. Of course this is not a positive argument, but merely an appeal to propriety in what one thinks to be a fit object of divine superintendence. And presumably the answer is that we are not the measures of the divine interest in our mundane existence. In the Old Testament the interest of God descended to ailments of the body and the handling of unclean vermin and animals in the Hebrew home. The view perhaps forgets that the God who cares for sparrows is much more concerned about warm clothing and lodging for his aged apostle. If God could superintend the arrow drawn "at random" which smote King Ahab "between the sections of his armor" in fulfillment of Micaiah's prophecy (2 Chron. 18:33), surely he is interested in our little problems, too, for in the life of a prophet or apostle, just as in our own, it is very difficult to separate the little from the big. It was a little thing that Paul happened to be in Jerusalem the day that Stephen was stoned and held the coats of his attackers, but it left an indelible impression which God doubtless used in the apostle's conversion. As a matter of fact, the little detail about the coat left at Troas, if it be accepted as genuine and believed, furnishes the clue to the later history of Paul. It proves correct the view that he was delivered from the first Roman imprisonment, then traveled about—at least to Troas—before being captured a second time for his execution a short time after 2 Timothy was written. Let us not despise the small things in the Bible or in any of God's work. Even the jots and tittles have their place. By verbal inspiration we merely mean that God superintended the process of writing so that the whole is true—the historical, the doctrinal, the mundane, the minor, and the major. The genealogies are not so ennobling as the Passion narratives, for instance, but they truly give the antecedents of him who was the Seed of David according to the flesh, but the Son of God with, according to the Spirit of holiness, Jesus Christ, the central subject of the whole sacred volume.

This, under various names, has been the doctrine of the Christian church from the earliest times, such unwilling witnesses as Sanday, Brunner, and

[39] Cf. the remark by G. Ernest Wright in *Interpretation* 3 (January 1949): 56f., where he says that the prevailing view of leaders of the World Council of Churches is that Fundamentalism holds a "mechanical inspiration," "analogous to the Mohammedan." For a denial of mechanical inspiration on the part of all leading conservative theologians, see R. Laird Harris, "Introduction," in *Inspiration and Canonicity of the Scriptures* (Greenville, SC: A Press, 1996), 12–13.

Alan Richardson being proofs.[40] Christ and the apostles believed it. So has the church, with the rarest of exceptions, until the rise of liberal theology in the nineteenth and twentieth centuries. This doctrine is by no means the hard and mechanical view it has been said to be. It has held before the church a Book with the message of God. In a dark and sinful world the Book has rebuked kings, comforted the poor, encouraged learning, freed the downtrodden, brought peace of heart, and ennobled men for missions of service and evangelism. Its rediscovery has brought new life and power. Its neglect has resulted in darkness, war, and sin. Of course we do not worship the Bible. The caricature of "bibliolatry" is manifestly unfair. We worship not the Book but Christ of the Book. But the Book is the gracious instrument God has given us for the spread of his gospel. And to that Book we do well to return for new supplies of grace and power.

> Holy Bible, book divine,
> Precious treasure, thou art mine;
> Mine to tell me whence I came,
> Mine to teach me what I am.

Christianity has always been a book religion!

[40] On Richardson, see above, note 14.

9

"The Witness of Scripture to Its Inspiration"

ALAN M. STIBBS

Revelation and the Bible

Previously published as "The Witness of Scripture to Its Inspiration," in *Revelation and the Bible: Contemporary Evangelical Thought*, ed. Carl F. H. Henry (Grand Rapids, MI: Baker, 1958), 105–18. Used by permission of Baker Books, a division of Baker Publishing Group.

The purpose of this chapter is to consider the witness of Scripture itself to its own inspiration. To begin with, there is need to distinguish clearly between two different meanings or possible implications of the word "inspiration" when it is thus used of Holy Scripture. The prevalent ideas associated with this term do not conform to that denotation of the word which has scriptural authority and justification, and which supplies the particular meaning which we have in view of a study of this kind.

Meaning of Inspiration

When the word "inspiration" is used of the Bible it is often thought to describe a quality belonging primarily to the writers rather than to the writings; it indicates that the men who produced these documents were inspired men. In contrast to this idea, which indubitably has its place, we find that the Scripture employs the word bearing this meaning primarily to describe not the writers but the sacred writings. Second Timothy 3:16 reads *pasa graphē theopneustos*. Thus the RSV renders "All scripture is inspired by God." Let us here notice three points about this statement. (1) The Greek adjective *theopneustos* (meaning literally "God-breathed") is a compound, which begins with an explicit recognition of God as the author; the inspiration is divine. (2) The human agents in the production of the Scripture are here not even mentioned. (3) The Scripture, or writing thus produced, is here described, and is intended to be thought of, as "divinely inspired," or as the KJV renders it, "given by inspiration of God." What, therefore, we are in this chapter to consider as inspired, or produced by divine inspiration, is not primarily the condition or activity of the biblical writers, but the biblical writings themselves, the actual written words of Scripture.

Place of Self-Authentication

Some will surely raise the objection that Scripture ought not thus to be appealed to for its own vindication. To quote Scripture in support of Scripture seems, admittedly, from one standpoint, to be arguing in a circle, and to be logically inconclusive. It is important, therefore, to see that in this particular case no occasion exists for such misgiving.

1. First, let us recognize that every man has surely a right to speak for himself; and that testimony to oneself ought not be ruled out as completely improper. Indeed, if men were not liars and deceivers, or not prejudiced and blind and lacking in full understanding, their own testimony about themselves would be sufficient. Consider the unique example of the perfect Man. Although Jesus recognized that the truth about himself needed confirmation by independent witness to satisfy normal human standards, he nevertheless said, "Even if I bear witness of myself, my witness is true" (RV; cf. John 5:31; 8:13–14).

2. Not only so, but some truths about people may never be known, unless the individuals concerned themselves bear witness to them. If what they thus say is unreliable, no other means of discovering the truth may exist. Somewhat similarly, the Bible discloses from God himself truths which cannot otherwise be discovered. For our knowledge of them we are wholly dependent upon divine revelation thus communicated through the Scriptures. Surely no justification exists for thus believing what the Bible teaches about other doctrines, wholly beyond independent human confirmation, if we cannot equally rely completely on what the Bible teaches about itself. Moreover, if we are to accept Scripture as our supreme rule of faith and understanding in the one, we ought similarly to do so in the other. In other words, we cannot rightly turn to the Bible for testimony to the otherwise unknown unless we do accept also its testimony to itself.

3. In the third place, if we believe that the Bible not only claims to be, but is, a book from God, then behind and beyond all its human writers and contributing agents God himself must be acknowledged as its author;

and God cannot lie. His word is always true and always trustworthy. The Bible's witness to itself ought, therefore, to be treated as authoritative and decisive; in a very real sense we need none other.

4. When men wish to confirm witness given about themselves, they appeal to one greater; they take an oath and swear by Almighty God. Similarly, when God wished to make men doubly sure of his word of promise, he confirmed it by an oath. But when he came to swear, since there was none greater by whom he could swear, he swore by himself (cf. Heb. 6:13–18). He thus made himself the guarantor of the truth and trustworthiness of his own word. This supremely illustrates the principle that in any realm of activity the supreme authority must be self-authenticating. It is impossible to get endorsement or confirmation of such utterances by appeal to some greater authority. Similarly, if the Bible is from God, and therefore possesses supreme authority among men in what it says, it cannot be other than self-authenticating. Truth is settled by what it says rather than by what others may say about it, or in criticism of it.

5. Finally, relief from the possible embarrassment of dependence upon a single witness—and that in this case the witness of Scripture to itself—is provided by the Trinity and the eternity of the Godhead. For God is three in one; and God still speaks. So the truth and trustworthiness of Scripture, as the authoritative and unbreakable divine word, are confirmed to the Christian believer by the witness during his earthly life of the incarnate Son of God and by the present continuing witness of the illuminating and indwelling Spirit of God.

What Scripture Declares about Itself

Let us now consider in detail some of the statements made in Scripture about itself and its production. Such statements, we shall note, inevitably bear witness also to Scripture's consequent distinctive character and authority.

All Scripture Is "God-Breathed"

We have noted that in 2 Timothy 3:16, "All scripture is inspired by God" (RSV), the Greek adjective *theopneustos* means literally "God-breathed," i.e., "inspired of God." The word "inspired," however, is not to be understood as indicating something "extra" superimposed on the writer or writing, to make the writing different from what it would otherwise be. It indicates rather *how* the writing came into being. It asserts that the writing is a product of the creative activity of the divine breath. The word thus goes right back to the beginning or first cause of the emergence of Scripture and indicates that Scripture has in its origin this distinctive hallmark, that it owes its very existence to the direct, creative activity of God himself. Although men wrote it, it is God who brought it into being. Its content and character have all been decisively determined by the originating and controlling activity of the creative Spirit. For this reason the context affirms that Scripture is profitable "for teaching, for reproof, for correction, and for training for righteousness," since its character and quality, and indeed its very existence, are God-determined.

This idea of God "breathing" and of the divine "breath" is familiar to students of the Old Testament. It is a graphic metaphor applied to the activity of God, especially to the Holy Spirit, who is the executor of the Godhead. So we read in Psalm 33:6, "By the word of the Lord were the heavens made; and all the host of them by the breath of his mouth." The breath of God is thus almighty to create. By this breath not only the heavens but also man was created. "And the Lord God formed man of the dust of the ground, and breathed into his nostrils the breath of life; and man became a living soul" (Gen. 2:7). Or again, we read in Job 33:4, "The Spirit of God hath made me, and the breath of the Almighty hath given me life." The breath or breathing of God speaks, therefore, of the activity of the one who is the first and final cause of all things. Scripture is said to be the product of his activity, the work of the Holy Spirit of God himself. Nor should we overlook that what is thus said to be Spirit-produced is the actual written Word. Its emergence and its enduring record were the consummation and intended goal of the Spirit's activity.

Men Spake from God

The ascription to Scripture of this special divine origin and consequent unique character is, either explicitly or implicitly, confirmed as true by many statements made elsewhere in the Bible. For instance, in 2 Peter 1:19–21 the prophetic word given to us in Scripture is said to be the more sure, and a source of light in our darkness to which we ought to give heed, because of its extraordinary and divine origin. Let us note carefully the sequence of thought in Peter's reasoning. "First of all," he writes, "you must understand this, that no prophecy of scripture is a matter of one's own interpretation, because no prophecy ever came by the impulse of man, but men moved by the Holy Spirit spoke from God" (RSV).

So the primary truth about Scripture, the very first thing we need to recognize about it, is that no prophecy in it was produced, or can be interpreted, through any individual man acting independently and alone. Genuine prophecies and their true interpretation do not just break forth "from man." The Spirit of God brings such prophecies to expression to reveal the mind of God; and the same Spirit alone can make plain, to those who hear and study these prophecies, what that mind is.

This essential dependence of true prophecy upon God and not upon man is primarily shown in the way in which it came to exist at all. For it was not brought into being simply by any man's desire, decision, and determination to give it utterance. It is not "from man." Man is not the prime mover in its production. Indeed, man acting independently, and solely on his own will and initiative, cannot produce it. For true prophecy has never emerged, except when men have been taken up into an activity of the Spirit of God, and borne along to the place, or into the circumstances and the conditions, where they gave utterance to words of which God was the primary originating cause. Clearly, therefore, what matters most for us is the actual words they were thus enabled to express. The enduring God-given witness to the truth is contained in, and conveyed by, the writing. These words, therefore, we ought to accept as brought into being by the Spirit of God for our instruction. They have supreme and final authority because they are from God himself. He is their real author.

In any attempt to appreciate the method of inspiration, or the way in which men specially chosen and prepared were moved to speak divinely intended words, it becomes us, as finite creatures, to recognize, in humility and with reverent awe, that the ways of God are past finding out. Men still cannot fully tell how a human child is brought to birth and a new independent personality created. In a very real sense a baby has human parents and is "born of woman." Yet in a deeper sense it is "of God." If this is true of ordinary childbirth, how very much more was it true of the birth of him who was "conceived of the Holy Ghost, born of the virgin Mary." Also, it seems in harmony with the revealed truth of God to suggest that a similarity in principle prevails between the manner of the birth of the incarnate Word of God and the method of the composition of the written Word of God. Scripture was, so to speak, "conceived or inspired of the Holy Ghost, and thought and uttered by human prophets." Scripture is obviously the work of human writers; and yet it is still more the product and result of a special and supernormal activity of the Spirit. So we may rightly believe it to possess a corresponding perfection.

In thus considering the divine inspiration of Scripture, the difficulty for the human mind is to reconcile the perfection of the divine determination of the finished product with the true freedom and inevitable imperfections of the human writers. How can these two characteristics both apply to the production of Scripture? In principle this problem is only a particular form of the general difficulty always involved in any attempt to reconcile divine predestination and human freewill.

A significant scriptural illustration of the joint working of human freedom and divine predetermination is provided by the one utterance of Caiaphas which is said to be prophecy. To his fellow members of the Jewish Sanhedrin he said, "It is expedient for us that one man should die for the people, and that the whole nation perish not" (John 11:50). In their immediate historical setting the meaning of these words is obvious enough. They were a counsel of political expediency. It was better, as Caiaphas saw it, to make Jesus a scapegoat and to sacrifice one life than to risk a popular messianic uprising. For such an uprising could only call forth a drastic Roman intervention, and then the priestly aristocracy, to which Caiaphas belonged, would be the first to suffer. Such was the meaning intended by human freedom.

These words of Caiaphas were thought worthy of a place in the gospel record for an entirely different reason, however. The evangelist interpreted them prophetically, as words not from Caiaphas but from God. He saw the meaning intended by the controlling Spirit. To him the words were a revelation—a revelation all the more remarkable because it was so completely hidden from the mind of the man who uttered the words. "And this spake he," writes John (11:51), "not of himself" (note the words); "but being the high priest that year, he prophesied that Jesus should die for that nation." For the high priest had a yearly office, which only he could fulfill, that is, on the day of atonement to make a propitiation for the sin of the people with the blood of sacrifice. And none other than he, fulfilling his own priestly office in a way far beyond his knowing, gave counsel to the Jews that in this year, the year when all types were fulfilled, it was expedient that a man, not an animal victim, die for the people. He designated, as it were, the sacrifice which was to take away sin and procure salvation. And so his words about the death of Jesus appear in the Scriptures not as an expression of the natural mind of Caiaphas, though on the lower level they are expressive of this, but as an expression of the mind of the Spirit, revealing the purpose of God thus to provide the sacrificial Lamb to take away the sin of God's people.

If, therefore, the inspiring Spirit can thus secure the utterance of divinely intended words from the mouth of an opponent of Christ, and words actually spoken by him in an entirely different sense from their divinely intended meaning, is it unreasonable to believe that all words of Scripture—many of them spoken and written by devout saints and uniquely illumined souls—are, all of them, to be received not chiefly nor exclusively as from man, but rather and primarily from God? It behooves us, therefore, submissively to receive them as an expression of the divine mind and as intended to contribute toward our better understanding of God's ways.

Words of Prophets and Apostles Were God-Given

If we are to do full justice to the witness of Scripture concerning its inspiration, another necessary and rewarding study pertains to the biblical use of the term "prophet," and the biblical indication of how true prophets function.

What distinguishes and characterizes the prophets of Scripture is that they were men unto whom "the word of God came." As simply stated by a writer a century ago, the biblical term "prophet" constantly designates "a man whose mouth utters the words of God" (L. Gäussen, *Theophneustia: The Plenary Inspiration of the Holy Scriptures,* p. 62). "A prophet in the Bible is a man in whose mouth God puts the words which he wishes to be heard upon earth." To illustrate this meaning on the more human level, let us notice the description given in Scripture of Aaron's relation to Moses as his spokesman. It is recorded that God said to Moses, "Thou shalt speak unto him, and put words in his mouth. . . . And he shall be thy spokesman unto the people; and he shall be . . . to thee instead of a mouth, and thou shalt be to him instead of God" (Ex. 4:15–16). Again later, God said, "See, I have made thee a god to Pharaoh: and Aaron thy brother shall be thy prophet" (Ex. 7:1). Clearly, therefore, a prophet is one who speaks words which God puts into his mouth.

Next, let us observe, from the record in 1 Samuel 3, how Samuel was "established to be a prophet of the Lord," and how "all Israel from Dan even to Beersheba knew." The chapter dramatically records his first experience of the word of God coming to him. It was not a private message for his own soul, but a word about Eli that had to be publicly uttered. He was thereby called to become a prophet and to speak forth the word which God had thus given to him. From then on this became his repeated experience. "The Lord revealed himself to Samuel in Shiloh by the word of the Lord. And the word of Samuel came to all Israel."

It was through the burden and constraint of such an experience of being given God's words to proclaim that prophets said with conviction, and unmistakable awareness, "Thus saith the Lord." It was clear that thereby they meant, "These are not my ideas, but words from God himself, which I simply must declare." Such was the irresistible urge, and at times the almost intolerable burden, of being compelled to become the Lord's mouthpiece. "The Lord God hath spoken, who can but prophesy?" (Amos 3:8).

Here we cannot do better than let Scripture provide its own explicit and repeated witness through a selection of quotations. All indicate in different ways that the prophets' spoken and written words were God-given. When they had declared their message, it was characteristic of the prophets for instance, to add "For the mouth of the Lord hath spoken it" (Isa. 40:5; 58:14; Mic. 4:4). Jeremiah looks for the man "to whom the mouth of the Lord hath spoken, that he may declare it" (Jer. 9:12). Aaron is said to have spoken to the elders of the children of Israel "all the words which the Lord hath spoken unto Moses" (Ex. 4:30). David declares, "The Spirit of the Lord spake by me, and his word was in my tongue" (2 Sam. 23:2). The Lord is said to have "put a word in Balaam's mouth" (Num. 23:5). Similarly "the word of God came upon Shemaiah the man of God" (1 Kings 12:22). And God said unto Jeremiah, "Behold, I have put my words in thy mouth" (Jer. 1:9); and to Ezekiel, "Thou shalt speak my words unto them" (Ezek. 2:7).

The unmistakable scriptural testimony, therefore, is that in their inspired utterances David and the prophets functioned as the mouth of the Holy Spirit. The apostle Peter explicitly acknowledged this in the very early days of the church. He appealed, for instance, to "this scripture . . . which the Holy Ghost by the mouth of David spake before concerning Judas" (Acts 1:16). He prayed to God as himself the author of Psalm 2, "who by the mouth of thy servant David hast said, Why did the heathen rage?" (Acts 4:25). Similarly Zacharias recalled what God "spake by the mouth of his holy prophets" (Luke 1:70). So according to the language and witness of the Scriptures its prophecies may be said to be the words of God put into, or expressed through, the mouth of man.

The evidence about prophetic utterance thus far adduced concerns primarily the period and the production of the Old Testament Scriptures. The New Testament also, however, contains some explicit witness to similar activity by the inspiring Spirit, giving to the apostles right utterance in the things of God for the edification of his church. When Christ himself had warned his commissioned witnesses about the opposition they would meet, and about the ways in which they would need to answer charges brought against them, he had said, "But when they deliver you up, take no thought how or what ye shall speak: for it shall be given you in that same hour what ye shall speak. For it is not ye that speak, but the Spirit of your Father which speaketh in you" (Matt. 10:19–20). Christ also promised his apostles similar divine cooperation in the recording of his own work and teaching when he said of the Spirit, "He shall teach you all things, and bring all things to your remembrance, whatsoever I have said unto you" (John 14:26). He similarly promised that the Spirit would guide them into all truth by speaking to them words from God and from Christ. For as Christ said, even the Spirit speaks "not of himself; but whatsoever he shall hear, that shall he speak . . . for he shall receive of mine and shall shew it unto you" (John 16:13–14).

We find, too, in confirmation of this, that Paul later testifies that his apostolic insight and utterance are wholly Spirit-given. He says that the purposes of God in Christ toward men, and the things prepared for them, are wholly beyond the natural perception and imagination of men; but that God has revealed them to his apostles by his Spirit, and that they are, by the same Spirit, enabled to give right expression to them "not in the words which man's wisdom teacheth, but which the Holy Ghost teacheth" (1 Cor. 2:9–13). So in New Testament and Old Testament alike, the very words of apostles and prophets were God-given.

In this connection it is also noteworthy that the men whom the Spirit of God thus used to utter his messages were conscious at times of the compulsion of both divine constraint and restraint. On the one hand, they had to declare all the God-given words; on the other, they could not add other words of their own choosing. This compulsion is particularly noticeable in the case of the prophets, who would have chosen to speak differently if they could; but they could not. So Balaam said, and repeated, "If Balak would give me his house full of silver and gold, I cannot go beyond the commandment of the Lord, to do either good or bad of mine own mind; but what the Lord saith, that will I speak" (Num. 22:18; 24:13). Similarly Micaiah, when urged to speak good unto King Ahab and not evil, answered, "As the Lord liveth, what the Lord saith unto me, that will I speak" (1 Kings 22:13–14).

The prophets' sense of compulsion to speak their God-given words, and these only, is significantly complemented in Scripture by a solemn injunction, and ultimately by a severe warning, to all who read God-given words, not to add to, or take away from, what is written. So in Deuteronomy 4:2

we read, "Ye shall not add unto the word which I command you, neither shall ye diminish ought from it"; and in Revelation 22:18–19, in the section which by God's providential overruling closes the whole canon of Scripture, we read, "For I testify unto every man that heareth the words of the prophecy of this book, If any man shall add unto these things, God shall add unto him the plagues that are written in this book: and if any man shall take away from the words of the book of this prophecy, God shall take away his part out of the book of life, and out of the holy city, and from the things which are written in this book."

Scripture Quoted in Scripture as the Word of God Himself

When parts of Scripture already recorded are quoted in Scripture by later writers, it is noteworthy that the words thus quoted are sometimes introduced simply as words spoken by God, or as being the entrance of the Lord given through a human prophet. Significantly, too, this characteristic applies not only to those words which in the Old Testament are explicitly said to be utterances of God, but also to words from other parts of the Scripture as well.

So in the Gospel according to Matthew, for instance, Old Testament questions are introduced which are said to have been "spoken by the Lord through the prophet" (RV) or "what the Lord has spoken by the prophet" (RSV) (cf. Matt. 1:22; 2:15). Also, our Lord himself, in his discussion with the Pharisees about divorce, according to Matthew 19:3–6, not only quoted Genesis 2:24 as an authoritative statement about marriage, but explicitly introduced it as a statement made by the Creator himself at the time of man's creation. "Have ye not read," said Jesus, "that he which made them at the beginning made them male and female, and said, For this cause shall a man leave his father and mother, and shall cleave to his wife: and they twain shall be one flesh?" Furthermore, our Lord treated this statement as a decisive, authoritative expression of the divine mind and purpose about marriage, sufficient in itself to justify the deduction that for man to separate those joined in marriage by divine appointment is wholly improper. Here, therefore, because divine in origin, words from these ancient Jewish writings are appealed to as determining for all time what is proper in the marriage relationship.

Later in Hebrews 1:7–8 words about God, spoken in praise by the psalmist, are quoted as spoken by God himself, and therefore, as carrying decisive weight and authority. We read, "And of all the angels he saith,

Who maketh his angels spirits, and his ministers a flame of fire" (a quotation from Psalm 104:4). "But unto the Son he saith, Thy throne, O God, is forever and ever" (a quotation from Psalm 45:6).

Not only are words from the Old Testament thus introduced as spoken by God himself, but sometimes in the New Testament they are used as words having present application, because the living, unchanging God is speaking them now. They are his present words for today. So, 2 Corinthians 6:16 quotes words from Leviticus 26:12: "I will dwell in them and walk in them, and I will be their God, and they shall be my people," to indicate God's present purpose for his redeemed people, and to justify Paul's appeal to his readers that they separate themselves from idolatry and uncleanness.

Similarly, in Hebrews 3:7, words from Psalm 95:7, "Today if ye will hear his voice," are quoted, not as words spoken by the psalmist long ago, but as words being spoken in the present by God the Spirit—"as the Holy Ghost saith."

Scripture, therefore—so Scripture itself bears witness—may be used as a means of present living communion between God and the individual soul. For what God has once said he may be regarded as still saying (except, of course, where his own fuller revelation has superseded what was previously given only in part or in figure); and responsive words which believers of old have thus been stirred to utter, believers today may rightly still make their own. For example, in Hebrews 13:5–6, we read, "Be content with such things as ye have: for he hath said, I will never leave thee, nor forsake thee [a quotation from Joshua 1:5]. So that we may boldly say, The Lord is my helper, and I will not fear what man shall do unto me [a quotation from Psalm 118:6]."

All this rich wealth of meaning and usage still to be found in Scripture is possible only because it can be treated and trusted as divinely provided for the permanent enrichment of God's people. It is, therefore, to be regarded and used as God-given, words issued on his authority, and therefore words of supreme and unchanging worth. Such, then, is Scripture's own witness to the character and consequence of its divine inspiration.

Divinely Intended Purpose of Scripture

Since the direction of too much attention to the details of the process of the production of Scripture by human writers may only perplex us with questions which we cannot answer, it is well that we should recognize that any workman's activity is to be properly understood and appreciated only in the light of his aim and ultimate achievement. This means that, in seeking to estimate the full significance of the divine inspiration of the Bible, we should not primarily look at the materials, the men, and the method used in its composition, but consider rather the finished product as a whole in the light of its divinely intended purpose. For the completed revelation of Scripture, taken as a whole, is meant to serve ends which cannot be served by its constituent parts or contributing human authors and sources taken independently.

Modern historical and literary criticism, with its excess of devotion to analysis and source criticism, has largely been a movement in the wrong direction, which has often involved a real disregard both of the true source and of the proper purpose of the inspiration of Scripture.

It is important, therefore, that we recognize the twofold end of Scripture as a divinely inspired whole. This is, in the first place, Christological, and, in the second, soteriological. The purpose of Scripture is, first, to testify of Christ, "For the testimony of Jesus is the spirit of prophecy" (Rev. 19:10). In the volume of the book it is written of him (cf. Heb. 10:7). The purpose of Scripture is, second, to make men "wise unto salvation through faith which is in Christ Jesus" (2 Tim. 3:15). Scripture has been inspired of God to promote the salvation of the world. The Scripture was written, and Christ died and rose again in fulfillment of its prophetic revelation, that repentance and remission of sins might be preached in Christ's name to all nations (cf. Luke 24:46–47). The New Testament was added to the Old Testament in fulfillment of the promise that the Holy Spirit would guide the apostles into all the truth about the Christ (cf. John 16:12–15). The full significance of the divine inspiration of Scripture can, therefore, be seen in its proper context only if it is seen as an essential part of the redeeming activity of God for the salvation of mankind.

Scripture serves this divine purpose by providing a true record of what God has done in history for man's salvation, and of those events which, under God's providence, have happened and been recorded for man's instruction. This record is by divine inspiration doubly true. On the one hand, it is historically reliable; it corresponds in its witness to what happened. On the other hand, it is sublime and perfect in its discernment and presentation of spiritual values. These two complementary senses in which the scriptural record is true are explicitly emphasized in John 19:35: "And he that hath seen hath borne witness, and his witness is true: and he knoweth that he saith true" ("he knows that he tells the truth," RSV), "that ye also may believe" (RV). Here John means that what he says is true or factually accurate, for he speaks as an eyewitness; and that his form of presentation is "ideal" (Gk. *alēthinos*), in harmony with, and an adequate expression of, the true meaning and value of the events thus recorded, a presentation intended to lead the reader to faith in the person and work of Christ.

For its proper use, Scripture, which bears such witness to its own divine inspiration, demands from those readers who are enlightened by God's Spirit to share in this conviction about it the submission of unquestioning acceptance. For Scripture provides, not data to be critically sorted out for acceptance or rejection before we can know the truth, but data to be treated as true and trustworthy and of supreme worth, data within whose witness all pursuit of the truth must work, if such pursuit is to progress in proper understanding and enjoyment of all the truth which God has thus been pleased to reveal.

Final Practical Authentication

Scripture itself explicitly mentions two distinguishing characteristics by which words which claim to be divine in origin may be recognized as genuine, because corresponding in character to their author.

One test is the test of *fulfillment* (cf. Deut. 18:21–22; Matt. 5:18). For God does not move indecisively. He never speaks without completing his purpose (cf. Num. 23:19). Fulfillment of Scripture is, therefore, one of the proofs of its divine inspiration. So, when Scripture witnesses to its own fulfillment, or declares that what it says must yet find fulfillment, it confirms its own witness that Scripture is divinely inspired.

The other test of the divine origin of words is the test of unchanging *endurance*, in contrast to the words of men which have their day and become obsolete. For, in the last analysis, all words are like their authors in character. Since men are like the grass that withers, their words similarly cease to carry weight, and become a dead letter. But not so with God. He lives and abides. He never changes. He is the same yesterday and today and forever. So, when he speaks, his words correspond in character to their author. They, too, have enduring and abiding worth. Therefore, Scripture's unfailing survival and strength as a fresh, living, undeniable word of truth in every generation confirm its divine origin. In a world of transient glory, in the midst of an insecure and impermanent created order, the scriptural Word, and the scriptural Word alone, not only continues to confront each generation anew, but increasingly vindicates its truth in fulfillment. "Heaven and earth shall pass away," said Jesus, "but my words shall not pass away" (Matt. 24:35). "For all flesh is as grass, and all the glory of man as the flower of grass. The grass withereth, and the flower thereof falleth away: but the word of the Lord endureth forever" (1 Pet. 1:24–25).

Part 4

Inerrancy

10

"Notes on the Inerrancy of Scripture"

ROBERT PREUS

Evangelicals and Inerrancy

Previously published as "Notes on the Inerrancy of Scripture," in *Evangelicals and Inerrancy: Selections from the Journal of the Evangelical Theological Society*, ed. Ronald Youngblood (Nashville, TN: Thomas Nelson, 1984), 91–104.

This study is offered as an approach to the problem of the inerrancy of Scripture as it concerns evangelical Protestantism today. The attempt is to present a position that agrees with Scripture's testimony concerning itself and with the historic position of the Christian church. At the same time the attempt is made to be timely and to take into account contemporary issues raised by modern biblical theology.

Here we shall try to delineate and clarify what is meant by the inerrancy of Scripture, what is the basis of this dogma, and what are its implications. It is not our purpose to become involved in the technicalities that have often obscured the doctrine or to traverse the labyrinth of intricate discussion that has not infrequently belabored studies of this basic theological truth.

Indeed, a brief treatment such as we are about to give cannot possibly solve the many hermeneutical and isagogical problems that touch upon the inerrancy of Scripture. Yet hermeneutical and isagogical concerns cannot be avoided in a study of this nature. Therefore we have endeavored to lay down general principles concerning these matters that will comport with the inerrancy and sole authority of Scripture.

Thesis

In calling the sacred Scriptures inerrant we recognize in them (a), as words taught by the Holy Spirit (b), that quality that makes them overwhelmingly (c) reliable witnesses (d–e) to the words and deeds of the God who has in his inspired spokesmen and in his incarnate Son disclosed himself to men for their salvation (f).[1]

Note: this definition is very general, seeking as it does to fit all the biblical data (for example, the bold language of prophecy and of adoration, the promises concerning the world to come for which human experience offers only imperfect and insufficient analogies, the expressive and indispensable anthropomorphisms and anthropopathisms used of God, the symbolic use of numbers and other referents in books like Daniel and Revelation, etc.). The definition also agrees, however, with what the church catholic has believed and confessed through her entire history. We offer a few typical examples to bring out this fact.

Augustine, *Epist.* 82 *to Jerome*: "Only to those books which are called canonical have I learned to give honor so that I believe most firmly that no author in these books made any error in writing. I read other authors not with the thought that what they have thought and written is true just because they have manifested holiness and learning!"

Thomas Aquinas, *In Ioh.* 13, *lect.* 1: "It is heretical to say that any falsehood whatsoever is contained either in the gospels or in any canonical Scripture."

Luther (W^2 15:1481): "The Scriptures have never erred." W^2 9:356: "It is impossible that Scripture should contradict itself; it only appears so to senseless and obstinate hypocrites."

Preface to the Book of Concord (Tappert, p. 8): "We have in what follows purposed to commit ourselves exclusively and only, in accordance with the pure, infallible and unalterable Word of God, to that Augsburg Confession which was submitted to Emperor Charles V at the great imperial assembly in Augsburg in the year 1530." *Large Catechism* (Baptism 57. Tappert, p. 444): "My neighbor and I—in short, all men—may err and deceive, but God's Word cannot err." *Formula of Concord* (Epitome, 7:13. Tappert, p. 483): "God's Word is not false nor does it lie."

Calov, *Systema locorum theologicorum* (Wittenberg, 1655–1677), 1:462: "Because Scripture is God's Word which is absolutely true, Scripture

[1] Majuscule letters A–F refer to the six ektheses that will shortly be given in support and clarification of the major thesis.

is itself truth (Ps. 119:43, 86, 142, 160; John 17:17, 19; 2 Sam. 7:28; Ps. 33:4; Gal. 3:1; Col. 1:5; 2 Tim. 2:18; 3:8; Titus 1:1; and James 1:8). Thus, whatever the sacred Scriptures contain is fully true and to be accepted with utmost certainty. Not only must we hold that to be true which is presented in Scripture relative to faith and morals, but we must hold to everything that happens to be included therein. Inasmuch as Scripture has been written by an immediate and divine impulse and all the Scriptures recognize Him as their author who cannot err or be mistaken in any way (Heb. 6:18), no untruth or error or lapse can be ascribed to the God-breathed Scriptures, lest God Himself be accused."

Turrettin, *Institutio Theologiae Elencticae* (Genevae, 1688), 1:79: "We deny that there are any true and real contradictions in Scripture. Our reasons are as follows: namely, that Scripture is God breathed (2 Tim. 3:16), that the Word of God cannot lie or be ignorant of what has happened (Ps. 19:8, 9; Heb. 6:18) and cannot be set aside (Matt. 5:18), that it shall remain forever (1 Pet. 1:25), and that it is the Word of truth (John 17:17). Now how could such things be predicated of Scripture if it were not free of contradictions, or if God were to allow the holy writers to err and lose their memory or were to allow hopeless blunders to enter into the Scriptures?"

Tromp, *De Sacrae Scripturae Inspiratione* (Romae, 1953) 121: "Everything which is contained in sacred Scripture, as attested by the author and in the sense intended by him, is infallibly true."

J. I. Packer, *"Fundamentalism" and the Word of God* (Grand Rapids, MI: Eerdmans, 1958), 95: "Scripture is termed infallible and inerrant to express the conviction that all its teaching is the utterance of God 'who cannot lie,' whose word, once spoken, abides forever, and that therefore it may be trusted implicitly."

Such statements written under different circumstances and at different times evince the remarkable unanimity on this matter that obtained in the church throughout her history. The statements also indicate or infer the following six ektheses, which will serve to delineate and further explain our definition.

Ekthesis A

This "recognition" of the truthfulness of the written Word of God is not primarily intellectual. It takes place in the obedience of faith. The truthfulness and reliability of the Scriptures is an article of faith.

Ekthesis B

The basis of inerrancy rests on the nature of Scripture as God's Word. Inerrancy is an inextricable concomitant of inspiration. Our conviction is that since Scripture is truly and properly speaking God's Word, it will not deceive nor err.[2] Admittedly this is an inference (as in the case of the doctrine of the Trinity or the two natures of Christ), but it is a necessary inference, because God is faithful and his Word (Scripture) is truth, and no Christian theologian until the period of rationalism ever shrank from this inference. It is to be noted that both Christ and the apostles drew the same inference (cf. not only John 10:34; Mark 12:24; Matt 5:18–19, but also Christ's and the apostles' use of the Old Testament: they simply cite it as unconditionally true and unassailable).

Ekthesis C

Our recognition of the reliability of the witness of Scripture is graciously imposed upon us by the Spirit of God, and this through the power of Scripture itself.

Ekthesis D

The nature of inerrancy is essentially twofold: Scripture does not lie or deceive, and Scripture does not err or make mistakes in any affirmation it makes (*falsum formale* and *falsum materiale*). In other words the holy writers, moved by the Spirit of God, infallibly achieve the intent of their writing (cf. the statement of Tromp above). This is what is meant when we say that Scripture is a *reliable witness* to the words and deeds of God. Of his people God demands in the second and eighth commandments that they tell the truth, of his prophets and apostles that they do not lie: God will not countenance lying and prevarication (Prov. 14:5; 19:22; Ps. 63:11; Jer. 23:25ff.; Zeph. 3:13; Acts 5:3; 1 John 2:21, 27). And God himself will not lie nor deceive (Prov. 30:6–7; Num. 23:19; Ps. 89:35; Heb. 6:18). In his written Word he will not break or suspend that standard of truth that he demands of his children. Thus we hear frequently from God's inspired witnesses the claim that they do not deceive, that they are not mistaken,

---

[2] Cf. M. Nicolau and I. Salaverri, S. J., *Sacrae Theologiae Summa* (Madrid, 1958), 1. 1095: "Inerrantiam Scripturae non derivari praecise ex fine scriptoris, ad illa tantum quae ipse docere intendit, sed derivari ex natura inspirationis, ad illa omnis quae vi huius influxus asseruntur." The alluding to many contemporary Roman Catholic sources in notes does not necessarily imply full agreement with these statements or that we should use these statements in any final study on inerrancy. The statements are for the most part quite sound and useful. The fact is that Roman Catholics are the majority of those who write on inerrancy today from a point of view similar to ours.

that they tell the truth (Rom. 9:1; 2 Cor. 11:31; Gal. 1:20; 1 Tim. 2:7). The whole impact of entire books of the Bible depends upon the authoritative and truthful witness of the writer (John 21:24; 1 John 1:1–5a; 2 Pet. 1:15–18). Pertinent to what was just said we must add the following: the truth of the sacred Scriptures must be determined from the sense that is intended (in verse, pericope, book) by the author. This sense in turn must be determined according to sound hermeneutical rules.

It is obvious that such a position on the nature of biblical inerrancy is predicated on a correspondence idea of truth, which in part means this: declarative statements (at least in those biblical genres, or literary forms, that purport to be dealing with fact or history) of Scripture are, according to their intention, true in that they correspond to what has taken place (for example, historical statements), to what obtains (for example, theological affirmations and other affirmations concerning fact), or to what will take place (for example, prophecy). It really ought to go without saying that Scripture, like all cognitive discourse, operates under the rubrics of a correspondence idea of truth (see John 8:46; Eph. 4:25; 1 Kings 8:26; 22:16, 22ff.; Gen. 42:16, 20; Deut. 18:22; Ps. 119:163; Dan. 2:9; Prov. 14:25; Zech. 8:16; John 5:31ff.; Acts 24:8, 11; 1 Tim. 1:15; cf. also the forensic picture that haunts all of Scripture—for example, such concepts as witness, testimony, judge, the eighth commandment, etc., John 21:24).

To speak of inerrancy of purpose (that God achieves his purpose in Scripture) or of Christological inerrancy of Scripture is indeed relevant to the general question of inerrancy but may at the same time be misleading if such a construct is understood as constituting the nature of inerrancy—for then we might speak of the inerrancy of Luther's Little Catechism or of a hymn by Paul Gerhardt, since they successfully achieve their purpose.

The first purpose of Scripture is to bring us to faith in Christ (John 20:31; 2 Tim. 3:15). Involved with this prime purpose of Scripture is Luther's doctrine of the Christocentricity of Scripture (Old Testament as well as New Testament). Such Christocentricity has a soteriological purpose. Only when I understand that Scripture and Christ are *pro me* will I understand the Scriptures (or the inerrancy thereof). But to say that Scripture is inerrant only to the extent that it achieves its soteriological purpose is a misleading position if it is made to be identical with inerrancy or confused with it. How does Scripture achieve this soteriological purpose? By cognitive language. By presenting facts, by telling a history (Old Testament as well as New Testament). To say that there is a purpose in Scripture but no intentionality (for example, intent to give meaning) in the individual books or sections or verses, or to maintain that Scripture is inerrant in its eschatological purpose but not in the intentionality of its individual parts and pericopes, would not only be nonsense (mysticism), reducing all Scripture to the level of some sort of mystical utterances, but would be quite unscriptural (Luke 1:1–4, etc.). The eschatological purpose of Scripture does not cancel or vitiate or render trivial and unimportant the cognitive and factual content of assertions (and the truth of assertions) throughout Scripture but requires all this (Rom. 15:4). And, on the other hand, formal and material inerrancy does not threaten or eclipse the Christological purpose of Scripture but supports it. Nor does such a position (formal and material inerrancy) become tantamount to reading Scripture atomistically. Language is a primary structure of lived experience and cannot be studied in isolation from it. Because the language of imagery in Scripture may not always be adequately analyzed or ever completely exhausted implies neither that it is meaningless (positivism) nor that it is errant ("Christian" positivism). Not orthodoxy but neoorthodoxy has a positivistic, wooden theory of language.[3]

Ekthesis E

Inerrancy is plenary or absolute. (1) It not only pertains to the substance of the doctrines and narratives in Scripture but pertains also to those things that are nonessential, adjunct or *obiter dicta* (Quenstedt, *Systema,* 1:77: "doctrine, ethics, history, chronology, topography or onamastics." (2) It covers not only the primary intent of the various pericopes and verses but also the secondary intent (for example, a passing historical reference within the framework of narrative—that is, that Christ was crucified between two thieves, that wise men visited him at his birth, that Joshua led the children of Israel into Canaan, that Ruth was a Moabitess, Nimrod a hunter, etc., etc.), not only soteriological, eschatological, and religious intent and content of Scripture but also all declarative statements touching history and the realm of nature.

There are various reasons for this strict position. (1) The New Testament cites what might often be considered to be passing statements or negligible items from the Old Testament, accepting them as true and authoritative (Matt. 6:29; 12:42; John 10:35). Jesus accepts the basic frame-

[3]Hoepfl insists that inerrancy is made irrelevant when it is said that historical errors do not affect the intent of Scripture. Cf. *Introductio Generalis in Sacram Scripturam* (Romae, 1958), 123: "Pro ipsis Protestantibus liberalibus magis 'conservatoribus,' qui inspirationis notionem saltem valde deprimunt, quaestio inerrantiae omnino non exsistit, cum errors historici fini S. Scripturae non noceant."

work of the Old Testament history, even those aspects of that history that seem unimportant to many today—for example, Sodom and Gomorrah (Luke 17:27), Lot's wife turning to salt, the murder of Abel (11:51), Naaman (4:27). The New Testament does not recognize levicula in the Old Testament (Rom. 15:4; 2 Tim. 3:16). (2) The primary intent of a passage or pericope is often dependent upon the secondary intent(s). This is so in the nature of the case. For instance, the exodus as a deliverance of God depends on the miraculous events connected with it. (3) The most common argument for the full inerrancy of Scripture as advanced by the older theologians was as follows: If errors are admitted in minor matters recorded in Scripture (matters that do not matter [?]), by what right may one then assume that there is no error in important or doctrinal concerns? How does one determine what matters are important? And does not, after all, everything pertain at least indirectly to doctrine (2 Tim. 3:16)? In other words, to maintain that "things that matter" in Scripture (doctrinal matters) are inerrant and "things that do not matter" (nondoctrinal matters) are errant is both arbitrary and impossible to apply (cf. Calov, *Systema,* 1:606ff.).

Ekthesis F

The practical importance of the doctrine must always be recognized. It consists in this: that, as God is true and faithful, the reader of Scripture can have the assurance that he will not be deceived or led astray by anything he reads in God's Word, Holy Scripture. In no discussion of inerrancy do we find merely an academic interest in maintaining purely a traditional position or in hewing to a party line. Such a practical concern must also be emphasized in our day. Any approach to Scripture or method of interpretation that would make of Scripture something less than trustworthy is sub-Christian and does not take Scripture at its own terms. It must also be borne in mind that the truthfulness of Scripture is never an end in itself but serves the soteriological purpose of Scripture.

Adjuncts to the Doctrine of Biblical Inerrancy

1. *Inerrancy does not imply verbal exactness of quotations* (for example, the words of institution, the words on Jesus' cross). The New Testament ordinarily quotes the Old Testament according to its sense only, sometimes it only alludes to a pericope or verse in the Old Testament, sometimes there are conflations, etc. In the case of extrabiblical citations we ought to assume that the holy writer stands behind and accepts the truth of his

quotation unless the context would indicate otherwise (cf. 2 Chron. 5:9; 8:8, where there are citations from documents that say that a situation obtains "to this day"—that is, when the original document was written). It is helpful to distinguish between the *veritas citationis* (lies, statements of evil men, or, for example, the statements of Job's friends, etc.) and the *veritas rei citatae* (Acts 17:28; Num. 21:14 and possibly 2 Kings 1:18).

2. *Inerrancy does not imply verbal or intentional agreement in parallel accounts of the same event.* For instance, the portrayal of creation in Genesis 1 and in Job 38 are radically different because of a radical difference in the aim of the author. Again, the different evangelists write about our Lord from different vantage points and out of different concerns. Therefore their accounts will differ not only in details (as in the case of any two or three witnesses of the same event) but in aim. We must exercise caution here lest we impose a point of view upon an author which cannot be drawn inductively from Scripture itself. For instance, there is no certain evidence that Matthew is writing for Jews, tying up Christ's life with Old Testament prophecy (John also cites the Old Testament often: 22 times). This is merely a rather safe conjecture. The same may be said concerning John writing on Christ's divinity against Cerinthus. We have no right or good reason to assume that the holy writer tampers with or distorts facts to maintain a point of view. The evangelists claim to be faithful and careful witnesses (John 21:24; Luke 1:1ff.). However, it must be clearly recognized that incomplete history or an incomplete presentation of doctrine in a given pericope is not false history or a false presentation.

3. *Scripture is replete with figures of speech*—for example, metonymy (Luke 16:29), metaphor (Ps. 18:20), personification (Matt. 6:4), synecdoche (Luke 2:1), apostrophe, hyperbole (Matt. 2:3), etc. It should go without saying that figurative language is not errant language. To assert that Scripture, by rounding numbers and employing hyperbole, metaphors, etc., is not concerned about precision of fact (and therefore subject to error) is to misunderstand the intention of biblical language. Figurative language (and not modern scientifically "*precise*" language) is *precisely* the mode of expression that the sacred writers' purposes demand. To imply that figurative language is *ex hypothesi* meaningless *or* that it cannot convey information—truthful and, from its own point of view, *precise* information—is the position of positivism, not the result of sensitive exegesis (for example, "Yanks slaughter Indians" is a meaningful and precise statement). How else does one speak of a transcendent God, of his epiphanies and revelations, than in metaphors and figures of speech? Demetaphorize,

deanthropomorphize, and you are not getting closer to the meaning of such expressions but losing their meaning. Figurative language, then, meets all the canons necessary: (1) that statements perfectly represent the author's meaning, (2) that statements do not mislead the reader or lead him into error of any kind, and (3) that statements correspond to fact when they purport to deal with fact—and this in the case of poetry as well as in the case of straight narrative.

Note: when we interpret or read Scripture we identify ourselves with the writers, not only with their *Sitz im Leben* and their use of language but with their entire spirit and their faith (which is more important, 1 Cor. 2:14–16). We not only understand them but feel and live and experience with them. We become totally involved. To stand back dispassionately and assess and criticize as a modern man would Shelley or Shakespeare or Homer is to fail to interpret Scripture.

4. *Scripture uses popular phrases and expressions of its day*—for example, bowels of mercy, four corners of the earth. Joseph is called the "father" of Christ, etc. No error is involved in the use of such popular expressions. Cf. Ps. 7:9; 22:10.

5. *In describing the things of nature Scripture does not employ scientifically precise language but describes and alludes to things phenomenally as they appear to our senses*—for example, the fixity of stellar constellations and the magnitude of the stars (Isa. 13:10; Judg. 5:20; Job 38:31; Amos 5:8; Job 9:9); the sun and moon called lights and the implication that the moon is larger than the stars (Gen. 1:16) [it *is* larger from our vantage point]; the earth as motionless in a fixed position (Eccles. 1:4; Ps. 93:1); the sun goes around the fixed earth (Eccles. 1:5; Matt. 13:6; Eph. 4:26; note that in Hebrew there is even a phrase for the rising of the sun: *mizralh šemeš*, which means "east," Num. 34:15). Phenomenal language also explains why the bat is classified with birds (Lev. 19:11; cf. Lev. 11:6; Ps. 135:6). Such a classification offers no attempt to be scientific. Many things in the realm of nature are spoken of in poetic language: the spreading out of the heavens (Isaiah 40; Job 9:8), the foundations of the earth (Job 38:6), the pillars of the earth (9:6) and of heaven (26:11), the ends of the earth (Ps. 67:7; 72:8). Note that there is much apostrophe and hyperbole (Mark 4:31) when Scripture speaks of the things of nature. In none of the above instances is inerrancy threatened or vitiated. The intention of the passages cited above is not to establish or vouch for a particular worldview or scientific explanation of things. Because the language is not scientific does not imply that it is not true descriptively.

6. *The various literary forms used by Scripture.* (1) Certain alleged forms are not compatible either with the purpose of Scripture or with its inerrancy. Specifically, any literary genre that would in itself be immoral or involve deceit or error is not compatible with biblical inerrancy and is not to be found in Scripture—for example, myth, etiological tale, midrash, legend, or saga according to the usual designation of these forms. None of these genres fits the serious theological purpose of Scripture. Thus we do not find Scripture presenting material as factual or historical when in truth it is only mythical (2 Pet. 1:16ff.; 1 Tim. 1:4; 4:7; 2 Tim. 4:4).[4]

(2) Apart from the above strictures any form of ancient literature is hypothetically compatible with biblical inerrancy—for example, allegory (Galatians 4), fable (Judg. 9:8–15), etc.—provided the genre is indicated directly or indirectly. At the same time it does no violence to inerrancy if the language of folklore or mythical elements serve as a means to clothe a biblical author's presentation of doctrine (for example, "helpers of Rahab" in Job 9:13; "Leviathan" in Job 3:8 and in Ps. 74:12–15; Idumea as inhabited by centaurs, satyrs, etc. [Is. 34:14], meaning that Idumea will be devastated so that only such animals can live there). We do the same today if in a sermon a pastor refers to a "dog in the manger." As for the midrash, there is no reason to maintain that Scripture cannot employ midrashim any more than other literary forms. In many cases midrash approaches parable in form and purpose. However, the fanciful examples of midrash with the indiscriminate admixture of truth and error and the production of pure fiction to stress a certain lesson is not compatible with the historical character and the inerrancy of Scripture; cf. J. M. Lehrmann, *The World of the Midrash* (London, 1961).[5]

[4] Cf. A Bea, *De Inspiratione et Inerrantia Sacrae Scripturae* (Rome, 1954) 44: "Myth is the expression of some religious or cultic idea through personifications which are regarded as divine entities (e.g., the fertility of the earth and of animals—Astarte). Such myths must be distinguished from mythic literary elements (metaphors, personifications) employed from selected mythology for illustrative purposes. Cf. Is. 27:1 (=Ugarit A+I, 1–2?); Ps. 74:12–17; 89:10–14; 48:3; Job 26:7; Ez. 32:20. Myth, properly so-called, cannot be found in the sacred Scriptures (cf. *EB* n. 60.333); however, that literary elements could be used to adorn or illustrate was already granted by the holy Fathers; cf. S. Greg. Nyss. *PG* 44, 973. On individual passages, see *Biblica* 19 (1938): 444–48; F. Porporato, *Miti e inspirazione biblica*, 1944; id. in *Civ. Catt.* 94 (1943/I): 329–40.
"*Midrashim* technically speaking are rabbinic literary efforts—writings from that era—which are not strictly exegetical but composed for establishing rules for living (*halachah*). 2 Chron. 13:22 and 24:27 do not use the term in this technical sense, but signify merely 'study' or 'work' (cf. Eissfeldt, *Einl.*, p. 605). Since it arbitrarily confuses true and false things, misdrash *per se* is excluded by the holy Scriptures (cf. *EB* n. 474). It can be admitted only if the holy writer clearly indicated that he is writing only for the sake of edification and not for setting forth properly history (cf. *EB* n. 154)."

[5] Cf. *Sacrae Theologiae Summa*, 1:1097: "All literary genres are quite compatible with inspiration, if they are not by their very nature immoral (as in the case of certain classical poetry) or if they do not tend to lead into error. Thus myths considered as false religious fables (e.g., the personification of natural things such as the fertility of the earth as divine beings is a literary form not consonant with inspiration). But a myth merely cited in Scripture or used as a mere literary adornment may be admitted, but as something merely cited, or as something purely metaphorical. . . . We can even allow that fictitious narratives (are present) in the Scriptures,

7. *Biblical historiography.* (1) Some biblical writers use and cite sources for their history. We must assume that the biblical author by the way in which he cites sources believes that these sources speak the truth, that they are reliable sources. Therefore he follows them. The contrary contention is certainly possible, but it must be proved in individual cases (implicit citations, cf. 2 Samuel). In the case of explicit citations (the words of a character in a history) we assume the truth of the matter cited, but this again depends upon the intention of the hagiographer. We can assume the truth of the matter cited only if the holy writer formally or implicitly asserts that he approved it and judges to be true what he asserts in the citation (cf. Acts 17:29).

(2) Historical events are not described phenomenally as are the data of nature.[6]

(3) The historical genre employed by Scripture is apparently a unique form. As it cannot be judged according to the canons of modern scientific historiography, it cannot be judged by the mythological and legendary or even historical forms of ancient contemporary civilizations—for example, we take the ancient Babylonian and Ugaritic accounts of creation as pure myth, but quite clearly the biblical cannot be taken as such.[7]

---

provided that they are recognized as such and that of necessity the truth related by the words of the story is in the proper sense not historical. Thus, there is the allegorical mode of speaking in Scripture, such as we find in Song of Songs which is an allegorical song describing the love and mystical union between Jahveh and His people. And it is true that in the different literary forms of Scripture, whether poetical or doctrinal or narrative, (fables) are interspersed."

[6] Cf. Bea, *De Inspiratione* 45: "'History according to appearance' is based upon a false foundation, namely this, that principles which obtain relative to matters of nature can be transferred to historical concerns. Historical sources or general opinion are not 'appearances of happenings'; the telling of a certain happening *per se* does not amount to announcing that something appeared to the senses, as in the realm of nature, nor is it tantamount to say what the common people think about a happening; rather it is the announcing of the happening itself." Cf. also *Sacrae Theologiae Summa*, 1:1097: "On the other hand, history is not concerned with phenomena which are continuously apparent and with things which men describe according to appearance, but history concerns itself with *things that have happened, just as they have happened*" (italics theirs.)

[7] Cf. Bea, *De Inspiratione* 46–48: "In its own characteristics Israelite writing of history far surpasses all other Semitic historiography . . . Albright, *The Archaeology of Pal.* (1932), 128. . . . In a certain sense Hebrew historiography can be compared with the Hittite (cf. *Annales Mursilis* II, ca. 1353–1325; *Apologia Hattusil.*, ca. 1295–1260), but the Israelitish writing of history surpasses this in liveliness, in its simple manner, and sincere way of narrating, in psychological depth and breadth; in particular it is not a 'courtly' or 'official' manner of narrating . . ."

"The manner of writing among the ancients definitely differs from the modern. Firstly, the ancients considered the writing of history to be an art (cf. Cicero). Thus it was adorned greatly, for instance, with fictitious speeches to express certain ideas. Such historiography pays more attention to give the sense of a speech than to bringing out the exact words; it employs numerical schemata (30, 40, 70); it uses mnemonic techniques (such as etymologies); it is careless concerning exact chronology; it uses genealogies as shortcuts to history; it narrates in 'concentric circles' rather than in straight continuous exposition, etc. Now all of these devices, provided that they are properly considered, in no way conflict with the integrity of the narratives. . . .

"Ancient history is not a genre of its own peculiar type which is less interested in telling the truth than modern history. Rather it has different aims, different ways of exposition from modern history. Therefore it is necessary in the case of all the individual authors to investigate accurately what sources they use, how they make judgments from these sources, what style they employ, what purpose they intend. Only then are we able to assess rightly and judiciously concerning their historical merit. . . .

(4) Chronology and genealogies are not presented in Scripture in the full and orderly manner in which we might present a chronicle or family tree today. Scripture often spreads out time for the sake of symmetry or harmony, hysteron proteron is often employed, and also prolepsis (John 17:4; 13:31. Again, genealogies often omit many generations (cf. 1 Chron. 26:24, where Moses, Gershorm, Shubael are given, covering a period of perhaps more than four hundred years; or cf. Heb. 7:9–10, where Levi is said to be in the loins of Abraham, his father, when Melchizedek met him. Thus any ancestor is the father of all his descendants).

8. *We must grant that there is often a sensus plenior in Scripture pericopae in the sense of 1 Peter 1:10–12*. That is to say, the writer of Scripture is not in every respect a child of his time, conditioned by his own cultural milieu, but he often writes for a later age. However, we cannot countenance a *sensus diversus et disperatus relate ad sensus litteralem obvium hagiographi*, which would conflict with biblical inerrancy and turn Scripture into a waxen nose. We hold only to a profounder and sometimes more distinct sense than the writer may have perceived as he expressed himself. This has serious implications relative to the New Testament use and interpretation of the Olf Testament. The New Testament does not misinterpret or do violence to the Old Testament when it interprets. *Sensus litteralis Scripturae unicus est* does not imply that the sacred writer understands the full divine implication of all his words.

9. *Pseudepigrapha*. Pseudonymity in the sense of one writer pretending to be another in order to secure acceptance of his own work is illicit and not compatible with inerrancy. That the motives for such action may be construed as good does not alter the fact that fraud or forgery has been perpetrated. The fact that such a practice was carried on in ancient times does not justify it nor indicate that the practice was considered moral. When in ancient times a pious fraud was found out and the authenticity of a work disproved, the work itself was suspect (cf. *Fragmentum Muratorianum* 5,

---

"The intention of the inspired historiographers is to write *true* history. When they made use of the narrative genre, this presupposes per se that they desire to tell of things that *have happened*. . . .

"That the facts connected with revelation are sometimes (for example, in the first eleven chapters of Genesis) presented in a simple manner, a manner accommodated to the comprehension of less cultured men, that they are presented figuratively and anthropomorphically, does not imply that we can call these narratives any less truly historical although they are not history in our modern technical meaning of the term; cf. *EB* 581, and *Verb. Dom.* 25 (1946): 354–56.

"The Judaic as well as the Christian tradition understood the biblical narratives in the strictly historical sense; cf. the sayings of Christ (Lk. 4:25; 6:3ff.; 17:32; Matt. 12:40) and the sayings of the apostles (Heb. 11:17–40; 2 Pet. 2:5–8), in which facts of minor or secondary importance are set forth as history. . . . That Christ and the apostles simply 'accommodated' themselves to their own contemporaries cannot be asserted a priori, but must be proved in each individual case where there might seem to be some special reason for granting this."

where the *finctae* letters of Paul to the Laodiceans and the Alexandrians were not accepted by the church for that very reason).

Pseudonymity must be carefully delimited. Pseudonymity is deliberate fraud (for any reason whatsoever). It has nothing to do with anonymity. Nor would it be pseudonymity if a later writer culled under inspiration all the wisdom sayings of Solomon, gathering them into a volume and presenting them for what they are—Solomon's wisdom. His contemporaries know that Solomon has not written the book but understand the sayings and the wisdom to be Solomon's (similar to this: that we have the words of Christ in the Gospels). In such a case no deception is involved. In the case of the Pastoral Epistles this could not be assumed by any stretch of the imagination. The letters are written to give the impression that they come directly from Paul, claiming his authority. If they were not in fact Pauline a deception has taken place, a successful deception until lately.[8]

10. Etymologies in Scripture are often according to sound and not (obviously) according to modern linguistic analysis. This fact does not affect inerrancy. The ancients are not thinking of etymologies in the modern sense.[9]

11. The inerrancy and the authority of Scripture are inseparably related. This fact has been consistently recognized by Reformation theologians who have often included inerrancy and authority under the rubric of infallibility. What is meant is that without inerrancy the *sola scriptura* principle cannot be maintained or practiced. An erring authority for all Christian doctrine (like an erring Word of God) is an impossible and impracticable *contradictio in adjecto*.

12. In approaching the Scriptures as children of God who are under the Scriptures it is well to recall and observe two basic principles of our Reformation fathers: (1) Scripture is *autopistos*—that is to say, we are to believe

[8] Cf. J. I. Packer, *"Fundamentalism" and the Word of God* (Grand Rapids, MI: Eerdmans, 1958), 182ff.

[9] Cf. J. Levie, *The Bible, Word of God in Words of Men* (New York, 1962), 220–21: "We know that in all countries the common people very often invent as an afterthought etymological explanations for the name of a given place or given tribe on the basis of quite arbitrary associations of ideas or words. Is it legitimate to admit that here too the sacred writer is content to hand down to us the popular derivations customary in his environment or should we be obliged to believe that, by virtue of inspiration, these derivations are the true linguistic explanations of the words in question, and should therefore be accepted by present-day scholars?

"It is now generally recognized that the inspired writer is only reporting these attempted etymologies as he found them in folklore of his country. The literary form he adopts, which is that of popular history, clearly shows that he has no intention of offering us scientific derivations of the modern kind, but popular derivations in the style of his own times.

"Here are a few examples taken from ten chapters of Genesis, 16 to 26:—16:13 (Atta el Roi); 16:14 (Lachai Roi); 17:17; 18:12–15; 21:6 which give three derivations of the name Isaac (these clearly show by their differences that the writer intended to give a simple report and to make no attempt at criticism); 19:22 (Segor); 21:31 (Bersabee); 22:14 (Yahweh Yireh); 25:25 (Jacob); 25:30–31 (Edom); 26:20 (Eseq); 26:21 (Sitna); 26:22 (Rechoboth); 26:33 (Schibea)."

its utterances simply because Scripture, the Word of God, makes these utterances (inerrancy is always to be accepted on faith!), and we are to believe without the need of any corroborating evidence. This would apply to statements about God, but also to statements about events in history.

(2) Scripture is *anapodeiktos*—that is, self-authenticating. It brings its own demonstration, the demonstration of the Spirit and of power. Again no corroborating evidence is necessary or sought for. Now *sola scriptura* means all this, and it means as well that there are no outside criteria for judging the truthfulness or factual content of scriptural assertions (for example, neither a modern scientific world view nor modern "scientific histonography"). We accept the assertions of Scripture on faith. For instance, the fact that the creation story or the flood or the story of Babel has some parallels in other Semitic and ancient lore gives no right to conclude that these accounts in Scripture are mythical (any more than we have the right to conclude that Christ's resurrection is not historical because there are mythical resurrections recorded in history). Such an interpretation would involve a violation of the *sola scriptura* principle. At the same time it is possible that a changed worldview (for example, our modern view as opposed to the Newtonian view of absolute time and space) will open for consideration a new interpretation of a biblical pericope, although it can never determine our interpretation of Scripture.

It is particularly important to maintain the above principles in our view of the tendency to allow extrabiblical data (particularly historical and archaeological data) to encroach on the absolute authority of Scripture.

11

"Inerrancy and Inspiration"

RENÉ PACHE

The Inspiration and Authority of Scripture

Previously published as "Inerrancy and Inspiration," in *The Inspiration and Authority of Scripture*, trans. Helen I. Needham (1969; repr., Chicago: Moody, 1974), 120–40. Reprinted with permission of Moody Press.

Definitions and Generalities

The definition of verbal, plenary inspiration (cf. chap. 7, subhead "Definitions")[1] implies that in drawing up the original manuscripts, the sacred authors were guided in such a way that they transmitted perfectly, without error, the exact message which God desired to communicate to men.

The terms "inerrancy" and "infallibility" seem to us practically interchangeable. There are those who think that the word "infallibility" smacks too much of the idea of papal authority, a treatment of the Bible as a piece of paper that automatically settles every question. The fact is that if Scripture is infallible, it cannot err; and if it is inerrant, this is because it contains no mistakes.

Inerrancy is the point of the *theopneustia*: it delineates sharply that which separates evangelical biblicists, on the one hand, from liberals and dialecticians (men who deny it) on the other. While faith rests on an ineffable and spiritual plane, the doctrine of inerrancy, on the level of observable facts, is the one more open to the attacks of unbelief (suggested by H. Blocher in a message given at Morges, Switzerland, in 1964).

---

[1] Editor's note: "We believe that in the composition of the original manuscripts, the Holy Spirit guided the authors even in their choice of expressions—and this throughout all the pages of the Scriptures—still without effacing the personalities of the different men." From René Pache, "Plenary and Verbal Inspiration of the Scriptures," in *The Inspiration and Authority of Scripture*, trans. Helen I. Needham (Chicago: Moody, 1974), 71.

We are not inventing this doctrine; it is found in the great confessions mentioned in more detail in chapter 20.[2] Our fathers in the faith, in fact, considered the Scripture as "the criterion of all truth" (la Rochelle), "the very Word of God" (Second Helvetic Confession), and "divine and canonical" (Waldensian churches of Piedmont). The Westminster Confession adds: "Our full persuasion and assurance of the infallible truth and divine authority thereof is from the inward work of the Holy Spirit. The Old Testament in Hebrew and the New Testament in Greek, inspired by God, and by His singular care and providence kept pure in all ages, are therefore authentical."

As for Calvin, he goes so far as to say: "It obtains the same complete credit and authority with believers, when they are satisfied of its divine origin, as if they heard the very words pronounced by God himself."

What is the source of the doctrine of inerrancy? It arises for us out of the nature and declarations of the Scriptures themselves. They everywhere present themselves as being the Word of God. When the Lord speaks, he cannot lie; neither can he teach truth by means of error. His veracity as well as his power are at stake. If he spoke erroneously at the beginning or mingled the true with the false, what could we think of him? With our eternal salvation standing or falling on it, what certainty could we find in a revelation like that? Or what if God, after giving to the sacred authors a message exact in every detail, had showed himself unable afterward to effect its transmission in a way worthy of confidence? Would this not mean that he had deceived us? And in that case, what would have been the use of his initial revelation?

The Bible's Testimony to Its Own Inerrancy

First of all, is it legitimate for us to base our faith in inerrancy on the Bible's own testimony? Isn't this just a vicious circle: like dispensing with debate simply on the declarations of the accused or of the interrogated witnesses? No, for here we have the Lord himself, the only source of all true knowledge. Just as we go to Scripture for all the doctrines concerning judgment, salvation, the future, etc., we can deduce only from the revelation a sure teaching concerning the written Word. Our first question regarding any subject must be "What do the Scriptures have to say about this?" (Rom. 4:3; Gal. 4:30).

[2]Editor's note: see "Testimony of the Church to the Inspiration of the Bible," in Pache, *The Inspiration and Authority of Scripture*, 233–47.

The authors of the Old Testament speak most explicitly: 3,808 times they claim to be transmitting the very words of God.

After the giving of the law, Moses declared: "Ye shall not add unto the word which I command you, neither shall ye diminish from it" (Deut. 4:2; cf. 6:1–2, 6–9; cf. 12:32).

The psalmist cries out over and over: "The law of Jehovah is perfect. . . . I trust in thy word. . . . I have seen an end of all perfection; but thy commandment is exceeding broad. . . . Thy word is very pure; therefore, thy servant loveth it. . . . Thy law is truth. . . . All thy commandments are truth. . . . The sum of thy word is truth; and every one of thy righteous ordinances endureth forever. . . . Let my tongue sing of thy word; for all thy commandments are righteousness" (Ps. 19:7; 119:42, 96, 140, 142, 151, 160, 172).

Christ specifically confirmed the whole Old Testament. He did not find any error that needed to be eliminated, nor did he express the slightest doubt about any part of it. He consistently based his arguments and exhortations on Scripture. He declared: "One jot or one tittle shall in no wise pass away from the law, till all things be accomplished" (Matt. 5:18). Discussing a single word with the Jews, He said: "The scripture cannot be broken" (John 10:35). And he exclaimed toward the end of his days on earth: "Sanctify them in the truth; thy word is truth" (17:17).

The apostles also gave witness to the perfection of the Scriptures. Paul said of the law that it is holy—"and the commandment [is] holy, and righteous, and good" (Rom. 7:12). The apostle's teaching is so explicit (e.g., Gal. 3:16–17) that any error in the Scriptures cited would take away the very foundation of that teaching.

For the author of the epistle to the Hebrews, the Word of God, living, effectual, and penetrating, goes so far as to judge even our feelings and our innermost thoughts (Heb. 4:12). It is not our prerogative to set ourselves up as its critic.

James, describing the Word, speaks of it as "the perfect law, the law of liberty" (1:22–25). Convinced of its supreme authority, he addresses to us this solemn warning: "Think ye that the scripture speaketh in vain?" (4:5).

John brings the written revelation to a close with these words: "If any man shall add unto them [the things which are written], God shall add unto him the plagues which are written in this book: and If any man shall take away from the words of the book of this prophecy, God shall take away his part from the tree of life" (Rev. 22:18–19). If it is the Lord who has given a message from himself, who could have the audacity to attempt to "complete" it or to despise any of it, even those parts which he might think of slight importance?

A testimony as clear and as unanimous as this is truly impressive. Nowhere does Scripture in one place declare erroneous what it gives in another place, and this holds true for even the smallest details. As it unsparingly recounts the faults and falls of men in general and of the people of God as well, its total silence about errors in the work of the sacred authors undeniably has great weight.

The Extent of Biblical Inerrancy

It is evident to anyone acquainted with the facts that the biblical text in our hands now is not without some problems. This is why, before going into the objections raised against the doctrine of inerrancy, we shall find it useful to specify what the doctrine refers to. Frank E. Gaebelein ably discusses this point.[3]

Inerrancy does not mean uniformity in all the details given in analagous accounts written by different authors. The books of Samuel, Kings and Chronicles all belong in large measure to the same historical period, but both their point of view and their expression vary sometimes. The four Gospels all recount the life of Christ, but with different details. In the Acts, each of the three treatments of the conversion of Saul of Tarsus (chaps. 8; 22; 26) is distinguished from the others in certain definite respects.

Such differences have often been greatly exaggerated: there are even those who promptly go on to call them contradictions and errors. In reality, although the doctrine of inspiration and inerrancy of the Scriptures requires that each author write according to truth, it leaves each one free in the choice of such actual incidents as illustrate what he purposes to teach.

If four independent witnesses in court parrot syllable by syllable the same story, made up of a series of complex facts, those men would at once be charged with collusion. Their very uniformity would make them suspect. For it is a psychological fact, due to inevitable differences in point of view and in observation, that several individuals, each completely honest, will tell the very same events in quite different ways. This can also be said of the biblical authors. Inspired, they wrote nothing false. Everything they saw and reported was true, even though they did not always see and report the same details. But each had his own personality and was far from being a mere robot.

[3]Frank E. Gaebelein, *The Meaning of Inspiration*, passim.

Take, for example, the accounts of the resurrection as recorded in the Gospels. The essential facts are identical: Christ arose; the tomb was empty; the Lord was seen alive by different groups of disciples in various places; his new body was not subject to the limitations of an ordinary human body; after a certain number of days, he went away from the earth again. This is the general framework on which all the Gospels agree. But they differ in certain details and in the presentation of some of the secondary facts. The accounts are nonetheless authentic for this, and the truth taught is well established.

Biblical inerrancy does not exclude the use of pictures and symbols. Although everything in the Bible is inspired, it does not follow that all of it must be taken literally. The plain meaning of many passages is clear from an historical, practical, legal, and moral point of view. But there are also many pages where the language is obviously symbolical: for example, many things in Psalms, the Song of Solomon, and the Prophets, as well as the parables in the Gospels and in Revelation. Besides, thousands of expressions in both the Old and New Testaments are closer to poetry than to prose. This is, moreover, why the style of the Bible always has a vital and magnetic quality. Therefore, belief in the inerrancy of Scripture in no wise requires a slavish adherence to an absolutely literal interpretation. Since when must belief in inerrancy impose a circumscribed, shackling prosaicness that shuts out those wider horizons where, in any age, picture and symbolism can strike fire to the imagination of men?

This repeated accusation of an obligatory literalness looms up partly from the false idea which critics hold about our position. They think that the concept of *verbal* inspiration forces us to consider every word by itself, irrespective of the context, as being the object of an independent inspiration. Nothing could be further from the truth. No language, no literature, could be subjected to such treatment. Words, vehicles of thought, are arranged and bound together to express one unified whole. The context will help to determine whether the interpretation is literal, spiritual, or symbolical.[4]

Biblical inerrancy does not imply the use of an exact technical vocabulary, conformed to present scientific terminology. The biblical authors were all men of antiquity. They employed the language of their times, not claiming to foresee modern science. But when they did set down facts in the realm of science, they expressed themselves without error in regard to fundamental principles. For example, the biblical record of the creation

[4] Cf. R. A. Finlayson, as cited in *Revelation and the Bible*, ed. Carl F. H. Henry, 223–24.

touches on the following areas: geology, astronomy, biology, meteorology, zoology, and physiology. The expressions used do not claim to be technical ones. Still, every page remains not only more sublime but also more logical than any other attempted explanation of the origin of the universe. Before coming back to this point (chap. 14),[5] let us give the opinion of two contemporary scholars. The famous geologist Dana declares that the first chapter of the Bible and science are "in agreement." Another geologist, Sir William Dawson, adds that the succession of creative acts indicated in Genesis is impeccable in the light of modern science and that many details show the most remarkable harmony with the results of science.[6]

It is also clear that Scripture uses popular expressions in the fields of astronomy, geology, and other scientific domains exactly the way our modern scholars do in current conversation. The preacher said, for example, that the sun rises and the sun goes down (Eccles. 1:5), precisely as we ourselves have kept on expressing the idea since the discovery of the rotation of the earth.

Apropos of inerrancy, the biblical message has to be put back into its own historical setting. Certain declarations of Scripture were true when they were made, although the circumstances are different now. When we read in the book of Joshua that the twelve stones set up in the midst of the Jordan "are there unto this day" (4:9), this obviously means that they *were* there at the time those things were written. One delicate subject is that of the chronology of the Old Testament, which has been judged as erroneous. What is certain is that the ancients did not count the way we do and had no fixed, universal calendar. The exact length of the reign of the kings is difficult to know, since the year at the end of one reign was often counted a second time as that of the beginning of the next one. At any rate, following the ancient ways of calculating and dating, one sees in Scripture a much greater precision than in the other ancient authors.[7]

The question of grammar and style is also in harmony with the historical framework. We do not have, on this point, a like statement by Muslims concerning expressions in the Koran. They think that their book came down complete from heaven, so for a long time they strongly opposed any translations being made of it. Our position for the Bible is that, according to the time or the author, the Hebrew is more or less pure and the Greek

[5] Editor's note: see "The Difficulties of the Bible," in Pache, *The Inspiration and Authority of Scripture*, 141–58.
[6] Cf. quotations by Albert Lüscher, *Wenn das Wort nicht mehr soll gelten*, 31.
[7] Suggested by Gaebelin, 16–22. Translator's note: See also E. R. Thiele, *The Mysterious Numbers of the Hebrew Kings*.

more or less correct (speaking, for example, of some of the writings of the prophets, or Revelation); and this concept does not signify any deviation from the integrity of the text. The style is not ceremonious or affected, as though it had been dictated. Although majestic or dramatic at times, it is often simple, varied, and even completely colloquial.

It is claimed that for some who wrote in the period following the Reformation, inspiration and inerrancy included even the points added to the consonants of the Hebrew text to indicate the vowels. Suffice it to say that the vowel points were invented by the Masoretes, starting with the fifth century AD.

Inerrancy has to do with the whole of the biblical message, within the limits specified above, and this not only for the part having to do with "faith and practice." If this were not so, would one not have to consider Scripture fallible in other respects? Take an example from history: God invaded our world. He initiated his plan of redemption in the incarnation and consummated it in specific historical facts. If the Bible is wrong about these facts, what is there for our faith to rest on? See what Paul says about the resurrection of Christ, as well as about the history of Israel (1 Cor. 15:14–19; 10:11; Rom. 15:4). The historical facts are so intimately tied in with spiritual realities that we would find it very hard to separate the two. We have seen that the same is true of the account of the creation, as touching the domain of the natural sciences (geology, astronomy, biology, etc.). The creation account, and also that of paradise, the fall, the deluge, etc., we find fully confirmed by Christ and the apostles. Unless we make myths out of these records, how could we separate them from the spiritual truths which have been drawn from them? Let us make it clear, however, that for us inerrancy extends to the text itself, not to the often absurd interpretations given to it (see chap. 14, subhead "The firmament," for an example).[8] In the realm of geography, likewise, the extraordinary exactitude of Scripture has been attested to by archaeology and by an improved understanding of antiquity.

One more word about the expression contained in a number of confessions of faith, whether ancient or recent: "Scripture is the Word of God, the only infallible rule of faith and practice." Clearly, the Bible does not claim to be a manual of science or history; its supreme domain is that of faith and life. It is the book of salvation; its aim is to lead us to God and to enable us to live with him, first down here and then forever in heaven.

[8] Editor's note: see "The Difficulties of the Bible," in Pache, *The Inspiration and Authority of Scripture*, 141.

Inerrancy does not imply omniscience on the part of the biblical authors. They were not acquainted with all facets of the subjects they treated. Thus their declarations are true without always being complete. One illustration is the case of the four Gospels. Each one has its part in filling in, adding to, and putting the finishing touches on the painting. This principle explains why the Bible does not always provide a full account of a given event or the well-rounded, all-comprehensive enunciation of a truth, such as one might expect from omniscience. The Scriptures were written by men who were kept from error, but who were not endowed with the perceptive faculties which belong to God alone.

It was, moreover, not necessarily the aim of the biblical records to tell absolutely everything. For example, the Gospels give us practically nothing about Jesus from the time he was twelve until the day he was baptized by John the Baptist. Such information would certainly have a popular appeal if we may judge by the apocryphal "gospels," but this might not be according to the purpose of either the Holy Spirit or the writers themselves.[9]

Objections to Inerrancy

Inerrancy is irreconcilable with the human nature of the biblical authors. Because "to err is human," everything is imperfect. And since the Bible did not fall straight down from the sky, God, in order to get it put into writing, led men whom he had at his disposal, the way an artist is limited in his expression by the materials he has available.

Now this is quite logical in view of man's fallen condition. But it does not at all take into consideration either God's omnipotence or his intervention in the providing of redemption. Just as revelation is a miracle on his part, so the inspiration which kept the sacred writer is another. If the utilization of human nature in itself necessarily implied sin, then Jesus Christ could not be the perfect Saviour; and this is exactly what unbelievers claim about him.

We have already seen that, had the sacred writers been abandoned to their natural fallibility, this would necessarily have extended to every domain, the spiritual as well as the historical and scientific. On the other hand, if they are inerrant in regard to spiritual truths, why would they not be also in other matters?

Again, if only human fallibility were to be reckoned with in the drawing

[9] See N. B. Stonehouse and Paul Woolley, eds., *The Infallible Word: A Symposium* (1946. Reprint, Grand Rapids, MI: Eerdmans, 1954), 198–99.

up of the biblical text, how could we discern the true from the false—we who are fallible ourselves? In that case there would be nothing left to us but skepticism.

Modern science has definitely destroyed the old idea of a perfect Bible. No cultivated person, they claim, can hold today to the inerrancy of the Scriptures. This tenet still remains subject to proof. It is true that the nineteenth century thought "science" was opposed to faith, whereas the truth is that, far from contradictory, the two are simply on different planes. A long list of great scholars could be mentioned who not only believe in God but also stoutly confess their faith in the Scriptures.

In the chapter entitled "Difficulties in the Bible,"[10] we shall see how some "errors" attributed to Scripture appear in the light of the better information which we now possess. Here is the opinion of Professor Robert Dick Wilson of Princeton, who held several doctorates and who knew forty-five languages and dialects of the Near East, including all of the Semitic languages: "I have come to the conviction that no man knows enough to attack the veracity of the Old Testament. Every time when anyone has been able to get together enough documentary 'proofs' to undertake an investigation, the biblical facts in the original text have victoriously met the test."[11]

Let us not forget, furthermore, the extent to which "science" is always relative and subject to change. It is a continuous and progressive attempt to explain the many mysteries of nature. It would be senseless, and even antiscientific, to reject everything we think of as up-to-date knowledge just because a good deal in it still needs to be clarified.

On the other hand, any scientific declaration is always open to revision and improvement. What scholars say today can be contradicted, or it can be completed, tomorrow. As for "theological knowledge," that is necessarily less controllable than the so-called natural sciences. It touches on the spiritual world; and, in that which concerns the Bible, it all too often takes its point of departure from eminently subjective philosophical and psychological suppositions. According to Lüscher, since 1850 biblical criticism has proposed more than 700 theories, all supposed to be the last word in science. By now more than 600 of these have become outmoded and discarded in the light of a more enlightened and extended scholarship.[12]

---

[10] Editor's note: see "The Difficulties of the Bible," in Pache, *The Inspiration and Authority of Scripture*, 141–58.

[11] Cited in Lüscher, 64.

[12] Ibid., 16.

We are ready to learn from what human science has to teach us, but we are not going to do it with our eyes closed. "Prove all things; hold fast that which is good" (1 Thess. 5:21). We do not claim the ability to explain everything; neither do we at all desire to seek a rationalistic support for our faith. Faith, based on solid facts, will always be created and nourished by a "demonstration of the Spirit and of power" (1 Cor. 2:4).

Mistakes made by copyists are evident from the variations in the different manuscripts. This is true, and we shall devote a subsequent chapter to the consideration of it.[13] But since these errors affect no more than about one one-thousandth part of the biblical text, we believe them far too insignificant to shake our faith in the inerrancy of the original manuscripts. (For the latter expression, see our explanation in this chap., subhead "Inerrancy of the Original Manuscript.")

The citations from the Old Testament as found in the New, taking liberties with the text, do not seem to consider it as inviolable. Again, this is a claim which we think should be closely examined. Let us at this point merely recall that Christ and his apostles, those responsible for the quotations, everywhere regarded the Scriptures with an attitude of total confidence and submission.

When one affirms inerrancy, he "petrifies" the biblical text. This is the expression used by J. K. S. Reid: "God's Word is petrified in a dead record."[14] Let us sum up S. Van Mierlo's view of the question: the theologians opposed to plenary inspiration say that it is a profound error to believe a thing simply because it is in the Bible. This is for two reasons: (1) There are doubtless historical and scientific errors in the Bible, and therefore one constantly exposes himself to controversies with science. (2) A Bible without error would be like an idol, exercising an inadmissible authority over our minds. We would then accept its teachings as true in a mechanical manner, without personal faith in the Lord Jesus Christ, who is the embodiment of the true divine revelation. This would make only a collection of doctrine and so a dead letter. We would then have to do with an authoritative religion which says what has to be believed, a teaching one must accept quite apart from any personal experience.[15]

Such reasoning as this seems to us untenable. Why would the biblical text be petrified merely because it contains divine truths rather than

---

[13] Editor's note: see "Transmission of the Text—The Variants," in Pache, *The Inspiration and Authority of Scripture*, 186–98.
[14] J. K. S. Reid, *The Authority of Scripture*, 279.
[15] S. Van Mierlo, *La révélation divine*, 234.

human error? God has provided "living oracles" as gifts to us (Acts 7:38). The written Word is the Word of the Holy Spirit (Heb. 3:7); and it has always been living and active (4:12). From it there emanates that quickening power, at once human and divine.

The doctrine of inerrancy hinders the exercise of faith. "The old Protestant doctrine of verbal inspiration transforms the living word of God into a sacred text and its consequent denial of the human character of Scripture evades and fails to appreciate not only the possibility of offense, but at the same time the reality of faith."[16] We have already given quite enough, assuredly, on the human side of Scripture and the part played by the personality of its composers. As for "real faith," is it actually true that "faith cannot be properly exercised unless and until we recognize that there are fallible elements in the Scripture"?[17]

The above arguments reveal a complete lack of understanding of the role of the Holy Spirit in the illumination and regeneration of the reader. The inspired text becomes intelligible to us only as we receive by faith the Saviour which it reveals and then as, by that faith, we allow the Holy Spirit to regenerate us. For all readers of the Scriptures, "a veil lieth upon their heart. But whensoever it [a man] shall turn to the Lord, the veil is taken away. . . . Now where the Spirit of the Lord is, there is liberty" (2 Cor. 3:15–17).

Further, what is this "Christ, the only true divine revelation" that the fully inspired text keeps people from knowing, unless it is a figment of the imagination born in the reader's subjective experience and, thus, different for each one, whether he be just an ordinary individual or some well-known theologian?

As for what concerns us, we should like to emphasize again what Warfield has to say. As is true for all other doctrines, our faith in verbal inspiration is based on the affirmations of Scripture itself. We do not ask: What do the confessions of faith say? What is the word of the theologians? What does the authority of the church declare? Rather: What does the Bible itself teach? We depend entirely, then, on an exegetical fact; that is to say, on a minute and reverent study of the text itself. If criticism by its discoveries should render untenable the doctrine of plenary inspiration, we would be forced to abandon not only "a particular theory of inspiration" but also the apostles and the Lord himself, as our doctrinal teachers and guides, for

[16] Heinrich Vogel, cited in R. A. Finlayson, *Revelation and the Bible*, ed. Carl F. H. Henry, 227.
[17] Ibid.

plenary inspiration was plainly their teaching.[18] This would mean nothing less than an actual renunciation of the attitude of faith, in which attitude, by God's help, we are determined to persevere.

There are those, indeed, who do not hesitate to say to us: "When you insist so much on the necessity for a totally inspired text, without which no one can be sure of anything, aren't you simply following the psychological and almost pathological need for security?" Once again, we reply that we must not reverse the priorities. Man, naturally in darkness, longs to be led in the way of light and truth, even as he could not live without an earthly and an eternal hope. This principle could not suffice as the foundation of the doctrine before us; but God, who has put such an aspiration in us, responds to it by a perfect revelation of his person, adapted to us in our present state. Obviously, he might be pleased to bring conversion to Christ to someone by means of a testimony in itself imperfect—an oral one, or possibly a written one, such as a tract. But these testimonies with their limitations could not "declare the whole counsel of God." It is the Lord himself who has indissolubly bound the message of salvation to a written revelation worthy of confidence. One automatically deprives himself of the first at the moment when he rejects the second.

The most objectionable aspect of inerrancy seems to be its limitation of the freedom of the critics. Now this objection clearly arises out of the declarations made above. People do not want to be bound by a verse, a collection of Bible doctrines, or a paternalistic and authoritarian religion. A Bible without error would squeeze our minds into an unendurable strait-jacket! Professor Emil Brunner says: "The fundamentalist is in bondage to the biblical text. . . . This makes the Bible an idol and me its slave."[19]

Obviously if everyone claimed the right to appraise any part of the text he happened to want to, affixing such erroneous labels as "contradictory," "legendary" or "mythological," he would be completely "free" in regard to it. If there were nothing to affirm that a given passage expresses a truth, the criterion of evaluation would be even more personal and subjective. Finally, the "religious conscience" of the individual and his mere reason would supplant the authority of the divine revelation. Experience shows that conscience and reason are not about to capitulate to authority. As for the inner witness of the Holy Spirit, it is clear that it follows along the line of truth which he himself has already revealed.

---

[18] B. B. Warfield, *The Inspiration and Authority of the Bible*, ed. Samuel G. Craig (Philadelphia: Presbyterian & Reformed, 1948), 179–80.
[19] Cited by Finlayson in Henry, 232.

Inerrancy produces a paper pope. One often hears it said that if Luther liberated Christianity from the pope at Rome, orthodox Protestants have replaced him by a "paper pope." We do not believe in an infallible church; and here, they say, you are trying to impose an infallible Scripture on us! Jesus Christ is alone infallible and ought to have this supreme authority. Protestants have put the Bible in the place of Christ, and this constitutes one of their greatest weaknesses.[20]

These are nothing but sophisms. Luther and the other evangelical believers did not invent anything. They simply went back to the scriptural position of Christ and his apostles (see chap. 18),[21] a position of unqualified submission to the fully inspired Scriptures. But this matter of authority is of supreme importance, and we shall shortly be coming back to it. Let us point out here that spiritual authority can have only three forms:

> the authority of the Lord
> and His written revelation;
> the authority of the church
> and its "infallible" pope;
> the authority of human reason,
> with its self-styled sovereignty

Did the Reformers really make the Scriptures supplant Christ? On the contrary, Christ cannot be known except through the Scriptures. Along with giving the world the open Bible, they wonderfully preached the gospel of grace in Jesus Christ. Edward J. Young says again on this subject:

> Those who are so concerned lest the Bible occupy a position which belongs to Christ have also themselves an "absolute" or "infallible" authority . . . the "infallible" mind of man. . . . This Jesus Christ whose position has supposedly been dethroned by the Bible, . . . is He the eternal Son of God, the second Person of the Holy Trinity, who for our salvation took unto Himself human nature, without sin, being born of the Virgin Mary . . . to die upon the cross in our stead and to rise from the dead? Is that the Christ about whom the modern theologian is concerned?[22]

In any case, this is not true for Brunner, Niebuhr, and Bultmann.

---

[20] Cf. Edward J. Young, *Thy Word Is Truth*, 104.

[21] Editor's note: see "Jesus Christ and Holy Scripture," in Pache, *The Inspiration and Authority of Scripture*, 215–23.

[22] Cf. Edward J. Young, *The Word Is Truth*, 107.

The only way to reverence the sovereignty of Christ is to learn to know him in that unique revelation which we have of him and then to obey his teachings, just as we do those of the prophets and apostles, which he invested with supreme authority.

A belief in inerrancy brings a danger of "bibliolatry." Those who take the Bible to be fully inspired and inerrant are also constantly accused of bibliolatry. "The fundamentalist makes an idol out of the Bible," they say, "and himself a slave to it." In reality, nothing is more untrue of sincere evangelicals, whose only desire is to worship and to glorify the Lord whom the Bible reveals. The Book is only his mouthpiece, the instrument forged by the Holy Spirit to make him known to us.

We shall develop in more detail this important matter of the sovereign authority of the Holy Scriptures (chaps. 18–19).[23]

Did not Paul himself admit that he was not always inspired? He wrote to the Corinthians: "The things which I write unto you, . . . they are the commandment of the Lord" (1 Cor. 14:37); "Unto the married I give charge, yea not I, but the Lord" (7:10); "To the rest say I, not the Lord" (v. 12); "So ordain I in all the churches . . ." (v. 17); "Now concerning virgins I have no commandment of the Lord: but I give my judgment, as one that hath obtained mercy of the Lord to be trustworthy" (v. 25).

Paul was touching on a very serious subject, where there was brought into the question of divorce a modification of the law of Moses. There is no doubt but that he knew himself to be fully inspired when he dared to say that some things were "the commandment of the Lord." However, he shows here that, although some rules are absolute, in other cases God lets man decide according to his conscience, his circumstances, and his particular gift (vv. 6–9, 36, 39). Paul, out of his great experience and special calling, felt free to offer faithful advice, given also by the Spirit of the Lord (v. 40). There is nothing false in that which he says, nothing to mar the inerrancy of the text.

Does not the Bible report some things which are false in themselves? Most certainly, for it cites the words of the Devil, as declarations of the enemies of God; and it even recounts the most enormous sins of believers, as well as some of the bad feelings of their hearts. This obviously does not mean that the Lord takes the responsibility for those things! He purposed, however, that they be written very exactly for our instruction, under the control of the Holy Spirit.

---

[23] Editor's note: see "Jesus Christ and Holy Scripture" and "The Apostles and Holy Scripture," in Pache, *The Inspiration and Authority of Scripture*, 215–23, 224–32.

Can one make inspiration and inerrancy applicable to truly insignificant details? Paul said to Timothy that he should take a little wine for his stomach's sake rather than to drink water (1 Tim. 5:23). From Rome the elderly apostle, as a prisoner, asked that before winter came on he might be brought the coat which he had left at Troas in the home of Carpus, as well as his books and parchments (2 Tim. 4:13). The passage in Romans 16:1–16 is full of friendliness and personal appreciation for the individuals whom Paul wished to greet at Rome. Some scholars have seriously called such details insignificant, trivial, and unworthy of inspiration. Scripture certainly finds it hard to satisfy everybody! Do not others become all worked up at times about emphasizing its human aspects? Passages like these, it seems to us, very definitely show the perfect naturalness of biblical style, along with traces left by the personality, affections, and circumstances of the authors. Such indications actually constitute proof that the Scriptures could not have been dictated mechanically.

In regard to 2 Timothy 4:13, let us mention an interesting comment by Erasmus: "See what the goods of the apostle consisted of: a coat for protection against the rain and a few books." And this one by Grotius: "See the poverty of the great apostle, who thought an article so slight in intrinsic worth and so far distant as a loss to himself."[24]

We could go on to find other objections to the inerrancy of Scripture, but they would only be a repetition in different forms of the same opposition in principle to the authority of the biblical revelation. Let us now bring up the other side of the subject, the positive and important one.

Inerrancy of the Original Manuscript

God watched over the writing down of the message to keep it faithful to the revelation he had given. We believe that it is in keeping with Scripture on the one hand and with the nature and honor of God on the other to affirm that in inspiring each sacred author, he jealously guarded his original manuscript to preserve it from error. What would be the good of saying that it was God who spoke if the written expression of that Word did not faithfully reproduce what he had said?

We have already seen to what point such an affirmation becomes an integral part of the notion of inspiration (cf. chap 7, subhead "Definitions").[25] If the whole Bible claims to be the Word of God, it certainly had to be

[24] Cited in Robert Haldane, *Dieu a parlé*, 70.
[25] Editor's note: see above, note 1.

wholly inspired; otherwise its authors either were deceived themselves or else deceived us.

It is evident, on the other hand, that in no case has the original manuscript been preserved. Our chapters on the transmission of the text and the variations and difficulties in the Bible explain in what state the text in our hands is at the present time, a text which one cannot call totally inerrant. Emil Brunner says that fundamentalism, faced with all the contradictions and non sequiturs discovered by the critics, had to resort to an infallible original, of which only two things are known: first, that it was the infallible Word of God; and second, that it was the same Bible as that which we have today—although quite different from it. Brunner condemns our explanations as "apologetical artifices." It goes without saying that his presentation of the facts is very much twisted; and we shall examine his position subsequently.

Why is it important that the original manuscript was itself free from error? Since God has not permitted us to have it, could we not get along all right without knowing what it was like? The scholars can refer to the Hebrew and Greek texts, as they were transmitted to us by the copyists. Now the ordinary reader in his own language has to content himself with a translation which is necessarily imperfect, one which is still further away from the original. But if God is blessing him anyway by means of what he has, what is the need of probing further?

First, we believe that the veracity of the Godhead is at stake, as well as his power to reveal himself—not only to an individual, but also to the whole of humanity. If God from the start had allowed error to slip into the composition of his message, what would we have to think of him? (The transmission of this written message down to our day is another problem, which we shall be taking up in chap. 16).[26] All this keeps making us revert to the same question: If the original manuscript already had mistakes in it, who can say now how far this element of error goes, and how are we to get the errors sorted out? We would be in complete confusion.

Second, it is evident that the writer of the original text had before him a task infinitely more difficult and more crucial than was the work of any copyist or translator afterward. Following Louis Gäussen, let us first of all consider the original text in relation to the translations made of it through the centuries.

1. The sacred authors had to give a human form to the divine message,

[26] Editor's note: see "Transmission of the Text—The Variants," in Pache, *The Inspiration and Authority of Scripture*, 186–98.

an operation mysterious, delicate, and open to error (if ever there was one); and for this responsibility the full assistance of the Spirit was needed. The mind of the Lord having been in a sense incarnated in human language, it was no longer a question, in translating, of giving it a body, but simply of changing its clothing, so as to make it say in our own language what it had said in Hebrew and Greek—that is, to modestly replace each word by an equivalent expression. This is an operation far inferior, comparatively, to the preceding one; it could conceivably be done even by a scrupulous unbeliever if he knew perfectly the languages in question.

2. The author of the original text, without entire inspiration, would have been far more in danger of error than the translators. The translators' work was done by a great many men, of every tongue and country, who could devote all their time to it and all their care, who were disciplining themselves through the centuries, and who were instructing and correcting one another. The original text, on the other hand, had to be written at a given time, by a single man, and once for all. No one was with that man except his God to hold him to the line and to furnish him with better expressions when his were faulty. If God had not done it, then nobody could have done it.

3. Whereas all the translators of the Scriptures were cultured people and specialists in the study of languages, many of the sacred authors were ignorant men, scarcely fluent in their own language. They would have been incapable of putting the divine revelation together with impeccable artistry all by themselves.

4. God's thought flashed like lightning across the mind of the prophet. It can be discovered again in our times only in the same rapid expression he gave to it as he wrote it down. If his transmission of it was inexact, how could the divine message ever be recaptured in all its pristine purity? The fault would be irreparable, for it would have hopelessly marred the eternal Book. The situation is quite different for the translations. Since we have today a biblical text extremely close to the original (see chap. 16),[27] our versions can be ceaselessly corrected and recorrected, with a view to conforming them to it with ever increasing precision. This work goes on from one century to another; and one can still revise today the Vulgate of St. Jerome after 1,500 years, Luther's translation after 450 years, and the English Authorized Version after 350 years. How important it was for the original to be without error and for it to have been transmitted to us with rigorous fidelity!

---

[27] Ibid.

Apropos of this, let us again consider a thought of Gäussen's.

> A book is from God, or it is not from God. In the latter case, it were idle for me to transcribe it a thousand times exactly—I should not thereby render it divine; and in the former case, I should in vain take a thousand incorrect copies; neither folly nor unfaithfulness on my part can undo the fact of its having been given by God. . . . If then the Book of Maccabees was a merely human book in the days of Jesus Christ, a thousand decrees of the Roman Catholic Church could not have any such effect thereafter as that, in 1560, becoming what it had never been till then, it should be transubstantiated into a divine book.[28]

5. If the original text was faulty, the streams of potential error flowing out from it would only tend to increase constantly. On the other hand, if it was inerrant, the possibility of error in the copies and in the translations would constantly diminish. The painstaking study of the innumerable copies of the Scriptures in our possession; the discovery of new manuscripts, such as those of Sinai and the Dead Sea; the progress in exegesis and philology; and the ceaseless revision of the translations—all these means have contributed in a wonderful way to confirm the basic text and to increasingly eliminate such mistakes in copying and translating as occurred through the centuries. Once again, such progress presupposes a dependable original manuscript as the source from which all the rest has proceeded, however far from it are the times in which we are living.

Gäussen concludes like this:

> Who now can fail to perceive the enormous distance interposed by all these considerations between those two texts [that of the Bible and that of the translations], as respects the importance of verbal inspiration? Between the passing of the thoughts of God into human words and the simple turning of these words into other words, the distance is as wide as from heaven to earth. God was required for the one; man sufficed for the other. Let it no longer be said, then, What would it avail to us that we have verbal inspiration in the one case [the original manuscript] if we have not that inspiration in the other case [the subsequent translation], for between these two terms, which some would put on an equality, the difference is almost infinite.[29]

Now let us consider a very recent voice, that of Dr. J. I. Packer.

---

[28] Louis Gäussen, *The Inspiration of the Holy Scriptures*, trans. David D. Scott, 165–66.
[29] Ibid., 160–61.

> It is sometimes suggested that we can have no confidence that any text that we possess conveys to us the genuine meaning of the inspired Word. . . . But faith in the consistency of God warrants an attitude of confidence that the text is sufficiently trustworthy not to lead us astray. If God gave the Scriptures for a practical purpose—to make men wise unto salvation through faith in Christ—it is a safe inference that He never permits them to become so corrupted that they can no longer fulfill it. It is noteworthy that the New Testament men did not hesitate to trust the words of the Old Testament as they had it, as a reliable indication of the mind of God. This attitude of faith in the adequacy of the text is confirmed, as far as it can be, by the unanimous verdict of textual scholars that the biblical manuscripts are excellently preserved; and no point of doctrine depends on any of the small number of cases in which the true reading remains doubtful. Professor F. F. Bruce expresses the verdict of scholarship as well as of biblical faith when he writes: "By the singular care and providence of God the Bible text has come down to us in such substantial purity that even the most uncritical edition of the Hebrew or Greek . . . cannot effectively obscure the real message of the Bible or neutralize its saving power."[30]

Why did God not let the original manuscripts be preserved for us? Might it be to keep us from making an idol of them? The Christians in Rome, for example, privileged to handle the very text of Paul's epistle, written by his own hand, based their faith directly on the inspired message (just as we are called upon to do today). But later, as this faith became less virile, might they not have been tempted to make of the material document that came from Paul's hands a sort of relic, even a fetish? The example of the brazen serpent which became an object of worship and which was finally destroyed by Hezekiah should cause us to reflect on such a possibility (Num. 21:8–9; 2 Kings 18:4).

Since we are deprived of the original manuscripts, we are all the more led to study the existing documents to compare them and to keep bringing them back to the primitive text, which, after all, is not so far from us. Having been laid hold on by the powerful message of Scripture, and feeling ourselves overwhelmed by its revelation of the living God, we can do no other than to cling to it wholly by faith. It is possible for us to adopt such an attitude, even if we are not able fully to explain, demonstrate, and harmonize the little which still seems obscure to us.

---

[30] J. I. Packer, *"Fundamentalism" and the Word of God*, 90. Editor's note: see also above, Packer.

We are, moreover, certainly obliged to accept in this same way all the great biblical doctrines:

> the Trinity: God revealed in three persons
> the incarnation: Jesus Christ, at once God and man
> the fall: man incapable of doing good, yet responsible
> justification: the believer at the same time a sinner and declared righteous
> predestination: the eternal election of man, who yet possesses free will
> resurrection: a new body—"body," but at the same time something spiritual
> eternal perdition: the question of reconciling this concept with the love of God.

We accept all these things by faith in the Scriptures, being fully convinced of its witness to the truth, even if we cannot explain every detail in it. Likewise, it is possible for us to take by faith the doctrines of inspiration and inerrancy: the Word wholly of God and at the same time of man, preserved from error to reveal the truth to us in no uncertain way.

This being said, faith in inerrancy is not at all conducive to an obscurantist attitude, which would blind us to plain problems or make us disparage the light that emanates from true science. Evangelical faith knows how to distinguish between positive and negative criticism. It endeavors to examine all things so as to retain that which is good. On the other hand, the thing that seems positively antiscientific to us is the flat rejection of the testimony to the integrity of the Scriptures which Christ himself gave and which the apostles and an impressive number of real facts substantiate.

12

"The Meaning of Inerrancy"

PAUL D. FEINBERG

Inerrancy

Previously published as "The Meaning of Inerrancy," in *Inerrancy*, ed. Norman L. Geisler (Grand Rapids, MI: Zondervan, 1980), 265–304.

Chapter Summary: The defense of the term and doctrine of inerrancy presupposes a clear definition. The aim of this paper is to specify the meaning of the doctrine. To this end a study of the methodology of theology is undertaken. The author concludes that the method of abduction or retroduction is most appropriate to theology as a whole and should be used in formulating a doctrine of inerrancy. Thus the phenomena of Scripture are examined, and a definition of the doctrine is formulated, in terms of truth, or truthfulness. Finally, there is a discussion of qualifications, misunderstandings, and objections.

It appears to me that in Ethics, as in all other philosophical studies, the difficulties and disagreements, of which its history is full, are mainly due to a very simple cause: namely to the attempt to answer questions, without first discovering precisely what question it is which you desire to answer.

G. E. Moore, Principia Ethica, *vii.*

While Moore undoubtedly overstates the case for discovering the precise question, he is nevertheless onto something very important. Without a proper understanding of the question, one has little hope of arriving at the right answer. Moreover, at the heart of clear and precise understanding is careful definition of the terms that make up the question. This is particularly true in theological contexts where words and dogma have a long and hoary history. The danger is always that emotions will be aroused unduly, with resultant failure to communicate the desired information adequately. All of this is to say that, without precise definition of the word *inerrancy* and of the related doctrine of inerrancy, it is difficult to answer the question as to whether or not the Bible is inerrant. That such clear and careful definition is necessary and can be seen even by a superficial reading of the literature of this debate. On both sides there have been attacks on straw men and failure to engage one another on the genuine Issues. Therefore, the task of this chapter is to define both the term and the doctrine of inerrancy as precisely as possible so that debate may genuinely proceed.[1]

Before turning to this task, however, it seems to me that some preliminary considerations are in order. First, I do not intend to defend all who have ever sought to advance a doctrine of inerrancy. Such is both impossible and unnecessary. Yet this fact needs to be emphasized, since there are some who have sought in the past, and some who are now seeking, to formulate the doctrine in an indefensible manner. Such attempts are often held up to ridicule and scorn, and all who hold to inerrancy are then tarred with the same brush. This is not to say that inerrantists have not done similar things but to emphasize a basic tenet of debate or argumentation—namely, that excessive or even false claims by some or even all defenders of a position do not prove that position to be false. To put it another way, a view may be poorly or incorrectly argued and yet be true. In order to disprove inerrancy, therefore, it must be shown that this doctrine in its most defensible formulation is false or at least that it is not as plausible as some other position.

Second, it is often claimed by those who support an inerrant Bible that they alone hold a high view of Scripture. This claim elicits the following response from Davis:

> I will criticize inerrancy, but my purpose is to strengthen not weaken the evangelical Christian cause by making a clear and, I hope, con-

[1] In dealing with the question of inerrancy, there are a number of closely related but distinct issues. In my judgment, failure to note the complexity of the problem has kept debate from being as precise as possible. Thus it is helpful to distinguish between the theological doctrine of inerrancy and the definition of the term *inerrancy*. In connection with the doctrine, there are the questions of how a doctrine is *constructed* and how it is *justified*. At the heart of these matters is the exegetical data from which the doctrine grows and against which it is tested. If indeed the Scripture teaches such a doctrine, there is then the matter of defining or establishing the precise meaning of the term *inerrancy*. It should be noted that a definition of *inerrant* can be given in a question-begging way. It would be question-begging and therefore wrong, to assert that if the Bible does teach its own inerrancy, a satisfactory definition of the term is impossible of attainment or else to state the definition so broadly that it is meaningless. The procedure that this discussion follows is intended to be consistent with the principles and objectives just mentioned.

> vincing case for an evangelical attitude toward the Bible that does not involve inerrancy. The "all or nothing" arguments of many defenders of inerrancy give the impression that there is no middle ground between inerrancy, on the one hand, and neo orthodoxy, liberal, or even atheistic attitudes toward the Bible, on the other.[2]

Davis's quote explicitly or implicitly raises at least three distinct but related questions. (1) Are there only two possible positions on Scripture? Must one hold either to (a) inerrancy, or (b) to neoorthodox, liberal, or atheistic attitudes toward the Bible? The answer to this question is easy. There are many possible attitudes toward Scripture. (2) What is the criterion for a high view of Scripture? Specifically, is inerrancy a necessary or sufficient condition, or both, for a high view of Scripture? The answer to this question is not easy. I would guess that there is disagreement on the answer among evangelicals. It is not within the scope of this chapter to answer this question. (3) Given a satisfactory criterion for a high view of Scripture, which of the many possibilities mentioned in question 1 qualify? Obviously, the answer to this question awaits a definitive answer to question 2, which we have not attempted to give. Thus we cannot give an answer to question 3. But again this is not the issue before us.

Third, it is claimed by some who defend the inerrancy of the Bible that forfeiture of the doctrine of inerrancy leads *inevitably* to the denial of other doctrines that are central to the Christian faith. This, of course, is not necessarily true, though there are numerous examples that can be cited where this has in fact taken place. Likewise, an orthodox doctrine of Scripture is not an *absolute* hedge against heterodoxy in other theological matters. Some cults, such as Jehovah's Witnesses, have as a part of their doctrinal statement an excellent position on Scripture. On the other hand, many who have vigorously opposed belief in the inerrancy of the Bible have remained orthodox elsewhere in doctrine.

Having said this, we have not settled the matter, since it would surely seem that the *first* step toward doctrinal purity would be a correct doctrine of Scripture. Nevertheless, there are many, even among the highly educated, who hold views for which they cannot give adequate justification. Thus the question to which we are addressing ourselves is not unimportant or insignificant. It cuts to the heart and foundation of Christian theology. It is the question of theological consistency.

The aim, then, of this chapter is to discuss methodology for formulat-

[2] Stephen T. Davis, *The Debate about the Bible* (Philadelphia: Westminster, 1977), 20–21.

ing and justifying the doctrine of inerrancy and then to define the term *inerrancy.* I will begin with a general discussion of the method by which a doctrine is constructed and justified. Then the exegetical evidence of Scripture that bears on the doctrine will be examined. This will be followed by a search for proper terminology and for a doctrine that best suits the scriptural phenomena, with special attention being given to qualifications and misunderstandings. Finally, I will reply to some important objections that might be raised against the doctrine of inerrancy but have not been treated in the course of the study.

The Problem of Method

Where do theologians begin in their efforts to set forth the meaning of inerrancy? One possible answer might be a good dictionary, such as the *Oxford English Dictionary*. If we were merely trying to define the word *inerrancy*, that suggestion would not be without merit. However, we are attempting to do more than merely define a *term*; we are seeking to define or formulate a *doctrine*. This task takes us to a most fundamental inquiry, a discussion of theological method. That is, how does the theologian go about formulating or constructing a doctrine? How does the theologian theologize? Indeed, it has not been uncommon to set the whole inerrancy conflict in the context of a debate over method. Just such a case in point is Beegle's treatment in *Scripture, Tradition and Infallibility*.[3]

Beegle begins by distinguishing between deductive and inductive methodology. While every argument involves the claim that its premises provide evidence for the truth of its conclusions, deductions and inductions differ in the nature of their premises and the relationship between the premises and the conclusion. The premise may be *general* assumptions or prepositions from which *particular* conclusions are arrived. The distinctive characteristic of deduction, however, is its demonstration of relationship between two or more propositions. Furthermore, a deductive argument involves the claim that its premises *guarantee* the truth of its conclusion. Where the premises are both the necessary and sufficient condition for the truth of the conclusion, the argument is said to be valid. Where the premise fails to provide such evidence, the argument is said to be invalid.[4]

With induction on the other hand, the relationship between premises and conclusion is much more modest. The premises only provide *some*

[3] Dewey M. Beegle, *Scripture, Tradition, and Infallibility* (Grand Rapids, MI: Eerdmans, 1973).
[4] Irving M. Copi, *Introduction to Logic*, 3rd ed. (New York: Macmillan, 1968), 20–21.

evidence for the conclusion. Inductive arguments are not valid or invalid. They are better or worse, depending on the degree of probability that their premises confer on their conclusions. Moreover, in induction the premises are *particulars,* and the conclusions are *generalizations*, the data being organized under the most general categories possible.[5]

Which of these methodologies is correct? Well, Beegle says that they are complementary. That is, both are needed. However this is not the end of the matter. There is, he thinks, a priority to the inductive. To illustrate this contention he discusses the way in which an archaeologist goes about excavating a tell. The primary task is to dig down through the strata and to label each item that is found, indicating its stratum. After thoroughly excavating and labeling the items, the archaeologist examines a group of objects, such as pottery, from a single stratum. As he correlates the characteristics of a level, he finds that the pottery has certain forms and other features that distinguish it from pottery in other strata. Thus he finds that each stratum has its own type or class of pottery. This classification procedure is called stratigraphy.[6] Now when the archaeologist goes to the next tell, especially if it is nearby, he does not follow quite the same process. Having already derived from the previously discovered phenomena a classification system, he immediately assigns a piece of pottery to a period and type on the basis of its characteristics. However, even here induction has a part. If, for instance, other factors begin to call into question the original classification, there is then need for revision. Beegle therefore concludes, "The best results are obtained when induction precedes deduction."[7]

Beegle now applies this discussion to the problem of inerrancy. Those who defend inerrancy are deductivists pure and simple. They begin with certain assumptions about God and the Scriptures, namely, that God cannot lie and the Scriptures are the Word of God. From these assumptions inerrantists deduce that the Bible is without error. This approach leads to an a priori determined conclusion, to dogmatism, and to disregard for the phenomena of Scripture. Regardless of the problems of the phenomena, the inerrantist stubbornly maintains his stance on Scripture.[8]

On the other hand, the inductivist cannot accept inerrancy. He begins with the phenomena of Scripture. There he finds errors of differing kinds. He comes across historical inaccuracies. Further, there is reflected in the

[5] Ibid.
[6] Beegle, *Scripture, Tradition and Infallibility*, 16.
[7] Ibid., 17.
[8] Ibid., 175–224. "Phenomena," as used by Beegle and others, refers to Scripture simply as it *appears*.

Bible a view of the world that is scientifically unacceptable today. And this is just the beginning. Thus, as the inductivist seeks to build a doctrine of Scripture, he must be true to the facts of the case. Therefore, try as he may, he cannot accept the idea of an inerrant Bible.[9]

Is this picture fair to the methodology of all defenders of inerrancy? I think not. There is no single methodology employed by inerrantists. In R. C. Sproul's excellent study "The Case for Inerrancy: A Methodological Analysis," he describes at least three general approaches to the problem of method. First, he cites the confessional method, by which the Bible is confessed to be the Word of God and is so recognized by faith alone. An exponent of this method is G. C. Berkouwer. Second, there is the presuppositional method of Cornelius Van Til. In this method defending the authority and inerrancy of the Bible includes accepting the absolute authority and inerrancy of Scripture as a foundational premise. The Bible is self attesting. Third, there is the classical method, which is both inductive and deductive, interested in external as well as internal evidence.[10]

Given that there are at least these three general approaches, Beegle is first of all wrong in lumping all defenders of inerrancy into the deductivist camp. Some, as we have seen, are more than deductivists. Moreover, even those that advocate a deductive methodology should not be so easily charged with dogmatism and closemindedness. For some, their theological a prioris are justified indirectly. Their proof is much like that used to justify the axioms of a geometric system. Since axioms are so basic, it is claimed they cannot be proven in terms of anything more primitive. Thus axioms are justified indirectly in terms of the theorems and propositions they generate and of the solutions they make possible. At any rate, while it is a priori, such methodology is concerned with the facts in some sense and, as such, should not be called "dogmatic."

That is not the end of the matter, however. The question still remains as to the correct method of formulating and testing a doctrine (i.e., of giving the meaning of the doctrine). It seems that the question of methodology with respect to inerrancy cannot be divorced from the broader considerations of a general methodology for theology.[11] Unfortunately,

---

[9] Ibid.

[10] R. C. Sproul, "The Case for Inerrancy: A Methodological Analysis," in *God's Inerrant Word: An International Symposium on the Trustworthiness of Scripture*, ed. John Warwick Montgomery (Minneapolis: Bethany Fellowship, 1973), 242–61.

[11] One might with some justification argue that the doctrine of Scripture is foundational. From this foundation, which is "theory natural," one has reasons for higher-order beliefs. One can see a recent exposition of this view, called foundationalism, in the work of John L. Pollock, *Knowledge and Justification* (Princeton, NJ: Princeton University Press, 1974). More recently, the picture that philosophers (particularly philosophers of

evangelicals do not usually discuss the matter of methodology, since they are generally more interested in the *content* of theology. There are, however, two very helpful articles by evangelicals on theological methodology. They are Arthur F. Holmes's "Ordinary Language Analysis and Theological Method,"[12] and John Warwick Montgomery's "Theologian's Craft: A Discussion of Theory Formation and Theory Testing in Theology."[13] Interestingly enough, there is a good measure of agreement between the two men. Both deny that either deduction or induction alone is the method of the theologian. Holmes is quite critical of the independent use of either methodology. Deduction is the logic of mathematics. If theology were circumscribed by this logic, (1) theological thought would have to be formalized into a deductive argument; (2) the historical narratives would merely be illustrative; (3) analogy, metaphor, symbol, and poetry in the Bible would all have to be restated in logical, univocal, universal form; and (4) all events in redemptive history, as well as their application of grace, would become logically necessary.[14]

Induction, on the other hand, is formulated in three differing ways. First, there is Aristotelian induction, which sought, through intuitive abstraction of familiar categorized data, to arrive at universal principles. Such a method presupposes, and would tie theology to, an Aristotelian view of nature and man. Second, there is the induction of Francis Bacon and John Stuart Mill, which is concerned with experimental identification of causes. This approach is hardly suited to theology. There is also the induction that uses a loose approximation of Aristotle's search for general concepts, based on observation of empirical data: his approach is rejected on two grounds: complete induction is impossible, and, in practice, this is not the way the theologian proceeds.[15]

Theological method is best described by a third and more informal approach. For Montgomery this is called *abduction* or *retroduction*, after Peirce's terminology,[16] although the idea can be found as early as Aristotle.[17]

science) have painted is quite different. At the heart of the change is the recognition that there is no such thing as theory-neutral experience; theory is operative at all levels. The importance of the point for the theologian is that theoretical considerations are at work in all levels of his task, even at the level of hermeneutics and exegesis. Much more could be said, but a good source for studying this issue is *The Structure of Scientific Theories*, ed. Frederick Suppe, 2nd ed. (Urbana: University of Illinois Press, 1977).

[12] Arthur F. Holmes, "Ordinary Language Analysis and Theological Method," *Bulletin of the Evangelical Theological Society* 11 (Summer 1968): 131–38.

[13] John Warwick Montgomery, "The Theologian's Craft: A Discussion of Theory Formation and Theory Testing in Theology," *The Suicide of Christian Theology* (Minneapolis: Bethany Fellowship, 1970), 267–313.

[14] Holmes, "Ordinary Language Analysis," 133.

[15] Ibid., 134.

[16] C. S. Peirce, *Collected Papers*, Harvard ed., 5:146; 5:171; 5:189; and 5:274; cf. 5:276.

[17] Aristotle, *Prior Analytics*, ii:25; cf. *Posterior Analytics*, ii:19.

On the other hand Holmes calls his method *adduction*.[18] The difference in terminology notwithstanding, both men expound a similar methodology. While both induction and deduction are employed, no easy formula is suggested for combining the two. A paradigm, or conceptual model, is formulated through an informed and creative thinking process, generally involving the data to be explained, and is then brought back, adduced, or tested against the data for "fit," or accuracy. The method is found in theory formulation and justification in science. The theory is not created strictly by induction from data or phenomena nor by deduction from first principles. Yet both induction and deduction operate in the imagination of the scientist so that a theory is born. The same general method in theology. The theologian may deal with the relationship between certain propositions, leading him to make deductive inferences. At the same time, he develops doctrine from his understanding of the scriptural phenomena. But it should be noted that neither deduction nor induction operates in any formal sense.[19]

Montgomery gives a helpful example of the operation of abduction or retroduction in science. He cites the story of James Watson and Francis Crick, who discovered the molecular structure of DNA. Watson was convinced by reasons based on genetics that the structure of DNA had to be built around two spirals. The key question was the arrangement of the spirals. Watson and Crick built a model and tirelessly sought to rearrange the spirals in such a way as to get it to work. One night Crick had an intuitive revelation: the two spirals had to be symmetrical—they coiled in opposite directions, one top to bottom and the other bottom to top. This theory seemed to reflect certain laws of crystallography. It turned out to be true! The thing that is noteworthy is that both induction and deduction were at work but, as said before, in a very informal way.[20]

The one point of difference between Montgomery and Holmes is that Montgomery says nothing about a doctrine of Scripture being formulated by this method. As a matter of fact, he seems to think that such a doctrine is a part of the data, outside of or before theologizing.[21]

---

[18] Holmes, "Ordinary Language Analysis," 135ff.

[19] Ibid.; Montgomery, "The Theologian's Craft," 276–79. For further references to the method see the following: Suppe, *Structure of Scientific Theories*; Mary Hesses, *Models and Analogics in Science* (South Bend, IN: University of Notre Dame Press, 1961); Stephen Toulmin, *Foresight and Understanding* (Hutchinson University Library, 1961); Norwood Hanson, *Patterns of Discovery* (Cambridge: Cambridge University Press, 1958); Ian Ramsey, *Models and Mystery* (Oxford: Oxford University Press, 1964) and *Religion and Science*; Frederick Ferré, "Mapping the Logic of Models in Science and Theology," *The Christian Scholar* 46 (1963): 9ff. It is important to note that I am not claiming that theology is science or vice versa, only that they employ a similar method.

[20] Montgomery, "The Theologian's Craft," 272–73.

[21] Ibid., 238–88.

On the other hand, Holmes is explicit that a doctrine of inerrancy is a product of this methodology. In about one page at the end of his article he sketches his view.[22] In a reply to Holmes, Norman Geisler objects to Holmes's treatment of the doctrine of inerrancy on two grounds: (1) the inadequacy of the bases for rejecting induction and deduction and (2) a discomfort with adduction as outlined by Holmes. Geisler concludes by arguing for a methodology that proceeds *inductively* to premises about the inspiration of the Bible guaranteeing that what it teaches is true and about the fact that the Bible teaches historical, factual material. From these premises one *deduces* that the Scripture is without error in matters of history and so on.[23]

I suspect that there is greater agreement between Holmes and Geisler than a first reading of the exchange might indicate. I think that a good deal of Geisler's concern is motivated by Holmes's unfortunate use of such terms as "extrapolation to round out the doctrine of Scripture," "a model," "a word game," and the unhappy characterization of the doctrine of inerrancy as a "second-order theological construct." Theologizing is all based on the text of Scripture and is not identical with it; so in this sense, all doctrine is "second order." In my judgment there is Scripture, and there is theologizing on it.[24] On the other hand, I guess that Holmes's objection to Geisler's suggestion is that in Holmes's judgment, Geisler cannot derive his conclusion without equivocation—due to the fact that the propositions from which inerrancy is deduced must be so loaded that the fallacy of equivocation is inevitable.[25] While one might be able to derive the proposition "the Bible is inerrant," this is far short of what theologians mean when they formulate the doctrine of inerrancy.

There is, however, a deep point of agreement between Geisler (and those who defend the classical method) and Holmes and Montgomery. This point of agreement is the need for the combined methods of induction and deduction, although admittedly these men would not relate the methods in the same way.

There are, in my judgment, a number of advantages in formulating

[22] Holmes, "Ordinary Language Analysis," 137–38.
[23] Norman L. Geisler, "Theological Method and Inerrancy: A Reply to Professor Holmes," *Bulletin of the Evangelical Theology Society* 11 (Summer 1968): 139–46. See also A. F. Holmes, "Reply to N. L. Geisler," *Bulletin of the Evangelical Society* 11 (Fall 1968): 194–95.
[24] See references in note 19 for arguments to this effect.
[25] Holmes, "Ordinary Language Analysis," 137. In a letter dated October 31, 1978, Holmes adds, "However much progress we make *inductively*, the resultant generalization still amounts to less than total inerrancy: at best probability will result. Further, I think that no set of biblical statements supplies sufficient premises to *deduce* total inerrancy as defined and qualified by careful theologians."

the doctrine of inerrancy by abduction or retroduction.[26] (1) Retroduction retains a methodological continuity with the rest of theology. If Holmes and Montgomery are right about retroduction being the correct method for theology in general, it is difficult, without some argument, to see why the specific doctrine of inerrancy should be methodologically different. (2) It retains both induction and deduction, albeit in an informal way, so that neither logic of the classical method is lost. (3) It places justification of the doctrine of inerrancy on a broader evidential base. In the next section I will examine the exegetical evidence of Scripture that serves as evidential justification for the doctrine of inerrancy. These considerations are more numerous than an inductive argument to two premises from which inerrancy is deducted. (4) The conclusion of a retroductive argument is much more difficult to disconfirm than that of the classical argument. This point can be illustrated in the distinction made by N. R. Hanson between pattern statements (the results of abduction) and detail statements (the results of induction alone):

> Pattern statements are different from detail statements. They are not inductive summaries of detail statements. Still the statement "It is a bird" is truly empirical. Had birds been different, or had the bird-antelope been drawn differently, "It is a bird" might not have been true. In some sense it is true. If the detail statements are empirical, the pattern statements which give them sense are also empirical—though not in the same way. *To deny a detail statement is to do something within the pattern. To deny a pattern statement is to attack the conceptual framework itself, and this denial cannot function in the same way.* (italics mine).[27]

If Hanson is correct—and I think he is—then concern about the certainty of the conclusion in retroduction is unnecessary. It should be remembered that the first steps in the logic of the classical method are inductive, so that the conclusion that is deduced is only from *probable* premises. (5) It gives a rationale as to why a defender of inerrancy might be justified in holding and defending the doctrine of inerrancy in spite of problems with some of the phenomena. A helpful analogue can be drawn from theory justification in science. No scientific theory is without anomalies. However,

[26] In advocating abduction as the method of formulating and justifying inerrancy, I am suggesting a modification of what has been called the classical method (see Sproul, "Case for Inerrancy"). Rather than following an ordered procedure of steps, all matters become a part of the data from which the doctrine is formulated and against which it is tested. Moreover, it should be quite clear that the charge of circularity against the doctrine of inerrancy is no more justified than the claim that our scientific theories are all circular. The evidential base contains both external and internal data. Beyond that, the doctrine is tested against the data for accuracy.
[27] Hanson, *Patterns of Discovery*, 87–90.

these anomalies do not necessarily disconfirm the theory if that theory fits most of the data. Rather, they show that the phenomena are not fully understood or that the theory needs further amplification. The same is true with the defender of inerrancy. Because the doctrine makes intelligible so much of the phenomena, the theologian works both with phenomena and doctrine to resolve the conflict. Such a procedure removes the doctrine of inerrancy from what some have called the "Maginot line mentality." The inerrantist can live with difficulties, knowing that one anomaly will not disconfirm or falsify his doctrine. This is as it should be, since the inerrantist claims only that when all things are known there will be no conflict between doctrine and data. (6) It retains an important distinction between the Scripture and interpretations of (hermeneutics/exegesis) and theologizing (biblical and systematic theology) on it. It is the Bible that is inerrant; neither our interpretations nor our theologizing are infallible. (7) Finally, if point 6 is correct, it leaves open the possibility that a better formulation of a doctrine may be made. This is not to deny that the phenomena and norms or models are primarily found in the Scripture. However, retroduction allows that some better way of setting forth the biblical data may be possible and can be sought. It does not mean that subjectivism and relativism are the rule of the day.

In closing the discussion of method, one final word is in order. I am not unduly optimistic that there will be agreement on methodology. This discussion too deeply touches theological and apologetical concerns where evangelicals differ widely in approach. However, it is important to notice that, while there is diversity in method, there is unity with respect to the place and importance of Scripture.

The Exegetical Evidence from Scripture[28]

In my judgment, the doctrine of inerrancy is built on five scriptural phenomena.

[28] At first I thought of entitling this section "The Phenomena of Scripture." However, although I still believe the material presented to be part of the phenomena of Scripture, I think such a heading would be misleading. "Phenomena of Scripture" has a very specific meaning in the history of the debate over inerrancy. It has been taken to mean a neutral or presuppositionless approach to the Bible simply as it appears. It is important to see that the biblical teaching about itself is a part of these phenomena and, as John Warwick Montgomery points out, it is exceedingly important to see which phenomena are primarily in the formulation of a doctrine. "To know how to treat biblical passages containing apparent errors or contradictions, we must determine what kind of book the Bible is. A doctrine of limited biblical authority derived from passages manifesting difficulties is as false an induction and as flagrant a denial of the analogy of Scripture as is a morally imperfect Christology derived from questionable acts on Jesus' part. In both cases, proper induction requires that we go to the express biblical teaching on the subject (Jesus' deity; Scripture's authority) and allow this to create the pattern for treating particular problems." (John W. Montgomery, "Inductive Inerrancy," *Christianity Today* [March 3, 1967], 48).

1. The Biblical Teaching on Inspiration

The importance of the doctrine of inspiration to inerrancy cannot be overstated. As a matter of fact, until the last century one was thought to be identical with the other. To deny inerrancy was to deny inspiration. Clearly the central passage for consideration here is 2 Timothy 3:16. While all parties to the debate recognize the importance of this verse to the doctrine, it is amazing how few actually exegete it carefully.

The interpretation of this passage involves four distinct but not unrelated questions. The first has to do with the meaning of *pasa graphē* (πᾶσα γραφή). *Pasa* may be translated either by "all" or by "every." The distinction between "all Scripture" and "every Scripture" is the difference between reference to the whole body of the Old Testament (see Gal. 3:8) and particular passages of Scripture (see Acts 8:35). It is the distinction between Scripture viewed collectively and Scripture taken distributively. Some argue emphatically for "every" on the ground that the article is absent. Others point to analogous cases where *pas* is used in a technical or semitechnical phrase and where "every" cannot possibly be meant (Acts 2:36; Eph. 2:21; 3:15; Col. 4:12). It may be, however, that in these exceptions attention is being drawn to the partitive aspect of the expression. If so, then "every" would be preferable, and the phrase would indicate that each separate part of the *graphē* is in view.[29]

There are three possible meanings here for *graphē*. It could mean any writing whatsoever, since the basic word simply means "writing"; it may refer to the Old Testament, *in toto* or in part; or it may be construed to include even recent Christian literature. It is highly unlikely that the first possibility is correct. The word *graphē* is found over fifty times in the New Testament and always means one thing—the sacred writings. Some have concluded that it has become a kind of *terminus technicus* for the sacred writings. Thus, if this occurrence refers only to *some* writing, it constitutes the sole exception. It might be objected, however, that such an exception is justified, since every other use of *graphē* has the definite article (*hē graphē*, *hai graphai*). The answer to that objection is that the absence of the article is due to the fact that the word has attained the status of a specialized term. With only one specific meaning it (*graphē*) can be used without the article, and the absence of the article here indicates this.[30]

The second question has to do with the meaning of *theopneustos*

[29] Donald Guthrie, *The Pastoral Epistles* (Grand Rapids, MI: Eerdmans, 1957), 1963.
[30] Ed L. Miller, "Plenary Inspiration and 2 Timothy 3:16," *Lutheran Quarterly*, XVII (February 1965): 57–58.

(θεόπνευστος). In my judgment, the importance of this word to any discussion of Scripture is decisive. *Theopneustos* is a member of a special class of adjectives called verbal adjectives. A group of these is formed by suffixing *-tos*. Further, this particular word is a compound of *theos* ("god") and *pneō* ("breathe"). The usual translation of the term is "inspired" or "inspiration." "Inspiration" may be somewhat misleading, since it could convey the idea of God's breath being infused into the Word—that is, energizing it. God does energize his Word, but that is not the point here. Adjectives of this class either (1) have meaning of a perfect passive participle or (2) express possibility. An example of the former is *agapētos* (ἀγαπητός, "beloved"); the latter can be seen in *anektos* (ἀνεκτός, "bearable, endurable"). The passive sense is far more common.[31] Warfield, whose exhaustive and often bypassed analysis has not been matched,[32] has concluded—after a thorough examination of eight-six words ending in *tos* and compounded with θεός—that *theopneustos* has nothing to do with *in*-spiring, but relates to the production of sacred, authoritative Scripture. The Scriptures are the spirated breath of God. For this reason, Paul can say that the Scriptures are God's speech (Gal. 3:8, 22; Rom. 9:17). God is the author of what is recorded (Acts 13:32–35), and the entirety of Scripture is the oracle of God (Rom. 3:2). Even if it could be shown that the active idea of God's breathing his breath into the Scriptures is preferable, a strong view of inspiration would not be hindered, so long as this inspiring took place once for all at the time of the writing of the text. The main thought then would be that the *graphē* is thoroughly permeated with the breath of God.

The third interpretative question has to do with the relationship between *graphē* and *theopneustos*. Our text says formally, or technically, that it is the Scriptures, not the writers, that are inspired or God-breathed. This point is important, since some who defend their belief that the Bible is not inerrant claim that it is false to assert that the writers of the sacred text never made errors of judgment. It seems quite clear that at least once one erred in what he did, for Paul tells us that he found it necessary to withstand Peter to his face (Gal. 2:11ff.). Furthermore, it is clear that at least three letters, possibly four, were written by the apostle Paul to the church at Corinth. However, only two (possibly three, depending on whether the

[31] Bruce M. Metzger, *Lexical Aids for Students of New Testament Greek*, New Edition (Princeton, NJ: Theological Book Agency, 1970), 44. See also F. Blass and A. Debrunner, *A Greek Grammar of the New Testament and Other Early Christian Literature*, trans. and rev. Robert W. Funk (Chicago: University of Chicago Press, 1961), 61–63; and Nigel Turner, *A Grammar of New Testament Greek* (Edinburgh: T & T Clark, 1963), 3:150–65.

[32] B. B. Warfield, *The Inspiration and Authority of the Bible* (Philadelphia: Presbyterian & Reformed, 1948), 281–83.

"severe letter" was a separate letter or whether it is a part of 2 Corinthians) are preserved in our present canon. Thus, all that is required is that *Scripture* be inspired and the extent of the inspiration be identical with our present canon.

The fourth question has to do with whether *theopneustos* is to be understood as standing (1) predictively or (2) attributively to the subject *graphē*. If the former is the case, Paul says that "every Scripture is inspired." On the other hand, if the latter is correct, the text should read, "Every inspired Scripture" or "Every Scripture is inspired." Both renderings are grammatically possible. It seems, however, that the predicative use of *theopneustos* is correct. These considerations are in its favor: (1) In the absence of a verb, it seems natural to construe the two adjectives (*theopneustos*, "God-breathed" and *ophelimos*, "profitable") in the same manner; (2) the construction of 2 Timothy 3:16 is identical to that of 1 Timothy 4:4, where the two adjectives are clearly predicative;[33] (3) in an attributive construction we would expect the adjective, in this case *theopneustos*, to appear before *graphē*; (4) words joined by *kai* ("and") are usually understood as linked by this conjunction; and finally, (5) the attributive interpretation seems to leave open the possibility that there may be some uninspired *graphē*.[34]

The primary argument in favor of the attributive construction is the supposed emphasis of the passage, which is said to lie not in the concept of inspiration but on the usefulness of Scripture.[35] Even if one accepts this less likely construction, it should be noted that the attributive sense does not necessarily lead to uninspired Scriptures, as Miller so clearly demonstrates:

> At this point I should like to suggest that the implication (namely, that there are some Scriptures which are not inspired) is not necessarily in the passage at all. *Graphē* can mean only three things: If it means any writing in general (which, as we have seen, it seems never to mean in the New Testament), then it is clearly reasonable to assert that only those which are God-inspired are useful for instruction, etc. If it means the authoritative Old Testament and/or Christian literature, then it amounts to a kind of reminder that we are talking, after all, about the Scriptures, that is, the inspired writings. To speak, for example of *mortal* man is not necessarily to imply that there is any other kind (italics his).[36]

[33] Miller, "Plenary Inspiration," 59.
[34] Ibid.
[35] Martin Dibelius and Hans Conzelmann, *The Pastoral Epistles*, trans. Philip Bultolph and Adela Yarbro (Philadelphia: Fortress, 1972), 120.
[36] Miller, "Plenary Inspiration," 59.

What then are the implications of this passage for our concern at hand? First, inspiration is something that has to do with the text of Scripture, surely not with the subjective interiority of the writer.[37] Such a view cannot square itself with this text. Second, the Scriptures *are* the very spirated breath of God. The view that the text becomes the Word of God when it speaks to me is, once again, outside biblical guidelines. Moreover, I think it is important to reaffirm that both the *form* and the *content* of Scripture are the very Word of God.[38] While it is true that we must resist the error of simply identifying the Word of God with an "aggregate of letters and sounds," it is nevertheless *nonsense* to think that you can separate them. The *Word* comes in *words*. Third, the doctrine of inspiration applies to *all* and to *every* Scripture. That is, the Scriptures in part and in the whole are God's Word. Note that there is no distinction between those things that are either Christological, salvific, or necessary for faith and practice and those things that are historical, scientific, or incidental. Such a distinction is sometimes called "limited inspiration." It is, however, not biblical. Lloyd-Jones puts the issues well:

> For the questions which immediately arise are these: Who decides what is true? Who decides what is of value? How can you discriminate between the great facts which are true and those that are false? How can you differentiate between the facts and the teaching? How can you separate this [*sic*] essential message of the Bible from the background in which it is presented? Not only so, but there is certainly no such division or distinction recognized in the Scripture itself. The whole Bible comes to us and offers itself to us in exactly the same way, and as a whole. There is no hint, no suspicion of a suggestion that parts of it are important and parts are not. All come to us in the same form.[39]

Although it is indeed a large and heavy burden to have to defend the Bible on all points, it is nevertheless necessary! It seems to me that those who could "relieve" us of this task overlook two quite important matters. The first is that it is simply impossible to separate the historical from the theological. They thoroughly interpenetrate one another. While the evangelical who believes the Bible is not inerrant may want to free us from the burden of defending the historical accuracy of the accounts of Pekah's

---

[37] Bernard L. Ramm, "Scripture as a Theological Concept," *Review and Expositor* 71 (February 1974): 157–58.
[38] Cf. this view with that of Charles A. Briggs, *The Bible, the Church, and Reason* (New York: Scribner, 1893), 91.
[39] D. M. Lloyd-Jones, *Authority* (Chicago: InterVarsity, 1958), 35.

reign because he cannot believe the accounts, the unbeliever cannot accept the historical nature of a resurrection. Why defend one and not the other? Certainly, the latter is much more difficult to accept than the former. The second point relates to the consequences of divorcing the historical and factual from the doctrinal and theological. Suppose for a moment that I am an unbeliever. You have just told me that the Bible has numerous inaccuracies of a historical, scientific, and possibly even ethical nature, but that it is absolutely without error in all of those wonderful, "unbelievable" things about God and heaven. Being a bit cynical, I would likely respond that you stretch the bounds of credulity in asking me to believe all these things that I have no possible way of confirming while at the same time allowing that there are numerous errors in areas that I *can* confirm. Can you blame me? It seems that our Lord sees more connection between the believability of earthly things and heavenly things (John 3:12) than do those who defend limited inspiration.

Before leaving this discussion of inspiration, let me point out that there seems to be at least one serious objection to our using this as such a strong datum in support of the doctrine of inerrancy. It has often been objected that a view such as the one I have been arguing is just too simple or one-sided. The objection is stated in a number of different ways. Sometimes it is argued that the inerrantist is guilty of an error analogous to the christological error of docetism (the denial that Christ had a human body). Others state it in terms of mechanical dictation. They argue that such a view of inspiration and inerrancy must of necessity involve not only the suspension of the abilities of the writers but also the word-by-word dictation of the *graphē*. Still others claim that this position overlooks the historical conditioning and human thought forms that must be used to convey the truth of God. Since each formulation of the objection requires a slightly different answer, I will reply to each in turn.

Does the doctrine of inerrancy lead to something like Docetism? I cannot see how. Some among those who believe in inerrancy may believe that the Bible came down from heaven in a heavenly language inscribed without human hand, but they are both in the minority and wrong. The problem for those who oppose inerrancy arises because they fail to keep the biblical balance between the human and the divine. It should be remembered that it is just as wrong to overemphasize the human at the expense of the divine as it is to exalt the divine to the negation of the human. The former can be done straightforwardly by denying that the Bible is the Word of God. It may also be accomplished quite subtly, as when Bloesch suggests that the Bible is not the *immediate* Word of God but rather comes through the human medium.[40]

The problem here, at its deepest level, is a misconception about the nature of humanity. Inerrantists often use the analogy of a sinless Christ and an errorless Bible. In Christ you have both the human and the divine without sin. In the Bible you have both the human and the divine without error. Beegle's response to this is instructive. He begins by pointing out two reservations that Warfield gives in citing this analogy. Warfield says that the analogy must not be pressed too far, since (1) in Christ there is the hypostatic union, while in inscripturation there is nothing parallel to such union, and (2) in Christ the divine and the human unite to constitute a divine-human *person*, but in Scripture they only cooperate to produce a divine-human *work*. Then Beegle quotes Vawter approvingly to the effect that the analogy between sinlessness and errorlessness breaks down because sin is a disorder in man, and error is not.[41] Furthermore, in another place Beegle declares that there is nothing more consistently human than to err.

But what both Beegle and Vawter do not realize is that their claim is not strong enough. For the human element in the Scripture to necessitate errors in the text of the Bible it must be shown that errancy is essential to humanity. If so, then Adam was not human until he erred, and we will not be human in the glorified state, since we will no longer sin or err. Thus, while care must be used in pressing the analogy between Christ and the Scripture, it does show the *possibility* of an inerrant Bible, given the essential nature of humanity. Inerrancy becomes *necessary* because of the divine element.

Does the doctrine of inerrancy demand mechanical dictation? Those who oppose the doctrine often seek to push inerrantists into this mold; but this is unnecessary and unfair. I think that the proper way to express the biblical teaching on the process that produced the inspired texts is *concurrence*. That is, God and man so cooperate that the product was God's Word in human language. The author's style and personality, as well as the distinctive characteristics of the language in which he wrote, are evident in the autographs. How could this be done? The closest that one can come to an answer is the statement found in 2 Peter 2:21, but beyond that it must be admitted that what took place was a miracle, just as was the virgin birth.

[40] Donald G. Bloesch, *Essentials of Evangelical Theology: God, Authority, and Salvation* (San Francisco: Harper & Row, 1978), 74–78.

[41] Beegle, *Scripture, Tradition, and Infallibility*, 289–90.

Finally, do historical conditioning or context and human thought forms count against inerrancy? Not unless historical conditioning and human thought forms and language *necessarily* falsify truth. I have not seen and do not expect to see such a proof. I will say more about this below.

2. The Biblical Teaching Concerning the Accreditation of God's Message and Messenger

The second aspect of the biblical data to which the doctrine of inerrancy should appeal is the criteria set down in Scripture for the accreditation of the prophet and his message. I think this is second in importance only to the biblical teaching on inspiration and has not been used as fully as it should have been. There is a good parallel between the prophet and the Scripture. In regard to the one the communication was usually oral, although it could have been written down either at the time of reception or later; in the other the communication is written. Further, in both cases the communication has the human element as an essential part.

There are two passages in the book of Deuteronomy that bear on the subject (13:1–5 and 18:20–22). These passages contain three criteria for accreditation: (1) The prophet must not speak in the name of another god (Deut. 13:1, 2; 18:20). This criterion is obviously easy to check. The extremely serious nature of this type of false prophecy is seen in the imposition of capital punishment for the offender. Such a prophet was guilty of breaking the first commandment and was thus deserving of death. (2) The prophet must not speak a word that is not true (Deut. 13:1–5; 18:22). This and the following criterion are meant to distinguish what is God's Word from what is merely human. In 18:22, "the word does not come true" (RSV) is literally "the word is not." The point is that the word has no substance or that it is not so. "That is, the word supposedly spoken by God through the prophet was not in accord with the word of God already revealed and it was therefore automatically suspect."[42] There is harmony within the revealed will of God. (3) The prophet must not speak what does not come to pass (Deut. 18:22). This criterion refers to the judgmental or predicative word of the prophet. The truth of his words would be demonstrated in their fulfillment or failure. The prophet is accredited by the *total, absolute* truthfulness of his words.

[42] P. C. Craigie, *The Book of Deuteronomy*, The New International Commentary on the Old Testament (Grand Rapids, MI: Eerdmans, 1976), 262–64.

3. The Bible's Teaching Concerning Its Own Authority

Evangelicals of all types are anxious to affirm the absolute authority of Scripture, making this an important consideration. Obviously many more passages could be cited,[43] but I will discuss only the two that, in my judgment, are most significant.

The first passage is Matthew 5:17–20. It is well known to those who have closely followed the debate over the Bible. Jesus is pointing out that a righteousness greater than that of the Pharisees is necessary for entrance into the kingdom (v. 20). In this context he talks about the authoritative and continuing nature of the law as a standard. He did not come to destroy it (v. 17). Moreover, until everything is fulfilled, heaven and earth will not pass away (v. 18). The Law's authority can be seen in the fact that every minutia will be fulfilled.

The second passage is John 10:34–35. In a disputation with the Jews, Jesus cites Psalm 82:6, after which he says that "Scripture cannot be broken" (v. 35). Our Lord here speaks of the absolutely binding nature of the authority of Scripture.

What kind of response do those who oppose inerrancy give? Hubbard's reply is significant. With respect to Matthew 5:17–20, his answer is twofold. First, he says that the context does not support a definition of inerrancy that entails absolute accuracy down to the smallest details, namely, the "smallest letter" and the "least stroke of a pen." "The heart of the argument, then, is . . . [the] binding, persevering quality of the divine commands that Jesus did not abolish but fulfilled."[44] Second, Hubbard maintains, much of the strong language in the Sermon on the Mount—such as "until heaven and earth disappear" and "smallest letter" and "least stroke of a pen"—is hyperbole. Of some of this language Hubbard says, "A literal interpretation would not only encourage self-maiming, it would surely limit the number of times that one could discipline himself in temptation."[45] Thus the binding or authoritative nature of the law is stressed.

While one may allow that there are *some* examples of hyperbole in the Sermon on the Mount, it is simply false to claim that everything is hyperbole. Hubbard must bear the burden of proof that the passage in question is hyperbole. I see no such proof.

[43] E.g., Acts 1:16; 3:24, 25; Rom. 9:17; 2 Cor. 6:16; Gal. 3:8.
[44] David Hubbard, "The Current Tensions: Is There a Way Out?," in *Biblical Authority*, ed. Jack Rogers (Waco, TX: Word, 1977), 172.
[45] Ibid., 173.

Hubbard gives similar treatment to John 10:34–35. Here the issue is authority, not inerrancy. Hubbard says:

> Jesus' argument seems to focus on the authority of his citation from Psalm 82:6. The statement "Scripture cannot be broken" is virtually an appeal on his part to what his Jewish opponents also believed. His aim was not to teach them new insights into the authority of Scripture, but rather to remind them of what they believed about the authority and applicability of the Scripture—an authority that made it lawful for him to be called the Son of God.[46]

I grant that these passages do not explicitly teach inerrancy and that they do not specify what a definition of inerrancy must contain. For instance, inerrancy clearly does not demand statements about "smallest letters" and "least strokes of a pen." However, Hubbard has left the ball park too early. The game is not yet over. To admit that these passages teach that the Bible is an absolute and binding authority is only to move the question one step backward. The question now before us is this: How can the Scriptures be such an authority? To what must we attribute this property? We could say that God just willed it so. However, is not a better explanation to be found in the inspiration and inerrancy of the Bible? To divorce inerrancy and authority is impossible. I have never been able to understand how one can be justified in claiming *absolute* authority for the Scriptures and at the same time deny their inerrancy. This seems to be the height of epistemological nonsense and confusion.

Let me try to illustrate the point. Suppose that I have an Amtrak railroad schedule. In describing its use to you, I tell you that it is filled with numerous errors but that it is *absolutely* authoritative and trustworthy. I think you would be extremely dubious. At least the schedule would have one thing going for it; it declares itself to be subject to change without notice. There is an objection to the point I am making, and it goes as follows: False in one thing does not make the Bible false in all it says.[47] Of course this objection is valid, but it overlooks the significant fact that if what has been said to this point is true, the Bible claims itself to be absolutely true. The Amtrak schedule makes no such claim. Beegle is aware of this reply. Thus, he says that even if his wife claims to tell the truth but is wrong, that does not mean that everything that she says is

[46] Ibid.
[47] Beegle, *Scripture, Tradition, and Infallibility*, 280ff.

false.[48] Again, what Beegle says is true, but he has overlooked another important fact. The person speaking with respect to the Bible is not his wife but *God*. This is not some finite god but a God who has essential attributes that include omniscience, perfect goodness, and omnipotence. These make a big difference.

4. The Way in Which Scripture Is Used by Scripture

A fourth important phenomenon to observe is the way in which Scripture uses other Scripture in argumentation. The instances may be divided into three classes. First, there are those instances where the whole argument rests on a single word. In Matthew 22:43–45, the entire argument rests on the word *Lord*. Jesus cites Psalm 110:1 and appeals to the use of "Lord" as support for his claim to deity. In John 10:34–35, Jesus' argument rests on the use of the single word *god* in Psalm 82:6.

Second, there is an instance where the entire argument depends on the tense of a verb. In Matthew 22:32, Jesus uses the present tense of the verb to demonstrate the truth of the resurrection. He says, "'I am the God of Abraham, the God of Isaac, and the God of Jacob.' He is not the God of the dead but of the living."

Third, in Galatians 3:16, we have an argument where the point depends on the singular number, *seed*, as opposed to the plural, *seeds*. Paul writes: "The promises were spoken to Abraham and to his seed. The Scripture does not say 'and to seeds,' meaning many people, but 'and to your seed,' meaning one person who is Christ." Now, if the text of Scripture is not inerrant, it is difficult to see the point in these arguments.[49] An easy rebuttal would be, "Well, the text may be wrong."

There is an objection that might be made against the argument just given. One might argue that there are many uses of Scripture by Scripture where the precision that I have spoken of is not demonstrated. For instance, certain uses of the Old Testament by New Testament writers seems to be very imprecise. A totally satisfactory answer to this objection would take far more space than allowed in this chapter. However, a meticulous study of these uses of the Old Testament reveals that the writers do not quote the Old Testament cavalierly but with great care.

---

[48] Ibid.

[49] Roger Nicole, "New Testament Use of the Old Testament," in *Revelation and the Bible*, ed. Carl F. H. Henry (Grand Rapids, MI: Baker, 1958), 139, gives twenty-four examples of the way in which New Testament arguments are based on one Old Testament word.

5. The Biblical Teaching Concerning the Character of God

More than once in Scripture we are told that God cannot lie (Num. 23:19; 1 Sam. 15:29; Titus 1:2; Heb. 6:18). Furthermore, in Romans 3:4 Paul emphatically declares that God is true and that his trustfulness cannot be changed by the lack of faith that some have. Jesus said to God, "Your word is truth" (John 17:17). If the Scriptures are from God and his character is behind them, it seems that they cannot be in error.

Having surveyed the exegetical data of Scripture that support doctrine of inerrancy, let us try to formulate a definition of inerrancy.

A Definition of Inerrancy

One of the factors that makes generalization about the biblical data concerning itself so difficult is the already-mentioned fact that Scripture makes no explicit statement on this matter. Although such a statement would not settle the matter decisively, as I have argued above, it would give us a running start. Lacking this, however, we must begin with a search for appropriate terminology. A number of terms have been suggested. The most common are: inspiration, indefectibility, infallibility, indeceivability, and inerrant, or without error. Let us now turn to an examination of these terms.

As has already been indicated, for at least a fair number of biblical and theological scholars of former days *inspiration* was synonymous with inerrancy. To say that the Bible is inspired was to say that it is absolutely accurate or inerrant. Two men among those who held such a view were B. B. Warfield, and Charles Hodge. Today such identification tends to be more confusing than helpful. Thus I think it wise to search for another, more appropriate, term.

A second possibility, suggested by Hans Küng, is *indefectibility*.[50] Indefectibility means abiding or remaining in the truth in spite of errors that touch even on doctrine. One can hardly do better than the judgment of Bloesch on this matter: "This seems to call into question the absolute normativeness of Scripture in the church's understanding of the truth of revelation."[51] This term is clearly at odds with the data presented above. We must find a better one.

Another possibility is *infallibility*, which has a long history of theo-

[50] Hans Küng, *Infallible? An Inquiry*, trans. Edward Quinn (Garden City, NY: Doubleday, 1971), 139ff., 181ff.
[51] Bloesch, *Essentials of Evangelical Theology*, 68.

logical use. Most likely the best place to begin a discussion of the term is with a definition from the *Oxford English Dictionary*. Infallibility means "the quality or fact of being infallible or exempt from liability to err" or "the quality of being unfailing or not liable to fall; unfailing certainty."[52] With the adjective *infallible* when predicated of things, this dictionary equates "not liable to fail, unfailing," "not liable to prove false, erroneous, or mistaken; that unfailingly holds good," or "not liable to fail in its action or operation."[53] Merely from the standpoint of definition, it would be difficult to maintain a *clear* distinction between this term and inerrancy, although it would always be possible to stipulate a distinction.

However, when we turn to the question of usage, the picture is more complex. Within Roman Catholic theology, *inerrant* is normally used when discussing the Bible, while *infallible* is used to designate the authority of the church, particularly with respect to the teaching function of the pope and the magisterium. Protestants, of course, do not claim infallibility for the church, and, more and more, *infallibility* has become associated with the Scriptures. More recently, it has become a term championed by many who support what has been called "limited inspiration," or what today might better be called "limited inerrancy." That is, those who often advance this word to the exclusion of inerrancy would, at most, defend the inerrancy of the Scriptures in areas that are "revelational," "soteriological," or are "matters of faith and doctrine." Because of the differing usages of *infallibility*, Stephen T. Davis in his recent book gives a stipulative definition reflecting this tendency. He says, "The Bible is infallible if and only if it makes no false or misleading statements on any matter of faith and practice."[54] At any rate, *infallibility* can and should properly be used of the Bible. In its lexical meaning it is not far from *inerrancy*.

Another candidate is *indeceivability*. It is questionable whether the term per se has been used to express the biblical attitude about itself. However, a long list of theologians—Briggs,[55] Berkouwer,[56] Rogers,[57] Hubbard,[58] and Bloesch[59]—like to affirm that the Bible is without error in the sense suggested by this term. These men are evangelical in their theology and have

[52] *Oxford English Dictionary*, s.v. "infallibility."
[53] Ibid.
[54] Davis, *Debate about the Bible*, 23.
[55] Briggs, *Bible, Church, and Reason*, 91–95.
[56] G. C. Berkouwer, *Holy Scripture*, trans. and ed. Jack Rogers (Grand Rapids, MI: Eerdmans, 1975).
[57] Jack Rogers, "The Church Doctrine of Authority," in *Biblical Authority*, ed. Jack Rogers (Waco: Word, 1977).
[58] Hubbard, "Current Tensions."
[59] Bloesch, *Essentials of Evangelical Theology*, 67–70.

a real love and respect for the Scriptures; but they think the Bible contains inaccuracies of various kinds and thus do not like the word *inerrancy*. They would rather stick with a designation such as "without error," defined in terms of indeceivability.

Let us take a moment to examine their argument, since this position seems to be gaining wider acceptance within evangelical circles. Usually the starting place is displeasure with the word *inerrancy*, for various reasons that are discussed below. Theologians like those mentioned above prefer to speak of the Bible's authority or even its infallibility. Some can live with a statement on Scripture like that found in the Lausanne Covenant, which states that the Bible is "without error in all that it affirms." There is a caveat. *Error* must be defined. Since it is such an important term, it is argued, we must not let just anyone specify its meaning. The place a definition must be sought is in the Scriptures themselves. The advantage, so it is claimed, is that we will not then be imposing an alien standard on the Bible. It is as though the imprecision of early historical writing is preserved in the meaning of the word *error*. For someone like Berkouwer, "without error" means free from lying and fraud.[60] For Rogers, "error" means "willful deception," and for Hubbard, "that which leads us astray from the will of God or the knowledge of his truth."[61] Thus, error becomes associated with (1) the intentionality of the writer or text and (2) the will of God, particularly as it has to do with religious or spiritual truth.[62]

What shall we say about such a proposal? There are at least two commendatory things that can be said about this attempt to reflect the attitude of the Bible toward itself. First, it recognizes that errorlessness in some sense must be attributed to the Scriptures. Second, it seeks to deal seriously with the biblical data.

There are, in my judgment, however, three reasons—methodological, biblical, and motivational—for thinking that this approach is inadequate in the final analysis. First, there is a methodological reason. As I have already stated, there is no explicit statement in Scripture to the effect that it is without error. If there were, then it would certainly be appropriate to start our definition with a study of the etymology and usage of the Hebrew and Greek terms used in this connection, but such is not possible. Error or inerrancy are theological concepts;[63] that is, they are used by the theologian

[60] Berkouwer, *Holy Scripture*, 184–94.
[61] Rogers, "Church Doctrine of Authority," 46.
[62] Hubbard, "Current Tensions," 168.
[63] Herman Ridderbos, "An Attempt at the Theological Definition of Inerrancy, Infallibility, and Authority," *International Reformed Bulletin*, 32 and 33, 11th year (January–April, 1968): 27–41.

to express what he thinks the biblical data demand. This fact, however, in no way counts a priori against *any* concept. For instance, *trinity* is in the same boat, since it is not to be found, *as a term*, anywhere in the Bible. As I have argued earlier, even biblical terms, when used in doctrinal or theological statements, are subject to the same constraints as are any formulations about inerrancy or error.

My second reason for rejecting the term *indeceivability* is biblical. It may be that some do not agree with the distinction between biblical and theological usage, but let us move to the level of the biblical for a moment. Let it be granted that Berkouwer, Rogers, et al., are methodologically right and I am wrong. I would still think that their conclusions are open to serious question. The reason is this: Any definition of error in terms of indeceivability as defined above appeals to too selective a sample of biblical vocabulary. To put it another way, indeceivability fails to reflect the polydimensionality of the biblical words for error. In both Hebrew and Greek the words may be classified into three groups: (1) errors where intentionality cannot possibly be involved; (2) errors where intentionality may or may not be involved; and (3) errors where intentionality must be involved. Let us take a quick look at each of these groups.

Clearly, the Bible teaches that some errors are made without intentionality.[64] Old Testament words coming from שָׁגַג (*shāgag*) and שָׁגָה (*shāgâ*) are good examples. The idea is "to stray," "to err," even to "transgress *inadvertently*."[65] In Job 6:24, Job says, "Teach me, and I will be quiet; show me where I have been wrong." In view of Job's contention that he was innocent he had to maintain that any error on his part was unintentional, since he was unaware of it. Again in Job 19:4 we read, "If it is true that I have gone astray, my error remains my concern alone." One cannot, without doing violence to the text, maintain that Job is referring to intentional error. It might be argued that Scripture does not hold an individual responsible for inadvertent error. But this too is simply false. From the Hebrew roots mentioned above, the Old Testament has words for sins of ignorance. Leviticus 5:18 says, "He is to bring to the priest as a guilt offering a ram from the flock, one without defect and of the proper value. In this way the priest will make atonement for him for the wrong he has committed *unintentionally*, and he will be forgiven." The same is true of Greek. The word for this kind of error is ἀγνοημα (*agnoēma*). It

[64] In Jer. 37:14, where there is an unintentional lie that is called a lie nevertheless.

[65] Francis Brown, S. R. Driver, and Charles A. Briggs, *A Hebrew and English Lexicon of the Old Testament*, trans. Edward Robinson (Oxford: Clarendon, 1907), 992–93.

means a "sin committed in ignorance."[66] In Hebrews 9:7 it is used of sins of ignorance: "But only the high priest entered the inner room, and that only once a year, and never without blood, which he offered for himself and for the sins the people had committed in ignorance."

The second class of terms has to do with errors where intentionality may or may not be involved. This seems to be the largest group. In the Old Testament a good example from this classification is שַׁל (*shal*). It means "a fault" or "error," and comes from the root שָׁלָה (*shālāh*, "to deceive" or "to be negligent").[67] It is used in 2 Samuel 6:7. Here it is difficult to tell if intentional deception or simply negligence is involved. The Greek ἀστοχέω (*astocheō*) means "to miss the mark."[68] The word is used three times in the New Testament (1 Tim. 1:6; 6:21; 2 Tim. 2:18). Here again, in my judgment, it is impossible to determine whether one misses the mark intentionally or unintentionally.

Finally, there is a group of words used for error that clearly includes the idea of intentionality. In the Old Testament תָּעָה (*ta āh*) and תַּעְתֻּעִים (*tāʿetuʿim*) are used. The first of these terms is used in the Hiphil and has as one of its meanings "to seduce,"[69] while the latter means "a fraud."[70] In the New Testament there are also two words that fall within this class, ἀποπλαγάω (*apoplagaō*) and πλανή (*planē*). The former term can mean "to seduce,"[71] the latter, "fraudulence."[72] Moreover, it is possible to cite at least two instances where lies are told with good intentions, but they are called lies nevertheless (Judg. 16:10). Authorial intention is indeed important, but its relevance is related to hermeneutics.

As should be noted from the discussion, greater emphasis has been placed on the first classification. This was done to show the inadequacy of the proposal before us. Fundamentally, the problem is this proposal seeks to retain a good term but at too high a price—a decided weakening of meaning. For instance, if we accept Rogers's understanding of error as "willful deception," then most books ever written are inerrant.

The third reason that I find the proposal of indeceivability inadequate is motivational. In practice there is the retention of the idea of errorlessness that has a long and important history, but it has been so diluted that it no

---

[66] W. Bauer, W. F. Arndt, and F. W. Gingrich, *A Greek-English Lexicon of the New Testament*, 2nd ed. (Chicago: University of Chicago Press, 1957), 11.
[67] Brown et al., *Hebrew and English Lexicon*, 117.
[68] Bauer, Arndt, and Gingrich, *Greek-English Lexicon*, 117.
[69] Brown et al., *Hebrew and English Lexicon*, 1,073.
[70] Ibid., 1074.
[71] Bauer, Arndt, and Gingrich, *Greek-English Lexicon*, 96.
[72] Ibid., 671.

longer retains its original meaning. The motivation behind this approach is not a more precise definition of *error* or *inerrancy* but ultimately the recognition of "unimportant" errors of history, science, and so forth. It is the first step in undermining the doctrine of inerrancy.

The final possibility that I have raised for an appropriate term is *inerrant*, that is "without error." *Inerrancy* itself is a relatively young word in the English language. At first it appears as though it might be a transliteration of the Latin word *inerrantia*, a participle from the verb *inerro*. However, such is not the case. *Inerrans* is used of fixed stars by Cicero and Lactanius. Boethius, who lived in the latter part of the sixth century and the early part of the seventh, used the Latin term *inerratum* in the sense of "absence of error."[73] The *Oxford English Dictionary* says that it was not until 1837 that the English *inerrant* was used in the modern sense of "exempt from error, free from mistake, infallible." Moreover, the noun *inerrancy* is said to have occurred for the first time in Thomas Hartwell Horne's formidable four-volume *Introduction to the Critical Study and Knowledge of the Holy Scriptures* (1780–1862).[74] In part 2 of volume 2 of the seventh edition (1834) he states, "Absolute inerrancy is impracticable in any printed book."[75] It is, however, possible that the word appeared as early as the first edition in 1818.

In current usage the *Oxford English Dictionary* offers this definition of *inerrancy*: "the quality or condition of being inerrant or unerring; freedom from error." For *inerrant* it gives "does not err; free from error; unerring."[76] On the other hand, *errant* is defined as follows: "the action or state of erring"; "the condition of erring in opinion; the holding of mistaken notions or beliefs"; or "something incorrectly done through ignorance or inadvertence; a mistake."[77] It is easy to see why some equate "without error" with "inerrant."

As I have noted, not all evangelicals like the designation *inerrancy*. Why is this so? Obviously, there are many reasons, stated and otherwise. LaSor says,

> Those who defend the "inerrancy of the Bible" generally mean by that word that the Bible contains no error of any kind, whether religious, historical, geographical, geological, numerical, or of any other category.

[73] *Oxford English Dictionary*, s.v. "inerrant."
[74] Ibid.
[75] Ibid.
[76] Ibid.
[77] Ibid., s.v. "errant."

> The term is not proper, for since it negates a negative idea, it does not leave room for a correct opposite.[78]

Inerrancy is unacceptable because it is essentially the negation of a negative concept. The consequence, LaSor goes on to say, is that the opposite of inerrancy is not errancy but the total infallibility of the Bible in matters of faith and practice. LaSor then points out what he thinks are scriptural problems, even inconsistencies, although he hesitates to call them outright errors.[79] One surely may wonder at this use of logic and language. Inconsistencies most certainly are errors.

Ridderbos[80] and Piepkorn[81] do not like the word *inerrancy* because it is not a biblical word. Piepkorn states the case clearly: "Lutheran clergymen and professors affirm everything that the Sacred Scriptures say about themselves and everything that the Lutheran symbols say about the Sacred Scriptures. It is significant therefore that the term 'inerrancy' does not correspond to any vocable in the Lutheran symbols."[82] Ridderbos thinks it is a theological concept.[83] On the other hand, Piepkorn classifies it as "an ecclesiastical term subject to definition by use."[84]

By far the most extensive criticism of the term *inerrancy* that I have seen comes from Pinnock. It should be noted that he has been one of the most able defenders of the doctrine of the inerrancy of the Bible and even now continues to claim that this is a good term.[85] His reasons for suggesting at least a moratorium on it are as follows. First, he sees the word as needing major qualifications. Such words are a liability and should be avoided where possible. Second, the term does not describe any Bible that we in fact use. It refers only to the original autographs. Third, since it refers to a nonextant text, it does not assert forcibly the authority of the texts that we do have. Fourth, it misfocuses attention on the small or minor difficul-

[78] William Sanford LaSor, "Life Under Tension—Fuller Theological Seminary and 'The Battle for the Bible,'" *Theology, News, and Notes*, Special Issue, Fuller Theological Seminary (1976), 23.
[79] Ibid., 23–25.
[80] Ridderbos, "Attempt at the Theological Definition."
[81] Arthur Carl Piepkorn, "What Does 'Inerrancy' Mean?," *Concordia Theological Monthly* 36 (1963): 577–93.
[82] Ibid., 577.
[83] Ridderbos, "Attempt at Theological Definition," 33ff.
[84] Piepkorn, "What Does 'Inerrancy' Mean?"
[85] Clark Pinnock's *Biblical Revelation: The Foundation of Christian Theology* (Chicago: Moody, 1971) is the able defense of inerrancy to which I refer. In his more recent works, Pinnock has been increasingly critical of the doctrine and its defenders, although he has claimed that he still holds the doctrine. One can trace this change in attitude, if not in substance, in the following articles: "Inspiration and Authority: A Truce Proposal," *The Other Side* (May–June, 1976), 61–65 (this article was sent to Theological Student Fellowship, and all references are to this latter publication); "The Inerrancy Debate Among the Evangelicals," *Theology, News, and Notes*, Special Edition, Fuller Theological Seminary (1976), 11–13; and "Three Views of the Bible in Contemporary Theology," in *Biblical Authority*, ed. Jack Rogers (Waco, TX: Word, 1977), 47–73.

ties in the text rather than on the truth it intends to explain. Finally, it has become a slogan and as such is a term of "conflict and ill feeling."[86] Thus Pinnock can conclude:

> It seems to me, in view of the serious disadvantages the term inerrancy presents, that we ought to suspend it from the list of preferred terminology for stating the evangelical doctrine of Scripture, and let it appear only in the midst of the working out of the details. It is sufficient for us in our public statements to affirm the divine inspiration and final authority of the Bible.[87]

One should not merely dismiss Pinnock's concerns without consideration. However, one may also wonder why *inerrancy* does not forcibly enough assert the authority of the Bible. Possibly there is need to express the biblical view in more than just *one* term. Nevertheless, this should not count against the use of a word if indeed it is appropriate. And the fact that it may be a slogan or may misdirect the attention of some is unfortunate, but if the concept that it seeks to convey is correct, then we must use it or a better term. All of this is just to say that I do not have an inalienable affection for the word. It is the concept of a *wholly true* Bible for which I contend. If some better word can be found, then let us use it.

But what is needed, I think, is a more clear and precise definition of inerrancy rather than a new term. People surely accept or reject the word without agreeing with or even knowing what someone else means by it.

It seems to me that the key concept both in the Scriptures and in the minds of those who use the term is truthfulness. Inerrancy has to do with *truth*. Hence, the positive side of the negative idea is that if the Bible is *inerrant*, it is *wholly true*. If this is the case, there are two ways in which the idea could be preserved. First, we could drop the term *inerrant* from the list of preferred terminology and substitute *always true and never false*. Rather than saying, "I believe the Bible is inerrant," we could say, "I believe the Bible is always or wholly true and never false." Second, we could continue using *inerrant* and clearly specify that it is always to be associated with *truth*.

Since the second is more likely to have widespread use, let me propose this definition of inerrancy. *Inerrancy means that when all facts are known, the Scriptures in their original autographs and properly interpreted will be*

[86] Pinnock, "Truce Proposal," 4.
[87] Ibid.

shown to be wholly true in everything that they affirm, whether that has to do with doctrine or morality or with the social, physical, or life sciences.

I would be willing to contend that inerrancy defined in terms of truth is a legitimate way of reflecting the biblical data. In Psalm 119, the most extended biblical statement on the Word of God, "truth" or "true" is used three times as a characterization: "Your law is true" (v. 142); "all your commands are true" (v. 151); and "all your words are true" (v. 160). Proverbs 30:5–6 say that "every word of God has proven true" (Berkeley Version). In John 17:17 Jesus says, "Your word is truth." It is this idea that is appropriate to the English word *inerrancy*. Such a definition has the advantage of defining a negative in terms of a positive concept. Conversely, it means that the Bible is never false.

Only half the job is now done. *Truth* or *true* must be defined. Although the Bible points to truth as an essential attribute of God, it does not give us a precise theological definition. We rather see the definition in the use of the word. However, truth is an abstract and possibly ambiguous term. There is always the danger that one will only move the debate from a discussion of *error* to a debate over the meaning of *truth* or *true*.

For pristine simplicity and clarity one can hardly beat Aristotle's definitions of true and false. He said, "To say what is, is, and what is not, is not, is true. And to say what is, is not, and what is not, is, it is false."[88]

More recently, the work of a Polish logician named Tarski has proved exceedingly helpful with regard to defining truth.[89] Tarski reduced the notion of truth to certain other semantic notions that were clearly—or better, widely—acceptable. The characteristics of Tarski's definition are as follows: (1) truth is defined in terms of *language*; (2) truth is defined in terms of *sentences* (that is, truth is a property of sentences), not of individual words; and (3) truth is defined in terms of *correspondence*.[90]

Observations, Qualifications, and Misunderstandings

Having defined the term *inerrancy*, now let me turn to its elaboration as a doctrine. This elaboration will take the form of some observations, some

[88] Aristotle, *Metaphysics*, 1011b, pp. 26ff.

[89] Alfred Tarski, "The Concept of Truth in Formalized Languages," in *Logic, Semantics, Metamathematics*, trans. J. H. Woodger (New York: Oxford, 1956).

[90] The introduction of Taski was suggested in an earlier draft of the chapter. Such a project seems to me to have some merit, but its full-blown explication and defense awaits further work. Some have suggested reservations since Tarski's work is formulated for formalized or ideal languages not natural languages. Some philosophers, however, have defended its applicability to natural languages as well. Cf. Donald Davidson, "Truth and Meaning," *Synthese* 17 (September 1967): 304–23; and Hartry Field, "Tarski's Theory of Truth," *Journal of Philosophy* 69 (July 13, 1972): 347–75.

qualifications, and finally some misunderstandings of the doctrine of inerrancy. The purpose of these considerations is to guide us in the application of the doctrine to the remaining phenomena of Scripture.

Observations

First, let me make two observations.

1. *No doctrine of inerrancy can determine in advance the solution to individual or specific problem passages.* The doctrine of inerrancy only gives guidelines or parameters for the handling of individual passages. It gives us the kind of phenomena over which a doctrine of inerrancy can range. It tells us that there is some sense in which what is affirmed is true. This does not guarantee universal agreement as to how a problem passage should be treated and the difficulty dissolved. Undoubtedly there will be debate as to which interpretation is best.

2. *Inerrancy is a doctrine that must be asserted, but which may not be demonstrated with respect to all the phenomena of Scripture.* There is in this definition of inerrancy the explicit recognition of both the fallibility and the finiteness of the present state of human knowledge. There are really only these two choices: either the theologian will trust the word of an omnipotent, omniscient God, who says that he controlled human agents, making it necessary for the theologian to admit his fallibility as critic, or in some sense he will declare that the aforementioned control is restricted and will affirm at least his own relative and finite omniscience as critic. Since Christ exhibited total trust in the Scriptures, can we do less? All that is claimed is that there is no final conflict with truth.

It might be objected that such a doctrine is unfalsifiable and therefore, if one were to use old positivist jargon, meaningless. There is, however, a twofold response that can and should be made against such criticism. First, such a view of inerrancy is not *in principle* unfalsifiable. There is no logical reason for our inability to gather all the facts. We can think of a world quite like ours but where we were actually in possession of all the facts. In such a world the Bible could be demonstrated as inerrant. Second, as a matter of fact, just such a world will be realized as the *eschaton. In practice* we will be in possession of all the facts, and then it will be shown that there is no final conflict.

Yet some might justifiably object that such a demonstration at the *eschaton* is of little help to them *now*. How is one to decide the question of the inerrancy of the Bible *now*? The answer is that there is evidence for inerrancy *now*, and that evidence is better than for any alternative view. First, there is the teaching of Scripture itself. Second, external evidence to the Bible (e.g., archaeology), while not without some problems, has confirmed the truthfulness of the Scripture over and over again.

Qualifications

There are, I think, just three qualifications that must be made to the doctrine of inerrancy. They are as follows.

1. *Inerrancy applies equally to all parts of the Scripture as originally written (autographa).* The doctrine of inerrancy applies only to the autographa, not to any copy of Scripture. This qualification is often objected to on the grounds that it serves as a neat hedge against disproving the doctrine. That is, any time that there is a difficulty, one can assign the problem to the copy, claiming it does not exist in the original. Indeed, such a qualification can be a hedge, *but it need not be.* The qualification simply grows out of the recognition that *any* copy will contain some errors due to transmission.

It might be argued that, if we no longer possess the autographs, the qualification is meaningless. Such an objection is only justified on one of two grounds, neither of which applies to the Bible. The first ground is the lack of an adequate discipline of textual criticism, which is hardly the case with Scripture. The second basis is a text so corrupt that even the canons of textual criticism could not make it intelligible. Again, such is not the case in regard to Scripture.

Still one might object that such a qualification is unnecessary, since the Spirit of God uses and blesses the existent, errant copies that we possess today. The reference to autographs is another example of evangelical overbelief. Again, I think the objection is false. Those who make this objection fail to recognize the difference between an original that is inerrant but to which errors have been added through transmission and an original that has substantive errors and has been further corrupted in transmission. With respect to the former, an inerrant text can be approached through textual criticism, while in the latter case, any attempt to discover an inerrant text would be hopeless. One can formulate a parallel objection with regard to a perfectly *interpreted* Bible, and a parallel answer can be given.

2. *Inerrancy is intimately tied up with hermeneutics.* Hermeneutics is the science of biblical interpretation. Though another chapter covers this topic specifically, three short comments seem appropriate here. First, the

common distinction between the Bible as given and as interpreted must be made. Though the Scriptures as given are completely true, no human interpretation of them is infallible. Second, inerrancy has as a precondition the proper application of hermeneutics. If one does not know the correct meaning of the text, he will never be justified in claiming that it is *false*. Third, a key principle in the application of hermeneutics is the analogy of faith as taught by the Reformers. This principle merely says that we should attempt to harmonize apparently contradictory statements in the Bible. That is, if there is a way of understanding a passage so that it is in harmony with the rest of Scripture and another way of understanding that conflicts with all other Scripture or parts of Scripture, the former is the correct interpretation. This often entails consideration of progress in God's revelation—not in the sense that later revelation ever falsifies, but that it often supplements, earlier revelation. Only in this way can it be affirmed that the Bible is true in the whole and in its parts.

3. *Inerrancy is related to Scripture's intention*. The point here has two aspects. First, Scripture accurately records many things that are false, for example, the falsehoods of Satan and of human beings. This point is often made in differing ways. Sometimes it is stated in terms of what the Bible *approves* as contrasted with what it merely *affirms*. Another way of putting it is to distinguish between *historical* or *descriptive* authority and *normative* authority.[91] Historical or descriptive authority applies equally to every word of an inerrant Bible. It merely means that whatever was said or done was in fact said or done. No judgment is passed as to whether it should or should not have been said or done. Normative authority, on the other hand, not only means that what was said or done was actually so but also that it should or should not have been said or done.

It should be noted again that there will not always be universal agreement as to whether a given statement falls within historical authority or normative authority. Gerstner makes the point this way:

> Suppose they [the biblical writers] think of a three-storied universe, which was the common view in their day, the Bible does not err unless it teaches such as a divine revelation of truth. In fact, by showing that the writers may have personally entertained ideas now antiquated it reveals its own historical authenticity without its normative authenticity suffering.[92]

[91] John Gerstner, *Biblical Inerrancy Primer* (Grand Rapids, MI: Baker, 1965), 49.
[92] Ibid.

Some may be a bit surprised at such a solution. Hence Pinnock's word is in order:

> The device is certainly a neat one, and gets us around some real difficulties. However, it conceals a hazardous principle. In admitting errors into the text itself, even into the body of teaching that text affords, the point is conceded to the critics of the Bible in every age; namely, that the teachings of Scripture may, or may *not*, be true.[93]

The point to be made here is that we cannot preclude in advance the possibility that some of the historically or descriptively authoritative material may contain errors.[94] This does not, however, admit errors into what I have called the *teaching of Scripture*. At the same time great caution may be used in invoking this solution, since it is fraught with hazards.

Second, Scripture's intention is found in the *meanings* of the biblical sentences. I use the term *Scripture's* rather than *author's* intention to make it clear that the latter is contained in the former, or, to put it another way, the determination of intention is a hermeneutical, not psychological, task.

Misunderstandings

Finally, I think it is helpful to enumerate and discuss some misunderstandings of the doctrine of inerrancy. For some who criticize inerrancy, these would be considered qualifications. One of the grounds on which they reject the doctrine is that to be maintained, it must be qualified in such a way that it becomes meaningless. I think the objection is false and specify why in the discussion below. The misunderstandings of which I speak are as follows.

1. *Inerrancy does not demand strict adherence to the rules of grammar.* One of the advantages of defining inerrancy in terms of truth and defining truth as a property of sentences is that the question of whether a grammatical error precludes an inerrant Bible is transcended. The answer is clearly no. This is as it should be. The rules of grammar are merely statements of normal usage of the language. Every day skilled writers break them in the interest of superior communication. Why should the writers of Scripture be denied this privilege?

---

[93] Pinnock, *Biblical Revelation*, 77–78.

[94] I wish to emphasize that before such a case could be claimed two things must be shown. First, we must show that something is simply affirmed and, second, that it is false. I do not assert that any such cases do in fact exist, only that such a possibility *could* be compatible with a doctrine of inerrancy. Given what the Bible teaches about itself, *if* such an error *were found*, then such an explanation would be necessary. I seriously doubt that this kind of solution is necessary.

2. *Inerrancy does not exclude the use either of figures of speech or of a given literary genre.* It is recognized by all that Scripture employs figures of speech. Some examples are meiosis (Gal. 5:14), hyperbole (Matt. 2:3), synecdoche (Gal. 1:16), personification (Gal. 3:8), and metonymy (Rom. 3:30). Figures of speech are common to ordinary communication and cannot be said to express falsehoods simply because they are not literal. While it may not always be easy to determine whether language is figurative or literal, there is nothing inherent in figurative language that prevents it from properly expressing truth and meaning.[95]

Moreover, various literary genres are employed in Scripture. There is narrative, dramatic, and apocalyptic literature. The Psalms are poetic in form. The literary style or form has nothing to do with the *truth* or *falsity* of the content conveyed in that style. Understanding of the form does, however, help in interpretation. Much more could be said here, but the issue is properly within the domain of hermeneutics.

3. *Inerrancy does not demand historical or semantic precision.* It is often stated that the doctrine of inerrancy cannot be accepted because the Bible does not reflect the canons of historical and linguistic precision recognized and required in the modern world. Like so many words used in the debate between inerrantists and errantists, *precision* is ambiguous. To some, *imprecision* has a connotation of error. This surely need not be so. As some of the divines of past ages put it, all that is necessary is that statements be adequate. I interpret this in terms of truth. Almost any statement is capable of greater precision. Any historiography, even a detailed chronicle, is still only an approximation. Let me illustrate. If we record an event as having transpired in 1978, we could obviously have said it more precisely—in the month of May, on the 15th day, at the hour of 10 p.m., and so on. But the original, simpler statement would still be true. The crucial point as I see it for inerrancy is this: Is a sentence as stated *true*? If so, there is no problem for the doctrine. Why should the modern criterion of precision be absolutized? Should we not expect Scripture to reflect the standards of its day? Is it not arrogant to think that our standards are right and theirs wrong?

4. *Inerrancy does not demand the technical language of modern science.* One should not expect the writers of Scripture to use the language of modern scientific empiricism. First, it was not their intention to provide a scientific explanation for all things. Second, popular or observational

[95] William R. Eichhorst, "The Issue of Biblical Inerrancy in Definition and Defense," *Grace Journal* 10 (Winter 1969): 8.

language is used even today by the common man. As a matter of fact, the modern scientist also uses it in certain contexts. We say, for example, that the sun "rises" and "sets." This in no way entails a theory of solar revolution. I am not convinced that this is not the way in which we are to understand the so-called "three-storied" universe. Unless one takes the statements of Scripture in crass geographic terms, I do not see the inappropriateness of such language. I think that much of the concern comes from a presumed similarity to certain contemporary myths. But why should this presumption be made? My contention is that if there is a sense in which the "scientific" language of Scripture is true, then the doctrine of inerrancy is not threatened. Third, it must be noted that there are many philosophers of science who would hold that all scientific theories about the nature of reality are not descriptive but solely instrumental or operational.[96] Thus, to absolutize the present language of science is to be out on a limb, with someone—perhaps even a scientist—sawing away at the branch!

Let me again state the possibility that certain alleged scientific problems may be accounted for in the distinction between descriptive or historical authority and normative authority.

5. *Inerrancy does not require verbal exactness in the citation of the Old Testament by the New*. In some ways this issue is obscured by discussing it in terms of the Old Testament *quotations* in the New. For this reason I have used what I hope is a more neutral word—*citation*. Quotation immediately gives one the picture of our present linguistic conventions of quotation marks, ellipses, brackets, and references. None of this was a part of the Hebrew and Greek of biblical times. When we quote today, we quote with verbal exactness, or we note that we have deviated from this through one of the aforementioned conventions. However, we cite statements in many ways besides quotation. We use indirect discourse, general reference, and summary. When we recall a statement or event, we often give only the gist or general idea of what was exactly said or done. Such practice was common in the New Testament (as it has been throughout literary history), and there are no conventions to advise us which method of citation is being employed in a given passage. Furthermore, citation of any kind in the New Testament involved translation. Since the Old Testament was in Hebrew, it had to be translated into Greek either by the New Testament writer himself or by someone else, such as a translator of the Septuagint.[97]

---

[96] Suppe, *Structure of Scientific Theories*.

[97] Eichhorst, "Issue of Biblical Inerrancy," 7. Cf. Roger Nicole, "New Testament Use of the Old Testament," in *Revelation and the Bible*, ed. Carl F. H. Henry (Grand Rapids, MI: Baker, 1958), 144.

6. *Inerrancy does not demand that the* Logia Jesu (*the sayings of Jesus*) *contain the* ipsissima verba (*the exact words*) *of Jesus, only the* ipsissima vox (*the exact voice*). This point is closely akin to the one just made. When a New Testament writer cites the sayings of Jesus, it need not be that Jesus said those exact words. Undoubtedly the exact words of Jesus are to be found in the New Testament, but they need not be so in every instance. For one thing, many of the sayings were spoken by our Lord in Aramaic and therefore had to be translated into Greek. Moreover, as was mentioned above, the writers of the New Testament did not have available to them the linguistic conventions that we have today. Thus it is impossible for us to know which of the sayings are direct quotes, which are indirect discourse, and which are even freer renderings.[98] With regard to the sayings of Jesus what, in light of these facts, would count against inerrancy? If the sense of the words attributed to Jesus by the writers was not uttered by Jesus, or if the exact words of Jesus are so construed that they have a sense never intended by Jesus, then inerrancy would be threatened.

7. *Inerrancy does not guarantee the exhaustive comprehensiveness of any single account or of combined accounts where those are involved.* This point is somewhat related to the early statement on precision. It must be remembered that from the standpoint of any discipline, even theology, the Scriptures are partial. Often partial is misunderstood to mean incorrect or false. But this idea itself is false. The Bible is a complete revelation of all that man needs for faith and practice. That is, there are many things we might like to know but which God has not seen fit to reveal. It is also true that God has not seen fit to record every detail of every account.

I think that this point has implications in another direction also, namely, that of the Gospel accounts. The problems in the Gospels are well known and cannot possibly be dealt with in the limited space available here. However, a giant step forward in the quest to resolve the problems will be taken when one realizes that none of the evangelists is obligated to give an exhaustive account of any event. He has the right to record an event in light of his purposes. Moreover, it must be remembered that the accounts of all four Gospel writers together do not exhaust the details of any event mentioned. There may be some unknown bit of information that

[98] Grant R. Osborne, "Redaction Criticism and the Great Commission: A Case Study toward a Biblical Understanding of Inerrancy," *Journal of the Evangelical Theological Society* 19 (Spring 1976): 83–85. I think Osborne is right in claiming that we do not need the exact words of Jesus in every instance. I have tried to explain why and under what conditions the voice of Jesus is sufficient. It might be helpful to say that when we lack the exact words of Jesus, we still have the *identical meaning*, which can be achieved in various ways. Thus, it should be clear that I disagree with the way Osborne applies the point in Matt. 28:18.

would resolve seeming conflicts. All that is required is that the sentences used by the writer be true.

8. *Inerrancy does not demand the infallibility or inerrancy of the noninspired sources used by biblical writers.* Form and redaction criticism of the biblical texts raised the question of sources as it had never been raised before. These forms of literary criticism make it necessary to face the possibility that the use of noninspired sources is much more widespread than was previously thought.[99] Thus, two comments are in order. The definition and doctrine of inerrancy here advocated does not rule out a priori the possibility, or even probability, that sources are cited with historical and descriptive authority but not normative authority. That is, the errors that these noninspired sources contain are accurately recorded, since Scripture's intention is not to approve those errors as true.[100]

Some Final Objections

Throughout the course of this chapter I have tried to deal at least with the major objections to the points made. Three additional objections are of sufficient weight to require some mention and answer. By far the most important is the first.

Has not your definition so qualified the concept of inerrancy that it is no longer meaningful? Pinnock thinks that the need for qualification is a liability and says, "This means that the discussion often has the air of unreality and even dishonesty about it."[101] Are we just avoiding the obvious fact that inerrancy is false? I do not believe so."

As a matter of fact, I seriously question whether these are qualifications at all. They are, as stated before, misunderstandings by those who reject inerrancy. If they were qualifications and they grew out of an ad hoc desire to prevent falsification of one's doctrine, then indeed Pinnock's and other such criticisms would be justified. However, since they are not, the picture is quite different. It must be remembered that words have more than one meaning. Thus it becomes necessary to specify which meaning is to be applied in a case in point. The more important the statement, the more precisely it needs to be specified. Notice the great care with which legal documents are prepared. What is important is the consistency of one's own

---

[99] Joseph A. Hill, "The Bible and Non-Inspired Sources," *Bulletin of the Evangelical Theological Society* 3 (Fall 1960): 78–100.

[100] Again, it should be noted that I am only talking about possibility. I have serious doubts that such a solution to biblical problems is needed, but this whole issue is a hermeneutical matter (e.g., the laying down of principles to decide which is descriptive and which is normative authority).

[101] Pinnock, "Truce Proposal," 4.

treatment of a doctrine, not whether it is consistent in light of certain views imposed on it by others. Clearly it is inconsistent to hold certain views and yet claim that the Bible is inerrant, but that is not the question here. The question here is this: Is this formulation inconsistent? Or, more generally, are all formulations inconsistent?

What would really constitute a qualified view of inerrancy? In my judgment, it would be a view that retains the word and develops a doctrine, but uses the word in a sense contrary to customary usage. Such an attempt would be a case of special pleading. As I see it, our definition does not do that. It seeks to employ the term *inerrancy* in connection with *truth*, and with the usual sense of truth. I do not think these are qualifications, only attempts to specify language more precisely.

Finally, if these are indeed qualifications, they are qualifications that apply to all books, particularly those of antiquity.[102] A case of special pleading is not being advocated for the Bible. I only ask that the principle of charity, which should be used in interpreting any type of text, be applied to the Bible.

Does not the Bible itself distinguish between the authoritative Word of God and the fallible opinions of its human authors? Seeming ground for such an objection is found in 1 Corinthians 7:10 where Paul says, "To the married I give this command (not I, but the Lord)," and in verse 12 he says, "To the rest I say this (I, not the Lord)." Is this not proof positive in the text of Scripture that the Word of God must be distinguished from the fallible opinions of its human authors? Although one may interpret what Paul has to say in this way, it is neither necessary nor best. In verse 10, Paul is pointing out that what he is saying has been said before by our Lord, while in verse 12 Paul is the vehicle of new revelation. That is, what he says has not been said before. Later, in 14:37, he says that what he wrote is the command of the Lord. Thus the distinction is not between revelation and nonrevelation, infallible and fallible, but is a distinction *within* revelation (the infallible) between what is repeated by Paul and what is original with him.

Does not the apostle Paul himself contradict inerrancy in 1 Corinthians 1:16? In this passage Paul says, "Beyond that, I don't remember if I baptized anyone else." How this is supposed to bear on errancy or inerrancy is not clear. Inerrancy merely demands that the Bible is all true; it does not require total recall. Gerstner puts it well: "If Paul remembered wrongly

[102] This can be substantiated by examining principles for the interpretation of literature. All that I am arguing is that the Bible is not a special case and thus does not involve special pleading.

we would have an uninspired Paul; but a Paul who does not remember is a Paul who is inspired to record that very fact for instruction (presumably, concerning the nature of Inspiration, what it does and does not include, what it does and does not exclude)."[103]

Conclusion

The task of this chapter has been to specify as clearly and precisely as possible what is meant by inerrancy—both the term and the doctrine. The approach used to achieve this goal was to examine the proper methodology whereby such a doctrine could be reached, then applying that method to the exegetical evidence or data. After examining a number of possible terms to express the attitude of the Bible toward itself, it was decided that among the words needed was a word to express the concept of "wholly true." It was suggested that this was the heart of the matter, whether one used *inerrancy* or not. There was, however, still a need to elaborate the way in which the doctrine functions in concrete instances. Finally, some previously unanswered objections were treated.

The conclusions of this paper concerning the doctrine of inerrancy may be summarized as follows: (1) the term *inerrancy*, like other words, is subject to misunderstanding and must be clearly defined; (2) inerrancy should be defined in terms of truth, making a number of the usual problems mute; (3) while inerrancy is not the only word that could express the concept here associated with it, it is a good word; and (4) inerrancy is not the only quality of the Bible that needs to be affirmed. After a study of the kind undertaken in this chapter, one cannot do better than to close with the words of Isaiah:

> The grass withers and the flowers fall,
> because the breath of the LORD blows on them.
> Surely the people are grass.
> The grass withers and the flowers fall,
> but the word of our God stands forever. (Isa. 40:7–8)

[103] Gerstner, *Biblical Inerrancy Primer*, 44.

13

"The Nature of Inerrancy"

ROGER R. NICOLE

Inerrancy and Common Sense

Previously published as "The Nature of Inerrancy," in *Inerrancy and Common Sense*, ed. Roger R. Nicole and J. Ramsey Michaels (Grand Rapids, MI: Baker, 1980), 71–95. Used by permission of Baker Books, a division of Baker Publishing Group.

Few areas in theology can be considered so plain and self-evident that little danger of deviation exists. In most cases, the path of soundness lies between two abysses, somewhat as a ridge on a steep mountain. Deviation to the right and deviation to the left need alike to be carefully avoided, even though the footing on the ridge itself is not always easy. Surely, this kind of situation is well illustrated in Christology, where the church learned, sometimes through painful losses, that it must maintain the full deity and the full humanity of Jesus Christ and acknowledge these as conjoined in the most intimate manner in the unity of his person. The subject of the inspiration of Scripture also falls in this category. Here it is essential to affirm the divine authorship of the Bible with all that this involves concerning the character of the product, and at the same time to recognize the reality of the contribution of the human authors, who were not used as robots or computers, simply to register mechanically some input placed into them by God, but who were commissioned to be the bearers of the divine Word in full keeping with their background, culture, personal training, language, and individuality. How these two can be combined remains a mystery to us. Yet the point of view that fails to do justice to both elements is bound to be an inadequate expression of the biblical doctrine of inspiration. Unfortunately, too many people have allowed themselves to move into areas of danger in which the truth of one or the other side was jeopardized. Sometimes, especially when logic has been permitted to have its full sway, this has taken them down into the abyss. Their downfall must stand as a warning to others.

Similarly, when we consider the topic of inerrancy, we must be wary of abysses lying on either side of us. On one side, there are those who, apparently in order to safeguard the human element involved in the writing of the Scripture, have thought it necessary to deny that the sacred writers were protected from error in everything they wrote. Those who hold this view sometimes say that the inspired writers were protected from serious error; or again that they were protected from error in matters related to faith and practice, while they remained susceptible to error in other areas; or again that they were free from error in their major message but subject to it in peripheral areas. The problem with this position is that it dilutes the authority of the Scripture and seems to open a way of escape from the impact of this authority, although undoubtedly limitations set upon inerrancy were not intended deliberately as a means to eschew the authority of the Word of God. This position also suffers from a lack of definitiveness, so that one is left to his own judgment concerning what is serious error; or again, what relates to faith and practice and what does not relate to them; or again, what is central and what is peripheral. If it is left to the individual's own judgment to determine what is authoritative and what is not, it is obvious that the supreme priority of the authority of Scripture will be damaged.

On the other side, some who have been very resolute advocates of inerrancy tend to provide the wrong strict definition of inerrancy, a definition often devised in terms of a rationalistic framework. Then they insist that this definition holds for all the phenomena of Scripture. In the process they sometimes press the phenomena of Scripture into conformity with this definition and thus open themselves to the charge of artificiality. Surely, this is not the appropriate approach to the Scripture. To move along these lines will not do justice to either the Bible or the God of the Bible.

The path of soundness will have to be recognized as falling between these two extremes. Inerrancy must be defined strictly in terms of Scripture's representation of what God is and does. At the same time we should not permit ourselves to entertain a view in which the frailties of the human authors impinge on the veracity of God. The present essay is designed specifically to ascertain the nature of inerrancy by exploring the biblical teaching and phenomena rather than to bring to the Scripture an arbitrary definition or rationalistic expectation concerning what God *should* do.

Areas of Common Misunderstanding

The Relationship between the Autographs and the Copies in the Original Languages

One could argue that if God were supremely interested in inerrancy he would have seen to it that those who copied the text were always infallibly kept from slips by the power of the Holy Spirit. In this case all our manuscripts would be precisely alike, and there would be no reason for a science of textual criticism. In fact, however, we do find that manuscripts differ. We find that those ancients who quoted or copied the Bible were subject to the same frailties which are found among those who copied other works. Probably no manuscript is entirely like any other manuscript, or when those who did their labors with painstaking care still introduced some slight deviations into their product. We need to take account of this in our understanding of inspiration. It was recognition of this fact which led evangelical theologians to emphasize the inspiration of the original autographs.[1] Sometimes those who object to the position of the advocates of inerrancy imagine that this qualification was designed to provide a huge loophole in case of serious difficulties that might be encountered. Then the advocate of inerrancy could always say, "This was not in the original." While he could not prove it, no one could prove otherwise.

Very definitely this is not the origin or the purpose of distinguishing between autographs and copies. Evangelicals who hold to inerrancy should be very careful not to raise questions rashly in relation to the text when no evidence is available that an error of transmission has in fact occurred. It is true, of course, that we cannot absolutely rule out the possibility of such an error even in the case of a great consensus of the various manuscripts. Yet the very great concurrence of the manuscripts of the Bible gives us strong warrant to rejoice in the assurance that God has safeguarded for us a text which is in substantial conformity with what was originally given.[2] At times in the presence of variants which leave the textual critic in a quandary, we may do well to acknowledge that certainty cannot be reached. Then we may not base any teaching or mandate upon the words which are in question. But in the overwhelming preponderance of cases

[1] B. B. Warfield, *The Westminster Assembly and Its Work* (New York: Oxford University Press, 1931), 236–51; François Turrettini, *Institutio Theologiae Elencticae*, Locus II, Q. X, vol. 1 (New York: Carter, 1847), 96ff.; Louis Gaussen, *Théopneustie*, 2nd ed. (Paris: Delay, 1842), 241–88.

[2] This is undoubtedly the meaning of the phrase "by his singular care and providence, kept pure in all ages" (Westminster Confession of Faith, 1.8). At times some of the theologians of the seventeenth century did show a certain restiveness in this area, as when they held that the force of the Hebrew vowel points had to be a part of the original deliverance (*Formula Consensus Helvetica*, 1675).

even the variants that we do have do not impinge on the message of the Scripture, and thus the frailties of man in the process of transmission have not deprived us of the divine authority we need in faith and practice.

It must be understood, however, that inerrancy in the Scriptures does not imply that we must posit a constant miracle in transmission by which anyone who copies, engraves, or quotes the Bible will be forever protected from any kind of slip. Some will wonder: since God has not seen fit to protect his Word in this way, is it important to insist that the Word as originally given was kept immune from all error? To answer this question, remember that the doctrine of inerrancy is inferred from the truth that God is the author of Scripture and that therefore God's veracity applies to the wording of the Bible. It may be helpful at this point to record some considerations which may bring the matter into focus.

1. *The fact that there are various transcriptional forms tends to confirm the reliability of the text in the very many cases where there is overwhelming agreement.* The situation is analogous to that of a series of witnesses in court. The diversity of presentations indicates that no collusion has taken place and that the various witnesses function independently of each other. Similarly, the variety of manuscripts and even of families of manuscripts reinforces our conviction that what we do have is not a trumped-up text but that the manuscripts in our possession are in fact related closely and vitally to the original. In this regard, our situation with the respect to the Old Testament was enhanced by the discovery of the Dead Sea Scrolls. Before that time the extant manuscripts had largely reflected the Masoretic School. Their close resemblance to each other gave us little basis for textual criticism, and a real possibility remained that the original texts at some points may have been replaced by something else which the Masoretes favored. The Dead Sea Scrolls are witnesses which antedate much of the Masoretic labors, and, while they introduce at times variant readings, they also substantially confirm the reliability of the text we have used for centuries. The possession of some autographs would, of course, be a boon, but in their absence, the textual variants may serve as a confirmation at most points of the authenticity of what we have.

2. *A slip in the transcriptional process is always subject to human correction.* This is an area in which men are competent to act and to express meaningful opinions. Errors in the original would not similarly respond to treatment by men. The analogy suggested by R. Laird Harris is helpful here. Loss or destruction of the standard yard at the Smithsonian Institution would not enormously affect the practice of measurement in the United

States, for a comparison of the multitudinous copies of that yard would lead us to something very close to the original standard. On the other hand, demonstration that the standard itself was not correct would have far-reaching implications for all measurements throughout the country.[3]

3. *Some problems in the transcriptional process were already in existence in the days of our Lord and his apostles; yet they did not hesitate to rely on the authority of Scripture.* Thus it is apparent that sufficient accuracy was present as to permit them to ground their teaching or arguments on what was transcribed.

4. *The possibility of transcriptional errors is not a late discovery*, even though it is only since the development of printing that the full range of possible errors became apparent. As early a writer as Augustine already was aware of the possibility of some flaws in this respect. In fact, he would use this as a possible explanation for some difficulties that he might find in Scripture.[4] Even in his case, however, this was hardly a loophole provided to insure that he would be safeguarded from embarrassment. In his practice as an exegete he scarcely ever suggests that the text was corrupted.

5. *If God had been pleased to preserve some autographs for us, there is reason to believe that some people might have been affected by a superstitious veneration for them.* The people would have viewed the autographs as sacred relics, and a kind of "bibliolatry" might have developed which would have been injurious to the soul. It is interesting that King Hezekiah destroyed the brazen serpent that Moses had made, and was commended for this action (2 Kings 18:4).

The Bible has been inspired to provide for us a message relating to spiritual matters, and on that account the measure of uncertainty which has been introduced by the presence of variants (e.g., deterioration in minute details; change in word order) does not really impair the authority of the Scripture. It can be said that copies of the Bible are inerrant to the extent that they agree with the original, and by all reasonable constructions, this extent is very considerable. It is so remarkable in fact that, except for inscriptions made on stone or on papyri, we do not have any text of antiquity which appears so well preserved as the Old and New Testaments.

It is frequently urged that, since the process of transmission has delivered to us a text which may not be in every respect identical with the autographs, it does not matter very much to us whether the autographs were, in fact, free from error. The point appears to have some force if one looks simply

[3] R. Laird Harris, *Inspiration and Canonicity of the Bible* (Grand Rapids, MI: Zondervan, 1957), 88f.
[4] Augustine, Letter 82.3 (to Jerome), *Nicene and Post-Nicene Fathers*, 1st series, vol. 1, p. 350.

at the character of the text that we possess. But even that force, we trust, is sharply limited by the considerations introduced just above. What seems to elude the minds of those who press the claim is the fact that in the Bible we do not have a written norm, but we have a claim of divine authorship as well. If the Bible is indeed the Word of God, can it be thought that in its original form it was blemished by numerous errors? A text of Cicero may have reached us with some attrition through the transcriptional process, and this may have damaged its style. But if a claim is made that the inferior character of a text in very poor Latin is an original feature, then the likelihood of Ciceronian authorship is reduced to the extreme. This seems to be the abiding difficulty of those who deny inerrancy. They proffer to us a text which is subject to challenge at some points, and whose authenticity as a divine document is placed in jeopardy by the blemishes which they allege.

The Process of Translation

Some people claim that translation inevitably tampers with an original pronouncement. It is true, of course, that in translation it is very difficult to provide a statement in another language which says absolutely no less and no more than the original and which conveys precisely the same impression to the hearer or the reader. Since most people do not have access to the Bible in the original languages, this may appear very disturbing, for they may fear that the human process of translating has substantially impaired the authority of the original Word of God. But here again the argument appears to raise fears that are not warranted by the facts of the case.

The same formula which we used in relation to textual variants may apply here as well: *Any translation is entitled to acceptance as the Word of God to the extent that it corresponds to the original.* This extent is very considerable for translations executed with appropriate care and without a subtle bias. If anyone should be inclined to interpret the Scripture in some unusual way on the basis of a translation, then he should check with the original to be sure that the meaning which he perceives is, in fact, present in the text. Individuals may easily fall into misunderstanding some portion of Scripture; it should be remembered, however, that the Bible is received from God not to be a strictly private instrument, but to be used and applied in the fellowship of God's people. Thus we can be protected from vagaries by the insights, the wisdom, and the scholarship of our fellow Christians.[5]

[5] One should be very careful not to develop this line of approach into a slavish acceptance of tradition, for the Bible must remain the judge of tradition rather than the other way around. In Matthew 15 and Mark 7 our Lord castigated human traditions which had moved far away from the intent of Scripture. He declared,

It is encouraging in this respect to see that the apostles in the preponderance of cases did not hesitate to use the Septuagint translation when referring in Greek to the Old Testament. Now the Septuagint was far from being a homogeneously excellent translation in terms of modern standards of translating, but it was well known, and was deemed adequate to convey to Greek readers the meaning of the Old Testament Hebrew. Thus we find that under the inspiration of the Holy Spirit the New Testament writers did not see fit to make a new authoritative and inspired translation, but they frequently made appeal to the Septuagint as embodying in sufficient manner what they wanted to emphasize. They did not, however, base the argument or their use of the text upon something which might be inferred from the Greek but which could not be found in the Hebrew.[6]

Spelling

In modern times certain standards of spelling are established in most languages. It is a part of the equipment of culture to be able to exhibit a reasonable conformity to these standards. An author or a publisher who does not abide by them opens himself to the charge of lacking culture or care. In this connection we often use the expressions "mistakes in spelling" or "spelling errors." It must be noted at once, however, that here we do not have an issue of conformity to or departure from factual truth. In fact, appropriate spelling varies from age to age and sometimes from one country to another. For instance, British writers will spell "favor" with a "u" (favour) which American writers omit. Obviously, extreme oddities of spelling might actually becloud a text, but this is a feature which we do

---

"You nullify the word of God by your tradition" (Mark 7:13 NIV). With due concern not to fall into a similar defect, we should recognize, however, that in the process of interpreting the Scripture, there are great benefits to be derived from a wholesome consideration of what other Christians have understood. If we take care to learn from them, we will not credit at once as God's Word certain eccentric interpretations which arise occasionally, particularly where there is no knowledge whatsoever of the original.

[6] It must be recognized that there are some passages where the New Testament writers have been charged with doing precisely that, although this view of their use of the Septuagint is by no means necessary. A passage in point might be Heb. 10:5, where Ps. 40:6 is quoted as saying, "A body you prepared for me" (NIV). The Masoretic Hebrew reads, "You have opened my ears." Some feel that later in the same context, when the author writes "through the sacrifice of the *body* of Jesus Christ" (v. 10), he is referring specifically to the form of language found in the Septuagint. The possibility does exist that the Septuagint bears witness to another form of the Hebrew text, which may be the original form. The Qumran scrolls have given us some examples of a Hebrew *Vorlage* for the Septuagint text, which some scholars consider as preserving the original form rather than the Masoretic text (e.g., Isa. 53:11). But in any case the author of Hebrews does not press the text of Psalm 40 beyond what could legitimately be inferred from the Masoretic text, for the presence of "ears" surely implies the existence of a "body." Therefore, one cannot maintain that the writer of Hebrews exploited a faulty Septuagint translation to prove something that the Hebrew text could not support. One could go so far as to say that the Masoretic text would be even more appropriate than the Septuagint form in emphasizing the voluntary obedience of Christ, the suffering servant, although this emphasis was not indispensable to the point of the author of Hebrews. This complex subject would warrant a fuller discussion which we do not have the space (nor the ability) to provide here.

not see in the Bible. At the same time, it is not necessary to imagine that the fact of divine authorship made it imperative that God should control the spelling habits of the human writers. Thus, in Matthew 27:46 the cry of dereliction of our Lord appears to have been spelled "Eli"; while in Mark 15:34, we encounter the spelling "Eloi." Here the Gospel writers were concerned to render for us the very sound of the voice of our Lord, but there was no necessity to secure identical phonetic symbols for this purpose. Similarly, many names, particularly those that are transcribed from another language, can be appropriately spelled in a variety of ways. The phenomena of Scripture will lead us to the conclusion that while the spelling practices of the sacred authors did not disfigure the sacred text, God appears not to have been concerned to supervise their handling of this matter as if they were participating in a spelling bee! This should not surprise anyone, since spelling is merely a human convention.

Grammar

Grammar may be defined as a codification of the principles generally accepted in the proper usage of language. It is indispensable for the purpose of communication and here again people of culture will manifest a certain conformity to the usage which is characterized as correct. A complete disregard of rules of grammar breeds ambiguity and in extreme cases opaqueness. We find that the Scripture was not written with such cavalier disregard. Yet there are at times puzzling cases, particularly in the state in which the texts have reached us, where it is difficult to ascertain the precise construction intended by the authors. It is also a matter of plain fact that they have used various turns of speech which from the point of view of grammar might not appear commendable. We have sentences that are suspended; we have verbs where the subject is in doubt; we have forms of speech which might have fallen under the condemnation of a classical Hebrew or Greek grammarian. There were some scholars in the seventeenth century who imagined that since the Bible is the Word of God, the Hebrew and Greek appearing in it must be deemed the supreme and perfect grammatical form of these languages. This, however, is not the case. Furthermore, there is no uniform standard in the Old Testament or the New. And there is no necessity to consider that the grammar of Koine Greek is lifted up above the usage of Plato and Thucydides.

Here again it must be emphasized that we do not have an area where truth is at stake but merely adherence to a human convention of language.

The convention itself fluctuates in both time and space. The biblical writers appear to have been permitted to express themselves in the idiom which was natural to them without receiving a supernatural help that would preclude expressions or turns of phrase that would offend a purist. It is therefore no disrespect to the Word of God to say that the author of Revelation in that book has used a form of Greek which is heavily colored by Hebraisms, expressions that would be rated incorrect in terms of standard Greek grammar.[7]

Phenomenological Use of Language

In our scientific age with the many advances which it has brought us with respect to dissemination of knowledge, access to information, and general acquaintance with scientific concepts, cultured people have developed ways of expressing themselves which take account of the best insights of human science. Even so, there are still expressions frequently used which reflect a phenomenological approach to reality. Very few people of culture, for instance, believe that the alternation of day and night is due to the movement of the sun. They realize that this phenomenon is produced by the rotation of the earth around its axis in twenty-four hours, and yet numerous expressions which might seem to imply the opposite are still considered quite appropriate: "the sun goes down," "the sun is high on the horizon," "sunrise," "sunset." The latter two appear even in astronomical publications! These are phenomenological uses of language where events are related from the vantage point of a spectator on the earth who describes what he observes rather than gives an explanation of the process by which the events in view are being caused. This is the situation throughout the Scripture. The Bible was not written in order to promote a particular view in scientific matters. It was meant as an address which would be understandable, regardless of the stance which one takes with respect to certain scientific theories. It is because the theologians of the seventeenth century failed to perceive this that they condemned Galileo. Both they and Galileo should probably have perceived that God was not taking sides in this matter and had not inculcated one particular view in Holy Writ. Warned by this egregious mistake, we should be careful to acknowledge the use of language prevailing at the time of the writing of the various books of the Bible, to accept the descriptions at face value, and not to read into the Scripture a commitment to positions about which the Bible does not give us a divine determination.

---

[7] To give only one example, Rev. 1:4 has ἀπὸ ὁ ὢν, which would be equivalent to "from *he* who is"!

Approximations

Because of the ready availability of information, we often pride ourselves in our day on strict accuracy. Even so, we commonly have recourse to approximations, which are recognized as being legitimate ways of presenting the truth. If someone asks me the population of Boston, I may reply "640,000," which is the nearest figure within 10,000 to the census of 1970. Very few people would expect me to say 641,071. That figure, in fact, would not be meaningful because it would not necessarily reflect the exact population at any one time and particularly not at the time of my answer. Similarly, when people are queried about their age, assuming that they wish to convey truthful information, they do not reply: "32 years, 5 months, 4 days, 2 hours, 52 minutes, and 35 seconds"; but they usually provide an approximate figure simply in terms of years. The integrity of truth is not at stake here. God, who knows all figures without approximation, has nevertheless seen fit to use approximations repeatedly throughout the Scripture. This is undoubtedly the case in all kinds of matters like numbers of people, size of armies, as well as in chronological measurements. Punctilious accuracy in the scientific sense is obviously not an aim of Scripture. As long as approximations are appropriate, no charge of failure to observe the truth can be leveled.

The same principle would apply with respect to the use of quotations and the relating of statements made in conversation. Our present practice of scholarship has led us to insist on a very high level of accuracy whenever we transcribe the words of another. But we have no ground to insist that this standard must have prevailed in biblical days. Thus we find that the New Testament writers, and presumably our Lord himself, quoted the Old Testament with a considerable measure of freedom, adapting the words of ancient writers in many cases to the contemporaneous situation. They freely omitted elements which did not appear relevant or inserted words that would elucidate more fully the sense in which they construed the ancient oracle. Similarly, in the four Gospels we have evidence that considerable freedom was used in the reporting of conversations in the days of our Lord. We have no right to posit a procedure which in our judgment the writers of the Bible should have used and then to proceed to judge them in terms of their conformity or lack of conformity to it. We need rather to observe the facts of the situation and to be satisfied with the way in which they were led to make their sacred record. Moreover, it would be wrong to imagine that one writer arbitrarily changed something which he found in another inspired writer on the ground that it did not conform to truth. Those who hold to inerrancy will retain the conviction that a real underlying harmony exists between various accounts which differ somewhat in details.

Fragmentary Information

It is very important to realize that absolute completeness is not indispensable for truth. If it were, we would despair of ever reaching truth at any point. The fragmentary character of information must be kept firmly in mind in relation to any account. This is the case also with respect to the Scripture. The writers led by God in their sacred writings selected data out of an immense pool of details which could have been given. This principle is specifically asserted in John 20:30, where we read: "Jesus did many other miraculous signs in the presence of his disciples, which are not recorded in this book." And again in John 21:25: "Jesus did many other things as well. If every one of them were written down, I suppose that even the whole world would not have room for the books that would be written" (NIV). The fragmentary nature of the information would encourage us to view the various writings as supplementing each other rather than as falling into a pattern of error due to incompleteness. A fair number of the difficulties that have been raised in relation to the Scriptures may perhaps find a solution when this principle is duly recognized.

Lack of Uniformity

Because a uniformity of standards frequently prevails in the modern scientific world, we usually expect that a well-written book will follow a uniform standard throughout. But this requirement cannot be placed upon the Scripture; we ought to recognize that varieties of standards may well prevail in measurements, in dating the reigns of kings, and in a number of other areas concerning which the ancient world had no uniform standard. Thus, a cubit may conceivably not mean exactly the same length in Genesis, Ezekiel, and the book of Revelation. It is also probable that the principles for the dating of the reigns of kings differed in the kingdoms of Israel and Judah.[8]

This does not lead us to the supposition that the biblical writers were permitted to incorporate without correction faulty data which they may have found in extant records, but it does not emphasize that we are not in

---

[8] The brilliant labors of Edwin R. Thiele appear to have established this (*The Mysterious Numbers of the Hebrew Kings*, 2nd ed. [Grand Rapids, MI: Eerdmans, 1965]).

a position to project upon their writings the expectation that in terms of accuracy they will conform to present canons of scientific writing.

Etymologies

Biblical etymologies have sometimes given difficulty to linguistic scholars. It is a possibility that it was never intended that we be able to trace the historical origin of certain names appearing in Scripture, as modern etymological science seeks to do. Scripture merely indicates some correspondence between the name of a place and certain important incidents which occurred there, or between the name of a person and a certain divine purpose in that person's life. To accomplish this a mere alliteration is effective, as well as a truly scientific linguistic etymology.

Transcendent Truths

There are elements of the Christian faith which so far transcend the comprehension of finite minds that it is probably impossible to formulate in terms of our finite perspective a wholly satisfactory rational harmonization of facets of the truth which confront us in the form of paradox or antinomy. By way of examples we might adduce the distinctness and integrity of the two natures in the unity of the person of Christ, or the confluence of the sovereign action of God and of the responsible decisions of rational agents, or again the unity of essence and trinity of persons in the Godhead. Obviously we should never commit the grievous mistake of regarding as error or contradiction in Scripture what simply transcends our finite minds by simultaneously asserting complementary aspects of the truth whose ultimate harmony is perceived in infinity but is not accessible to finite rational investigation.

A Definition of "Inerrancy"

Other aspects of the veracity of the Bible might be investigated, but for the present purposes this will suffice.[9] When the phenomena adverted to above are duly taken in consideration, certain parameters for the meaning of "error" may begin to appear, parameters established not on the basis of

[9] Further very helpful elaboration may be found in Robert Preus, "Notes on the Inerrancy of Scripture," *Bulletin of the Evangelical Theological Society* 8, no. 4 (Autumn 1965): 127–38. One should also consult his important chapter on "The Truthfulness of Scripture" in *The Theology of Post-Reformation Lutheranism* (St. Louis: Concordia, 1970), 339–62, 394–400. Of great interest also, although not supporting inerrancy as we view it here, is the article by G. Courtade, "Inspiration et Inerrance," in L. Pirot, *Supplément au Dictionnaire de la Bible*, vol. IV (Paris: Letouzey & Ané, 1949), 482–559.

a preconceived opinion as to what the Bible may or may not contain, but at least in good part on the basis of the phenomena manifestly exhibited in the performance of those who wrote. Within this framework it appears possible to assert with confidence the "inerrancy" of the Bible as an inevitable implication of the veracity of God and of the divine authorship of Scripture. Inerrancy will then mean that at no point in what was originally given were the biblical writers allowed to make statements or endorse viewpoints which are not in conformity with objective truth. This applies at any level at which they make pronouncements. Notably, this will serve to corroborate the truth of external sources which they might have used in the preparation of their text and whose data were embodied in the text. Obviously, this does not confer a divine endorsement on all statements made by all the individuals who appear in the drama of the Bible. Surely the words of Satan, the friends of Job, Esau, Pharaoh, Sanballat, and the unbelieving leaders in Palestine in Christ's day do not receive God's approval by the mere fact that they are recorded in Scripture.[10] Similarly, some written documents quoted in Scripture would not necessarily receive divine endorsement.[11] In these cases the inerrancy of Scripture means that the writers of Holy Writ were guided by God to record in a perfectly adequate way what the people in question said or wrote. Throughout history this point was always clear in the mind of wise advocates of inerrancy.[12]

Those, however, who have attempted to expand this principle into the position that God does not vouch for the accuracy of material from other sources which the sacred writers used and transcribed appear to us to dilute the authority of Scripture.[13] If God did not guide the sacred writers in the choice of the material that they decided to incorporate into their own text, then it will be forever impossible to distinguish between what is truly God's Word and what may be simply an accurate record of a fallible source. To the extent that any material appears endorsed by the sacred writer, it must be viewed as endorsed by God as well.

[10]In 1 Cor. 3:19 Paul quotes with approval a statement of Eliphaz the Temanite (Job 5:1), but it may well be urged that here Paul does not rely on this statement as a divine authority for asserting the limitations of human wisdom, but simply finds in the ancient text an impressive formulation of that truth, which he adopts for his present purpose. This might well be analogous to certain quotations from extrascriptural sources (cf. Aratus in Acts 17:28, Menander in 1 Cor. 15:33, and Epimenides in Titus 1:12).

[11]2 Kings 19:10–13; Ezra 1:2–4; 4:11–16, 17–22; 5:7–17; 6:3–12; 7:12–26; and Acts 23:26–30 might be examples in point.

[12]Turrettini, *Institutio*, Locus II, Q. IV, #IV (vol. I, pp. 59f.); R. Pache, *The Inspiration and Authority of Scripture* (Chicago: Moody Press, 1969), 133f.; Tenis Van Kooten, *The Bible: God's Word* (Grand Rapids, MI: Baker, 1972), 97; John H. Gerstner, *A Bible Inerrancy Primer* (Grand Rapids, MI: Baker, 1965), 55f.

[13]James Orr, *Revelation and Inspiration* (London: Duckworth, 1910), 179–81, 213–15; E. J. Carnell, *The Case for Orthodox Theology* (Philadelphia: Westminster Press, 1959), 102–9; Courtade, "Inspiration," 549–50.

The Problem of Apparent Discrepancies

Some scholars strongly emphasize that the phenomena of Scripture *do* lead us to posit errors of fact, and for this reason these scholars naturally wish to avoid the whole language of inerrancy. Undoubtedly, there are some cases in which the statements of Scripture might appear to fall in this category, and one can easily understand how it might seem more tempting to account for the "error" by assuming an original mistake in a peripheral matter rather than to have to labor to explain away the apparent contradiction between what the Scripture says in one place and other passages of Scripture or some elements of truth that we have culled from other avenues of endeavor. In our judgment this temptation must be resisted, because the assumption that original erroneous material was introduced into Holy Writ jeopardizes both the authority of the Bible as a norm and the divine authorship. Meanwhile, it should be strongly emphasized, as B. B. Warfield has done,[14] that the authority and inerrancy of Scripture are not dependent upon our ability to provide in every case a rational explanation of difficulties encountered. The authority of Scripture is not dependent upon the ability or resourcefulness of any man to vindicate its truth at every point. Therefore, we should never be reluctant to acknowledge that we may not at the present time be in possession of the solution of particular difficulties. This would surely be a wiser course of action, and more conformed to scholarship, than to present a scheme of harmonization that would be so obviously contrived and artificial that those who hear it might gain the impression that we are insincere and that we can hardly entertain seriously the thought that such an explanation is valid. This kind of approach would only promote suspicions concerning our own integrity, and it is surely far better occasionally to acknowledge ignorance, than to incur the distrust of people who will think that we are not dealing squarely with them.[15]

At times there may be a variety of ways in which a particular difficulty may be resolved, none of which may be so manifestly superior to the others that we are compelled to judge that it must be *the* solution. In such cases it has been a common practice in the history of biblical exegesis to present

[14]Benjamin B. Warfield, *The Inspiration and Authority of the Bible* (Philadelphia: Presbyterian & Reformed, 1948), 127f., 215f., 219ff., 225, 439. "Our individual fertility in exegetical expedients, our individual insight into exegetical truth, our individual capacity of understanding are not the measure of truth. If we cannot harmonize without straining, let us leave unharmonized" (219). Cf. also J. I. Packer, *Fundamentalism and the Word of God* (London: Inter-Varsity, 1958), 108f.

[15]John Calvin did not hesitate to acknowledge that he was puzzled in the presence of certain difficulties of Scripture. But far from viewing any of these as indicative of a mistake in the original, his language implies precisely the opposite.

these various explanations together with their strong and weak points, and to leave it to the reader to decide which one, if any, he prefers. Even if none of the suggestions advanced commends itself at the present time to the point of acceptance, this fact does not constitute an invalidation of the truthfulness of the sacred records, which may be presumed true unless they are so cogently demonstrated to be in error that not only is no acceptable solution presently in view, but no conceivable solution can even be envisioned.[16]

In the wise providence of God many features of Scripture which were very puzzling in previous times received satisfactory explanation when additional knowledge was secured which permitted us to understand better the purpose of the writers. It doesn't seem unreasonable to expect that the small residue of problems that presently remain will similarly be solved by an increase in the knowledge of Bible times. As it is, God has shed enough light on his Word so that we may recognize it as undoubtedly the Word of God; and he has permitted sufficient difficulties to remain so that those who wish to dose their eyes may seem to have some reason for doing so.[17]

In some respects the sinlessness of our Lord Jesus Christ presents an analogous situation. The reality of his deity completely precludes the possibility that he should commit any sin, and the Scripture bears witness to the fact that he remained sinless throughout his days (John 8:46; 14:30; 2 Cor. 5:21; Heb. 4:15; 9:14; 1 Pet. 2:22; 1 John 3:5). Now, there are some actions which he did or words that he uttered which in the life or on the lips of any other person might be deemed questionable. Our assurance of the sinlessness of Christ inevitably leads us to interpret these incidents keeping with his deity, or else serious heresies will follow. Meanwhile, we do not go about fretting in the fear that some sin in the person of Christ might be discovered, but we maintain with confidence the sinlessness of our Lord in the assurance that the data will ultimately support our faith. The same principle applies to our attitude toward Scripture: even though we may not at present see the complete harmony at every point, we trust that

---

[16] Cf. the fine statement by Warfield, *Inspiration and Authority of the Bible*, 225. Calvin frequently lists a variety of explanations in his *Commentaries*, sometimes indicating his own preference for one among them. The concern which he shows to provide explanations for apparent discrepancies (e.g., in relation to the raising of Jairus's daughter [Matt. 9:18ff., etc.]; or the healing of the blind near Jericho [Matt. 20:29–34, etc.]; or in the narratives concerning the resurrection of Christ [Matt. 28:2ff., etc.]) manifests clearly that he did not entertain the possibility that the Scripture might be in error. It is strange that some of these passages of Calvin have been quoted by some (notably Emile Doumergue) as implying that Calvin did not hold to inerrancy. This evidence boomerangs, as was well shown by John K. Mickelsen, "The Relationship between the Commentaries of John Calvin and His *Institutes of the Christian Religion*, and the Bearing of that Relationship on the Study of Calvin's Doctrine of Scripture," *The Gordon Review* 5, no. 4 (Winter 1959): 155–68.

[17] Cf. Blaise Pascal, *Pensées*, no. 736 (Brunschvicq, no. 564) (London: Harvil Press, 1962), 332.

such harmony does exist and that it will in due course be made manifest by God himself.

Inerrancy and Evangelical Truth

Some strong advocates of inerrancy have occasionally expressed themselves as if this doctrine were the necessary and sufficient standard of evangelical truth. Important as this tenet is, we should say here that it is not strictly either sufficient or necessary.

It is not sufficient because there are many other tenets that need to be maintained if a person is to be seen as clearly evangelical. Some who have turned to cults still adhere to the inerrancy of Scripture.[18] Thus, while the Evangelical Theological Society has made its confession of faith to pivot in this area,[19] this is not to say that no other doctrine matters. Meanwhile, our Roman Catholic friends who do use the word *inerrant* a good deal and have it incorporated in certain official statements[20] seem to have shown at times considerable laxity in the critical approach toward the Scripture.[21] The restrictions on the concept of inerrancy presently in vogue in many circles of the Roman Catholic Church are not reassuring. Thus, no one should imagine that the use of the word *inerrant* is an infallible preservative against any loosening of the faith. It is indeed a link in the chain but it does not constitute the whole chain.

On the other hand, inerrancy is not strictly a necessary tenet of evangelical truth. Some people who assert a limited errancy remain in other respects very solidly aligned with the evangelical movement. Here the much cited case of James Orr might be advanced. He did not rule out the possibility of errors of detail, but he averred that he never found anything in Scripture which would compel him to say that the Bible was wrong.[22] It would seem unfortunate to frame a definition of evangelical faith that

[18] E.g., Jehovah's Witnesses and the Mormons, to name only two groups by their popular designation.

[19] "The Bible alone, and the Bible in its entirety, is the Word of God written, and therefore inerrant in the autographs."

[20] Leo XIII, Encyclical *Providentissimus Deus*, 18 November 1893, Denz 1952–53 (3292–93); Benedictus XV, Encyclical *Spiritus Paraclitus*, 15 September 1920, Denz 2186 (3652); Pius XII, Encyclical *Divino Afflante Spiritu*, 30 September 1943, Denz 2294 (3830); "Dogmatic Constitution on Divine Revelation," #11, in *The Documents of Vatican II*, ed. W. M. Abbott (New York: Guild Press, 1966), 119.

[21] Jean Levie, *The Bible, Word of God in Words of Men* (New York: P. J. Kenedy & Sons, 1962), 214–46; J. T. Burtchaell, *Catholic Theories of Biblical Inspiration Since 1810* (Cambridge: Cambridge University Press, 1969); Hans Küng, *Infallible? An Inquiry* (Garden City, NY: Doubleday, 1971), 209–21.

[22] Orr wrote: "'Inerrancy' can never be demonstrated with a cogency which entitles it to rank as the foundation of a belief in inspiration" (*Revelation and Inspiration* [London: Duckworth, 1910], 199). Yet he also wrote a few pages later: "The Bible, impartially interpreted and judged, is free from demonstrable error in its statements, and harmonious in its teachings, to a degree that of itself creates an irresistible impression of a supernatural factor in its origin" (216).

would oblige us to deny the title of membership to a man like James Orr. Warfield himself, who surely showed no hesitancy in his advocacy of inerrancy, was ready to recognize in Orr a man of faith with whom he was pleased to collaborate.

What is supremely at stake in this whole discussion is the recognition of the authority of God in the sacred oracles. Are we going to submit unconditionally to the voice of God who has spoken? Or, are we going to insist on screening the message of the Bible, accepting only what appears palatable and remaining free to reject what does not conform to our preconceived criteria? This is really the great divide, and those who stress inerrancy are simply aiming to maintain what they view as the consistent biblical stance on this issue.

At the close of the Chicago Statement on Biblical Inerrancy this point is admirably expressed:

> In our affirmation of the authority of Scripture as involving its total truth, we are consciously standing with Christ and his apostles, indeed with the whole Bible and with the main stream of church history from the first days until very recently. We are concerned at the casual, inadvertent and seemingly thoughtless way in which a belief of such far-reaching importance has been given up by so many in our day.
>
> We are conscious too that great and grave confusion results from ceasing to maintain the total truth of the Bible whose authority one professes to acknowledge. The result of taking this step is that the Bible which God gave loses its authority, and what has authority instead is a Bible reduced in content according to the demands of one's critical reasonings and in principle reducible still further once this has started. This means that at bottom independent reason now has authority as opposed to scriptural teaching. If this is not seen and if for the time being basic evangelical doctrines are still held, persons denying the full truth of Scripture may claim an evangelical identity while methodologically they have moved away from the evangelical principle of knowledge to an unstable subjectivism, and will be hard put not to move further.[23]

The confession of biblical inerrancy, in the biblical sense of that concept, is simply one emphatic way to assert that what Scripture says, God says. To him be the glory and the authority. Amen.

[23] "Chicago Statement on Biblical Inerrancy," 10–11. Printed, e.g., in Carl F. H. Henry, *God, Revelation, and Authority*, vol. 4 (Waco, TX: Word, 1979), 219.

Part 5

Infallibility

14

"What Does Biblical Infallibility Mean?"

GORDON R. LEWIS

Evangelicals and Inerrancy

Previously published as "What Does Biblical Infallibility Mean?" in *Evangelicals and Inerrancy: Selections from the Journal of the Evangelical Theological Society*, ed. Ronald Youngblood (Nashville, TN: Thomas Nelson, 1984), 35–48.

The purpose of this study is to investigate the meaning of infallibility, not to establish the grounds on which infallibility rests. The writer, however, questions the view that inerrancy is not "required" by the biblical teaching of its own inspiration.[1] Rather, he here assumes with Frederick C. Grant that in the New Testament "it is everywhere taken for granted that Scripture is trustworthy, infallible and inerrant. . . . No New Testament writer would ever dream of questioning a statement contained in the Old Testament."[2]

Neither does the paper intend to lay a foundation for the doctrine of propositional revelation. We assume a position similar to that of Bernard Ramm.[3] Nor is it the purpose of this paper to discuss the implications of textual criticism for the nature of inspiration. It is assumed that textual criticism has generally confirmed the trustworthiness of by far the greatest part of the Greek and Hebrew texts. References to the Bible may be regarded as being to those passages on which there is not such variation in the mss as to affect in any material way the meaning conveyed.

An important distinction between the Bible as given and the Bible as interpreted should also be noted. The doctrine of infallibility applies to the

[1] E. F. Harrison, "The Phenomena of Scripture," in *Revelation and the Bible*, ed. C. F. H. Henry (Grand Rapids, MI: Baker, 1958), 238, 250.
[2] F. C. Grant, *Introduction to New Testament Thought* (New York: Abingdon-Cokesbury, 1950), 75.
[3] B. Ramm, *Special Revelation and the Word of God* (Grand Rapids, MI: Eerdmans, 1961).

Bible as given, not to the interpretation of any individual. Therefore it is not the province of this paper to deal with the complex issues of hermeneutics, although they cannot be avoided entirely. It is assumed, however, that an objectively infallible standard is not in vain. Although no interpreter can claim inerrancy for himself, interpreters are not equally in a morass of subjectivity since there is an objective standard of comparison in Scripture. The Bible's meaning can be approximated by the use of sound principles of hermeneutics, the witness of the Holy Spirit, and the help of previously Spirit-illumined interpreters in the history of the church.

Positively this paper explores a means of understanding and communicating the significance of biblical infallibility to our generation. One of the most influential schools of thought is called philosophical analysis, recent development from earlier logical positivism. In order to help young people familiar with philosophical analysis to understand the import of biblical infallibility we may employ its terms as far as possible for meaningful communication. In so doing our own concept of the applicability of the doctrine of biblical infallibility to our times may be enriched and expressed with increased precision.

Meaning and Language

Contemporary philosophical analysis and semantics vigorously stress the difference between logical meanings and the verbal sentences conveying them. Long ago Augustine had classically expressed the distinction in his dialogue "On the Teacher" (*De Magistro*). The words uttered by a teacher are not identical with the thought he hopes to teach or the realities to which they refer. As a result of this analysis Augustine cautioned against confusion of linguistic signs with their meanings or with the things they signify. The New Testament itself distinguishes to some extent *logos* (emphasizing the meaning of words) from *rhēma* (underlining the uttered or written terms).

Although this distinction has a long and noble ancestry, it has frequently been ignored in discussions of biblical inerrancy. Logically, errorlessness or truth is a quality not of words but of meanings. Ben F. Kimpel explains, "Language . . . is only a means for articulating a proposition. Hence the truth-character of an affirmed proposition is not a feature of its language-form. . . . Language is not essential for having true beliefs. It is essential only for *affirming* them."[4] How can this important distinction be

[4] B. F. Kimpel, *Language and Religion* (New York: Philosophical Library, 1957), 93.

related to the doctrine of inspiration? May we not preserve it by employing "inerrancy," which explicitly claims truth, only for the propositional content of Scripture, and by using "infallibility," which may mean "not liable to fail," only for the verbal expressions of Scripture?

Acknowledging that the Bible is both inerrant in content and infallible in expressing it, we do not maintain mere conceptual inspiration or mere "record" inspiration[5] but both. That seems to have been the point of verbal inspiration. Furthermore we shall seek to determine how verbal inspiration may be understood plenarily in these terms. It will be helpful to note not only the distinction between content and wording but also a number of subdivisions within each of these categories. To facilitate reference to these classifications in the remainder of the paper, the following chart lists rather widely accepted kinds of meaning in the left-hand column and parallel uses of language in the right-hand column.

An Analysis of Meaning and Language[6]

KINDS OF MEANING	USES OF LANGUAGE
A. Cognitive Meanings Assertions that are either true or false.	A. Informative Sentences Usually declarative
1. Formally The truth or falsity is determined by the definitions, the principles of logic, or principles of mathematics.	1. Formally informative Convey nothing about matters of fact but only about definitions of words and logical mathematical relations.
2. Empirically The truth or falsity is determined by observable, sensory, scientific evidence. Any proposition that is cognitively meaningful must be verifiable. Some empirical evidence must be relevant to the confirmation or disconfirmation of it. Such meaning may also be designated as literal.	2. Empirically informative Convey propositions regarding matters of fact, states of affairs, existence, or reality.
B. Noncognitive Meanings	B. Noninformative Sentences
1. Emotive Vent the speaker's emotions or evoke similar emotions in others.	1. Expressive Convey emotive meaning (e.g., poetry).
2. Motivational Stimulate volitional action.	2. Directive Convey exhortations, commands.

[5] E. J. Carnell, *The Case for Orthodox Theology* (Philadelphia: Westminster, 1959), 92–112.

[6] These classifications are not presented as final or absolute but suggestive. Additional categories may well be required by the scriptural materials. See H. Feigl, "Logical Empiricism," in *Twentieth Century Philosophy*, ed. D. D. Runes (New York: Philosophical Library, 1943), 379.

KINDS OF MEANING	USES OF LANGUAGE
3. Interrogative	3. Questions
4. Exclamatory	4. Exclamations
5. Pictorial, imaginative	5. Figures of speech
C. Meaningless Nonsense Alleged assertions about unverifiable existences or realities.	C. Pseudo-Sentences Declarative sentences conveying nonsense.

Inerrancy and Kinds of Meaning

The term inerrancy here specifically designates meaning that is not false but true. By definition cognitive meanings alone can be true or false of objective reality—that is, reality independent of the speaker. Noncognitive meanings on the other hand express something only of the speaker. We shall consider the relation of inerrancy first to those biblical meanings that are related to the objective world. Cognitive meanings themselves have a twofold classification, as the chart reveals. There are those assertions that may be regarded as true or false formally—that is, by reason of their definition or by reason of the principles of mathematics or logic. In the second place, there those cognitive propositions which are true or false empirically—that is, by reason of some observable scientific evidence which tends either to confirm or disconfirm them. Are there such cognitive propositions in the Bible? And if so, what does it mean to say to our contemporaries that they are inerrant?

1. *Formally cognitive meanings.* In order to keep the discussion within reasonable limits, we shall consider of the formal types of cognitive assertions only the logical. Formal logical principles seem to be implied in Romans 11:6. The content of the verse is clearly dependent upon such basic laws of logic as the principle of identity, the principle of excluded middle, and the principle of noncontradiction. Israel's election, Paul argues, is by grace, not works. "And if by grace, then is it no more of works: otherwise grace is no more grace. But if it be of works, then is it no more grace: otherwise work is no more work." No experimental inquiry need be instituted here. The argument is settled by application of these logical principles. Assuming the principle of identity, grace is grace and works are works; assuming the validity of the principle of excluded middle, Israel's election must be either by grace or works; and assuming the validity of the principle of noncontradiction, it cannot be by grace and not by grace. What, then, does inerrancy mean in a passage like this? If the Scriptures

teach inerrancy concerning their own content, then are not their assertions in didactic passages formally true and not false?

Syllogistic reasoning appears in the argument of Galatians 3:15–17. Paul argues: No confirmed covenant is one that is disannulled or altered. The covenant with Abraham is a confirmed covenant. Therefore the covenant with Abraham is not one that is disannulled or altered (by the law 430 years later). Again Paul's case depends upon formal principles; it does not require any experiential confirmation. The truth of his conclusion rests squarely on the validity of the principles of syllogistic reasoning. The rules of a valid syllogism are followed. In a passage like this, what does inerrancy mean? Would not the doctrine of inerrancy mean that assertions dependent on formal logical principles in didactic passages are cognitively true and not false? Can the reasoned case of an inspired author be based on fallacious logic?

Although this is not the place to examine the status of formal logical principles, a few words are necessary. According to the analysts, propositions true on formal logical grounds are true because (1) we have arbitrarily ruled that the game be played that way, or (2) we have surreptitiously hidden the conclusion in the premises so that our argument is tautologous. However, Paul in the two biblical passages mentioned hardly seeks to spell out the implications of arbitrarily conceived rules of thought or first premises. Rather, he employs formal logic to support what is in fact the case concerning God's gracious election and the Abrahamic covenant. How can these passages be made to fit the analyst's shibboleths of "merely formal," "arbitrary" and "tautologous"? Indeed they are formally valid, but the contexts imply more than that. These propositions are both formally and actually true. And how can these passages be made to fit the neoorthodox shibboleth of "mere witness" to the mighty covenant acts of God? They are that, but they are more than that. They spell out the propositional implications of these divine acts. If these passages are inerrant, the truth of their propositional content is certified both formally and actually.

2. *Empirically cognitive meanings*. Some cognitive assertions are true or false not in virtue of formal logical principle but in virtue of empirically observable evidence. The Bible contains many assertions whose truth is not formally validated but could be tested through human experience. Under the continuing influence of logical positivism, many contemporary analysts still limit human experience that attests cognitively true propositions to the witness of the five senses. And the Bible includes many such propositions. The descriptive statement of Acts 1:12 is a verifiable one. The disciples,

after the ascension, "returned to Jerusalem from the Mount called Olivet which is from Jerusalem a Sabbath day's journey." That event was testable by the senses on the day it occurred. And by means of sensory observation, the disciples had confirmed the bodily resurrection of Christ from the dead. They heard him speak; they saw him eat before them; and they were invited to touch him (Luke 24:36–43; John 20:25–28). What then can it mean to say that such passages are inerrant? It cannot mean merely an accurate record of what may not have happened. Rather, if inerrant the assertions are true and therefore the facts specified real. The disciples did take the trip from Olivet to Jerusalem; Christ in his scarred body did talk, walk, and eat with the disciples after his death.

Now to account for Scripture data it is necessary to broaden the criterion of verifiability as held by positivistically inclined contemporaries. The positivists themselves have been forced to adopt a weakened form of the verification principle, such as that of A. J. Ayer in his *Language, Truth and Logic*. Nonpositivists consider it arbitrary to limit the meaningful experience to that of our bodily senses. Because of the complexity of human experience, the verification principle as applied to the five senses may be only one clue to meaning; there may be many others. Empirical philosophies of religion like that of the late Edgar S. Brightman have stressed the richness of all human experience, including experience of values and of God. We may well expand the verification principle after the pattern suggested by F. W. Copleston to the effect that there must be some difference between that situation in which an empirically meaningful proposition would be true and those in which it would be false. "We can conceive or imagine facts that would render it true or false," or "some experiential data are relevant to the formation of the idea."[7] It cannot dogmatically be asserted that no prehistorical and no metaphysical proposition satisfies this general requirement. Nor does this criterion open the door to snarks and boojums that make no conceivable difference in any situation whether alleged to exist or not.

On such a broadened criterion, the following biblical statements must be considered as empirically cognitive. "They were all filled with the Holy Spirit" (Acts 2:4). The disciples' reception of the invisible Spirit on the Day of Pentecost made an experiential difference in their lives. The assertion to that effect is either true or false, and if inerrant it is true. In such a passage as Genesis 2:10–14, describing four rivers flowing out from Eden,

[7] F. W. Copleston, *Contemporary Philosophy* (London: Burns & Oates, 1956), 46, 48.

the content is not verifiable on a strict positivistic view of history. The alleged state of affairs antedates extant writing from the time, and there is no known way now of confirming or disconfirming such propositions. However, if the Scriptures in fact intend to assert the actual existence of the four rivers, then what does inerrancy of such statements imply? Must we not conclude that there were such rivers? There is conceivable empirical difference between the ancient world that had these four rivers and an ancient world that did not have them.

The Scriptures also make assertions concerning the being of God as in Exodus 3:14, "I AM THAT I AM," or Heb. 11:6, "He that cometh to God must believe that he is, and that he is the rewarder of them that diligently seek him." What does inerrancy mean in relation to these passages? Does it not imply the truth of the propositions even though they are not verifiable in the strict positivistic sense? Is it not the case that, although no man has seen him at any time, an eternally active God exists? Admitting frequent metaphor, parable, and other figures of speech, must we not acknowledge that if a concept of inerrancy applies at all, every literal assertion made by didactic passages of Scripture is true? If so, the state of affairs or the reality designated actually existed, exists, or will exist as the Scriptures specify.

Again it is impossible here to attempt anything like a full justification of this position or its enormous implications. However, a brief consideration may indicate the writer's position on some of the problems involved. To assert inerrancy is not to assert full comprehension of any of the events or things designated. Granting propositional revelation and a high view of inspiration, we still know only in part. But we *know* in part! Following the biblical writers, can we not call knowledge of God truth?

Someone may object that the limited character of the concepts God had available as he began to reveal himself rule out cognitive truth ontologically. A father puts things in a very circumscribed way to "get through" to his child—even to the point of distortion. How much more then does God have to abandon infinite truth to get through to finite man! Such an argument fails to take into account several important factors. God did not decide to communicate with man after all possible temporal conditions contributed to make this impossible. Communication with man was among his eternal purposes, was it not? Providence from the moment of the first creative act worked toward the realization of that purpose in the cultures, the moral ideas, the thought patterns, and the languages. Revelation was not frustrated by unforeseen limitations of earlier creative activity!

On a biblical view, provision for communication was planned and equipment for it was included in the mind of man from the beginning.

Overlooking these points, Eugene Heideman argues that verbal inspiration necessarily implies fallibility. In choosing to use Hebrew, God was limited to its available erroneous concepts. The belief that the sun went around the earth and low moral concepts exemplify his point.[8] May we ask Heideman if he has considered sufficiently the fact that truth claims must always be evaluated in terms of the writer's purpose? It could be no part of the biblical writer's intention to scoop Copernicus' view of the solar system. The language of phenomenal appearance (the sun going around the earth) is true within its intended realm of discourse. But what about the concept of Hebrew justice? Did not God have to make use of a crude, vengeful idea in revealing his justice? No, the principle of an eye for an eye also must be judged in its historical setting and purpose. The law did not provide freedom for all to take personal vengeance on wrongdoers. Whereas people had taken justice into their own hands, the national judges were now provided with an objective law of retribution. Its point was that in Israel's courts the punishment should fit the crime, a principle not foreign to our allegedly high views of justice nor to that of the divine judgment seat. Admittedly in the progress of revelation God took the Israelites where they were and accomplished amazing things with them for his redemptive purposes. But where they were at the beginning was no accident. God in his providence had long before intended the use of the Hebrew language and its concepts for a medium of his revelation to mankind.

No attempt is made here to deny that the divine revelation does, like the divine incarnation, stoop to man and make use of anthropic and cosmic modes of revelation. It is claimed, however, that these forms of revelation are true as far as they go and not distortive. They are true, however, not as the very archetypal ideas in the mind of God himself, but as a copy of them expressed to man, his image. The knowledge of propositional revelation then is true as a copy or ectype of the original, because revealed truth is the object of worship. However, it is no service to worship to deny the accuracy of biblical propositions concerning God. Neither is it the part of piety to allege that the Bible is full of nonsense.

3. *Noncognitive meanings*. Noncognitive propositions, according to the analysts, are those that do not assert any matter of fact in the objective world but simply express something about the speaker. While the earliest

[8] E. W. Heideman, "The Inspiration of Scripture," *RefR* 15 (September 1961): 29.

positivists may have denied the meaningfulness of emotive, motivational, interrogative, exclamatory and pictorial types of meaning, recent analysts have extended their concept of meaning to include at least these. On this theory, when a football fan screams "Hurrah!" he is not asserting a verifiable state of affairs but simply venting his emotions and possibly seeking to evoke a similar reaction in others. Are there statements in the Bible that do not intend to assert states of affairs in publicly observable reality but rather to express the writer's emotions? Such a meaning may be in view when a prophet like Isaiah cries, "Woe is me!" We shall not expect archaeology to confirm or disconfirm the truth of that proposition. What then does inerrancy mean for content like this? If these biblical expressions are inerrant, is not their point about the speaker or writer in fact true concerning him? Emotive meanings may be said to be inerrant in that they adequately convey what the writer felt or sought to evoke in others.

There are also in the Bible other noncognitive materials, such as motivational statements, exhortations and commands, expressing the speaker's will and stimulating others to action. Is it not beside the point to look for confirmation or disproof of these meanings on the part of any objective science? If so, then it is irrelevant to assert their cognitive inerrancy in the sense analysts commonly understand. However, such a phrase as "Love one another" (John 15:17) may meaningfully be considered inerrant in truly stating the speaker's will and desire. Interrogative meanings also tell us something true of the questioner. A question from Satan, for example, inerrantly expresses his challenge of God's word: "Yea, hath God said ye shall not eat of every tree of the garden?" (Gen. 3:1). Exclamations also adequately state the speaker's feeling: "Woe unto you, scribes and Pharisees . . . !" (Matt. 23:14). If such noncognitive thoughts are inerrant, do they not truly assert what was the desire, the question and the emphatic feeling of the one who said them at the time they were spoken? Pictorial language inerrantly portrays the author's view of a given thing. The metaphor "The tongue is a fire" (James 3:6) does not teach a literal matter of fact but vividly illustrates James' concept of the potential dangers of speech.

What then does inerrancy mean in such noncognitive passages of the Bible? In these cases the point of infallibility is simply that we have a true assertion of what the writer felt, commanded, asked, exclaimed or pictured. The question of whether those feelings and exclamations are exemplary must be determined by the context. If there is no explicit indication of approval or disapproval in the immediate context, then we must resort to the broader context of the thought of the Bible in its entirety. The applicability of commands must be similarly judged.

These noncognitive categories of the analysts may seem arbitrarily to exclude implicit cognitive elements in them. Men like E. L. Mascall, university lecturer in philosophy of religion at Oxford, argue that there are no completely noncognitive forms of language. Mascall goes so far as to say that art is essentially a cognitive activity revealing truth.[9] If the noncognitive types of meanings here listed do carry some implicit objective implications that may be regarded true or false in an external state of affairs, as the points of figures of speech clearly do, then all that we have said concerning cognitive inerrancy applies to those implications. However, what has been said concerning the inerrancy of the emotive, motivational, interrogative, exclamatory, and pictorial types of subjective meaning also holds. In other words, to the extent that the biblical materials are noncognitive they are here regarded as inerrant in reference to the speaker, and to the extent that they teach cognitive assertions they are also regarded as inerrant objectively. The knotty problem of determining what is cognitively taught and what is not can only be resolved in individual passages by devout scholars employing sound principles of hermeneutics and respecting the judgment of other Spirit-led exegetes throughout the church's history.

Some may fear possible consequences of leaving to interpreters the distinguishing of objectively inerrant propositions from the subjectively inerrant ones. Admitting the dangers of misinterpretation in determining the objective or subjective reference of biblical statements, we cannot escape the responsibility. Such decisions are as unavoidable as those between what is literal and figurative, or between narratives that are exemplary and those that are not. There is no virtue in denying the necessity of facing these issues of interpretation with louder affirmations of belief in inspiration. Even a stalwart like A. T. Pierson frankly acknowledged, "Every student must observe what in Holy Scripture carries authority and what only accuracy." After citing Satan's words to Eve and the questionable counsel given Job by his friends, Pierson adds, "Even prophets and apostles apart from their character and capacity as such, being only fallible men, were liable to mistakes (1 Kings 19:4; Gal. 2:11–14)." What is Pierson's conclusion? "Any theory would be absurd that clothes all words found in Scripture with equal authority or importance. But whatever is meant to convey God's thought is used with a purpose and adapted to

[9] E. L. Mascall, *Words and Images* (London: Longmans Green, 1957), 93.

its end, so that, as the angel said to John on Patmos: 'These are the true sayings of God' (Rev. 19:9)."[10]

We might well ask what criteria Pierson used to determine which narrative passages carried authority and which only accuracy of recording. In some cases, he suggests, God's disapproval is evident in the context, whereas in other cases the sentiments and acts are obviously controlled by the Holy Spirit and represent the mind and will of God. Where no such contextual indications are available the judgment must be made in accord with general scriptural teaching on the subject. May we not suggest similar standards for judging passages cognitive or noncognitive? If contextual evidence indicates that a proposition has no cognitive import, we abide by that. If an assertion that displays the characteristics of cognitive propositions is taught by Christ himself, or prophets and apostles, the content inerrantly conveys truth concerning reality. If the context fails to clarify the cognitive intent of a proposition, its intention can only be determined in accord with the general tenor of Scripture on the subject or related subjects. The interpreter who faces these issues will work with sound principles of hermeneutics and avail himself of the judgment of Spirit-led exegetes from the past as safeguards against dangerous misinterpretation.

4. *Inerrancy and meaninglessness or nonsense.* If inerrancy applies to the Bible in any respect, does it not mean that in any didactic passage there can be no nonsense? Although there may be serious assertions incapable of verification on a strict positivistic principle, if the Holy Spirit kept the thought of Scripture free from error he preserved the writers from including any assertions that were not true to the facts. Employing a broadened sense of verification, we may say that inerrancy means that there is no intended assertion of Scripture that does not make some difference in the total complex of reality.

Let us sum up the discussion of inerrancy and the content of Scripture. As inspiration is applied to Scripture content it guarantees the objective inerrancy not of every thought conveyed in the Bible but of everything cognitively taught in it.[11] Insofar as the Bible chooses to assert the existence of scientifically verifiable or unverifiable realities, the Bible is true; the events or realities specified are actual. Furthermore there is no nonsense in Scripture. This is not to say, however, that the Bible's propositional truth is presented with twentieth-century technical precision. Its accuracy must

[10] A. T. Pierson, *Knowing the Scriptures* (Los Angeles: Biola Book Room, 1910), 16–17.

[11] Cf. J. I. Packer, *"Fundamentalism" and the Word of God* (Grand Rapids, MI: Eerdmans, 1958), 169, and Smedes' comment.

be judged in terms of the writer's own purpose. Needless to say, the Bible writers' purpose was not to address specialists in an honorary scientific society. In accord with the popular purpose, if the Scriptures are inerrant at all we must conclude that their didactic assertions are true. Furthermore noncognitive assertions about the speaker or writer are held to be inerrant for their particular purposes. From the consideration of the content of Scripture, we turn to a discussion of the verbal expressions through which the meanings are conveyed.

Infallibility and Uses of Language

Infallibility is here used to emphasize the nonfailing character of God's written Word as a vehicle for its meanings. This concept applies fruitfully to biblical sentences. The Word of God through the prophets and apostles will not return void; it will accomplish the purpose for which he sent it (Isa. 55:11). Not one jot or tittle will fail until all God purposed through it is fulfilled (Matt. 5:17–18; Luke 16:17; John 10:35).

How then does infallibility apply to informative sentences that convey formal or empirical truth? B. B. Warfield has well stated the point: "Inspiration is a means to an end and not an end in itself; if the truth is conveyed accurately to the ear that listens to it, its end is obtained."[12] In other words, to assert the infallibility of Scripture is to assert that it is grammatically adequate in conveying the divinely intended meanings. "A sentence is grammatically adequate when it clearly articulates meaning, and it is grammatically inadequate when it does not do so."[13]

Viewed in this light, the writers' sentences are infallible even though their purpose may be not to present cognitive propositions but to convey noncognitive meanings. Thus noninformative sentences are clear and adequate to their respective tasks. Emotive expressions in the poetical books are as infallible as empirically informative statements in Acts. The directive sentences of the Ten Commandments are as infallible as the informative statement that God cannot deny himself. The meaning of questions is conveyed as accurately as the content of John 3:16. Exclamations clearly portray the intended spirit, and figures of speech adequately present their point. All of the Bible, whatever its kinds of sentences, is equally infallible and equally effective in conveying the various meanings intended by the Holy Spirit through the inspired writers. From the fact that the Bible con-

[12] B. B. Warfield, *The Inspiration and Authority of the Bible* (Philadelphia: Presbyterian & Reformed, 1948), 438.
[13] Kimpel, *Language*, 138.

tains no nonsense it follows that the writers were preserved from penning any pseudo-sentences.

As a result of this understanding of infallibility we may appreciate the Reformers' doctrine of the Scriptures' perspicacity. In terms common to our generation, would not the Reformers assert that the Bible is capable of adequately accomplishing its goal of communication apart from any external interpretive authority?

In view of contemporary understanding of the limitations of culturally conditioned languages, is such a concept of infallibility tenable? Are the grammatical structures of Hebrew and Greek so readily adaptable for mediating the divine meanings? Many contemporary theories of the origin of language assume that meaningful sounds evolved from earlier grunts and that all terms were devised with physical or phenomenal referents. If that be assumed, it is indeed difficult to transmit infinite meanings through finite vocables. But must a Bible believer accept the naturalistic theories of the origin of language? Eugene Nida assumes that we must.[14] He claims that language was first used for the naming of animals. And language originated not by God's naming of them but Adam's. This, he argues, means that language is primarily a human convention participating in the finiteness of all that is human. We would not deny that the naming of the animals may be the origin of certain human words, but what of the communication between God and Adam? Dialogue between God and man presupposes that two-way conversation is possible. May not the Bible believer also hold that God created man's capacity for linguistic communication? Of course this is impossible on a positivistic worldview! But on a theistic worldview, Gordon Clark argues, God created man and revealed himself to him in words. Language is adequate for theology.[15]

It may be well then to observe some of the advantages of the view proposed in this paper for the use and understanding of the terms "infallibility" and "inerrancy." One benefit of regarding truth a quality of propositions rather than sentences is a diminishing of the problem of some of the variations in the gospel accounts, in other historical passages relating to the same event (Kings and Chronicles) and in the New Testament wordings of Old Testament references. One and the same logical content can be expressed by different wordings—that is, active or passive, direct or indirect discourse, etc. The major point of inerrancy is to assert the truth

[14] E. Nida, *Message and Mission* (New York: Harper, 1960), 224–25, as summarized by E. Heideman, "Inspiration."

[15] G. H. Clark, *Religion, Reason, and Revelation* (Philadelphia: Presbyterian & Reformed, 1961), 146.

of the meaning rather than the wording. Verbal inspiration in this context stresses the functional value of whatever sentences are used to convey accurately the intended meaning. Verbal inspiration would not imply that alternative expressions are necessarily falsifying.

A second value of this analysis may be a clarification of the role of the witness of the Holy Spirit. A factual or cognitive proposition has both an intension and an extension. "Its intension is its meaning. Its extension is the reality to which its meaning refers."[16] Independently of the witness of the Holy Spirit a grammarian can examine biblical sentences and a logician analyze their precise intension. But only via the witness of the Holy Spirit can any man come into personal communion with God himself, the reality to whom the sentences refer. This at any rate was Augustine's view of illumination, which stimulated Calvin's thought on the testimony of the Spirit.

What then are the conclusions of this paper?

1. Although there is a clear distinction today between meaning and sentences, inspiration may be viewed as implying neither merely conceptual nor merely verbal supervision on the part of the Holy Spirit. Inspiration in this realm of discourse applies to both content and wording, meanings and sentences.

2. "Inerrancy" may be used most clearly for meanings that are cognitively taught by those with delegated authority as spokesmen for God, and for noncognitive meanings relating to the speakers themselves.

3. "Infallibility" most helpfully designates the verbal media of the Scriptures as effective communicators of the Spirit-intended meaning through the biblical writings.

4. All that is written in Scripture is infallible. All that Scripture teaches cognitively is objectively true. All that Scripture teaches noncognitively is subjectively true—that is, true of the one whose idea is expressed. This then is a plenary view of verbal inspiration. All sentences are infallible, and all meanings are inerrant for their respective purposes.

---

[16] Kimpel, *Language*, 134.

For Further Study

Geisler, Norman L. Geisler, ed. *Inerrancy*. Grand Rapids, MI: Zondervan, 1980. (Contains the papers from ICBI Summit I and "The Chicago Statement on Inerrancy," 1978.)

Hannah, John, ed. *Inerrancy and the Church*. Chicago: Moody, 1984. (A collection of essays that review inerrancy from the early, postapostolic church to c. 1970.)

International Council on Biblical Inerrancy (ICBI) Collection.

Radmacher, Earl, and Robert Preus, eds. *Hermeneutics, Inerrancy, and the Bible*. Grand Rapids, MI: Zondervan, 1984. (Contains the papers from ICBI Summit II and "The Chicago Statement on Hermeneutics," 1982.)

Recent Releases

DeYoung, Kevin. *Taking God At His Word*. Wheaton, IL: Crossway, 2014.

Edwards, Brian H. *Nothing but the Truth*, 3rd edition. Faverdale North, Darlington, UK: Evangelical Press, 2006.

Frame, John M. *The Doctrine of the Word of God*. Phillipsburg, NJ: P&R, 2010.

Geisler, Norman L., and William C. Roach. *Defending Inerrancy*. Grand Rapids, MI: Baker, 2011.

Scripture Index